Business Taxation and Financial Decisions

Deborah Schanz • Sebastian Schanz

Business Taxation and Financial Decisions

Springer

Prof. Dr. Deborah Schanz
WHU – Otto Beisheim School of Management
Chair of Taxation and Accounting
Burgplatz 2
56179 Vallendar
Germany
deborah.schanz@whu.edu

Prof. Dr. Sebastian Schanz
University of Magdeburg
Chair of Business Taxation
Universitätsplatz 2
39106 Magdeburg
Germany
sebastian.schanz@ovgu.de

ISBN 978-3-662-51947-9 ISBN 978-3-642-03284-4 (eBook)
DOI 10.1007/978-3-642-03284-4
Springer Heidelberg Dordrecht London New York

Cover design: WMX Design GmbH, Heidelberg

Printed on acid-free paper

Springer is part of Springer Science+Business Media (www.springer.com)

To Anni Sophie

Foreword

Taxes matter! Nobody seriously doubts this. Yet many finance textbooks keep entirely quiet about tax issues. It is well-known that investors and enterprises strive to maximize their income net of taxes, yet business schools rarely teach their students how tax effects impact business decisions. Ignoring tax effects will typically lead to investor decisions that are wrong from a real world perspective. A lack of student knowledge also makes fiscal policy more difficult: How can a financial system offer targeted tax incentives given that managers, former business school students, do not know how to rationally incorporate them into their decisions?

So far, it has been unnecessarily difficult to offer tax courses at business schools because of a lack of comprehensive textbooks covering tax effects on investment and financing decisions. With a vast number of accounting and finance textbooks to choose from, professors faced a comparable dearth of tax management textbooks. Lack of importance certainly is not the reason. Planning costs partly explain the relative neglect of tax planning so far. Incorporation of taxes makes problems inherently more complex. Also, tax systems around the world differ considerably. While the financial sector exhibits the same economic structures globally, and accounting rules are converging, tax systems still impact investment and financing decisions differently. Many business schools tend to provide a simple answer to the challenging question of which tax system to teach their students: They omit taxes entirely from their curriculum. Any conclusions about the tax impact of a tax system are obviously confined to that country. Ignoring taxes however is certainly wrong everywhere.

Because of this, the education of investment bankers, financial managers and strategy consultants frequently proceeds without taking tax issues into account. Deborah and Sebastian Schanz want to fix this obvious gap in the international textbook market.

They highlight in a universal treatment the tax influence on investment and financing decisions by following the common division into time-, tax base- and tax-rate effects. In contrast to the supposition that taxes only lend themselves to verbal discussion by lawyers, their approach is grounded in analytical rigor. The advantages of tax planning vis-à-vis a neglect of taxes can thus be calculated. All results are consistently clarified via numerical examples.

Their book benefits from numerous previous contributions to the literature which have so far been only partly made available in English. It is intended for graduate students with a basic knowledge of taxation. I hope and expect this book to be widely incorporated into business school curricula, enabling business schools to give tax issues the attention they deserve.

Tübingen *Franz W. Wagner*
August 2010

Preface

During the last 30 years, finance and accounting knowledge has been more and more extended by integrating taxes. At universities throughout the world, tax classes are taught, which integrate tax knowledge with financing decisions. Very often, these decisions are best made based on financial plans, but textbooks covering those contents are rare. Therefore, we decided to write this book, which combines tax background and basic financial decisions. The lack of tax knowledge in financial decisions may lead to serious problems if students evaluate investment options, as real-world decisions always involve tax consequences.

This book seeks for bridging the gap between (tax) accounting and financial decisions. We take the basic ideas of financial decision criteria and integrate income taxes. This approach stresses how taxation affects investment and financing decisions. We do not focus on tax law details, because tax rules are very dynamic and are continuously adjusted to the economic environment. The idea is to provide simple standard models and explain how the models might be adjusted to tax law. More complex financing issues such as uncertainty are mostly neglected in this book. Regarding taxes, readers are not required to have tax prerequisites. We set up and explain the content step by step. Therefore, the book is also recommended to students who do not wish to follow a "tax career". On the contrary, this textbook helps to develop an understanding of effects caused by taxes which is important for many students, e.g., in the areas of corporate finance, accounting, investment banking, and strategy consulting.

We cover contents from Bachelor of Science-, Master of Science-, and MBA-classes. We address students from different levels, but some chapters fit to specific target groups only. Chapters 1 and 3 are important for all readers as an introduction to the topic and to understand the technique of applying financial plans. Chapter 2 should be treated in Bachelor classes. It introduces decision criteria such as the net present value and the future value as well as financial plans without taking taxes into account. Typically, Master of Science students are familiar with those contents. The Fisher–Hirshleifer-Sections (Sects. 2.5, 3.7, and 5.2.3) are not suitable for MBA programs. They derive theoretically why we use the net present value criterion and can be neglected if students accept this criterion without a derivation. Chapter 4 is only relevant when students are interested in gaining basic tax knowledge about different countries, such as Member States of the European Union, the United States, or OECD countries. If students want to apply the models shown in this book to one specific country, they can skip Chap. 4. Chapters 5 to 9 can be chosen separately and are not built upon each other. At the end of each chapter, we provide some questions and mathematical exercises to reiterate the main ideas and topics. Moreover, we give basic solutions to the mathematical exercises in the Appendix at the end of the book.

This book renders contents thoroughly tried and tested in our tax planning and tax strategy classes at the Universities of Bielefeld and Magdeburg (Germany), Graz (Austria) and WHU – Otto-Beisheim-School of Management in Vallendar (Germany). But experiences with major parts of the content go far beyond our teaching: They have been developed and improved by our academic teacher Professor Dr. h.c. Franz W. Wagner at the University of Tuebingen (Germany), to whom we owe deep thank and respect. We also want to thank Professor Dr. Rainer Niemann. Both laid the cornerstones of our knowledge we bring down on paper with this work.

Special thanks go to our research assistants Sara Keller, Frederick Krummet, and Holger Theßeling who did the proofreading and calculated and corrected our examples in enduring perseverance. Thank you for your unresting mission to improve the content of the book.

Koblenz
October 2010

Deborah Schanz
Sebastian Schanz

Contents

Part II Integrating Taxation into Investment Decision Making

List of Abbreviations

ACE	Allowance for Corporate Equity
AMT	Alternative Minimum Tax
CEO	Chief executive officer
Chap.	Chapter
c.p.	ceteris paribus (other parameters do not change)
Cr	Credit account
Dr	Debit account
DRD	Dividend received deduction
EA	Equity account
EBT	Earnings before taxes
EPS	Earnings per share
ESt	German income tax
EStG	German income tax code
EU	European Union
Ex.	Example
EVA	Economic Value Added
fifo	First in first out
Fig.	Figure
GAAP	General Accepted Accounting Principles
GewSt	German local business tax
HGB	Handelsgesetzbuch (German local GAAP)
IBFD	International Bureau of Fiscal Documentation
IFRS	International Financial Reporting Standard
IMF	International Monetary Fund
IRC	Internal Revenue Code
IRS	Internal Revenue Service
KStG	German corporate income tax code
lifo	Last in first out
NOK	Norwegian Krone
OECD	Organisation for Economic Co-operation and Development
P&L	Profit and loss account
SEC	Securities & Exchange Commission
Sect.	Section

SME	Small and medium-sized enterprizes
SPE	Special purpose vehicle
US-GAAP	United States General Accepted Accounting Principles
VAT	Value Added Tax

List of Symbols

a	Dividend payout ratio
A	Amortization of debt
AF	Annuity factor
AGI	Adjusted gross income
ANN	Annuity
APC	Additional paid-in capital
BV	Book value
c	Index representing corporate level
C_0	Consumption
$C^{\max}$	Maximum consumption
CE	Capital endowment
CIF	Cash inflow
COF	Cash outflow
CF	Cash flow
CF^L	Cash inflow from debt financing
$CF^{\tau,c}$	Cash flow after corporate income tax
CG	Capital gains
CRF	Capital recovery factor
δ	Loss carry forward timing restriction
Δ	Absolute difference of the value of a parameter
d	Disagio as a percentage of the nominal debt value; year of fair value depreciation
$disc$	Index representing discounted numbers
D	Depreciation
$D^{disagio}$	Depreciation of disagio
D^{GW}	Depreciation of goodwill
D^{SU}	Depreciation of step-up amount
DF	Discount factor $DF = (1 + i^{\tau})^{-t}$
$Dist$	Distribution
Div^{FI}	Dividend from financial income
Div^{P}	Dividend from current profits
Div^{RE}	Dividend from retained earnings
ε	Interruption value
ED	Economic depreciation

EP	Economic profit
ER	Earnings
EXP	Expenses
$f(.)$	Investment function
F	Fixed capital
F_0	Financial initial investment
$FairVD$	Fair value depreciation
FBS	Final balance sheet
FI	Financial investment
FV	Pre-tax future value
FV^{τ}	After-tax future value
$FVAD$	Future value of an annuity in advance
$FVAR$	Future value of an annuity in arrears
g	Growth rate
GCV	Going-concern-value
GW	Goodwill
i	Pre-tax interest rate, pre-tax discount rate
i^*	Internal rate of return
i^{τ}	After-tax interest rate, after-tax discount rate
$i^{\tau,c}$	After-tax interest rate on corporate level
$i^{\tau,flat}$	After-tax interest rate taxed at the reduced flat tax rate
$i^{\tau,p}$	After-tax interest rate on personal level
I_0	Initial investment
II	Imputed interest
Int	Absolute interest
IP	Interest payment
$IP^{\tau,flat}$	Interest payment taxed at a reduced flat tax rate
j	Index
k	Period in which loss occurred
λ	Lagrangian parameter
$\mathscr{L}(.)$	Lagrangian function
L	Liability (debt)
LCB	Loss carry back
LCF	Loss carry forward
LD	Loss deduction
LO	Loss offset
LO^{AGI_k}	Loss offset resulting from a loss in period k
LP	Leasing payments
MP^B	Marginal price of buyer
MP^S	Marginal price of seller
MRR	Marginal rate of return
MTR	Marginal tax rate
n	Planning horizon, useful life of assets
n_{GW}	Useful life of goodwill
n_A	Useful life of assets
n_{SU}	Useful life of step-up

NFV	Pre-tax net future value
NPV	Pre-tax net present value
NPV^L	Net present value of debt financing
NPV^τ	After-tax net present value
$NPV^{\tau,c}$	After-tax net present value on corporate level
$NPV^{\tau,disagio}$	After-tax net present value of disagio
$NPV^{\tau,loan}$	After-tax net present value of loan (excluding disagio)
$NPV^{\tau,L}$	After-tax net present value of debt financing
$NPV^{\tau,p}$	After-tax net present value on personal level
p	Index representing owner's personal level
P	Profit
PRO	Provision
PV	Present value
$PVAD$	Present value of an annuity in advance
$PVAR$	Present value of an annuity in arrears
q	$1+$ interest rate i before taxes
q^τ	$1+$ interest rate i^τ after taxes
ρ	Pre-tax borrowing rate, debit interest rate; time preference rate
ρ^*	Effective borrowing rate (including interest and disagio costs), internal rate of return
r	Pre-tax rate of return
r^B	Modified internal rate of return (Baldwin rate of return)
RE	Retained earnings
REC	Receivables
RI	Residual income
RRA	Rate-of-Return-Allowance
S	Sum of digits
S_0	Savings
SP	Selling price
$s.t.$	Subject to
t	Time index
τ	Tax rate
τ^c	Corporate income tax rate
τ^{CG}	Tax rate on capital gains
τ^{CI}	Tax rate on capital income
$\tau^{c,p}$	Combined tax rate on corporate and personal level
τ^{flat}	Flat tax
τ^p	Personal income tax rate
T	Tax payment
T^c	Corporate taxes
T^p	Personal taxes
TB	Tax base
$U(.)$	Utility function
W_0	Wealth/Endowment
W_t	Withdrawal

Part I
Introduction to Investment Decision Making

Chapter 1
Introduction to Tax Planning

Abstract In this chapter we explain why integrating taxation into decision making processes is not negligible. Using simple examples, we show that taxation affects optimal investment decisions. We present the two most important objectives of tax research: Tax planning and identifying tax impact on decisions. We discuss main assumptions of an investment decision process briefly and introduce the important terms of tax planning and tax minimization. Moreover, we provide basic concepts of tax planning and discuss different types of decision settings and planning approaches. After studying this chapter, you are able to evaluate the importance of taxation in investment decisions and distinguish between tax planning and tax minimization.

1.1 Why Taxes Matter in Investment Decision Settings

Let us start with explaining the importance of taxes in decision making based on an example.

Example 1.1. Taxes Influencing Investment Decisions

Suppose you inherit € 10,000 after inheritance tax from your beloved rich aunt in year $t = 0$. Striving for wealth, you are excitedly looking for lucrative investment alternatives. Fortunately, your investment alternatives are reduced to two financial securities

Security	Yield
A	4%
B	6%

At first assume that no taxes are levied on the yield of the securities considered. In the absence of taxation, future values FV of your investment alternatives rise to

D. Schanz and S. Schanz, *Business Taxation and Financial Decisions*,
DOI 10.1007/978-3-642-03284-4_1, © Springer-Verlag Berlin Heidelberg 2011

$$FV^A = 10{,}000 \times (1 + 0.04) = 10{,}400$$
$$FV^B = 10{,}000 \times (1 + 0.06) = 10{,}600.$$

in $t = 1$. The decision in this case is trivial. Because security B leads to a higher future value you are well advised to invest in security B.

Now suppose tax authorities decide to levy taxes on security B with a marginal tax rate of $\tau = 50\%$. The return on security A stays tax exempt. Now, wealth in $t = 1$ is determined as:

$$FV^A = 10{,}000 \times (1 + 0.04) = 10{,}400$$
$$FV^B = 10{,}000 \times (1 + 0.06) - 10{,}000 \times 0.06 \times 0.5 = 10{,}300.$$

In this case, security A leads to a higher return after taxation. You will certainly invest in security A.

Although the presented example is quite simple, it shows that taxation might distort optimal investment decisions. In the pre-tax case you choose investment B. If taxes are levied and you calculate without taking the consequences of taxation into account you will make the wrong decision. If you ignore taxation you will also invest in investment B which is definitely worse than investment A in case taxes are imposed. In summary:

1. Investment decisions are distorted by taxation.
2. Individuals act differently when taxes are levied compared to the case where no taxes are levied.
3. If taxes are neglected, incorrect investment decisions might occur and unprofitable investments might be carried out.

We now know that taxes matter in investment decision settings.[1] However, to understand the following chapters we need to determine how distortion is measured and how decision settings are characterized.

1.2 Two Objectives of Tax Research: Optimizing Tax Planning and Identifying Tax Impact

This section introduces the two objectives of tax research: On the one hand, the aim of tax research is to help individuals and firms optimize their tax planning. On the other hand it aims at identifying how individuals and firms really behave and whether taxes have an impact on their decisions.

The normative tax planning doctrine answers the question how individuals *must* behave in order to reach their post-tax overall objective, which is typically maximization of their utility. Normative optimal behavior can be identified by formulating

[1] See *Schneider* [1], *Wagner* [3], and *Scholes* et al. [2].

decision models. These models have to be built on a set of assumptions. Under those assumptions, it is possible to identify optimal investment or financing decisions. The investment decision in Ex. 1.1 is an example for a small tax planning model which helps identifying optimal behavior.

In contrast, the descriptive tax impact doctrine measures the impact of taxation on the behavior of individuals. This reveals how individuals *do* behave. Research in this area is based on empirical methods.

In reality, we often find behavior which deviates from the optimal solutions we identify in our tax planning models. On the one hand, people neglect taxes in their decision making. This can lead to suboptimal behavior resulting in individuals or firms losing money as they realize suboptimal decisions. On the other hand, the effect of taxes can be overestimated. Very often, individuals want to save taxes at any price. This behavior can be suboptimal as they might not realize that they are losing more money than they are saving.

Example 1.2. The Foolish Tax Attorney

Mr. Smith owns a small garage where he repairs old cars and provides other car related services. There is a lifting ramp in his garage. The lift makes it easier to, e.g., change tires and do some welding work. The ramp concerned is quite old but works well. By accident, Mr. Smith is assigned to maintain your car, too.

While changing the tires of your car Mr. Smith tells you that he just fired his tax attorney. What happened? Mr. Smith realized that the book value for tax purposes of his lifting ramp accounted for zero resulting in a current depreciation of zero. He argued that his tax attorney had forgotten to tell him to buy a new lifting ramp in order to generate tax deductible depreciation. This supposed bad consulting led to the loss of Mr. Smith as the tax attorney's client. You pay the bill and drive home while thinking about the fool Mr. Smith.

What's wrong about the argument of Mr. Smith? In order to generate tax deductible depreciation Mr. Smith has to buy the new asset (ramp). However, the resulting cash outflow causes less potential in consumption and reduces Mr. Smith's wealth or utility, respectively. But as the lifting ramp still works well, its economic useful life has not been reached yet. Thus, it is not necessary to replace the lifting ramp by a new one.

The example is based on a true story. It shows that individuals may act irrational just to reduce their tax liability.

In this book, we will focus on tax planning rather than on identifying the impact of taxes on an individuals' behavior. We introduce tax planning models in detail and deduce the optimal decisions and optimal behavior on the basis of those models.

1.3 Tax Planning vs. Tax Minimization

There are two different basic categories of tax planning models that can be distinguished: Tax planning models in the narrow sense and tax minimization models.[2]

First, we consider models where we integrate taxes into decision making to choose the right alternative out of a pool of different investment opportunities. This type of model is called tax planning model. This tax planning category is a part of the preinvestment analyses. In this case the decision setting is explicitly modelled and the individual chooses the best opportunity according to the decision criterion used. The decision has not been made yet. Therefore, we can say that this kind of model belongs to the category of ex-ante optimization models. Figure 1.1 shows the tax planning period as the period until the actual start of the project in $t = 0$. To make the correct decision, the decision criterion or objective function has to be adjusted by taxes. In a one-period context, the individual strives to maximize his after-tax cash flow to maximize utility. Therefore, the individual chooses the opportunity generating the highest after-tax cash flow

$$(CF - T) \rightarrow \max, \tag{1.1}$$

where CF stands for cash flow before taxes and T represents the absolute tax payments due. During this book, we will use the expressions "after-tax" and "post-tax" as synonyms. Correspondingly, we will use "before-tax" and "pre-tax" as synonym expressions.

The second type of model is called tax minimization model and has to be assigned to the category of suboptimization models. The individual has already carried out an investment and wants to minimize the liability at the end of the taxable period. The individual usually consults a tax attorney. In this case the investment decision might be wrong because it was made without considering taxes or just taking simple assumptions into account. Taxation solely plays an ex-post role at the end of the year. In a one-period context, the individual tries to minimize taxes after the decision was made. Therefore, cash flow CF is constant

$$CF = const. \quad \Rightarrow \quad T \rightarrow \min. \tag{1.2}$$

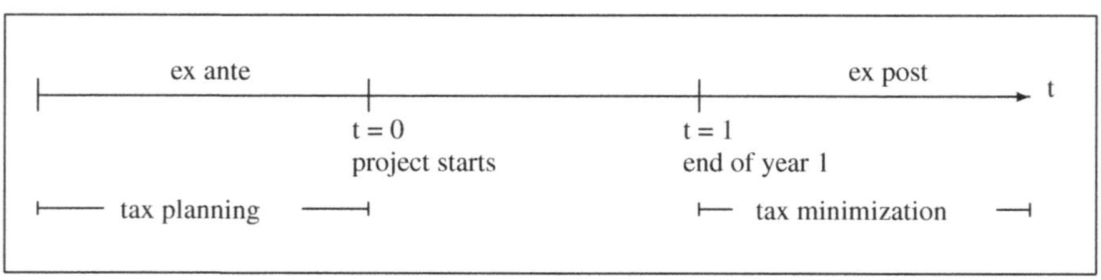

Fig. 1.1 Tax planning vs. tax minimization

[2] See *Wagner* [3], pp. 446–453.

The investor starts to care about taxes for the first time at the end of the first taxable period. This point is illustrated by $t = 1$ in Fig. 1.1. At this point of time the investor has to file his first tax report covering his new project.

Example 1.3. Investment before and after Taxes

Suppose an investor faces three investment opportunities A, B, and C. The investments generate pre-tax cash flows of $CF^A = 8, CF^B = 10$ and $CF^C = 12$ and induce absolute tax liabilities of $T^A = 1, T^B = 4$, and $T^C = 8$. The post-tax cash flows of these alternatives are

Investment	CF	T	$CF - T$
A	8	1	7
B	10	4	6
C	12	8	4

An investor using a tax planning model for optimization reasons will choose investment A, because investment A yields the highest post-tax cash flow.

To design a decision setting for an investor who has already chosen an investment without taking taxes into account, we assume that an investor chose investment C paying pre-tax cash flows of $CF^C = 12$. Now, at the end of the taxable period – usually 1 year – the investor has to go through the income tax code together with his tax advisor in order to identify possibilities to reduce his tax liability. The absolute tax payments for investment C, $T^C = 8$, is assumed to be the payment due before consulting the tax advisor. After using discretion provided by the income tax code, e.g., choosing the optimal depreciation rate, absolute tax payments could be reduced to say $T^C_{after} = 7$. In this case the post-tax cash flow accounts for $CF^C - T^C_{after} = 5$ which is still lower than the post-tax cash flow of investment A or B.

In a multiperiod setting, investors choosing the tax planning model use the decision criterion "net present value after taxes" (NPV^τ) or similar criteria. In this case the decision rule is to realize the investment that generates the highest net present value after taxes, which is calculated as:

$$NPV^\tau = -I_0 + \sum_{t=1}^{n} \frac{CF_t - T_t}{(1 + i^\tau)}, \qquad (1.3)$$

where I_0 denotes the initial investment, n the time horizon of the project, i the interest rate, and τ represents the tax rate on interest income. We will discuss the NPV and decision rules in the following chapters in detail.

Investors choosing the ex-post suboptimization model are minimizing the present value of future tax liabilities

$$\sum_{t=1}^{n} \frac{T_t}{(1 + i \times (1 - \tau))^t} \rightarrow \min. \tag{1.4}$$

1.4 The Tax Planning Process

To determine profitability of an investment project and the impact of taxation we need to follow five steps as described later.

1. Identification of the decision maker

   First, it is important to identify who is in charge of the decision. Who is able to make decisions? Who is the decision maker? We know that "the company" as an institution is not able to make decisions. Hence exclusively individuals are able to make decisions. Relevant individuals for our decision problems might be a company's management or the shareholders. When we think of smaller companies with only few shareholders or of basic decisions of larger firms, like finding the optimal legal form or the optimal location of the firm, the owners are the ones in charge of the decision. Their decision is influenced by both the taxes levied on profits at the corporate level as well as the taxes they pay as an individual. Therefore, from now on our typical point of view is the investor's perspective taking both levels into account. This is clarified in Fig. 1.2.
   Figure 1.2 shows the relationship of investors, companies, and environment. The company is endowed with funds by the investor. Due to interactions with the environment, cash is generated which is at the end withdrawn by the investor, who uses the company as investment vehicle.

2. Identification of the objective

   It is assumed that each individual strives to maximize its consumption utility. Possible consumption is maximized if the wealth of the investor is maximized.[3]

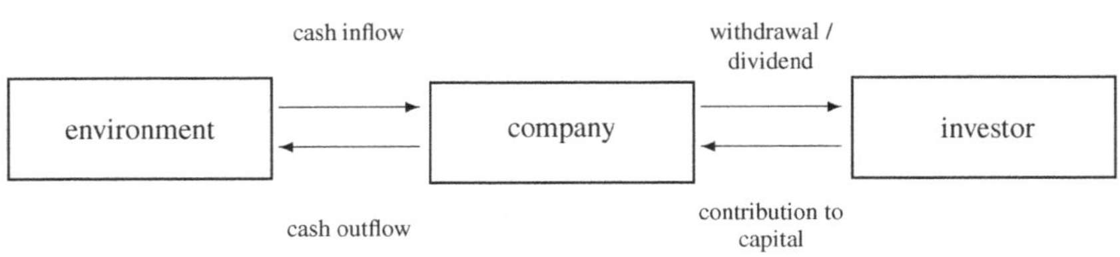

Fig. 1.2 Company as an investment vehicle
Source: Based on *Wagner* [3], p. 413

[3] See Sect. 2.5 on p. 36 for proof.

3. Identification of the appropriate decision model

   As we will prove later on, the after-tax net present value criterion assures maximum consumption utility.

4. Tax planning or tax minimization?

   Based on the two possibilities described in Sect. 1.3 we have to decide whether our problem is a real tax planning problem or just a tax minimization problem. If the investment decision or financing decision has not been made, our problem is a real tax planning problem. In this case, we need to collect information about cash flows, interest rates and the time horizon of our investment as well as tax information. If the investment decision or financing decision has already been made and the project is carried out, we are dealing with tax minimization. In this case we only have to gather information concerning taxes, i.e., the tax base, the tax rates and the after-tax interest rate. Depending on the decision model, tax data and nontax data are integrated into our models.

5. Investment decision and tax impact

   Finally, we are able to evaluate the profitability of available investment alternatives before and after taking taxes into consideration. We are able to identify the impact of taxation on the individual's optimal investment decision. The necessary calculations are made on the basis of appropriate formulas or on the basis of a financial plan. Both are described in Chaps. 2 and 3.

Questions

1.1. An individual is endowed with € 10,000 and faces two investment alternatives A and B. The rate of return on security A (B) accounts for 10% (8%). The marginal tax rate for investment A (B) is 30% (0%). Show that the individual makes an incorrect decision if taxation is neglected.

1.2. What are the two objectives of tax research?

1.3. What types of tax planning models can be distinguished? Give examples for decision settings and assign the different types of tax planning models. Distinguish one-period and multiperiod decision settings.

1.4. What assumptions have to be accepted in case of suboptimization models?

References

1. Schneider, D.: Investition, Finanzierung, Besteuerung. 7th edn. Gabler, Wiesbaden (1992)
2. Scholes, M.S., Wolfson, M.A., Erickson, M., Maydew, E.L., Shevlin, T.: Taxes and Business Strategy. A Planning Approach. 4th edn., Prentice Hall, Upper Saddle River (2009)
3. Wagner, F.W., Besteuerung. In: Bitz, M., Domsch, M., Ewert, R., Wagner, F.W. (eds.) Vahlens Kompendium der Betriebswirtschaftslehre, vol. 2, 5th edn., pp. 407–477, München (2005)

Chapter 2
Principles of Investment Decisions

Abstract This chapter focuses on fundamental concepts of decision making in capital budgeting and financing. These concepts – as described here – neglect taxes, but it is important to understand them to be able to follow the after-tax models in the following chapters. We assume that the content of this chapter is basically known from other courses. Therefore, we provide a very brief summary of the different concepts. Furthermore, we provide a justification for using the net present value concept as a Standard Model for investment decision problems. After reading this chapter, you are able to evaluate the profitability of different investment options. Moreover, you know the advantages and shortcomings of the decision criteria described.

2.1 Overall Assumptions

A decision problem can be structured as a pool of two alternatives from which the investor has to choose one. In the following we assume one alternative to be a real investment and the other one a financial investment opportunity. Endowed with enough equity, the investor can choose to carry out the real investment or not to invest. In the case that he is not willing to carry out real investment, it is assumed that there is a financial market where he can invest his money at an assured fixed interest rate. That financial investment is called the alternative financial investment. However, the situation can also demand the investor to make a decision out of several real investment options. In both types of decision problems described earlier, the investor needs a concept that tells him which investment alternative has the highest payoff. Therefore, he has to rank all investment options according to their profitability. In the following, alternative concepts to solve this problem are introduced and discussed.

Before we start deriving models for preinvestment analysis, we need to talk about more assumptions. *First*, we work with time discrete models. The *second* assumption deals with the capital market. Capital market is assumed to be perfect without arbitrage opportunities. We neglect transaction costs and assume perfect information symmetry. In our setting, perfect capital markets can only occur if interest rates for borrowing and lending are equal and if there are no limits of borrowing. For

D. Schanz and S. Schanz, *Business Taxation and Financial Decisions*,
DOI 10.1007/978-3-642-03284-4_2, © Springer-Verlag Berlin Heidelberg 2011

sure, the assumption that there are no taxes will be eased in this book. With regard to the assumption of perfect capital markets, we surely know that reality tells us something else, but the main focus of this book is to illustrate distortions by taxes. Problems of imperfect capital markets are discussed in standard finance textbooks. *Third*, we assume certainty regarding interest rates, tax rates, and future cash flows. We know that reality is dynamic, stochastic, and complex. However, in our opinion this assumption has to be made for the sake of being able to present tax distortions in an intuitive manner.[1] *Fourth*, we assume the overall objective of individuals is to maximize consumption utility.

2.2 Financial Plans

Long-term decision making is challenging for management because in reality decision makers do not just face one decision but have to decide about investment alternatives that might interact in future. To quantify monetary consequences of decisions, capital budgeting with financial plans is used.[2]

Let us look at a simple example without taxes.

Example 2.1. Financial Plan without Taxes

You setup a business and invest € 1,000 equity to buy a machine which is used for producing toys. You sell the toys in the next 3 years and assume certain future cash flows from sales in $t = 1, \ldots, 3$ to be $CF = (400; 350; 700)$. You invest free cash flows in a bank account yielding 10% interest. You want to know how much money is available after 3 years.

The following financial plan helps calculating the future value (in €)

t	0	1	2	3
CF_t	−1,000	400	350	700
Financial Investment $t = 1$		400		
thereof interest			40	
Financial Investment $t = 2$			790	
thereof interest				79
Financial Investment $t = 3$				1,569
Withdrawals		0	0	0

In year $t = 1$, cash flow CF_1 is 400 that is reinvested in a financial investment FI_1 yielding 10% interest. $10\% \times 400 = 40$ is earned as interest payment IP_2 in $t = 2$. Financial investment in year $t = 2$ amounts

[1] Uncertainty is discussed in detail in *Kruschwitz/Löffler* [5].

[2] See *Kruschwitz* [5], pp. 122–132 and *Grob* [3].

to $FI_2 = FI_1 + IP_2 + CF_2 = 790$. Yielding 10% interest in year $t = 3$ and earning $CF_3 = 700$ accumulates to $FI_3 = 1{,}569$. This future value is available for consumption at the end of year $t = 3$.

The same calculation can be carried out using the future value formula as presented later in Sect. 2.3.3.

2.3 Basic Concepts of Decision Criteria

In the following sections, we focus on dynamic methods of capital budgeting decision criteria. Dynamic models – also known as time-adjusted models or multiperiod models – take periodic conditions into account, whereas static models use a single standard period for decision purposes or reduce reality to just few basic elements that affect the decision. Static models are also referred to as one-period models.

2.3.1 *Net Present Value Before Taxes*

The net present value (*NPV*) – one of the most important preinvestment decision criteria in management decisions – is defined as present value of future cash flows (*CF*) less the cash outflow for initial investment I_0. Notice that cash outflow might not only occur in $t = 0$ but also in following periods, leading to a negative cash flow. If n represents the total planning period – also called time horizon – and i the fixed (flat) interest rate of a risk free alternative financial investment project, the *NPV* in a time discrete environment is

$$NPV = -I_0 + \sum_{t=1}^{n} \frac{CIF_t - COF_t}{(1+i)^t}. \tag{2.1}$$

For the sake of convenience we combine cash inflow (*CIF*) and cash outflow (*COF*) simply to cash flow (*CF*). The cash flow of the real investment is reflected in the numerator. The denominator represents the alternative financial investment, where a flat yield curve is assumed. This implies that in case we do not invest our money in any real or specific financial investment, we always can choose the financial investment yielding the certain fixed interest rate usually represented by securities issued by the government. *NPV* is called a dynamic decision criterion because it takes future conditions into account at the time the decision has to be made. Furthermore, *NPV* is a relative decision criterion. It does not demonstrate the absolute advantage when carrying out the investment under consideration but the relative advantage compared to the alternative financial investment.

Let's give a brief economic interpretation of the *NPV*. The *NPV* states the additional wealth available for consumption purposes in terms of utility compared to the alternative financial investment at the time of decision ($t = 0$).

The decision rule based on the *NPV* criterion is already known from finance courses and states:

$NPV > 0$: Investment opportunity is better compared to the fixed interest rate of the financial investment alternative → invest!

$NPV < 0$: Investment opportunity is worse compared to the fixed interest rate of the financial investment alternative → do not invest!

$NPV = 0$: There is no difference between the *NPV* of the real investment opportunity and the alternative financial investment (This investment opportunity is also called marginal investment because the return of the real investment equals the return of the alternative financial investment.) → indifferent!

In case several investment opportunities generate different positive net present values, the investor should carry out that investment resulting in the greatest *NPV*.

Example 2.2. Net Present Value Calculation

Suppose, an investor faces a real investment opportunity with a cash flow vector of $CF = (-100; -30; 50; 70; 90)$ in € for $t = 0, \ldots, 4$. The interest rate is assumed to be $i = 5\%$. The pre-tax *NPV* then amounts to

$$\begin{aligned} NPV &= -100 + \frac{-30}{1.05} + \frac{50}{1.05^2} + \frac{70}{1.05^3} + \frac{90}{1.05^4} \\ &= 51.29 > 0. \end{aligned}$$

Interpretation: The investment is carried out because $NPV > 0$. The real investment opportunity is better compared to the financial investment with a fixed rate of return of $i = 5\%$. Moreover, in terms of consumption the present value of additional consumption by carrying out the real investment option is evaluated with €51.29.

In the following, we will present other variations of the net present value criterion. Nevertheless, the *NPV* will always be our most important decision criterion, if we are able to calculate it.

2.3.2 *Present Value and "True" Economic Profit*

Now, you are able to determine the net present value of an investment. But often, it is interesting to find out the value in other periods. The concept for evaluating investment at any point of time remains the same compared to the *NPV*: We look at future cash flows. To take the time effect of money into account, future cash flows are discounted until t. The resulting value is called the present value PV_t of an investment. The present value (PV_t) is defined as the sum of discounted cash flows $CF_{t+1}, \ldots, CF_n$ at time t, which yields:

$$PV_t = \sum_{j=t+1}^{n} \frac{CF_j}{(1+i)^{j-t}}. \tag{2.2}$$

The present value in $t = 0$ accounts for

$$PV_0 = \sum_{j=1}^{n} \frac{CF_j}{(1+i)^j} = NPV + I_0,$$

which is equivalent to NPV plus the payout relating to the initial investment I_0.

Based on the present value concept, we can define the economic profit. The economic profit EP_t is the return i on the investment's value in each period. The profit is defined as the return on the present value of the previous period $i \times PV_{t-1}$. This profit concept cannot be compared to accounting profit concepts, because they look at cash flows and accruals from the past, such as depreciation of assets bought in previous periods. The economic profit is calculated based on future cash flows.

The previous period's present value PV is

$$PV_{t-1} = \sum_{j=t}^{n} \frac{CF_j}{(1+i)^{j-t+1}}. \tag{2.3}$$

Using $1 + i = q$, (2.3) changes to

$$PV_{t-1} = \frac{CF_t}{q} + \frac{CF_{t+1}}{q^2} + \frac{CF_{t+2}}{q^3} + \ldots + \frac{CF_n}{q^{n-t+1}}. \tag{2.4}$$

Multiplying (2.4) by q, we get

$$q \times PV_{t-1} = CF_t + \underbrace{\frac{CF_{t+1}}{q} + \frac{CF_{t+2}}{q^2} + \ldots + \frac{CF_n}{q^{n-t}}}_{PV_t} = CF_t + PV_t. \tag{2.5}$$

Equation (2.5) states that the return on wealth expressed as the present value in $t - 1$ multiplied by $q = (1 + i)$ is equivalent to wealth in t and cash flow in t.

Example 2.3. Compounding Values

If the investment represents a stock, the market value of the stock plus dividend in $t + 1$ has to be equivalent to the compounded market value of t.

Changes in wealth are described by

$$\Delta PV_t = PV_{t-1} - PV_t.$$

Subtracting PV_{t-1} from both sides of (2.5) yields

$$i \times PV_{t-1} = CF_t - \Delta PV_t = EP_t \tag{2.6}$$

which is called economic profit. The difference between PV_t and PV_{t-1} is called economic depreciation ED

$$ED_t = PV_{t-1} - PV_t. \tag{2.7}$$

(2.6) and (2.7) imply

$$EP_t = CF_t - ED_t. \tag{2.8}$$

Taking (2.5), the relation between PV_t and PV_{t-1} is

$$PV_t = (1+i) \times PV_{t-1} - CF_t$$

or

$$PV_{t-1} = \frac{PV_t + CF_t}{(1+i)}.$$

PV_t might increase, decrease, or be constant over time:

$$\begin{aligned}
&\text{If } CF_t < i \times PV_{t-1} \longrightarrow PV_t \text{ increases}\\
&\text{If } CF_t > i \times PV_{t-1} \longrightarrow PV_t \text{ decreases}\\
&\text{If } CF_t = i \times PV_{t-1} \longrightarrow PV_t \text{ stays constant.}
\end{aligned}$$

Example 2.4. Present Value and Economic Profit

Using the assumptions of Ex. 2.2 on p. 14, PV_t accounts for

$$\begin{aligned}
PV_4 &= 0\\
PV_3 &= \frac{90}{1.05} = 85.71\\
PV_2 &= \frac{70}{1.05} + \frac{90}{1.05^2} = 148.30\\
PV_1 &= \frac{50}{1.05} + \frac{70}{1.05^2} + \frac{90}{1.05^3} = 188.86\\
PV_0 &= \frac{-30}{1.05} + \frac{50}{1.05^2} + \frac{70}{1.05^3} + \frac{90}{1.05^4} = 151.29.
\end{aligned}$$

From $t = 0$ to $t = 1$ PV increases. This is because $0.05 \times 151.29 = 7.56 > CF_1 = -30$. From $t = 1$ to $t = 2$ PV decreases. This is because $0.05 \times 188.86 = 9.44 < CF_2 = 50$. As we know PV_t, we are able to derive the economic depreciation

$$\begin{aligned} ED_1 &= PV_0 - PV_1 = 151.29 - 188.86 = -37.57 \\ ED_2 &= PV_1 - PV_2 = 188.86 - 148.30 = 40.56 \\ ED_3 &= PV_2 - PV_3 = 148.30 - 85.71 = 62.59 \\ ED_4 &= PV_3 - PV_4 = 85.71 - 0 = 85.71. \end{aligned}$$

Economic profit in each period then accounts for

$$\begin{aligned} EP_1 &= CF_1 - ED_1 = -30 - (-37.57) = 7.57 \\ EP_2 &= CF_2 - ED_2 = 50 - 40.56 = 9.44 \\ EP_3 &= CF_3 - ED_3 = 70 - 62.59 = 7.41 \\ EP_4 &= CF_4 - ED_4 = 90 - 85.71 = 4.29. \end{aligned}$$

The NPV of the project equals the present value in year $t = 0$ minus the payout relating to the initial investment $NPV = PV_0 - I_0 = 151.29 - 100 = 51.29$.

The following financial plan visualizes the results

t	0	1	2	3	4
CF_t	−100.00	−30.00	50.00	70.00	90.00
PV_t	151.29	188.86	148.30	85.71	0.00
ED_t		−37.57	40.56	62.59	85.71
EP_t		7.57	9.44	7.41	4.29

What is the infinite consumption potential that is generated by this project? To answer this, we are looking for an infinite annuity ANN leading to a present value that is equivalent to the present value of the investment. Therefore, we get

$$\sum_{t=1}^{\infty} ANN \times (1 + i)^{-t} = PV_0.$$

The present value of an infinite annuity is defined as $\frac{ANN}{i}$.[3] Hence we get

$$ANN = i \times PV_0. \tag{2.9}$$

[3] That result is proved in Sect. 2.4.

Example 2.5. Infinite Consumption Potential

Using the assumptions of Ex. 2.2 on p. 14, the infinite annuity for consumption accounts for

$$i \times PV_0 = 0.05 \times 151.29 = 7.56.$$

t	0	1	2	3	4	5	...	∞
CF_t	−100.00	−30.00	50.00	70.00	90.00	0.00	...	0.00
C_t		7.56	7.56	7.56	7.56	7.56	...	7.56
IP_t			−1.88	0.15	3.28	7.56	...	7.56
FI_t		−37.56	2.99	65.58	151.29	151.29	...	151.29

with

C_t = consumption
IP_t = interest payments
FI_t = financial investment.

Free cash flow after consumption of $C_t = 7.56$ is reinvested in the financial investment $FI_t = FI_{t-1} + CF_t - C_t + IP_t$ yielding 5% interest. The financial investment increases over time as it consists of the current free cash flow plus the preceding financial investment. From year $t = 5$ on, interest earned IP_t equals consumption C_t. The consumption level is infinitely financed.

2.3.3 Net Future Value and Future Value

The net future value (*NFV*) is defined as the compounded cash flows until time horizon n. *NFV* gives

$$NFV = \sum_{t=0}^{n} CF_t \times (1+i)^{n-t} \tag{2.10}$$

which is equivalent to

$$NFV = NPV \times (1+i)^n,$$

using (2.1) for calculating the *NPV*. Please note that in (2.10) we sum up from $t = 0$ not from $t = 1$ as in (2.1). Hence, the initial payment I_0 is included. *NFV* follows the same decision rule as *NPV*. If positive, invest, if negative, do not invest, if zero, be indifferent.

Example 2.6. Net Future Value

Using the assumptions of Ex. 2.2 on p. 14, *NFV* is

$$NFV = 51.29 \times (1 + 0.05)^4 = 62.34.$$

The future value (*FV*) is defined as the compounded present value PV_0

$$FV = PV_0 \times (1+i)^n = \sum_{t=1}^{n} CF_t \times (1+i)^{n-t} = (NPV + I_0) \times (1+i)^n. \quad (2.11)$$

The future value can also be denoted by terminal value.

The future value *FV* itself is not applicable for decision making, because no comparison with an alternative investment is made. However, it can serve as a decision criterion, if the difference to the future value of the alternative investment is derived

$$\Delta FV = FV - I_0 \times (1+i)^n = PV_0 \times (1+i)^n - I_0 \times (1+i)^n = NFV.$$

FV is called an absolute decision criterion because it states the absolute wealth in terms of consumption or utility in $t = n$, respectively.

Example 2.7. Future Value

Using the assumptions of Ex. 2.2 on p. 14, we get for *FV* and ΔFV

$$FV = PV_0 \times (1+i)^n = 151.29 \times (1 + 0.05)^4 = 183.89$$
$$\Delta FV = 183.89 - I_0 \times (1+i)^n = 183.89 - 100 \times (1.05)^4 = 62.34.$$

As *FV* is an absolute decision criterion with $FV = 183.89$, we cannot evaluate profitability of the real investment exclusively based on this information. As we know that we can generate an alternative rate of return of 5% while investing in a financial investment, the future value of our financial investment is $100 \times 1.05^4 = 121.55$. Now, we have two comparable future values. As the future value of our real investment option is greater than that of the financial investment, the real investment is carried out.

2.4 Present Value of an Annuity

Suppose, you get paid an amount of €*ANN* at the end of every year from $t = 1$ until $t = n$. Let $1 + i = q$, then the present value in $t = 0$ of that annuity *ANN* is

$$PV_0 = \sum_{t=1}^{n} ANN \times q^{-t}. \tag{2.12}$$

Equation (2.12) can be written as:

$$PV_0 = ANN \times q^{-1} + ANN \times q^{-2} + \ldots + ANN \times q^{-n+1} + ANN \times q^{-n}. \tag{2.13}$$

If we exclude *ANN*, (2.13) is simplified to

$$PV_0 = ANN \times (q^{-1} + q^{-2} + \ldots + q^{-n+1} + q^{-n}). \tag{2.14}$$

Equation (2.14) multiplied by q gives

$$q \times PV_0 = ANN \times (1 + q^{-1} + \ldots + q^{-n+3} + q^{-n+2} + q^{-n+1}). \tag{2.15}$$

Now, we subtract (2.13) from (2.15) and get

$$\begin{aligned} q \times PV_0 - PV_0 = {} & ANN \times (1 + q^{-1} + \ldots + q^{-n+3} + q^{-n+2} + q^{-n+1}) \\ & -ANN \times (q^{-1} + q^{-2} + \ldots + q^{-n+2} + q^{-n+1} + q^{-n}). \end{aligned} \tag{2.16}$$

Equation (2.16) can be simplified to

$$PV_0 \times (q - 1) = ANN \times (1 - q^{-n}). \tag{2.17}$$

Equation (2.17) can be transformed to

$$PV_0 = ANN \times \frac{1 - q^{-n}}{(1 + i) - 1} \quad = \quad ANN \times \frac{q^n}{q^n}\frac{1 - q^{-n}}{i} \quad = \quad ANN \times \frac{q^n - 1}{i \times q^n}.$$

Suppose, $ANN = 1$, then we can derive the present value factor of an annuity in arrears (*PVAR*) as

$$PVAR = \frac{q^n - 1}{i \times q^n}. \tag{2.18}$$

Now, suppose an infinite annuity ($n \to \infty$). Then (2.18) would be

$$\lim_{n \to \infty} \frac{q^n - 1}{i \times q^n} = \lim_{n \to \infty} \frac{1 - q^{-n}}{i} = \frac{1}{i}. \tag{2.19}$$

Up to now, we just focused on annuities *in arrears* and present values. However, there are also annuities *in advance* and moreover, we can also compute future values. If we take (2.18) and determine the future value, the future value factor of an annuity in arrears (*FVAR*) is defined as:

$$FVAR = \frac{q^n - 1}{i \times q^n} \times q^n = \frac{q^n - 1}{i}. \tag{2.20}$$

An annuity in advance is defined as an annuity of payments made at the beginning of each year. If the present value of an annuity in advance has to be determined, (2.12) changes to

$$PV_0 = \sum_{t=1}^{n} ANN \times q^{-t+1}, \tag{2.21}$$

because payments have to be discounted 1 year less.

Hence the present value factor of an annuity in advance ($PVAD$) is formally described as:

$$PVAD = \frac{q^n - 1}{i \times q^{n-1}} \tag{2.22}$$

while the future value factor of an annuity in advance ($FVAD$) is determined by

$$FVAD = \frac{q^n - 1}{i \times q^{-1}}. \tag{2.23}$$

Figure 2.1 summarizes the annuity factors derived.

Example 2.8. Annuity Factor

Since little Lutz is an extraordinary well-behaved student, his rich aunt Hillary transfers an amount of €5,000 to his always overdrawn bank account as a contribution to his expenses for his studies at the end of each year for a period

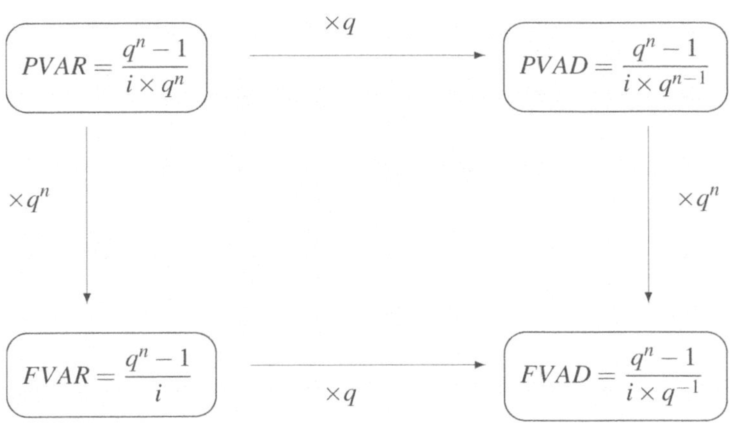

Fig. 2.1 Annuity-square

of 12 years (starting in $t = 1$). Lutz is very pleased but wants to invest the money in a Mercedes in $t = 0$. If $i = 5\%$, what amount can he spend for the Mercedes in $t = 0$?

$$PV_0 = ANN \times PVAR = 5{,}000 \times \frac{1.05^{12} - 1}{0.05 \times 1.05^{12}} = 44{,}316.26.$$

What amount will Lutz be able to spend for a new car in $t = n$ if he saved the money?

$$FV = ANN \times FVAR = 5{,}000 \times \frac{1.05^{12} - 1}{0.05} = 79{,}585.63.$$

2.4.1 Capital Recovery Factor

The reverse case to the present value of an annuity, as derived in the previous section, is to derive an annuity (ANN) out of a given NPV. In this case the annuity in arrears is given by:

$$ANN = NPV \times \frac{1}{PVAR} = NPV \times \frac{i \times q^n}{q^n - 1}, \tag{2.24}$$

where

$$CRF = \frac{1}{PVAR} = \frac{i \times q^n}{q^n - 1} \tag{2.25}$$

is called capital recovery factor (CRF).

Example 2.9. Capital Recovery Factor

Using the assumptions of Ex. 2.2 on p. 14, we get an NPV of 51.29. Transforming that NPV into an annuity in arrears would give

$$ANN = 51.29 \times \frac{0.05 \times 1.05^4}{1.05^4 - 1} = 14.46.$$

If an annuity of 14.46 is consumed each year, there is no money left at the end of $t = 4$.

2.4.2 Internal Rate of Return

The internal rate of return i^* is defined as the rate of return which results in an *NPV* of zero.

$$NPV = -I_0 + \sum_{t=1}^{n} \frac{CF_t}{(1+i)^t} \stackrel{!}{=} 0 \quad \Leftrightarrow \quad i^* = i \left| \sum_{t=1}^{n} \frac{CF_t}{(1+i^*)^t} - I_0 = 0 \right. . \quad (2.26)$$

Obviously, for any $i < i^*$, *NPV* is positive; for $i > i^*$, *NPV* is negative and if $i = i^*$, there is indifference. In summary

$$i \begin{Bmatrix} > \\ = \\ < \end{Bmatrix} i^* \Leftrightarrow NPV \begin{Bmatrix} < \\ = \\ > \end{Bmatrix} 0.$$

The internal rate of return cannot be found with a simple calculator. You can either use a programmable calculator or use the Excel Solver function. An advanced approach is to calculate the internal rate of return based on Newton's Solution. This method will be explained in Sect. 2.4.3 on p. 28.

Nevertheless, we cannot use the internal rate or return i^* as a decision criterion, because several problems might occur:

1. It is not unique.
   To solve (2.26), a polynomial to the nth-power has to be solved. This gives n possible internal rates of return. Such a result does not lead to a clear economic interpretation because an investment cannot grow at different rates. Moreover, there are investment opportunities that have no internal rate of return, neither a positive nor a negative one, and finally there are cases in which mathematically no real number results when the internal rate of return is calculated.
2. It is implicitly assumed that all intermediate cash flows are treated as if they were reinvested at the rate i^*.
   The implicit assumption of reinvestments at the rate i^* is very abstract. There are rarely cases in which the return of the financial reinvestment alternative equals exactly the internal rate of return of the real investment. Only in the case where no free cash flows are generated and reinvested until the time horizon, this assumption does not produce any problems.
3. The investment option resulting in the highest internal rate of return is not necessarily the best option.
   This can be seen in Ex. 2.10.

Example 2.10. Internal Rate of Return

You have to decide whether a forest should be chopped in 1 or 2 years. The initial investment is assumed to be 1. The capital market interest rate is 10%. Estimating the corresponding cash flows leads to

t	0	1	2
CF_t^{early} (chop forest early)	−1	2	0
CF_t^{late} (chop forest late)	−1	0	3

Chopping the forest early would result in a net present value of

$$NPV^{early} = -1 + \frac{2}{1.1} = 0.82.$$

However, chopping the forest late would give

$$NPV^{late} = -1 + \frac{0}{1.1} + \frac{3}{1.1^2} = 1.48.$$

The net present value criterion suggests to chop the forest in $t = 2$ as this results in a greater positive net present value.

What would the investment decision look like if the internal rate of return was applied? That criterion demands, that if two mutually exclusive investment projects differ from each other then invest in the project with the greater internal rate of return. We get

$$NPV^{early} = -1 + \frac{2}{1+i^*} \stackrel{!}{=} 0 \quad \Rightarrow i^{*,early} = 1$$

$$NPV^{late} = -1 + \frac{0}{1+i^*} + \frac{3}{(1+i^*)^2} \stackrel{!}{=} 0 \quad \Rightarrow i^{*,late} = 0.73.$$

The internal rate of return criterion suggests chopping the forest early because of a greater internal rate of return than chopping in $t = 2$.

Why do the suggestions differ? Remember, the internal rate of return contains the implicit assumption that free cash flows are reinvested at this rate, independent of the capital market interest rate. For this reason, the return of the alternative investment project (opportunity cost of capital in the denominator) is assumed to be 1 or 0.73, respectively. But this is not necessarily the case: The investor has no opportunity to earn the same rate of return with the free cash flow! In this case, the internal rate of return criterion does not reflect reality.

Example 2.11. Nonuniqueness of the Internal Rate of Return

Suppose a three-period investment option resulting in a stream of cash flows of

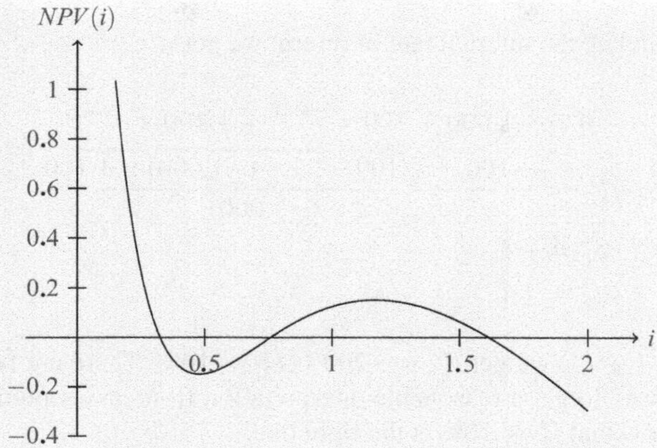

Fig. 2.2 Nonuniqueness of the internal rate or return

t	0	1	2	3
CF_t	−10	57	−104	61

If

$$NPV = -10 + \frac{57}{(1+i^*)} + \frac{-104}{(1+i^*)^2} + \frac{61}{(1+i^*)^3} \stackrel{!}{=} 0$$

is solved for i^*, there are three results ($i^* = 32.65\%, i^* = 75.85\%$, and $i^* = 161.49\%$). So the internal rate of return is not unique (Fig. 2.2). Moreover, the intermediate cash flow of € 57 must definitely be reinvested externally, e.g., in a financial investment that accidentally could have a rate of return equivalent to one of the internal rates of return.

Example 2.12. Negative Internal Rate of Return

There are some more examples which show that the internal rate of return should not be used to evaluate the profitability of investment alternatives. If you put money in a bank account, let's say € 1,000 and get € 100 interest every year, it is intuitively clear that the internal rate of return has to be 10%. If we take 2 years into account, we invest € 1,000, receive a return of € 100 in $t = 1$ and receive the return of € 100 plus the invested funds of € 1,000 in $t = 2$. The cash flow stream is

t	0	1	2
CF_t	−1,000	100	1,100

If we calculate the internal rate of return, we get

$$\begin{aligned}
0 &\stackrel{!}{=} -1{,}000 + 100 \times q^{*-1} + 1{,}100 \times q^{*-2} \\
q^*_{1,2} &= \frac{-100 \pm \sqrt{100^2 - 4 \times (-1{,}000) \times 1{,}100}}{2 \times (-1{,}000)} \\
q^*_1 &= -1 \\
q^*_2 &= 1.1.
\end{aligned}$$

With $q^* = 1 + i^*$, we get $i^*_1 = -200\%, i^*_2 = 10\%$. There are two internal rates of return. To get a reasonable interpretation from an economic point of view we know that $i^*_2 = 10\%$ is the right one.

Two mutual exclusive projects A and B can be compared to each other by calculating the internal rate of return based on the difference investment of the two investments. The profitability of the two investment alternatives depends on the assumed interest rate i. To determine the critical i where $NPV^B(i)$ intersects $NPV^A(i)$, we might set the two functions equal. Another approach is to compute the difference investment $NPV^{A-B}(i)$ and find the root of that new function. The cash flow structure of the difference investment is then

$$A - B = (CF^A_0 - CF^B_0; CF^A_1 - CF^B_1; CF^A_2 - CF^B_2; \ldots; CF^A_n - CF^B_n).$$

The new curve $NPV^{A-B}(i) = NPV^A(i) - NPV^B(i)$ is plotted in Fig. 2.3. Figure 2.3 is based on the following cash flows

$$\begin{aligned}
A &= (-1{,}400; 500; 500; 500; 500) \\
B &= (-1{,}000; 700; 600).
\end{aligned}$$

Notice if $NPV^{A-B}(i) > 0$ and $NPV^A > 0$ investment A is profitable otherwise if $NPV^{A-B}(i) < 0$ and $NPV^B > 0$ investment B should be carried out. The reverse case, the difference investment of $NPV^{B-A}(i)$ would lead to a cash flow structure of

$$B - A = (CF^B_0 - CF^A_0; CF^B_1 - CF^A_1; CF^B_2 - CF^A_2; \ldots; CF^B_n - CF^A_n).$$

and advise us to carry out B if $NPV^{B-A}(i) > 0$ and $NPV^B > 0$ or A if $NPV^{B-A}(i) < 0$ and $NPV^A > 0$. The internal rate of return of the difference investment is $i^* = 12.88\%$.

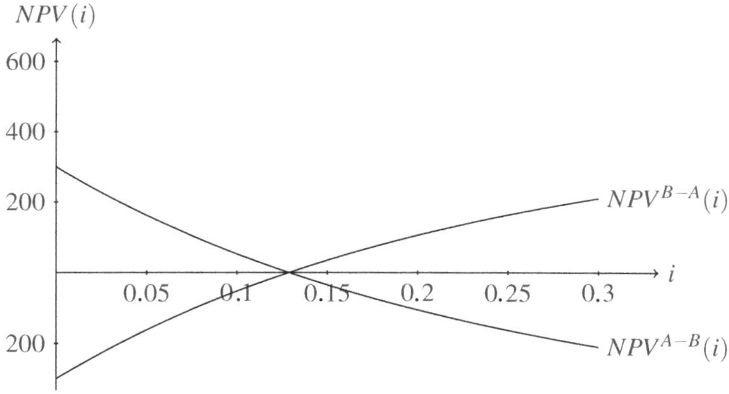

Fig. 2.3 Difference investment $NPV^{A-B}(i)$ and $NPV^{B-A}(i)$

Example 2.13. Internal Rate of Return of Difference Investments

Suppose, there are two investment options A and B that are mutually exclusive alternatives, e.g., two different types of oil pumps, an expensive one that generates constant receipts over a period of 4 years and a cheaper alternative that generates high receipts over a period of 2 years. The cash flows resulting from these investment options are given as:

$$A = (-1{,}400; 500; 500; 500; 500)$$
$$B = (-1{,}000; 700; 600).$$

A plot of the two alternative options against i draws the following picture (Fig. 2.4).

The internal rate of return of investment alternative A gives $i^{*,A} = 15.97\%$, the internal rate of return of alternative B accounts for $i^{*,B} = 20.00\%$. So far, if the investor decides on that basis, he will prefer investment B because it states a higher internal rate of return. In fact, the profitability of the two investment alternatives considered depends on the interest rate i. Subtracting alternative B from alternative A results in a stream of cash flows of $A - B = (-400; -200; -100; 500; 500)$. Now, the internal rate of return is $i^{*,A-B} = 12.88\%$ and represents that rate of return where the graph of investment A intersects the graph of investment B. So, if we calculate the internal rate of return of the so-called difference investment, we are able to evaluate the profitability of the two investments. If $i < 12.88\%$ investment A should be carried out, otherwise if $i > 12.88\%$ investment B is the best choice. If $i = 12.88\%$ the investor is indifferent between investment A and B.

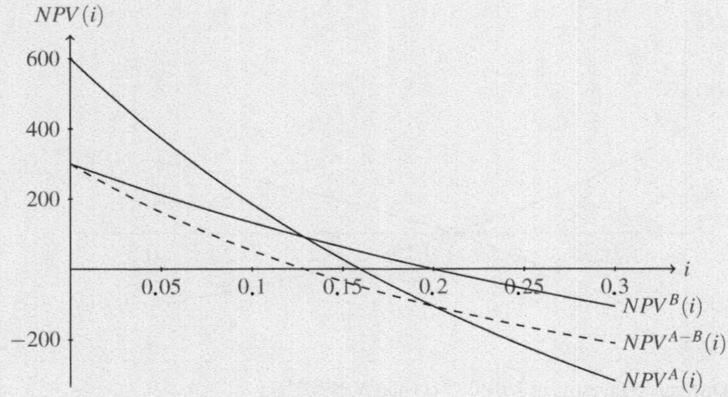

Fig. 2.4 Net present value and internal rate or return

2.4.3 Newton's Solution

The internal rate of return can be determined by using Newton's Solution.

The basis of Newton's Solution is the linear tangent line approximation. If $y(x)$ is differentiable at x_0 then for small changes of x defined as Δx the following equation delivers a good approximation

$$y(x_0 + \Delta x) \cong y(x_0) + y'(x_0) \times \Delta x. \tag{2.27}$$

Proof. To prove the statement of (2.27) let's start illustrating the problem. In the graph shown in Fig. 2.5, starting from the point (x_0, y_0) the variable x changes to the extent of Δx.

Now, the question is, to what extent does y change if x changes by Δx units? Formally, the change in y can be described as:

$$\Delta y = y(x_0 + \Delta x) - y(x_0).$$

Further the difference coefficient answers the question to what extent y changes per change of one unit of x

$$\frac{\Delta y}{\Delta x} = \frac{y(x_0 + \Delta x) - y(x_0)}{\Delta x}.$$

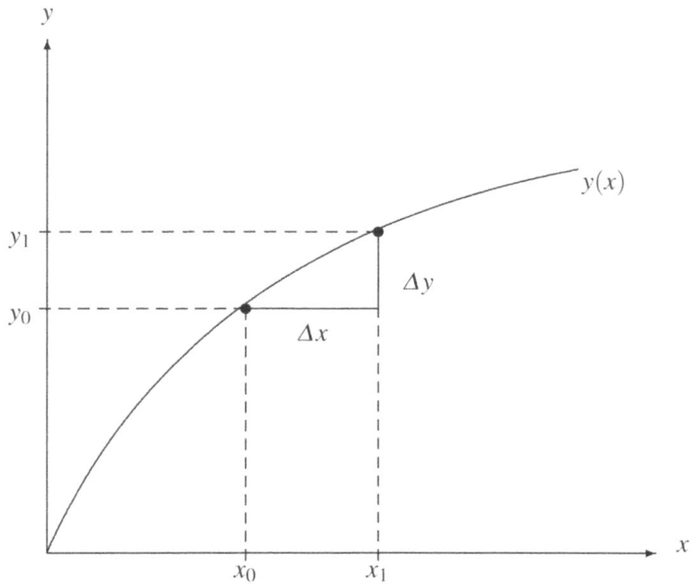

Fig. 2.5 Illustration of changes in x and y

For $\Delta x \to 0$ we get

$$y'(x_0) = \lim_{\Delta x \to 0} \frac{\Delta y}{\Delta x} = \lim_{\Delta x \to 0} \frac{y(x_0 + \Delta x) - y(x_0)}{\Delta x}. \tag{2.28}$$

Ignoring terms of higher order, (2.28) can be rewritten as:

$$y(x_0 + \Delta x) = y(x_0) + y'(x_0) \times \Delta x. \tag{2.29}$$

□

Newton's idea was to take the linear tangent line approximation to determine the point where a function intersects the x-axis. Setting (2.29) equal to zero we get

$$\begin{aligned} y(x_0 + \Delta x) = y(x_0) + y'(x_0) \times \Delta x &= 0 \\ y(x_0) + y'(x_0) \times \Delta x &= 0 \\ \Delta x &= -\frac{y(x_0)}{y'(x_0)}. \end{aligned} \tag{2.30}$$

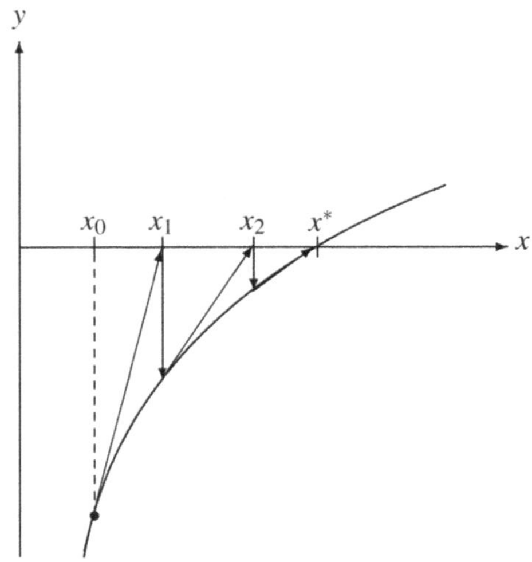

Fig. 2.6 Graphical illustration of Newton's iteration

If $\Delta x = x_{k+1} - x_k$, (2.30) changes finally to

$$x_{k+1} = x_k - \frac{y(x_k)}{y'(x_k)}. \tag{2.31}$$

Figure 2.6 shows the iteration graphically. The starting point is x_0.

Example 2.14. Newton's Solution

To calculate the internal rate of return of Ex. 2.2 on p. 14 we use the standard solution for mixed quadratic equations. But suppose, we face an investment opportunity that gives a cash flow vector that is equal to our standard example and therefore would be $CF = (-100; -30; 50; 70; 90)$. As in this case we do not get a quadratic equation but an equation to the power of four, we are not able to solve the problem in the way we solved our mixed quadratic equation. To determine the internal rate of return there are several algorithms to solve that problem. We want to use Newton's Solution. In that case we have to follow four steps to get the right solution:

1. Estimation of a starting point i_k for $k = 0$ and definition of an interruption value for stopping the calculations: $| i_{k+1} - i_k | < \varepsilon$ ($|\Delta i| < \varepsilon$),
2. Determination of the function value at i_0 ($f(i_0)$),

3. Determination of the function value of the first derivative of the net present value ($f'(i_0)$),
4. Calculation of the new return i_{k+1} taking (2.31) into account

$$i_{k+1} = i_k - \frac{f(i_k)}{f'(i_k)}$$

5. Repetition of steps two to four until the interruption value is reached.

Taking the cash flow vector $CF = (-100; -30; 50; 70; 90)$, we get a net present value function of

$$f(i) = -100 - \frac{30}{(1+i)} + \frac{50}{(1+i)^2} + \frac{70}{(1+i)^3} + \frac{90}{(1+i)^4}.$$

The first derivative gives

$$f'(i) = \frac{30}{(1+i)^2} - \frac{100}{(1+i)^3} - \frac{210}{(1+i)^4} - \frac{360}{(1+i)^5}.$$

1. Estimation of a starting point i_0 and definition of an interruption value: We estimate that the internal rate of return is around 20%, for example. Therefore, we choose $i_0 = 0.2$. We are interested in approximately knowing the correct internal rate of return. We accept a deviation of maximum 0.1 percentage points: $\Delta i < 0.1\%$-points),
2. Determination of the function value at i_0, $f(i_0)$

$$f(0.2) = -100 + \frac{-30}{1.2} + \frac{50}{1.2^2} + \frac{70}{1.2^3} + \frac{90}{1.2^4} = -6.36574,$$

3. Determination of the function value of the first derivative of the net present value $f'(i_0)$

$$f'(0.2) = \frac{30}{1.2^2} - \frac{100}{1.2^3} - \frac{210}{1.2^4} - \frac{360}{1.2^5} = -282.98611,$$

4. Determination of i_1:

$$i_1 = 0.2 - \frac{-6.36574}{-282.98611} = 0.177505.$$

5. The interruption criterion is not reached because $\Delta i = 0.2 - 0.177505 = 0.022495 > 0.001$, therefore we repeat steps two to four:

$$f(i_1 = 0.177505) = 0.27521$$

$$f'(i_1 = 0.177505) = -307.88401$$

$$i_2 = 0.177505 - \frac{0.27521}{-307.88401} = 0.176611.$$

Now, the interruption criterion is reached, because the difference between our solutions resulting from the last two rounds is less than our interruption value of 0.1 percentage point:

$$0.177505 - 0.176611 = 0.000894$$

or 0.0894 percentage points.
The internal rate of return is 17.6611%. We can calculate the *NPV* to check how exact the approximated value is:

$$f(0.176611) = 0.55 \approx 0.$$

2.4.4 Modified Internal Rate of Return (Baldwin Rate of Return)

The modified rate of return (or Baldwin rate of return) can be used to evaluate the profitability of an investment.[4] The advantage compared to the internal rate of return method is that we do not need the assumption that free cash flow is reinvested at the internal rate of return. Instead, it can be reinvested at the capital market interest rate.

Calculation of the Baldwin rate of return depends on the time the investment takes place. If the investment is only carried out in $t = 0$, we can proceed as follows:

Our calculation is based on the future value which we have already computed in Sect. 2.3.3.

The Baldwin rate of return r^B is now defined as the geometrical average rate of return of the initial investment

$$I_0 \times (1 + r^B)^n = FV. \tag{2.32}$$

If (2.32) is solved for r^B as the Baldwin rate of return, we get

$$r^B = \sqrt[n]{\frac{FV}{I_0}} - 1.$$

[4] See *Baldwin* [1].

If the investment payout is spread over several years, we have to split cash flows into positive cash flows which are used to calculate the future value of the investment and into negative investment payments which are used to calculate the present value of the investment in $t = 0$.

First, the present value of all negative cash flows and the future value of all positive cash flows has to be calculated. The present value of the cash outflows gives

$$PV^{CF^-} = \sum_{t=0}^{n} CF_t^- \times q^{-t}$$

whereas the future value of the cash inflows is

$$FV^{CF^+} = \sum_{t=0}^{n} CF_t^+ \times q^{n-t},$$

respectively.

The Baldwin rate of return is now defined as the geometrical average rate of return of the initial investment

$$PV^{CF^-} \times (1 + r^B)^n = FV^{CF^+}. \quad (2.33)$$

If (2.33) is solved for r^B as the Baldwin rate of return, we get

$$r^B = \sqrt[n]{\frac{FV^{CF^+}}{PV^{CF^-}}} - 1. \quad (2.34)$$

For both methods – the net present value and the modified rate of return – the decision rule is as follows: For any $i < r^B$, *NPV* is positive; for $i > r^B$, *NPV* is negative. In summary

$$NPV \begin{Bmatrix} > \\ = \\ < \end{Bmatrix} 0 \Leftrightarrow r^B \begin{Bmatrix} > \\ = \\ < \end{Bmatrix} i.$$

Now, we know, that the net present value (our standard decision criterion) leads to the same result as the Baldwin rate of return. However, this is only true, if the expected useful life n, the capital market interest rate i and the initial investment I_0 of the investment alternatives are the same for each investment opportunity considered. If there are different expected useful lives, interest rates or initial investments, the decisions made based on the net present value criterion and the Baldwin rate of return might differ.

In these cases, the time horizon of the longer lasting project and the initial investment of the more expensive investment have to be used to calculate the modified internal rate of return. Then the modified internal rate of return can be used as a decision criterion equivalent to the *NPV* criterion.

Example 2.15. Modified Internal Rate of Return when the Initial Investment is Spread Over Several Years

Calculating the Baldwin rate of return using the assumptions of Ex. 2.2 on p. 14, we get for PV^{CF^-}

$$PV^{CF^-} = 100 + \frac{30}{1.05} = 128.57.$$

The future value of cash inflows during the time horizon accounts for

$$FV^{CF^+} = 50 \times 1.05^2 + 70 \times 1.05^1 + 90 \times 1.05^0 = 218.63.$$

Therefore, the Baldwin rate of return gives

$$r^B = \sqrt[4]{\frac{218.63}{128.57}} - 1 = 14.19\%.$$

Because $i = 5\% < r^B = 14.193\%$ the investment should be carried out.

Example 2.16 shows which problems occur if the useful lives and the initial investments of two projects differ from each other.

Example 2.16. Modified Internal Rate of Return

Suppose, two mutual exclusive investment projects A and B are available. Economic life of project A (B) is assumed to be 6 (3) years. Acquisition costs of project A (B) are 2,400 (1,000). The cash flow structures are

t	0	1	2	3	4	5	6
CF_t^A	−2,400	700	700	700	700	700	1,100
CF_t^B	−1,000	800	600	450	-	-	-

To determine the modified internal rate of return, we first have to calculate the future value of the cash flow stream starting from $t = 1$. Assuming $i = 12\%$ we get

$$FV^A = 700 \times \frac{1.12^5 - 1}{0.12} \times 1.12 + 1,100 = 6,080.63$$
$$FV^{B,t=3} = 800 \times 1.12^2 + 600 \times 1.12 + 450 = 2,125.52.$$

Under these conditions the modified rate of return is

$$r^A = \sqrt[6]{\frac{6{,}080.63}{2{,}400}} - 1 = 0.1676$$
$$r^B = \sqrt[3]{\frac{2{,}125.52}{1{,}000}} - 1 = 0.2857.$$

The results indicate that investment project B should be preferred because r^B exceeds both r^A and the rate of return i of the alternative financial investment. However, net present values give

$$NPV^A = -2{,}400 + 700 \times \frac{1.12^5 - 1}{0.12 \times 1.12^5} + \frac{1{,}100}{1.12^6} = 680.63$$
$$NPV^B = -1{,}000 + \frac{800}{1.12} + \frac{600}{1.12^2} + \frac{450}{1.12^3} = 512.90.$$

The result suggests that investment project A should be preferred. As the economic life of the two investments differ, some adjustments are necessary. First, we have to compute the future value of project B at $t = 6$ not at $t = 3$. Assuming a yield of $i = 12\%$ during the last three periods, we get

$$FV^{B,t=n} = 2{,}125.52 \times 1.12^3 = 2{,}986.20$$
$$r^B = \sqrt[6]{\frac{2{,}986.20}{1{,}000}} - 1 = 0.2000.$$

We still favor investment B. Now, consider the second adjustment dealing with the acquisition costs. Project A needs funds of 2,400, investment B can be carried out with just 1,000. Supposing acquisition costs of 2,400 for project B we need to consider 2,400 – 1,000 = 1,400 more initial costs. The additional 1,400 are invested at the capital market interest rate i. The modified internal rate of return finally decreases to

$$FV^{B,t=n} = 2{,}125.52 \times 1.12^3 + 1{,}400 \times 1.12^6 = 5{,}749.55$$
$$r^B = \sqrt[6]{\frac{5{,}749.55}{2{,}400}} - 1 = 0.1567.$$

Because we made necessary adjustments to project B in order to calculate profitability in a correct way, the result now advises to choose project A ($r^A = 16.67\% > r^B = 15.67\%$).

2.5 The Fisher Model

In the last sections, we presented the net present value criterion as our standard decision criterion to evaluate the profitability of investment alternatives. But as we learned in our microeconomics lectures, individuals use their individual utility functions to determine their optimal consumption. But so far we presented a decision criterion without considering utility functions. Therefore, it's time to justify the net present value criterion theoretically as a valid decision criterion. The answer why no utility functions were used in the last sections is quite simple. It is possible to show that an investor who maximizes net present value simultaneously maximizes his utility. The following explanations make clear why maximizing net present value is equal to the maximization of the individual utility of the investor (*Fisher* [2]). The basic assumption here is, that utility is exclusively based on material consumption.

2.5.1 Maximization of Utility in Case of Real Investment in the Absence of a Capital Market

Suppose, you have to invest your money solely in real investments, meaning no banks or other financial institutions where you can put money in an account or buy financial assets are available. To derive the investment function assume an investor who is endowed with funds of € 80,000 and faces four discrete investment projects A, B, C, and D. Initial payments I_0 in $t = 0$ as well as returns in terms of total cash flows in $t = 1$ (CF_1) and marginal returns MRR are displayed in Table 2.1. The marginal rate of return is calculated as:

$$MRR = \frac{CF_1 - I_0}{I_0}.$$

The projects in Table 2.1 are already sorted according to their marginal rates of return. Project A yields the highest return, project D the lowest. The marginal rate of return decreases with each additional project carried out.

In this case, facing discrete investment opportunities, the investment function will look like the one illustrated in Fig. 2.7.

In Fig. 2.7 four investment opportunities A, B, C, and D are given. If an investor invests in investment opportunity A, his initial investment would be $\overline{0A}$. Out of that

Table 2.1 Investment projects

Project	I_0	CF_1	MRR
A	20,000	26,000	30%
B	20,000	25,000	25%
C	20,000	24,000	20%
D	20,000	23,000	15%

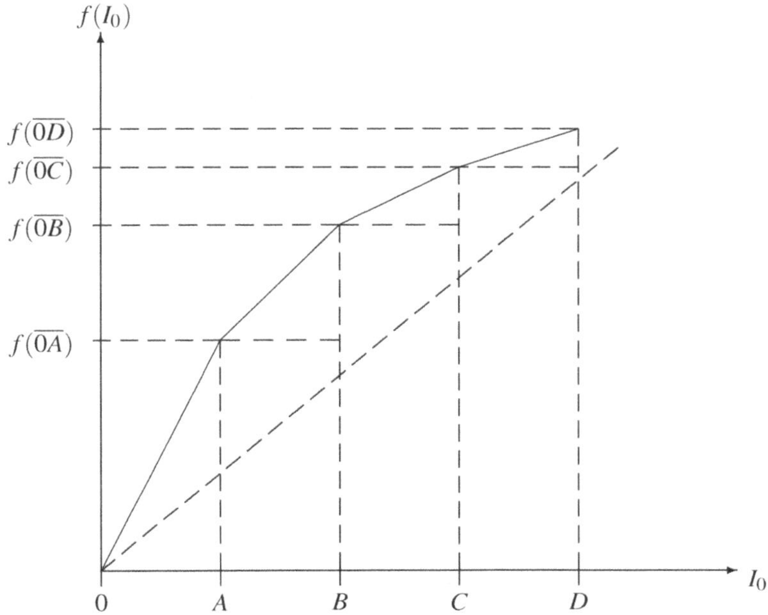

Fig. 2.7 Investment function

investment his return is $f(\overline{0A})$. Therefore, the rate of return is represented by the slope of the first line $(0, f(\overline{0A}))$. Because the first line has the steepest slope, the rate of return of investment A is greater than the rate of return of investment B, C, and D. The rate of return decreases with every additional investment. The dashed line that starts at the origin represents the 45° line. If the return of investments decreases below that line, the investments would not be carried out, because the value of the investment would be lower than the initial investment.

Now, suppose the investor is endowed with funds of W_0 (wealth) in $t = 0$ and has to decide how much to spend for consumption in $t = 0$ (C_0) and how much to invest in $t = 0$ (I_0). The more he invests in $t = 0$, the more he is able to consume in $t = 1$. Consumption is C_0 in $t = 0$. It is assumed that his wealth is consumed completely at the end of $t = 1$. Therefore, we get

$$C_0 = W_0 - I_0.$$

In Fig. 2.8 the transformation curve is illustrated. As you can see, it just represents the mirrored investment function of Fig. 2.7. To keep it simple, we changed from discrete to continuous investment projects.

Two assumptions concerning the investment function have to be made. First, the marginal rate of return must be positive

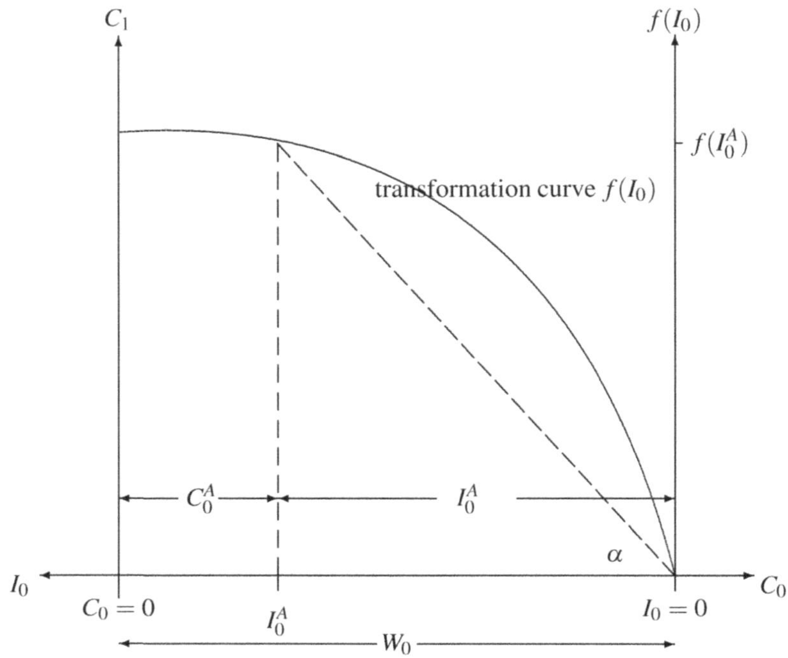

Fig. 2.8 Transformation curve

$$\frac{df(I_0)}{dI_0} > 0.$$

Second, the marginal rate of return decreases

$$\frac{d^2 f(I_0)}{dI_0^2} < 0.$$

On the left side in Fig. 2.8 the ordinate stands for consumption purposes. On the right side the ordinate shows the return of the initial investment. The axis of abscissae shows both C_0 and I_0. Where C_0 increases to the right, I_0 increases to the left. The line between the two ordinates represents the wealth in $t = 0$ (W_0).

Now, suppose an investor invests I_0^A. The money left for consumption therefore accounts to $C_0^A = W_0 - I_0^A$. The return of his initial investment is $f(I_0^A)$ which amounts to the possible consumption in period 1

$$C_1 = f(W_0 - C_0) = f(I_0^A).$$

The rate of return for his initial investment I_0^A is given by the tangent of α

$$r^A = \tan\alpha - 1 = \frac{f(I_0^A)}{I_0^A} - 1. \tag{2.35}$$

Obviously, an investor can consume at each point of the transformation curve. If he consumes all his wealth in $t = 0$, he would not be able to invest some money, therefore $I_0 = 0$ and $C_1 = 0$. If the investor did not consume anything in $t = 0$ and his investment equals his wealth $I_0 = W_0$, his consumption in $t = 1$ accounts for $f(W_0)$ and lies at the point where the transformation curve intersects the ordinate which represents consumption in $t = 1$ (C_1). The transformation curve represents the return on the investment $f(I_0)$. If the investor did not consume all his wealth, his consumption point would lie between the origin of consumption $(C_0 = 0, C_1 = 0)$ and the transformation curve. As we assumed that all his wealth is consumed by the end of period 1, this case is not considered. On the other hand, he cannot consume more than W_0 in $t = 0$. His consumption is restricted to the transformation curve $f(I_0)$ in $t = 1$, because according to our assumptions there is no capital market. Because there is no capital market, he is not able to afford consumption bundles beyond the transformation curve. Hence, all possible consumption patterns lie on the transformation curve.

Now, the question that the investor faces is, to what extent does he have to invest in $t = 0$ in order to be best off? As there are infinite solutions what would be the best one? The best solution would be the one that maximizes his utility of consumption. To determine the utility of consumption, utility has to be quantified. The investor has to maximize the intertemporal utility function. The intertemporal utility function is described by:

$$U(C_0, C_1).$$

It is supposed that the individual derives positive marginal utility out of an additional unit of consumption. However, the marginal utility per additional unit of consumption decreases.

Example 2.17. Marginal Utility

Suppose, you face a hot day in summer. Consuming the first cooled bottle of beer would give you a very big additional utility of consumption. Now, suppose you reached the tenth bottle of beer. The marginal utility of the eleventh beer would definitely not be as big as the marginal utility of the first beer.

The assumption of positive marginal utility also includes, that a billionaire still faces positive marginal utility if he earns his one billion and first Euro.

To accept the assumption of positive, but decreasing marginal utility, we have to accept the postulate of rational behavior. As we do not want to give a complete lecture in microeconomics we focus on the four most important attributes of that postulate.

1. Comparability
   Suppose, there are two bundles of consumption goods A and B. Now, it is true that $A \succ B$, or $B \succ A$, or $A \sim B$, i.e., A is preferred over B, B is preferred over A, or the investor is indifferent between the two goods.

> *Example 2.18.* Comparability of Consumption Bundles
>
> Suppose, there is a world with exclusively two goods of consumption, cheese and wine. The investor is able to evaluate every thinkable mix of these two goods relatively to another mix of those goods, e.g., the bundle A consisting of 10 lbs cheese and 6 bottles of wine is better than bundle B that consists of 8 lbs of cheese and 12 bottles of wine.

2. Transitivity
   If A, B, and D are different bundles of consumption goods and it is assumed that $A \succ B$ and $B \succ D$ then it has to be true that $A \succ D$.

> *Example 2.19.* Transitivity
>
> If 6 lbs cheese and 5 bottles of wine (= consumption bundle A) are better than 5 lbs cheese and 4 bottles of wine (B) and if 5 lbs cheese and 4 bottles of wine (B) are better than 4 lbs cheese and 3 bottles of wine (D), than 6 lbs cheese and 5 bottles of wine (A) are better than 4 lbs cheese and 3 bottles of wine (D).

3. Nonsaturation
   The investor prefers bundle A, that does not contain less from any good but contains more from at least one good than another bundle.

> *Example 2.20.* Nonsaturation
>
> If bundle A contains 4 lbs cheese and 10 bottles of wine, it is better than bundle B that contains 3 lbs cheese and 10 bottles of wine.

4. Decreasing marginal rate of substitution
   If the investor is indifferent between the two different consumption bundles A and B ($A \sim B$, but $A \neq B$) and D is a combination of λ of A and $(1 - \lambda)$ of B ($D = \lambda \times A + (1 - \lambda) \times B$ with $1 > \lambda > 0$) as shown in Fig. 2.9, then it is true that $D \succ A, B$.

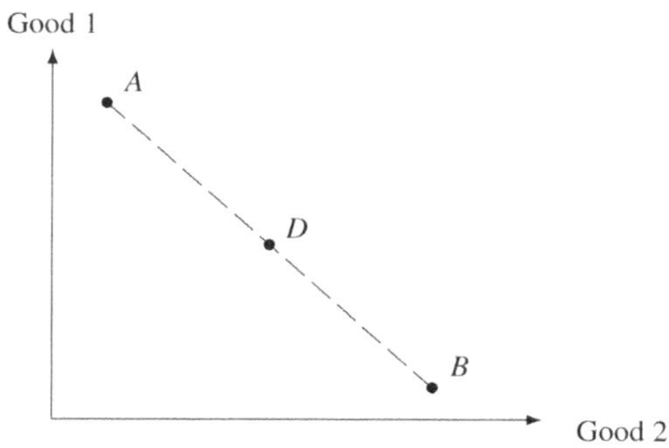

Fig. 2.9 Linear transformation of consumption bundles

Example 2.21. Decreasing Marginal Rate of Substitution

If bundle D is a linear transformation of bundle A and B where the investor is indifferent between A and B then it is assumed that D is better than A and B.

Nonsaturation and decreasing marginal rate of substitution are not necessary for rational behavior. They are assumptions about the attributes of the utility function.

Now, we are able to derive the graph of consumption bundles for which the investor is indifferent. If we start with bundle A in Fig. 2.10, we see that bundle A is located right at the intersection of Sects. I, II, III, and IV. Suppose, we are looking for a bundle B where the investor is indifferent to A. Bundle B cannot lie in Sect. II because all bundles in Sect. II are strictly better than bundle A because in order to be located in Sect. II, more of good 1 and good is needed. The reciprocal case is true for Sect. III. Bundle B cannot be located in Sect. III because in Sect. III all bundles are strictly worse than bundle A because less of good 1 and good 2 is needed to be located in Sect. III. How about Sects. I and IV? To be located in Sect. IV, more of good 2 but less of good 1 is needed. Therefore, in Sect. IV there must be a bundle B that is evaluated indifferent to bundle A by the investor. However, there must also be some bundle D in Sect. I that is indifferent to bundle A because in order to be located in Sect. I more of good 1 but less of good 2 is needed. If we combine all indifferent consumption bundles to bundle A we get the so-called utility indifference curve.

Impossible utility indifference curves are illustrated in Fig. 2.11. Consider the left part of Fig. 2.11 where two utility indifference functions intersect. Suppose, an investor consumes at consumption bundle D. He has to be indifferent to consumption bundle A. So far there is no logical mistake because consumption bundle A represents more consumption of good 2 but less consumption of good 1 and therefore A can possibly be indifferent to bundle D. However, consumption bundle A is

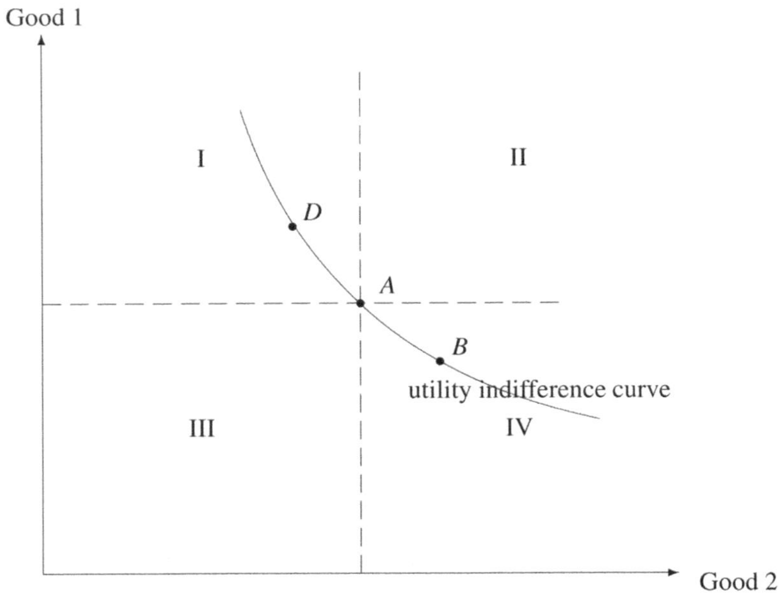

Fig. 2.10 Indifference between consumption bundles

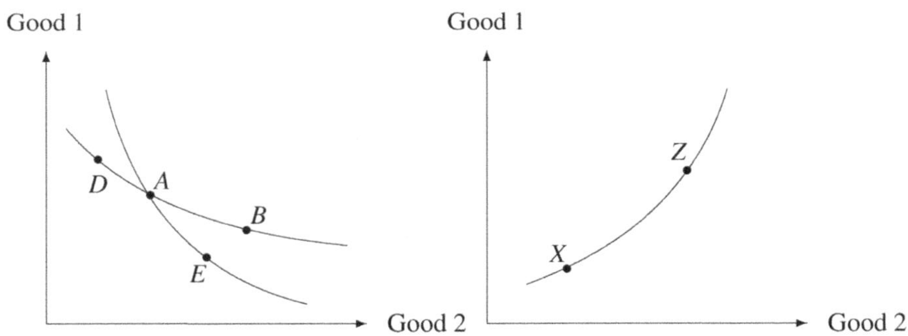

Fig. 2.11 Impossible curves of utility indifference functions

also indifferent to bundle E and B which cannot be possible. As a result, bundle E has to be indifferent to bundle B which cannot be true. Because of the assumption of nonsaturation, bundle B has to be better than E because at B the investor is able to consume more of good 2 and more of good 1. As a result, utility indifference functions cannot intersect.

Let's have a look at the right part of Fig. 2.11. The function drawn implies that an investor is indifferent between consumption bundle X and Z. Because we assumed nonsaturation that conclusion cannot be true. Therefore, the slope of utility indifference functions cannot be positive.

Let's switch to our intertemporal utility model with consumption in $t = 0$ (C_0) and consumption in $t = 1$ (C_1). Figure 2.12 illustrates utility indifference functions in a $C_0 - C_1$-coordinate system. If the function moves to the north east, a higher utility level is reached. If the function moves to the south west, a lower utility level is reached. The level of utility is for example determined by the endowment in $t = 0$. The higher the wealth in $t = 0$, the higher the overall utility level.

Technically, the utility indifference function in a $C_0 - C_1$-coordinate systems is described by:

$$U(C_0, C_1).$$

Figure 2.13 describes the marginal rate of substitution. The marginal rate of substitution is the slope of the utility indifference function at a specific point. It describes the ratio at which the investor is willing to give up consumption in $t = 0$ for consumption in $t = 1$. In our wine and cheese example, it would be the ratio of how much cheese the investor is willing to give up in order to consume more wine. Let's consider consumption bundle A in Fig. 2.13. The slope at point A is defined as the ratio of the change of consumption in $t = 1$ that is ΔC_1^A to the change of consumption in $t = 0$ that is ΔC_0^A. Because the coordinate plane shows the dependence of C_1 from C_0 and we express the give-up of consumption in $t = 1$ for consumption in

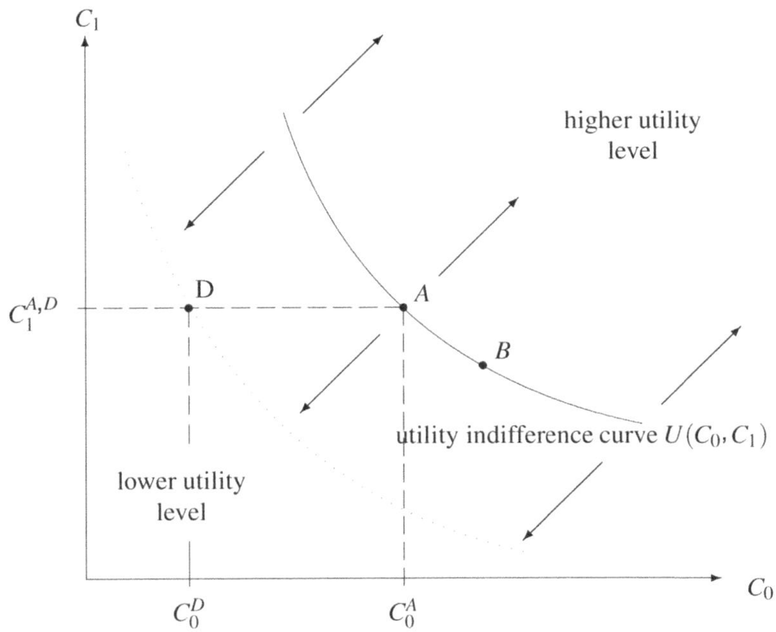

Fig. 2.12 Utility indifference functions

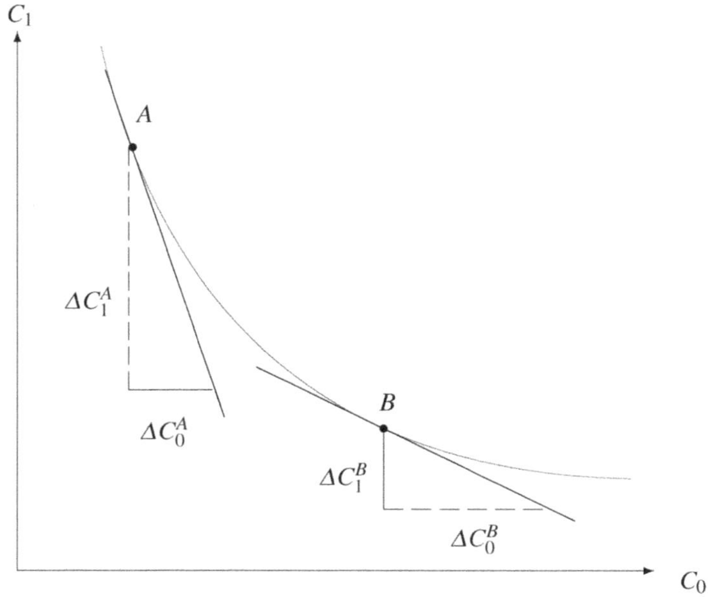

Fig. 2.13 Marginal rate of substitution

$t = 0$, the change of consumption in $t = 1$ is negative. Therefore, we get $\Delta C_1^A < 0$ and hence a negative slope.

Technically, the marginal rate of substitution is expressed by the total differential of the utility indifference function. That is

$$U(C_0, C_1)$$

$$dU = \frac{\partial^2 U}{\partial C_0 \partial C_1} = \frac{\partial U}{\partial C_0} \times dC_0 + \frac{\partial U}{\partial C_1} \times dC_1 = 0$$

$$\Leftrightarrow \frac{\partial U}{\partial C_0} \times dC_0 = -\frac{\partial U}{\partial C_1} \times dC_1$$

$$\frac{\frac{\partial U}{\partial C_0}}{\frac{\partial U}{\partial C_1}} = -\frac{dC_1}{dC_0}. \tag{2.36}$$

The first derivative of the marginal rate of substitution is positive

$$\frac{\partial \left(-\frac{dC_1}{dC_0}\right)}{\partial C_0} > 0,$$

that means that the marginal rate of substitution decreases if consumption in $t = 0$ decreases. Consider Fig. 2.13 again. The slope of the utility indifference function at consumption bundle B is less steep than the slope at bundle A. To get some more consumption in $t = 1$ at point B he is not willing to give up that much of consumption in $t = 0$.

Example 2.22. Marginal Rate of Substitution

Consider an extreme consumption bundle where you have 1,000 lbs of cheese and just 1 bottle of wine. It's clear, that you are willing to give up a lot of cheese to get some more wine. However, if you have 5 lbs of cheese and 6 bottles of wine you may be not willing to give up that much cheese in order to have some more wine.

Now, we are able to combine our results of Fig. 2.8 – the transformation curve – and Fig. 2.10 – the utility indifference function. Starting with Fig. 2.8, remember that the investor still faces the problem that he does not know how much he should invest in $t = 0$ to be best off. In Fig. 2.10, we derived the utility indifference function and are able to plot that function in a $C_0 - C_1$-coordinate plane (see Fig. 2.12). The result was the optimal investment decision drawn in Fig. 2.14. We already know that the utility level increases if there is a parallel translation to the north east. However, the consumption bundles are restricted by the investment function, meaning the investor can just afford consumptions bundles that lie between the origin $C_0, C_1 = 0$ and the investment function or on the investment function. Hence, consumption bundle E is not affordable whereas consumption bundle B implies that the investor has not consumed his whole wealth by the end of $t = 1$. As we assumed that all wealth is consumed by the end of $t = 1$, the consumption bundle or the optimal investment in $t = 0$, respectively, has to be right on the investment function.

Now, consider consumption bundle A which is located right on the investment function. The utility indifference function shows, that the investor is indifferent between bundle A and bundle B. Therefore, bundle A cannot be optimal because the investor will be indifferent between a bundle at which he consumes all his wealth (bundle A) and a bundle where still some wealth is left at the end of $t = 1$ (bundle B). If we now move along the investment function from bundle A to bundle C^*, the wealth that is left at indifferent bundles that are located in the area between the origin $C_0 = 0$ and the investment function decreases. On the other hand, there is a parallel translation of the utility indifference function representing a higher level of utility while moving along the investment function from point A to point C^*. Therefore, the optimal bundle is represented by bundle C^*, where the utility indifference function is tangent to the investment function.

If we go back to Fig. 2.8, we remember that there are two ordinates. The second one, the one that represents the absolute return in $t = 1$, cannot be found in Fig. 2.14 but is still there. The origin of investment in $t = 0$ ($I_0 = 0$) can be found where the investment function touches the axis of abscissae. To the left, the investment in $t = 0$ increases. Now, if we know the optimal consumption bundle C^*, we can

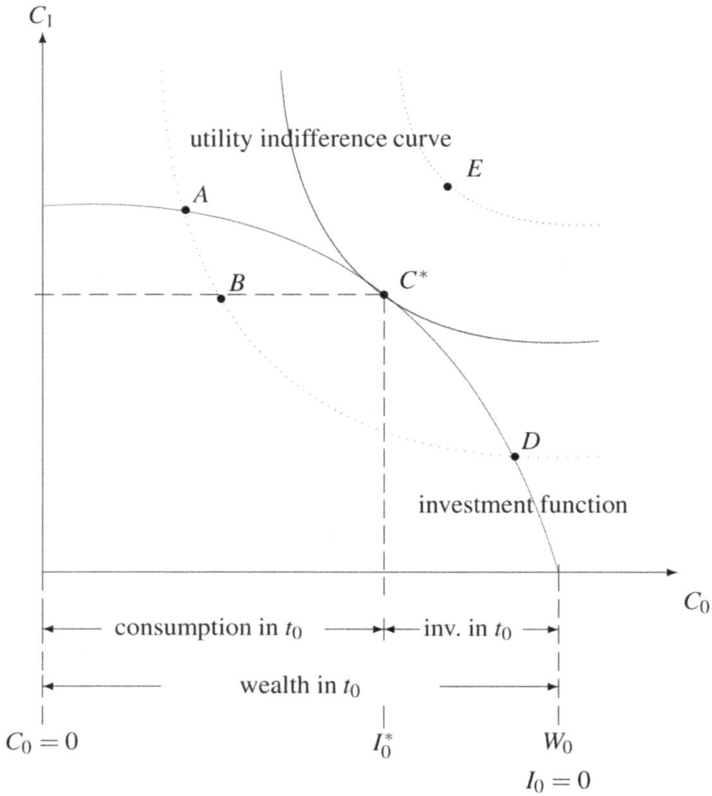

Fig. 2.14 Optimal investment decision

derive the optimal investment in $t = 0$ (I_0^*). After determination of I_0^* we can derive optimal consumption C_0^* in $t = 0$ that is

$$C_0^* = W_0 - I_0^*.$$

Technically, the optimal consumption bundle is derived by the maximization of the utility function with subject to the budget restriction. If the utility function is represented by $U(C_0, C_1)$ where C_0 and C_1 represent the decision variables, the problem of optimization is described by:

$$\max_{C_0, C_1} \quad U(C_0, C_1) \tag{2.37}$$

$$\begin{aligned} \text{s.t. } C_1 &= f(I_0) \\ I_0 &= W_0 - C_0. \end{aligned}$$

Notice, the restrictions bind. The Lagrangian function gives with $f(I_0) = f(W_0 - C_0)$

$$\mathscr{L}(C_0, C_1, \lambda) = U(C_0, C_1) + \lambda \times (f(W_0 - C_0) - C_1).$$

The partial derivatives of C_0 and C_1 account for

$$\frac{\partial \mathscr{L}}{\partial C_0} = \frac{\partial U}{\partial C_0} + \lambda \times \frac{df}{dI_0} \times \frac{\partial I_0}{\partial C_0} = \frac{\partial U}{\partial C_0} - \lambda \times \frac{df}{dI_0} = 0 \tag{2.38}$$

$$\frac{\partial \mathscr{L}}{\partial C_1} = \frac{\partial U}{\partial C_1} - \lambda = 0. \tag{2.39}$$

To simplify (2.38), we use $I_0(C_0) = W_0 - C_0$ as one of the restrictions of (2.37). The first derivative of that restriction is $\frac{\partial I_0}{\partial C_0} = -1$. Solving (2.38) and (2.39) for λ and setting equal to zero we get

$$\frac{\frac{\partial U}{\partial C_0}}{\frac{\partial U}{\partial C_1}} = \frac{df}{dI_0}$$

$$\Leftrightarrow$$

$$\frac{\frac{\partial U}{\partial C_0}}{\frac{\partial U}{\partial C_1}} = -\frac{dC_1}{dC_0} = \frac{df}{dI_0}.$$

The result shows that the optimum is reached if the marginal rate of substitution equals the marginal rate of transformation (the slope of the real investment function). If the slope of the real investment function is defined as the rate of return r (which is actually equal to the internal rate of the return) of the initial investment we get

$$-\frac{dC_1}{dC_0} = \frac{df}{dI_0} = 1 + r.$$

Example 2.23. Optimal Real Investment

Suppose, an investor is endowed with funds of equity of $W_0 = 100$ in $t = 0$. In $t = 0$ he has to decide how to split up the money for consumption and real investment. The money that is invested will be consumed – including the return – in $t = 1$. He tells you that his utility function is

$$U(C_0, C_1) = C_0 \times C_1,$$

where C_0 stands for consumption in $t = 0$ and C_1 for consumption in $t = 1$. If he invests money in $t = 0$ in a real investment the amount ready for consumption in $t = 1$ is assumed to be

$$f(I_0) = 20 \times \sqrt{I_0}.$$

It is assumed that there is no money left for consumption at the end of $t = 1$. Hence, the restriction in $t = 1$ is $C_1 = f(I_0)$ (see (2.37)). Further, investment in $t = 0$ must be $I_0 = W_0 - C_0$. The Lagrangian function then gives

$$\mathscr{L}(C_0, C_1, \lambda) = C_0 \times C_1 + \lambda \times \left[20 \times \sqrt{(W_0 - C_0)} - C_1\right].$$

The partial derivatives with respect to C_0, C_1, and λ are

$$\frac{\partial \mathscr{L}}{\partial C_0} = C_1 - \lambda \times \frac{10}{\sqrt{(W_0 - C_0)}} = 0 \tag{2.40}$$

$$\frac{\partial \mathscr{L}}{\partial C_1} = C_0 - \lambda = 0 \tag{2.41}$$

$$\frac{\partial \mathscr{L}}{\partial \lambda} = 20 \times \sqrt{(W_0 - C_0)} - C_1 = 0. \tag{2.42}$$

Solving (2.40) and (2.41) for λ and setting equal we get

$$\frac{C_1 \times \sqrt{(W_0 - C_0)}}{10} = C_0. \tag{2.43}$$

Now, solving (2.43) for C_1 gives

$$C_1 = \frac{10 \times C_0}{\sqrt{(W_0 - C_0)}}. \tag{2.44}$$

Now, we insert (2.44) in (2.42), use $W_0 = 100$ and solve for C_0

$$\begin{aligned} 0 &= 20 \times \sqrt{(W_0 - C_0)} - \frac{10 \times C_0}{\sqrt{(W_0 - C_0)}} \\ 0 &= 20 \times (W_0 - C_0) - 10 \times C_0 \\ C_0 &= \frac{20 \times W_0}{30} \\ C_0 &= 66.67. \end{aligned} \tag{2.45}$$

Equation (2.45) in (2.44) gives

$$C_1 = \frac{10 \times C_0}{\sqrt{(W_0 - C_0)}} = \frac{10 \times 66.67}{\sqrt{(100 - 66.67)}} = 115.48.$$

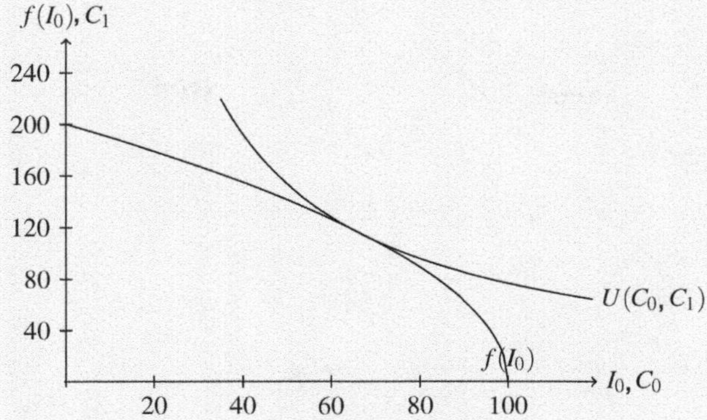

Fig. 2.15 Optimal consumption bundle in absence of a capital market

Investment in $t = 0$ is then calculated as:

$$I_0 = W_0 - C_0 = 100 - 66.67 = 33.33$$

whereas consumption C_1 must be $20 \times \sqrt{(W_0 - C_0)} = 115.46$. The result is shown graphically in Fig. 2.15.

2.5.2 *Integration of a Capital Market*

The result of the previous section assumes the absence of a capital market. Therefore, investors cannot lend money from others or invest money in financial investments in order to improve their level of utility. All money that is not consumed has to be invested in real investment projects. Because we excluded a negative return, investing money is always better than keeping money under the pillow.

2.5.2.1 Lending Rate Equals Borrowing Rate

Figure 2.16 shows the investment function if an investor invests in a financial investment with a fixed interest rate i. If assets of F_0^A are invested in $t = 0$, the investor will get back $F_1^A = f(F_0^A)$ in $t = 1$ or

$$f(F_0^A) = (1 + i) \times F_0^A.$$

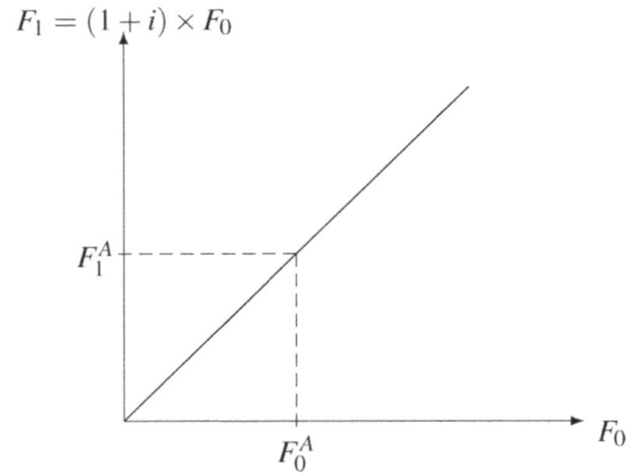

Fig. 2.16 Financial investment

The slope of the financial investment function is

$$\frac{\partial f(F_0)}{\partial F_0} = 1 + i.$$

Figure 2.17 represents the counterpart to Fig. 2.8 and shows the determination of the optimal financial investment in $t = 0$. If the assumption that the whole wealth of the investor is consumed by the end of $t = 1$ is maintained, the consumption bundles the investor has to choose are right on the financial investment curve. The area of possible consumption bundles is restricted to the area between $C_0, C_1 = 0$ and the financial investment function. Consumption bundles above the financial investment function are not reachable for the investor – he cannot afford those bundles. The procedure to determine the optimal consumption bundle is the same compared to the determination of the optimal real investment. The optimal point A is where the utility indifference function is tangent to the financial investment function. Now, consumption in $t = 0$ would be

$$C_0^A = W_0 - F_0^A$$

whereas consumption in $t = 1$ is

$$C_1^A = F_0^A \times (1 + i).$$

That leads to the consumption bundle

$$A = (C_0^A, C_1^A) = (W_0 - F_0^A, F_0^A \times (1 + i)).$$

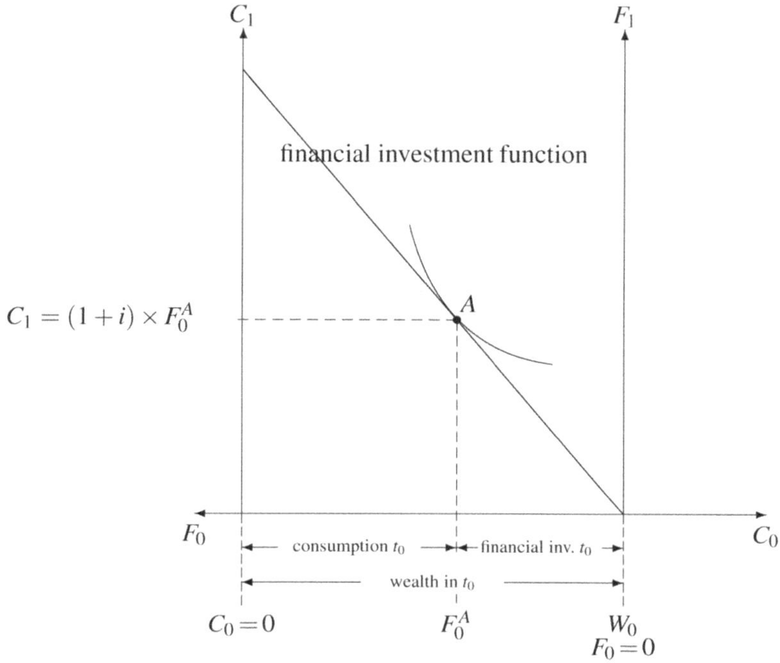

Fig. 2.17 Optimal financial investment

Technically, the optimization problem is defined as:

$$\max_{C_0, C_1} \quad U(C_0, C_1) \tag{2.46}$$

$$\text{s.t. } C_1 = f(F_0)$$
$$F_0 = W_0 - C_0.$$

The Lagrangian function gives

$$\mathscr{L}(C_0, C_1) = U(C_0, C_1) + \lambda \times (f(W_0 - C_0) - C_1).$$

Remember that $\frac{\partial F_0}{\partial C_0} = -1$. The partial derivatives of C_0 and C_1 account for

$$\frac{\partial \mathscr{L}}{\partial C_0} = \frac{\partial U}{\partial C_0} + \lambda \times \frac{df}{dF_0} \times \frac{\partial F_0}{\partial C_0} = \frac{\partial U}{\partial C_0} - \lambda \times \frac{df}{dF_0} = 0$$

$$\frac{\partial \mathscr{L}}{\partial C_1} = \frac{\partial U}{\partial C_1} - \lambda = 0.$$

Hence we get

$$\frac{\frac{\partial U}{\partial C_0}}{\frac{\partial U}{\partial C_1}} = -\frac{dC_1}{dC_0} = \frac{df}{dF_0} = 1 + i.$$

Example 2.24. Optimal Financial Investment

Suppose, an investor is endowed with funds of equity of $W_0 = 100$ in $t = 0$. In $t = 0$ he has to decide how to split up the money for consumption and financial investment. There are no real investment opportunities. The money that is invested will be consumed – including the return – in $t = 1$. He tells you that his utility function is

$$U(C_0, C_1) = \sqrt{C_0} \times C_1,$$

where C_0 stands for consumption in $t = 0$ and C_1 for consumption in $t = 1$. If he invests money in $t = 0$ in a financial investment (F_0), the amount ready for consumption in $t = 1$ is

$$f(F_0) = F_0 \times 1.1.$$

It is assumed that after consumption in $t = 1$, there is no money left. Hence the restriction in $t = 1$ is $C_1 = f(F_0)$ (see (2.46)). Further, investment in $t = 0$ must be $F_0 = W_0 - C_0$. The Lagrangian function then gives

$$\mathcal{L}(C_0, C_1, \lambda) = \sqrt{C_0} \times C_1 + \lambda \times [(W_0 - C_0) \times 1.1 - C_1].$$

The partial derivatives with respect to C_0, C_1, and λ are

$$\frac{\partial \mathcal{L}}{\partial C_0} = \frac{C_1}{2 \times \sqrt{C_0}} - 1.1 \times \lambda = 0 \tag{2.47}$$

$$\frac{\partial \mathcal{L}}{\partial C_1} = \sqrt{C_0} - \lambda = 0 \tag{2.48}$$

$$\frac{\partial \mathcal{L}}{\partial \lambda} = (W_0 - C_0) \times 1.1 - C_1 = 0. \tag{2.49}$$

Solving (2.47) and (2.48) for λ and setting equal we get

$$\frac{C_1}{2 \times \sqrt{C_0} \times 1.1} = \sqrt{C_0}. \tag{2.50}$$

Now, solving (2.50) for C_1 gives

$$C_1 = 2.2 \times C_0. \tag{2.51}$$

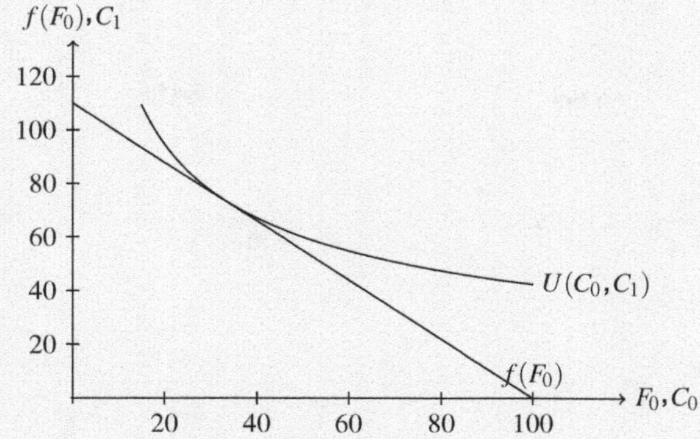

Fig. 2.18 Optimal consumption bundle in absence of a real investment opportunity

Now, we insert (2.51) in (2.49), use $W_0 = 100$ and solve for C_0

$$\begin{aligned} 0 &= (100 - C_0) \times 1.1 - 2.2 \times C_0 \\ C_0 &= 33.33. \end{aligned} \tag{2.52}$$

Equation (2.52) in (2.51) gives

$$C_1 = 2.2 \times C_0 = 2.2 \times 33.33 = 73.33.$$

Investment in $t = 0$ is then calculated as:

$$F_0 = W_0 - C_0 = 100 - 33.33 = 66.66$$

whereas consumption in C_1 must be $F_0 \times 1.1 = 66.66 \times 1.1 = 73.33$. The result is shown graphically in Fig. 2.18.

In this case, the financial market can only be used to lend money. Borrowing money is not intended.

Figure 2.19 shows the combination of the real investment function and the financial investment function. The situation is illustrated where the investor has to lend money from the financial market in order to be able to reach his desired consumption bundle. First of all you can see, that the area of possible consumption bundles increases. The possible consumption bundles are now restricted by both the real investment function and the financial investment function. Therefore, integrating a financial market improves utility for investors. Now, there are three coordinate planes drawn in just one figure. We have the coordinate planes for consumption, real investments and financial investments. The origin for consumption ($C_0 = 0$) is

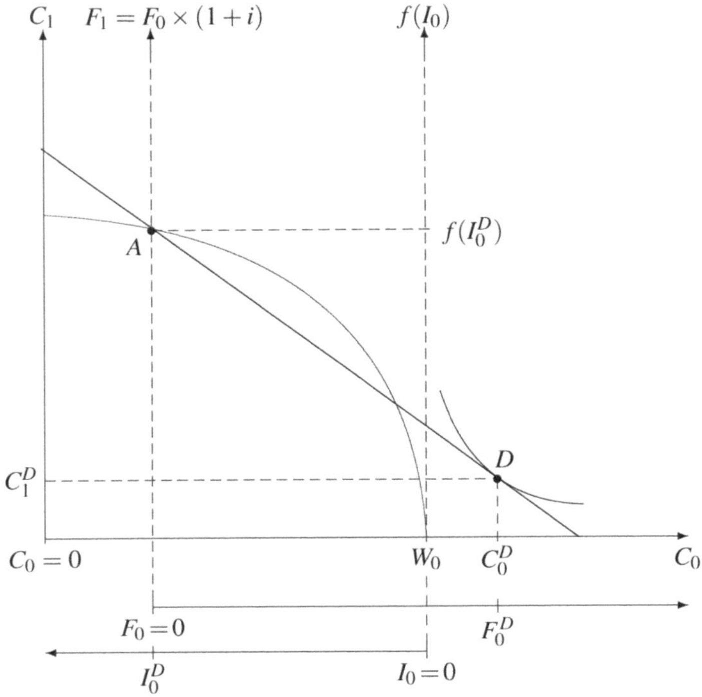

Fig. 2.19 Combination of real investment and financial investment (lending situation)

located at the very lower left end of the coordinate plane. The origin for real investments is located where the investment function touches the axis of abscissae. And as we will see later, the origin for financial investments ($F_0 = 0$) is located at the coordinate of abscissae at the point of the real investment I_0.

Now, assume that an investor wants to consume at point D. At that point he faces the problem that consumption in $t = 0$ (C_0^D) is definitely greater than his endowment in $t = 0$ (W_0). Therefore, it is true that $C_0^D > W_0$. To be able to afford consumption C_0^D he needs to borrow money from the financial market. At the same time he has to decide what part of his endowment in $t = 0$ he wants to invest in real investments. To invest in real investments and at the same time borrow money from the financial market makes sense because the rate of return of these two types of investments is not the same.

Let's first consider the real investment decision. Suppose, the investor invests I_0^D. That leads to a return in $t = 1$ of $f(I_0^D)$. However, investing I_0^D means that there is just $W_0 - I_0^D$ left for consumption. The investor cannot reach his desired consumption bundle at point D. To reach D he has to borrow F_0^D from the capital market. Now, he is able to consume more than his initial endowment in $t = 0$, that would be

$$C_0^D = W_0 - I_0^D + F_0^D.$$

In $t = 1$ he has to pay back the credit inclusive interest. At the same time he collects the return of his real investment made in $t = 0$. Consumption in $t = 1$ is restricted to the return of the real investment less the compounded credit.

$$C_1^D = f(I_0^D) - F_0^D \times (1 + i).$$

Now, consider the situation in Fig. 2.20. In that case the investor wants to realize consumption bundle B and, therefore, does not borrow money from the financial market but invests money in the financial market. He first has to decide to what extent he invests money in the real investment. Suppose, he chooses the real investment I_0^B. However, if choosing I_0^B there is still some money left, because his consumption in $t = 0$ is lower than $W_0 - I_0^B$. So the difference has to be invested in the financial market. Consumption in $t = 0$ is then

$$C_0^B = W_0 - I_0^B - F_0^B.$$

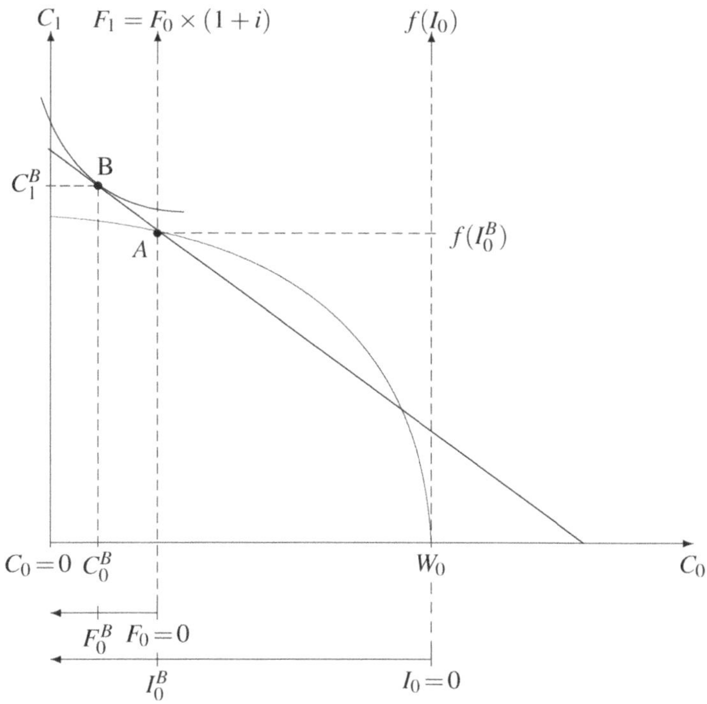

Fig. 2.20 Combination of real investment and financial investment (financial investment situation)

The return of the real investment in $t = 1$ accounts for $f(I_0^B)$ whereas the payoff of the financial investment is $F_0^B \times (1+i)$. Consumption in $t = 1$ therefore accounts for

$$C_1^B = f(I_0^B) + F_0^B \times (1+i).$$

In Figs. 2.19 and 2.20 we described the two possible cases an investor can face if he strives for his optimal consumption bundle. However, we have not presented the overall optimal solution. We already mentioned that the existence of a financial market expands the possible consumption bundles and therefore increases utility. Now, it's easy to see that a parallel translation of the financial investment function to that extent that it is tangent to the real investment function would maximize the area of possible consumption bundles and therefore maximizes utility. Another explanation for maximal consumption is, that an investor will invest his initial endowment into real investments as long as the internal rate of return exceeds the rate of return of the financial investment. That is investment in real investment to that point where the slope of the transformation curve equals the slope of the financial investment function.

The case where the investment function is tangent to the transformation curve is drawn in Fig. 2.21. The only case where the existence of a capital markets does not lead to a higher utility level is when consumption bundle A represents the optimal consumption bundle. Now, suppose an investor wants to consume at point D. In $t = 0$, he then invests I_0^* to the real investment and borrows money from the capital market to the amount of F_0^D. However, if he wants to consume at point B, in $t = 0$ he also invests I_0^* but puts money on the capital market to the amount of F_0^B. Hence, it does not matter where on the capital market curve the investor wants to consume, he always invests I_0^* into real investments. That means that he is able to make his investment decision independently of his consumption preferences which is the main conclusion of the so-called Fisher Theorem. If that is true, in order to determine the optimal consumption bundle, the investor can separate his decision into two steps:

1. Determination of the optimal investment decision represented by the determination of the optimal level of the initial investment I_0^* without considering preferences or utility functions.
2. Determination of the optimal consumption bundle according to the individual preferences or utility function.

Figure 2.21 also shows the maximum additional consumption in $t = 0$ and $t = 1$ if a financial market exists. The maximum consumption in $t = 0$ is represented by C_0^{max}. The additional potential consumption through the existence of a financial market would be $C_0^{max} - W_0$.

We know from Fig. 2.21 that graphically, the investors are best off if the financial market line is tangent to the transformation curve (real investment function). However, we have not shown yet why we are allowed to use the net present value as a decision criterion without taking individual utility functions into account. To be able to do so, we have to derive the optimal solution.

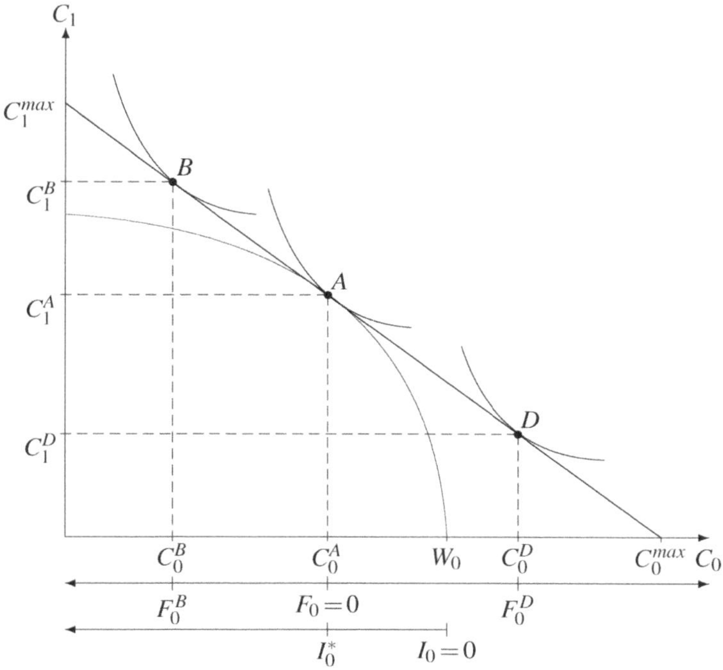

Fig. 2.21 Optimal real investment decision

Suppose, an investor faces consumption bundle A at Fig. 2.22. We know that the slope of the financial market function is $-(1+i)$. Therefore, we get

$$\tan\alpha = \frac{f(I_0^A)}{F_0} = \frac{f(I_0^A)}{C_0^{max} - (W_0 - I_0^A)} = 1 + i$$

$$C_0^{max} - (W_0 - I_0^A) = \frac{f(I_0^A)}{1+i}$$

$$C_0^{max} - W_0 = -I_0^A + \frac{f(I_0^A)}{1+i}. \tag{2.53}$$

The right-hand side of (2.53) now represents the net present value. The initial investment is I_0^A. The cash flow generated by that initial investment in $t = 1$ is $f(I_0^A)$ discounted at rate $1+i$

$$NPV(I_0^A) = -I_0^A + \frac{f(I_0^A)}{1+i}.$$

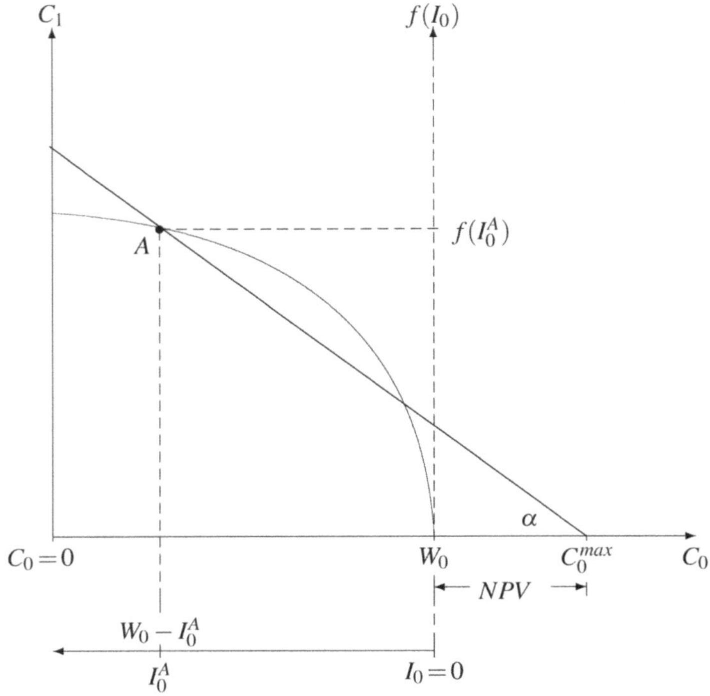

Fig. 2.22 Net present value

Therefore, additional consumption potential caused by the existence of a capital market is represented by the net present value.

An alternative way to derive the net present value is to start exclusively with a financial investment. Therefore, in $t = 1$ consumption is given by:

$$C_1^A = (1+i) \times F_0^A \quad \Rightarrow \quad C_1^A = (1+i) \times (I_0^A + C_0^{max} - W_0). \tag{2.54}$$

Remember that $(I_0^A + C_0^{max} - W_0)$ equals F_0^A. If the investor invests exclusively in a real investment we get

$$C_1^A = f(I_0^A). \tag{2.55}$$

If we set equal (2.54) and (2.55) we get

$$f(I_0^A) = (1+i) \times (I_0^A + C_0^{max} - W_0)$$

$$\frac{f(I_0^A)}{(1+i)} = I_0^A + C_0^{max} - W_0.$$

$$C_0^{max} - W_0 = -I_0^A + \frac{f(I_0^A)}{(1+i)}. \tag{2.56}$$

Now, if (2.53) represents the net present value then the net present value reaches its maximum if $C_0^{max} - W_0$ is at maximum. In turn, $C_0^{max} - W_0$ reaches its maximum if there is a parallel translation of the capital market line until it is tangent to the transformation function. As we can see, the net present value represents the additional consumption possibility compared to the alternative investment. The result also shows, that the net present value criterion goes conform with the maximization of utility. However, the most important insight of that result is, that for investment decisions based on the net present value criterion no individual utility functions are necessary, because choosing the project with the highest *NPV* always guarantees maximal utility.

Up to this point, we derived the solution of the Fisher-Separation graphically. We still have to derive it technically – taking financial and real investments into account – in order to justify the use of the net present value criterion. The investor faces the problem that he has to decide in $t = 0$ how much to invest in real investments in order to maximize utility over a two period time horizon.

$$\max_{C_0, C_1, F_0, I_0} \quad U(C_0, C_1) \tag{2.57}$$

$$\text{s.t. } C_1 = f(I_0) + F_0 \times (1 + i)$$
$$I_0 = W_0 - C_0 - F_0.$$

As I_0 can be derived by $I_0 = W_0 - C_0 - F_0$, (2.57) is reduced to

$$\max_{C_0, C_1, F_0} \quad U(C_0, C_1) \tag{2.58}$$

$$\text{s.t. } C_1 = f(W_0 - C_0 - F_0) + F_0 \times (1 + i).$$

The Lagrangian function gives

$$\mathcal{L}(C_0, C_1, F_0) = U(C_0, C_1) + \lambda \times (f(\underbrace{W_0 - C_0 - F_0}_{I_0}) + F_0 \times (1 + i) - C_1).$$

The partial derivatives of C_0, C_1, and F_0 account for

$$\frac{\partial \mathcal{L}}{\partial C_0} = \frac{\partial U}{\partial C_0} + \lambda \times \frac{df}{dI_0} \times \frac{\partial I_0}{\partial C_0} = \frac{\partial U}{\partial C_0} - \lambda \times \frac{df}{dI_0} = 0 \tag{2.59}$$

$$\frac{\partial \mathcal{L}}{\partial C_1} = \frac{\partial U}{\partial C_1} - \lambda = 0 \tag{2.60}$$

$$\frac{\partial \mathcal{L}}{\partial F_0} = \lambda \left(\frac{df}{dI_0} \times \frac{\partial I_0}{\partial F_0} + (1 + i) \right) = 0. \tag{2.61}$$

Because of nonsaturation, the budget restriction always binds and therefore $\lambda^* \neq 0$ and $\frac{\partial I_0}{\partial F_0} = -1$. Equation (2.61) is equivalent to

$$\frac{df}{dI_0} = 1 + i.$$

Again, the result shows, that in order to determine the optimal initial real investment level, the investor just has to know the real investment function and the rate of return of the alternative financial investment. Moreover, the result is also the essential constraint for a maximum net present value. If we differentiate the net present value function

$$NPV(I_0) = -I_0 + \frac{f(I_0)}{1+i}$$

we get

$$\frac{dNPV(I_0)}{dI_0} = -1 + \frac{\frac{df}{dI_0}}{1+i} = 0$$
$$\frac{df}{dI_0} = 1 + i.$$

Example 2.25. Optimal Consumption Bundle

Suppose, an investor is endowed with funds of equity of $W_0 = 100$ in $t = 0$. In $t = 0$ he has to decide how to split up the money for consumption and real investment. The money that is invested will be consumed – including the return – in $t = 1$. The utility function is assumed to be

$$U(C_0, C_1) = C_0^2 \times C_1.$$

We assume that the real investment function is

$$f(I_0) = 15 \times \sqrt{I_0}.$$

It is assumed, that after consumption in $t = 1$, there is no money left. According to (2.57) there are two restrictions to consider. First, consumption in $t = 1$ has to be equivalent to the return of the real investment plus the return of the financial investment which – in case of borrowing – might be negative. The first restriction is hence

$$C_1 = f(I_0) + F_0 \times (1 + i).$$

The second restriction deals with the amount that is invested in the real investment. That amount is restricted to initial wealth less consumption in $t = 0$ less positive or plus negative financial investment in $t = 0$. Hence

$$I_0 = W_0 - C_0 - F_0.$$

Now, we have to maximize the Lagrangian function with respect to C_0, C_1, F_0, and λ. We get

$$\mathscr{L}(C_0, C_1, F_0, \lambda) = C_0^2 \times C_1 + \lambda \times \left[15 \times \sqrt{(W_0 - C_0 - F_0)} + F_0 \times (1+i) - C_1\right].$$

The partial derivatives with respect to C_0, C_1, F_0, and λ are

$$\frac{\partial \mathscr{L}}{\partial C_0} = 2 \times C_0 \times C_1 - \lambda \times \frac{7.5}{\sqrt{(W_0 - C_0 - F_0)}} = 0 \tag{2.62}$$

$$\frac{\partial \mathscr{L}}{\partial C_1} = C_0^2 - \lambda = 0 \tag{2.63}$$

$$\frac{\partial \mathscr{L}}{\partial F_0} = \lambda \times \left[-\frac{7.5}{\sqrt{(W_0 - C_0 - F_0)}} + (1+i)\right] = 0 \tag{2.64}$$

$$\frac{\partial \mathscr{L}}{\partial \lambda} = 15 \times \sqrt{(W_0 - C_0 - F_0)} + F_0 \times (1+i) - C_1 = 0. \tag{2.65}$$

Solving (2.62) and (2.63) for λ and setting equal we get

$$\frac{2 \times C_0 \times C_1 \times \sqrt{(W_0 - C_0 - F_0)}}{7.5} = C_0^2. \tag{2.66}$$

Now, solving (2.66) for C_1 gives

$$C_1 = \frac{7.5 \times C_0}{2 \times \sqrt{(W_0 - C_0 - F_0)}}. \tag{2.67}$$

For $\lambda > 0$ we can solve (2.64) for F_0 and get

$$F_0 = W_0 - C_0 - \left(\frac{7.5}{(1+i)}\right)^2. \tag{2.68}$$

We insert (2.67) and (2.68) in (2.65) and solve for C_0:

$$0 = 15 \times \sqrt{\left[W_0 - C_0 - \left(W_0 - C_0 - \left(\frac{7.5}{(1+i)}\right)^2\right)\right]}$$

$$+ \left(W_0 - C_0 - \left(\frac{7.5}{(1+i)}\right)^2\right) \times (1+i)$$

$$- \frac{7.5 \times C_0}{2 \times \sqrt{\left[W_0 - C_0 - \left(W_0 - C_0 - \left(\frac{7.5}{(1+i)}\right)^2\right)\right]}}$$

$$0 = 15 \times \frac{7.5}{(1+i)} + \left(W_0 - C_0 - \left(\frac{7.5}{(1+i)}\right)^2\right) \times (1+i) - \frac{(1+i) \times C_0}{2}$$

$$C_0 = \frac{15 \times \frac{7.5}{(1+i)} + \left(W_0 - \left(\frac{7.5}{(1+i)}\right)^2\right) \times (1+i)}{(1+i) + \frac{(1+i)}{2}}.$$

With $i = 0.2$ and $W_0 = 100$, C_0 is

$$C_0 = 92.71. \tag{2.69}$$

We insert (2.69) in (2.68) and get

$$F_0 = 100 - 92.71 - \left(\frac{7.5}{1.2}\right)^2 = -31.77. \tag{2.70}$$

Obviously the individual is in a situation where money is borrowed in $t = 0$. Now, we get C_1 by inserting (2.69) and (2.70) in (2.67)

$$C_1 = \frac{7.5 \times 92.71}{2 \times \sqrt{(100 - 92.71 + 31.77)}} = 55.63. \tag{2.71}$$

Real investment in $t = 0$ is

$$I_0 = W_0 - C_0 - F_0 = 100 - 92.71 + 31.77 = 39.06. \tag{2.72}$$

Because, we know that real investment in $t = 0$ is profitable up to the amount where the marginal return is equivalent to the marginal return of the financial investment we can reproduce the result of (2.72) by differentiating $f(I_0)$ with

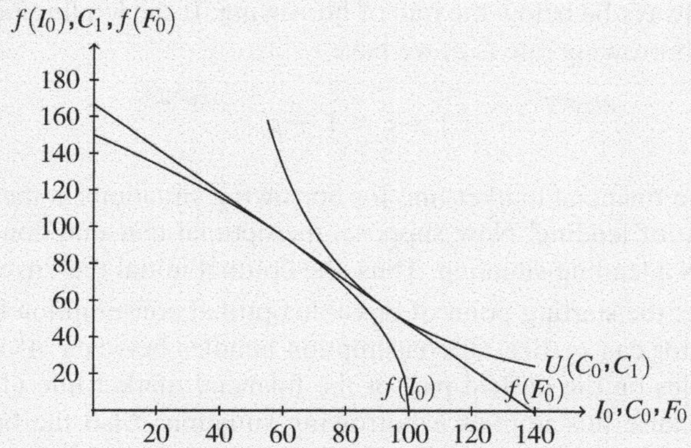

Fig. 2.23 Optimal consumption bundle if investor is in a borrowing situation

respect to I_0 and set it equal to the constant marginal return of the financial investment which is

$$\frac{\partial f(F_0)}{\partial F_0} = 1.2.$$

We get

$$\frac{\partial f(I_0)}{\partial I_0} = 1.2 \quad \Leftrightarrow \quad \frac{7.5}{\sqrt{I_0}} = 1.2$$

$$I_0 = 39.06.$$

Net present value of the real investment is

$$NPV = -I_0 + \frac{f(I_0)}{(1+i)} = -39.06 + \frac{15 \times \sqrt{39.06}}{1.2} = 39.06.$$

The result of the present example is illustrated in Fig. 2.23.

2.5.2.2 Lending Rate Falls below Borrowing Rate (Hirshleifer-Case)

So far we assumed the borrowing and lending rate to be identical. However, *Hirshleifer* mentioned that the determination of the optimal real initial investment in $t = 0$ does not hold, if the borrowing and lending rate differ.[5]

---

[5] *Hirshleifer* [4].

Suppose the situation drawn in Fig. 2.24. In reality, if you lend money, your rate of return will always be below the rate of borrowing. If the lending rate is assumed to be i and the borrowing rate is ρ, we have

$$1 + i < 1 + \rho.$$

The slope of the financial market line for borrowing situations is therefore steeper than in the case of lending. Now suppose, the optimal consumption bundle of an investor implies a lending situation. Thus, the optimal initial real investment would be I_0^{A*l}. Hence, the starting point of possible optimal consumption bundles is A^l. Now, the investor can realize all consumption bundles between A^l and X^l. Consumption bundles on the dashed part of the financial market line $(1 + i)$ are not considered, because this implies a borrowing situation. Also the bundles on the dashed part of the financial market line $(1+\rho)$ are not realizable because this implies a lending situation where the lender lends money at the borrowing rate.

If the optimal consumption bundle of an investor implies a borrowing situation, the optimal initial real investment will be I_0^{A*b}. Hence, the starting point of possible optimal consumption bundles is A^b. The investor can realize all consumption bundles on the capital market line $(1 + \rho)$ between A^b and X^b. Consumption bundles on the dashed part of the financial market line $(1 + \rho)$ are not considered because this implies a lending situation. Also the bundles on the dashed part of the financial

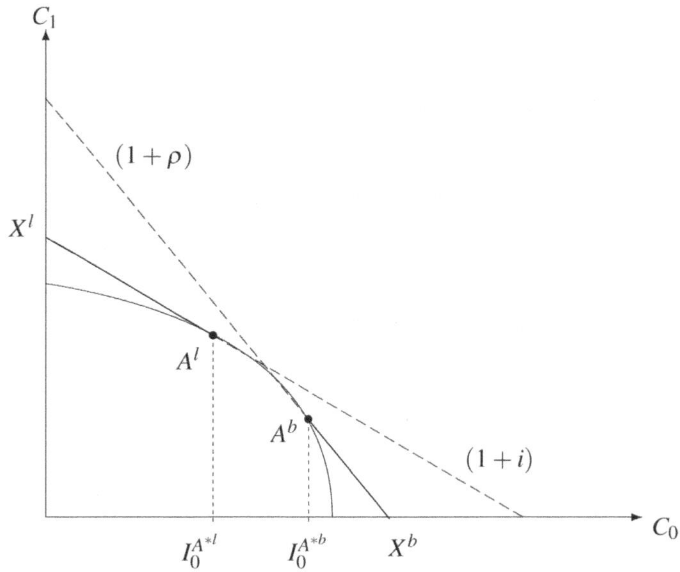

Fig. 2.24 Different taxation of borrowing and lending

market line $(1 + i)$ are not realizable because this implies a borrowing situation where the borrower borrows money at the lending rate.

2.6 Maximizing Withdrawals and Future Value

The previous sections deal with different decision criteria. We learned that net present value is our main decision criterion to evaluate the profitability of investment alternatives. We also discussed the net future value which is a transformation of the net present value. We know that the net present value reflects the additional consumption possibility of the considered investment compared to the alternative financial investment. But what happens if a consumption vector is given by the investor? Is there still equivalence between maximizing consumption or withdrawals and wealth maximization? Wealth maximization means maximizing future value. Hence, there are no withdrawals for consumption until the end of the investment's useful life.

Example 2.26. Maximizing Consumption and Wealth

An investor owns funds of equity of € 1,000 and is offered two mutual exclusive investments A and B. Both investments require acquisition costs of $I_0 = 1{,}000$. The stream of future cash flows generated by the two investments can be taken from the following table:

t	0	1	2	3	4
CF_t^A	−1,000	200	300	430	500
CF_t^B	−1,000	500	350	300	200

The investor is able to reinvest money yielding $i = 6\%$. In this case net present values before taxes – if cash flows are consumed at the end of each period immediately – are

$$\begin{aligned} NPV^A &= -1{,}000 + \frac{200}{1.06} + \frac{300}{1.06^2} + \frac{430}{1.06^3} + \frac{500}{1.06^4} = 212.76 \\ NPV^B &= -1{,}000 + \frac{500}{1.06} + \frac{350}{1.06^2} + \frac{300}{1.06^3} + \frac{200}{1.06^4} = 193.50. \end{aligned} \quad (2.73)$$

Now, the investor asks you which investment will be profitable if he wants to

(a) withdraw a constant annual amount in $t = 1, \dots, \infty$.
(b) withdraw a constant annual amount in $t = 1, \dots, 4$.
(c) maximize withdrawals in $t = 4$.

(d) consume an annual amount of €330 in $t = 1, 2, 3$, maximize the remaining withdrawal in $t = 4$ and he faces a borrowing rate of $\rho = 12\%$.

(a) The first case deals with a situation we already know from Ex. 2.5 on p. 18. We need to transform the present value (see (2.2) on p. 15) in $t = 0$ into an infinite constant series and use (2.9) on p. 17. Present value in $t = 0$ for investment A (B) amounts to $PV_0^A = 1{,}212.76$ ($PV_0^B = 1{,}193.50$). Hence, maximum constant withdrawals W in $t = 1, \ldots, \infty$ are

$$\max W_t^A = PV_0^A \times i = 1{,}212.76 \times 0.06 = 72.77$$
$$\max W_t^B = PV_0^B \times i = 1{,}193.50 \times 0.06 = 71.61.$$

As a result, investment A leads to higher constant withdrawals and should be preferred. The following financial plan is based on investment A. Notice, financial investment in t is $FI_t = FI_{t-1} + CF_t - W_t + i \times FI_{t-1}$ and $FI_0 = 0$.

t	0	1	2	3	4	5	...	∞
CF_t^A	−1,000.00	200.00	300.00	430.00	500.00			
PV_t^A	1,212.76	1,085.53	850.66	471.70	0.00			
FI_t		127.23	362.09	741.05	1,212.76	1,212.76	...	1,212.76
$i \times FI_{t-1}$		0.00	7.63	21.73	44.46	72.77	...	72.77
$\max W_t^A$		72.77	72.77	72.77	72.77	72.77	...	72.77

The complete financial plan for investment B is shown in the following table. As in the case of investment A, financial investment from $t = 4, \ldots, \infty$ is constant. Withdrawals are equal to the return of the financial investment.

t	0	1	2	3	4	5	...	∞
CF_t^B	−1,000.00	500.00	350.00	300.00	200.00			
PV_t^B	1,193.50	765.11	461.02	188.68	0.00			
FI_t		428.39	732.48	1,004.82	1,193.50	1,193.50	...	1, 193.50
$i \times FI_{t-1}$		0.00	25.70	43.95	60.29	71.61	...	71.61
$\max W_t^B$		71.61	71.61	71.61	71.61	71.61	...	71.61

(b) The situation in case (b) is similar to case (a). However, withdrawals in terms of an annuity are maximized. Now, we have to transform the present value in $t = 0$ in an annuity covering four periods. Assume an annuity in arrears and take the formula for the capital recovery factor from (2.25) on p. 22. We get

$$ANN^A = PV_0 \times \frac{i \times q^n}{q^n - 1} = 1,212.76 \times \frac{0.06 \times 1.06^4}{1.06^4 - 1} = 349.99$$
$$ANN^B = PV_0 \times \frac{i \times q^n}{q^n - 1} = 1,193.50 \times \frac{0.06 \times 1.06^4}{1.06^4 - 1} = 344.43.$$

Again, investment A allows higher constant withdrawals over time than investment B. The following financial plans show that if the annuities computed earlier are withdrawn, financial investment is zero at the end of $t = 4$. To reproduce the financial plans recall that we still face an equivalent borrowing and lending rate.

t	0	1	2	3	4
CF_t^A	−1,000.00	200.00	300.00	430.00	500.00
PV_t^A	1,212.76	1,085.53	850.66	471.70	0.00
FI_t		−149.99	−208.98	−141.51	0.00
$i \times FI_{t-1}$		0.00	−9.00	−12.54	−8.49
$\max W_t^A$		349.99	349.99	349.99	349.99

t	0	1	2	3	4
CF_t^B	−1,000.00	500.00	350.00	300.00	200.00
PV_t^B	1,193.50	765.11	461.02	188.68	0.00
FI_t		155.57	170.47	136.27	0.00
$i \times FI_{t-1}$		0.00	9.33	10.23	8.18
$\max W_t^B$		344.43	344.43	344.43	344.43

(c) In this case the investor wants to maximize withdrawals at the end of $t = 4$. The same objective would be maximizing wealth at the end of $t = 4$. This implies $W_t = 0$ for $t = 1, \ldots, 3$. The future value is computed by compounding the present value in $t = 0$, we get

$$FV^A = W_4^A = PV_0^A \times q^4 = 1,212.76 \times 1.06^4 = 1,531.08$$
$$FV^B = W_4^B = PV_0^B \times q^4 = 1,193.50 \times 1.06^4 = 1,506.77.$$

Again, investment A of course, has to be preferred. The following tables compute the future value of our two investments.

t	0	1	2	3	4
CF_t^A	−1,000.00	200.00	300.00	430.00	500.00
FI_t		200.00	512.00	972.72	0.00
$i \times FI_{t-1}$		0.00	12.00	30.72	58.36
W_t^A		0.00	0.00	0.00	1,531.08

t	0	1	2	3	4
CF_t^B	-1,000.00	500.00	350.00	300.00	200.00
FI_t		500.00	880.00	1,232.80	0.00
$i \times FI_{t-1}$		0.00	30.00	52.80	73.97
W_t^B		0.00	0.00	0.00	1,506.77

(d) So far the results are as expected. But what happens if withdrawals are given and borrowing and lending rates differ? We assume constant withdrawals of $W_t = 330$ for $t = 1, 2, 3$. In case of investment A, consumption in terms of withdrawals has to be financed by external funds, e.g., borrowing from a bank. The loan in $t = 1$ is $W_1 - CF_1^A = 330 - 200 = 130$. In $t = 2$ interest on debt is $\rho \times \text{borrowing}_1 = 0.12 \times 130 = 15.60$. Debt from $t = 1$ is amortized in $t = 2$. Debt in $t = 2$ then is $W_2 - CF_2^A + \text{interest}_2 + \text{amortization}_2 = 175.60$. In $t = 3$ the loan is 96.67. In $t = 4$, maximum withdrawals are $CF_4^A + \text{interest}_4 + \text{amortization}_4 = 391.73$.

t	0	1	2	3	4
CF_t^A	−1,000.00	200.00	300.00	430.00	500.00
borrowing in $t = 1$		130.00			
thereof interest			−15.60		
amortization			−130.00		
borrowing in $t = 2$			175.60		
thereof interest				−21.07	
amortization				−175.60	
borrowing in $t = 3$				96.67	
thereof interest					−11.60
amortization					−96.67
W_t^A		330.00	330.00	330.00	391.73

Net present value of the withdrawals of investment A is

$$NPV^A = -1{,}000.00 + \frac{330.00}{1.06} + \frac{330.00}{1.06^2} + \frac{330.00}{1.06^3} + \frac{391.73}{1.06^4} = 192.38.$$

Of course, the total net present value can be separated in the net present value of the real investment and the net present value of the loans. If the net present value is separated we get

$$\begin{aligned} NPV^{A,real} &= -1{,}000.00 + \frac{200.00}{1.06} + \frac{300.00}{1.06^2} + \frac{430.00}{1.06^3} + \frac{500.00}{1.06^4} \\ &= 212.76 \end{aligned}$$

$$NPV^{A,loan} = \frac{130.00}{1.06} - \frac{130.00 + 15.60 - 175.60}{1.06^2} - \frac{21.07 + 175.60 - 96.67}{1.06^3} - \frac{96.67 + 11.60}{1.06^4} = -20.38$$

We get $NPV^{A,real} + NPV^{A,loan} = 212.76 - 20.38 = 192.38$ which is equivalent to the net present value of the withdrawals. Notice, borrowing means cash inflow, whereas amortization means cash outflow. E.g., consider $t = 2$ in case of the loan. Cash flows that are assigned to the external funds in $t = 2$ are: amortization (€ 130), interest (€–15.60), and new debt (€–175.60).

In case of investment B the investor does not have to claim external funds to finance desired withdrawals. As a result, the net present value does not differ from the original one computed in (2.73). The financial plan for investment A can be derived from the following table.

t	0	1	2	3	4
CF_t^B	−1,000.00	500.00	350.00	300.00	200.00
FI_t		170.00	200.20	182.21	0.00
$i \times FI_{t-1}$		0.00	10.20	12.01	10.93
W_t^B		330.00	330.00	330.00	393.14

Now, withdrawal W_4 is 393.14. As a result, investment B is more profitable than investment A, because withdrawals in $t = 4$ are higher ($W_4^B > W_4^A$) and all other withdrawals are identical. In the previous situations (a), (b), and (c) investment A was preferred. The rank order changes due to different borrowing and lending rates. Please keep in mind that we still are operating in a world without taxes. Hence, distortion cannot be assigned to taxation.

The following table summarizes the considered situations (a) to (d).

	A	B	choose
(a) max $W_t, t = 1, \ldots, \infty$	72.77	71.61	A
(b) max $W_t, t = 1, \ldots, 4$	349.99	344.43	A
(c) FV ($W_t = 0, t = 1, 2, 3$)	1,531.08	1,506.77	A
(d) W_4 ($W_t = 330, t = 1, 2, 3$)	391.73	393.14	B

As long as the borrowing rate (debit interest rate) and lending rate (credit interest rate) are identical, maximizing net present values is always equal to maximizing withdrawals, not depending on the structure of the withdrawals (consumption vector). The previous example has shown that the ranking of different investment projects will differ depending on the given consumption vector, if borrowing rates and lending rates fall apart.

In the following, we will ignore the specific withdrawal needs of the investor. Based on this, we can always use net present value maximization to make investment decisions.

Questions

2.1. What are the main characteristics of dynamic and static decision criteria? Give examples.

2.2. What is a relative and an absolute decision criterion? Give examples.

2.3. How can a "real investment" and a "financial investment" be characterized? Derive criteria in order to distinguish the two types of investments.

2.4. What does the discount rate (i) represent?

2.5. Why are cash flows that occur in different periods not directly comparable?

2.6. What are the main assumptions that have to be accepted if investors make their decision according to the net present value criterion? Discuss the assumptions critically.

2.7. What does the net present value state in terms of consumption? To what type of investment criterion does the net present value belong to and why? Under which conditions does the *NPV* advise to invest, not to invest or suggest indifference?

2.8. What type of investment decision criterion does the future value represent? What is the main difference between the net present value and the future value? What role does the alternative financial investment play?

2.9. What is the net future value? What is the main difference between the net future value and the future value?

2.10. Why do we use time discrete models for tax planning reasons?

2.11. Provide an interpretation of the "economic profit".

2.12. How does the pre-tax net present value change if c.p.

(a) The acquisition costs I_0 increase
(b) The interest rate i decreases
(c) The level of cash flows decreases?

2.13. What does the internal rate of return imply? What are the main problems? What is the internal rate of return of a financial investment with a fixed interest rate?

2.14. Explain the main differences between the internal rate of return and the modified rate of return. What deficiencies of the internal rate of return do not occur at the modified rate of return?

2.15. Determine the internal rate of return and the modified rate of return for a self-made example of one period (initial investment in $t = 0$ and return in $t = 1$). Explain your result.

2.16. Draw the investment function in the Fisher model with absence of a capital market. What are the basic assumptions? Show the maximum consumption in $t = 1$ if the investor neither invests nor consumes anything in $t = 0$.

2.17. Draw the transformation curve in a $C_0 - C_1$ coordinate system in absence of a capital market. Explain the characteristics of the curve. How can the internal rate of return be determined? Which consumption bundles are reachable, which of them are not? Where is the optimal consumption bundle located if it is assumed that the investor consumes his total initial endowment?

2.18. Why are preferences or utility functions needed for the Fisher model? What are the main assumptions of the utility functions? Draw a utility indifference function in a $C_0 - C_1$ coordinate system and explain the characteristics of the curve. Explain, why utility indifference functions cannot intersect. Explain why the slope of the utility indifference functions is assumed to be negative.

2.19. What is the marginal rate of substitution?

2.20. Draw the curve of the financial investment in the Fisher model in a $C_0 - C_1$ coordinate system. Describe the area of reachable consumption bundles. Where is an investor supposed to consume if his utility function is not known? Show the internal rate of return graphically.

2.21. Combine the real investment and the financial investment function in the Fisher model in a $C_0 - C_1$ coordinate plane. Assume that the financial investment curve intersects the transformation curve twice. Now show where an investor should have his optimal consumption bundle if he is (a) in a borrowing position (b) in a lending position (c) if he does not need the capital market.

2.22. Graphically derive the optimal initial real investment in the Fisher model and show where the net present value is located.

2.23. Will all investors be better off if a capital market is introduced? Explain your result graphically.

2.24. What happens with Fisher's optimal initial investment if different borrowing and lending rates are assumed (Hirshleifer-case)? Show the reachable consumption bundles in that case.

Exercises

Solutions are provided starting on p. 389.

2.25. Interest Computation

You invest € 900 in a financial investment yielding 4%. How much money do you have after 7 years?

2.26. Interest Computation

Your savings deposit of € 10,000 yields 2.5% the first 5 years and 5% the following 3 years. What's the actual state of your account at the end of year 8?

2.27. Interest Computation

You invest € 12,000 in a financial investment in $t = 0$. In $t = 5$ your investment adds up to € 15,000; in $t = 8$ to € 18,000. Calculate the interest rate for the first 5 years and the next 3 years. What does interest amount to in year 6?

2.28. Annuities

Suppose, you put an amount of € 300 in your bank account annually for a period of 11 years. Determine the future value at an interest rate of 6% in case an annuity is paid

(a) in arrears,
(b) in advance.

2.29. Annuities

Your bank account amounts to € 300,000. Calculate the annuity that would be paid

(a) in arrears,
(b) in advance

at an interest rate of 4% for a period of 15 years.

2.30. Annuities

Carl is 30 years old. He has just finished his studies at the University of Columbia in Missouri. He knows for sure that he is going to retire at the age of 60. He wishes to have a retirement pension of € 30,000 annually. The interest rate is supposed to be 7% and assumed to be constant over time. What amount will Carl have to save annually the next 30 years, if he expects to die at an age of 85? Now suppose, Carl starts saving at an age of 35 and will retire at an age of 60. What amount does he have to save annually in order to get the € 30,000 for the rest of his life?

2.31. Annuities

Andrew wants to sell his business. An investor is willing to pay € 500,000. However, Andrew wants to have constant annual payments for about 20 years. Suppose, the interest rate is 5%. What could the investor pay at maximum to be indifferent between one initial payment and an annuity in arrears?

2.32. Annuities

A retired person pays a rent of € 12,000 annually in advance. He is offered the following: If he pays € 135,000 right now he will get a residence for the rest of his life. What is your advice to that person? The interest rate is $i = 8\%$. What happens if the interest rate is $i = 10\%$?

2.33. Annuities

You inherit € 120,000. If the capital market rate of return is 3% what amount will you be able to withdraw to infinity?

2.34. Net Present Value

Choose a self-made example covering three periods and show that the net present value is (a) > 0, (b) < 0, (c) = 0.

2.35. Economic Depreciation

Define the term economic depreciation. Compute the economic depreciation based on a self-made numerical example.

2.36. Alternative Decision Criteria

For the given cash flow stream $CF_0 = -120$, $CF_1 = 40$, $CF_2 = -20$, $CF_3 = 60$, $CF_4 = 30$ determine the

(a) net present value,
(b) future value,
(c) net future value,
(d) present value for each period,
(e) amount that can be withdrawn to infinity,
(f) annuity in arrears that can be withdrawn provided no money is left by the end of $t = 4$,
(g) internal rate of return,
(h) modified rate of return if CF_2 is (h1) discounted, (h2) compounded.

Please assume an interest rate of $i = 5\%$.

2.37. Formal Derivation of an Annuity

Derive the present value factor of an annuity in arrears.

2.38. Present Value: Own Example

Create examples covering three periods and show that the present value (a) increases in period one and decreases in period two, (b) decreases in period one and increases in period two and (c) stays constant in period one and two.

2.39. Present Value: Own Example

Create a stream of cash flows covering five periods provided that the present value stays constant from $t = 0$ to $t = 1$, decreases from $t = 1$ to $t = 2$, increases from $t = 2$ to $t = 3$, and decreases from $t = 4$ to $t = 5$.

2.40. Economic Profit

What will happen to the economic profit if c.p. (a) the level of cash flows increases, (b) the interest rate increases, and (c) the present value increases.

2.41. Formal Derivation of the Marginal Rate of Substitution
Derive the marginal rate of substitution.

2.42. Evaluating Profitability
There are two mutually exclusive real investment alternatives A and B and an alternative financial investment.

SUM^A, SUM^B : not discounted sum of future cash flows
$i^{*,A-B}$: internal rate of return of the difference investment $A - B$
NPV^{A-B} : net present value of the difference investment $A - B$

If the investor's general objective is to maximize the future value, what investment alternative will be carried out? (A, B or the alternative financial investment FI; if there is not enough information to make a decision, place a cross at "?")

	A	B	FI	?
1. $NPV^A < NPV^B < 0$				
2. $r^{B,B} > i > r^{B,A}$				
3. $SUM^A < SUM^B < 0$				
4. $NPV^A > SUM^B > 0$				
5. $NPV^{A-B} > 0$				
6. $i > r^{B,B} > r^{B,A}$				
7. $r^{B,B} > r^{B,A} > i$				
8. $NPV^{A-B} > 0$ and $NPV^A > 0$				
9. $NPV^{A-B} < 0$				
10. $NPV^{B-A} < 0$ and $NPV^A > 0$				

2.43. Evaluating Profitability
Suppose, your beloved rich aunt wants to test your knowledge in evaluating the profitability of different presents for your birthday. She lets you choose one out of four alternatives

(a) Immediate payment of €600,
(b) Three constant annual payments of €320,
(c) An initial payment of €200 and €470 in 3 years or
(d) One payment in 3 years of €700.

Facing an interest rate of 6%. What's the best option?

2.44. Modified Rate of Return
An investor is offered two mutually exclusive real investments with the following stream of cash flows:

t	0	1	2	3	4
CF_t^A	−1,000	200	270	350	400
CF_t^B	−800	400	500		

The capital market rate is $i = 7\%$.

(a) Compute the net present value and the modified rate of return of the two projects if the time horizon for investment A (B) is $n^A = 4$ ($n^B = 2$) and the initial cost of investment A (B) is $I_0^A = 1,000$ ($I_0^B = 800$). What's the problem with your result?
(b) Now suppose, the investor is endowed with equity amounting to € 1,000. In case of investment B he invests the € 200 that are left in a financial investment yielding 7%. Time horizons are assumed to be the same as in (a). Determine the net present values and the modified rates of return.
(c) Now suppose the same assumptions as in (b). However, the time horizon for investment B is now $n^B = 4$, too. Compute the net present values and the modified rates of return again. What's the difference to your results from (a) and (b)?

2.45. Modified Rate of Return

Suppose, there are two mutually exclusive real investment opportunities A and B which have the following streams of cash flow:

t	0	1	2	3	4
CF_t^A	−1,000	200	−330	700	900
CF_t^B	−1,000	400	−330	700	750

If $i = 10\%$ determine

(a) the net present value,
(b) the modified rate of return in case CF_2 is compounded,
(c) the modified rate of return in case CF_2 is discounted,

for both investments.

(d) Is the rank order of profitability affected if different types of the modified rate of return in (b) and (c) are used? Why?
(e) What arguments can be made to justify compounding, what arguments can be made for discounting CF_2?

2.46. Fisher Model

Suppose, two investors A and B with an initial endowment of $W_0 = 200$. Both face the following utility functions

$$U^A(C_0, C_1) = C_0^3 \times C_1$$
$$U^B(C_0, C_1) = C_0 \times C_1^3.$$

The real investment function is

$$f(I_0) = 20 \times \sqrt{I_0}.$$

(a) Derive the transformation curve.
(b) Determine optimal C_0, C_1 for investor A if there is no capital market. What does I_0 amount to? What's the internal rate of return?
(c) Now a capital market with a lending and borrowing rate of $i = 10\%$ is introduced. Determine optimal C_0, C_1, I_0, and F_0 for both investors and determine the increase in utility for investor A compared to case (b). Determine the net present value for both investors.
(d) What happens to optimal C_0, C_1 and the utility level for investor A if the borrowing rate is $\rho = 20\%$?

2.47. Withdrawals and Wealth Maximization

An investor has equity amounting to € 120,000 and is offered two mutual exclusive investments A and B. Both investments require acquisition costs of $I_0 = 120,000$. The future stream of cash flows generated by the two investments are shown in the following table:

t	0	1	2	3	4
CF_t^A	−120,000	10,000	40,000	50,000	60,000
CF_t^B	−120,000	38,000	38,000	38,000	38,000

The investor is able to reinvest money in a financial investment yielding $i = 8\%$. Now the investor asks you which alternative is profitable in case he wants to

(a) Maximize net present value.
(b) Withdraw a constant annual amount in $t = 1, \ldots, \infty$.
(c) Withdraw a constant annual amount in $t = 1, \ldots, 4$.
(d) Maximize withdrawals in $t = 4$.
(e) Consume the following amounts in $t = 1, 2, 3$: $W_1 = 45{,}000$, $W_2 = 35{,}000$, and $W_3 = 25{,}000$. Now the borrowing rate is $\rho = 12\%$.

References

1. Baldwin, R.H.: How to assess investment proposals. Har. Bus. Rev. 98–104 (1959)
2. Fisher, I.: The theory of interest. As determined by impatience to spend income and opportunity to invest it. Macmillan, New York (1930)
3. Grob, H.L.: Capital Budgeting with Financial Plans. Gabler, Wiesbaden (1993)
4. Hirshleifer, J.: On the theory of optimal investment decision. J. Political Econ. **66**(4), 329–352 (1958)
5. Kruschwitz, L., Löffler, A.: Discounted Cash Flow: A Theory of the Valuation of Firms. Wiley, Chichester (2005)
6. Kruschwitz, L.: Investitionsrechnung. 12th edn. Walter de Gruyter, Berlin, New York (2009)

Part II
Integrating Taxation into Investment Decision Making

Chapter 3
Integrating Income Taxes into Finance

Abstract Investment decisions may be wrong when they are made without taking taxes into account. In this chapter, we present the well-known Standard Model. The Standard Model is a simple investment model that integrates income taxes. The previous chapter deals with various investment criteria before taxes; now, we present different investment decision criteria extended by taxes. Using the Standard Model we explain why taxes distort investment decisions. In this context, we explain the income tax paradox which describes increasing after-tax net present values due to taxes. The reason for this distortion can be found in three effects: The tax rate effect, the tax base effect, and the timing effect. Furthermore, we define marginal tax rates and average tax rates. Due to nonlinearity of typical individual income tax rate functions, they differ from each other. Depending on the type of the decision, the marginal or the average tax rate needs to be calculated. At the end of the chapter, we extend the Fisher–Hirshleifer Model from the previous chapter by integrating taxes.

3.1 Why Integrate Taxes?

If investors make their investment decisions on the basis of the criteria before taxes developed in Chap. 2, their decisions might be wrong. Taxes can cause the ranking of different investment projects to change compared to the pre-tax case. Therefore, integrating taxes in decision making is important. But be careful, an investment decision never can be carried out just for the purpose of saving taxes. The relevant information is the after-tax value of an investment. This after-tax value depends on the pre-tax value as well as the treatment of the investment income according to the relevant income tax code. Let's have a look at an example.

Example 3.1. The After-Tax Return of an Investment

The two brothers Daniel and Steven Sink want to invest € 100,000 in shares. After 1 year they have to sell their shares because they want to start their own business. Daniel Sink chooses to invest in Deutsche Telekom and in the energy supply company RWE, while Steven invests in Infineon and Singulus.

D. Schanz and S. Schanz, *Business Taxation and Financial Decisions*,
DOI 10.1007/978-3-642-03284-4_3,

The shares are privately held and amount to less than 1% of total shares of the companies. After 1 year, Steven and Daniel sell their shares and realize that they both earned € 5,000. Steven's income consists of capital gains because his Infineon shares and Singulus shares increased from € 100,000 to € 105,000. No dividends were paid during the year. Daniel's income consists of dividends paid by Deutsche Telekom and RWE. The share prices went back to € 100,000. Let's evaluate the yield of the investments by taking taxes into account.

The evaluation depends on the relevant tax system. Assume the brothers live in Austria. Capital gains from shares held for more than 1 year are tax exempt (§§ 30, 31 Austrian income tax code). Dividends are taxed at the flat rate of 25% (§§ 93 (2) No.1, 95 (1), 97 (1) Austrian income tax code).

In the one-period context, we can use the after-tax return as a decision criterion. Daniel's tax liability amounts to $0.25 \times$ € 5,000 $=$ € 1,250. His return after taxes is

$$\frac{5{,}000 - 1{,}250}{100{,}000} = 3.75\%,$$

while Steven's capital gain is tax exempt. Steven's after-tax return is

$$\frac{5{,}000}{100{,}000} = 5.00\%.$$

Thus, Steven's investment decision is advantageous.

3.2 Standard Model

The so-called "Standard Model" is based on the pre-tax net present value criterion adjusted by income taxes. After deriving the "Standard Model" we give a brief discussion about the main assumptions of the model.

3.2.1 The Model

In the previous section, we saw that neglecting taxes may lead to wrong investment and financing decisions. Therefore, we want to integrate taxes into our decisions. Real-world tax systems are very complex and can never be integrated in detail. Instead, we take the most relevant parts of tax rules and integrate them into a simplified model. The best-known model is called the Standard Model.[1] The Standard

[1] See *Wagner/Dirrigl* [14] and *Kruschwitz* [6].

Model is an extension of the pre-tax *NPV* calculation[2] and integrates taxes concerning the real investment (numerator) and the financial investment alternative (denominator)

$$NPV^{\tau} = -I_0 + \sum_{t=1}^{n} \frac{CF_t - T_t}{(1+i^{\tau})^t} = -I_0 + \sum_{t=1}^{n} \frac{CF_t - \tau \times \overbrace{(CF_t - D_t)}^{tax\,base\,TB_t}}{(1 + i \times (1-\tau))^t}. \tag{3.1}$$

I_0 denotes the initial investment as known from the *NPV* formula. Typically, investments in assets such as land and buildings, technical equipment and machinery are not immediately tax deductible. Therefore, I_0 is subtracted as a cash expense in $t = 0$.

In the numerator of (3.1), the investment's cash flows CF_t are reduced by taxes T_t. The tax liability is calculated as the product of the tax base TB_t and the tax rate.[3] In the Standard Model, we assume a constant marginal tax rate τ. The tax base only consists of two elements, cash flows CF_t and depreciation allowances D_t. The tax base is called taxable profit. The taxable profit calculation typically differs from profit calculation according to financial accounting standards.

The depreciation D_t is the most important noncash tax base element. Noncash elements are also referred to as accruals. Depreciation stands for tax deductibility of an investment I_0 over time. As mentioned before, assets are not immediately tax deductible. Instead they are depreciated over the expected useful life of the asset. For example, the expected useful life of personal computers typically is 3 years, and is between 20 and 100 years for buildings. Useful life for tax purposes differs from country to country and is defined in the tax codes or other regulations. In the Standard Model, we assume linear depreciation of the asset's initial value I_0 over n years. Depreciation is calculated as:

$$D_t = \frac{I_0}{n}. \tag{3.2}$$

The yearly tax base differs from cash flows due to accruals. Accruals are caused by accelerating or deferring tax deductibility or recognition of the corresponding cash flows. In the Standard Model, only depreciation allowances are taken into account as accruals. All kinds of accruals have one important matter in common: As they are based on cash flows recognized at another point of time, the sum of cash flows over the whole investment period ($t = n$) equals the sum of tax bases. This is known as congruence principle

$$\sum_{t=0}^{n} CF_t = -I_0 + \sum_{t=1}^{n} CF_t = \sum_{t=0}^{n} TB_t. \tag{3.3}$$

---

[2] The *NPV* formula is discussed in Sect. 2.3.1 starting on p. 13.

[3] Real-world tax rates of selected countries are presented in Sect. 4.3 starting on p. 141.

The tax base of year zero ($t = 0$) is always zero because the initial investment is not tax deductible.

Tax effects are also integrated in the denominator of (3.1). They have to be taken into account, because taxes influence the opportunity cost of capital of the investor. The investor compares his real investment project with an alternative financial investment.[4] Financial investments are taxed differently in comparison to real investments. The most simple financial investment, an interest-bearing bank account, is taxed on a cash basis. Yearly interest income is subject to tax. The net return of the investor decreases from i to $i \times (1 - \tau)$. Such a tax system, where interest income is taxed, is called a comprehensive income tax.

Example 3.2 demonstrates how the Standard Model is used to evaluate investment projects.

Example 3.2. Applying the Standard Model: The After-Tax Net Present Value of an Investment

Assume an investment which generates a cash flow vector of $CF = (-150; 80; 90; 80)$. The capital market interest rate and the opportunity cost of capital of the investor is $i = 0.1$. The net present value before taxes is

$$NPV = -150 + \frac{80}{1.1} + \frac{90}{1.1^2} + \frac{80}{1.1^3} = 57.21.$$

The investor decides to carry out the real investment. But taxes are ignored in his decision.

To take taxes into account, we need to know the depreciation schedule and taxable useful life of the investment, and the tax rates on profits and on interest income. We assume a constant marginal tax rate $\tau = 0.5$ for both real and financial investmens. We assume straight-line depreciation of the investment over $n = 3$ years. Hence, depreciation amounts to

$$D_t = \frac{150}{3} = 50.$$

The after-tax net present value amounts to

$$\begin{aligned} NPV^{\tau} &= -150 + \frac{80 - 0.5 \times (80 - 50)}{(1 + 0.1 \times (1 - 0.5))} + \frac{90 - 0.5 \times (90 - 50)}{(1 + 0.1 \times (1 - 0.5))^2} \\ &\quad + \frac{80 - 0.5 \times (80 - 50)}{(1 + 0.1 \times (1 - 0.5))^3} = 31.55. \end{aligned}$$

[4] See the discussion in Sect. 2.3.1 starting on p. 13.

The after-tax net present value is smaller than the *NPV* before taxes, but it is still positive. The investor decides to carry out the real investment.

Another way to determine the after-tax net present value is based on a simple financial plan

t	0	1	2	3
(1) Cash flows CF_t	–150	80	90	80
(2) Depreciation D_t		50	50	50
(3) Tax base TB_t = (1)–(2)		30	40	30
(4) Tax liability T_t		15	20	15
(5) CF_t^τ = (1)–(4)	–150	65	70	65

The tax base is composed of cash flows minus the depreciation. The tax liability is calculated by multiplying the tax base and the tax rate. After-tax cash flows CF_t^τ consist of cash flows before taxes minus the tax liability. The NPV^τ is derived by discounting the net cash flows

$$NPV^\tau = -150 + \frac{65}{1.05} + \frac{70}{1.05^2} + \frac{65}{1.05^3} = 31.55.$$

Using the financial plan or the formula always leads to the same result. The after-tax net present value amounts to 31.55.

Now, we want to demonstrate a third method to calculate the after-tax net present value. Assume that net cash flows are reinvested in a financial investment within the company. Therefore, in our next financial plan, financial investment is therefore explicitly calculated. We derive the future value of the investment and discount it over n periods in order to calculate the after-tax net present value.

t	0	1	2	3
(1) Cash flows CF_t	–150.00	80.00	90.00	80.00
(2) Depreciation D_t		50.00	50.00	50.00
(3) Financial investment FI_t		65.00	138.25	210.16
(4) Interest income IP_t		0.00	6.50	13.83
(5) Tax base TB_t = (1)–(2)+(4)		30.00	46.50	43.83
(6) Tax liability T_t		15.00	23.25	21.92
(7) CF_t^τ = (1) + (4) – (6)	–150.00	65.00	73.25	71.91
(7) Withdrawal	–150.00	0	0	210.16

Interest income is derived as the product of the financial investment of the preceding year and the pre-tax interest rate i. Under our assumptions, interest income is fully taxable and increases the tax base which is now calculated as

$$TB_t = CF_t - D_t + IP_t.$$

The net cash flows are calculated by adding interest income to cash flows and subtracting tax payments. The net cash flows increase the previous year's financial investment. In $t = n$, when the project finishes, the financial investment of 210.16 is withdrawn. The financial investment is the after-tax future value of the project.

The NPV^τ is derived by adding the discounted final withdrawal to the negative initial investment

$$NPV^\tau = -150 + \frac{210.16}{1.05^3} = 31.55.$$

Using the after-tax net present value formula according to (3.1) is equivalent to using after-tax financial plans as demonstrated in Ex. 3.2.

The Standard Model can also be used to compare different real investment projects to each other.

Example 3.3. Comparison of Two Investment Projects

The mutually exclusive projects A and B are available and yield the following cash flow streams (in €)

t	0	1	2	3	4
$A : CF_t$	–1,000	600	250	250	250
$B : CF_t$	–1,000	350	350	350	350

In $t = 0$ the machines A and B have to be acquired for € 1,000 each. We assume an interest rate of $i = 10\%$ and a tax rate of $\tau = 40\%$. The machines are depreciated over 4 years using the straight-line method.

Neglecting taxes, the $NPVs$ of the two projects are

$$NPV^A = -1{,}000 + \frac{600}{1.1} + \frac{250}{1.1^2} + \frac{250}{1.1^3} + \frac{250}{1.1^4} = 110.65.$$

$$NPV^B = -1{,}000 + \frac{350}{1.1} + \frac{350}{1.1^2} + \frac{350}{1.1^3} + \frac{350}{1.1^4} + \frac{350}{1.1^5} = 109.45.$$

The NPV of project A is slightly higher, therefore, we would choose investment A when taxes are neglected in our decision.

Taking taxes into account, the after-tax net present values can be calculated using a financial plan

t	0	1	2	3	4
Cash flows CF_t	−1,000	600	250	250	250
Depreciation D_t		250	250	250	250
Tax base TB_t		350	0	0	0
Tax liability T_t		140	0	0	0
CF_t^τ	−1,000	460	250	250	250

Discounting net cash flows gives an $NPV^{\tau,A}$ of 64.39. Notice, in this case the after-tax discount rate is $i \times (1 - \tau) = 0.1 \times (1 - 0.4) = 0.06$.

Project B's profitability is calculated as follows

t	0	1	2	3	4
Cash flows CF_t	−1,000	350	350	350	350
Depreciation D_t		250	250	250	250
Tax base TB_t		100	100	100	100
Tax liability T_t		40	40	40	40
CF_t^τ	−1,000	310	310	310	310

Discounting net cash flows yields $NPV^{\tau,B} = 74.18$.

The ranking of the two investments has changed. In our after-tax calculation we prefer project B.

The Standard Model is a very simplified model, but it reflects real investment decision models quite well. We know from empirical investigations that large companies' tax planning is very similar to the Standard Model. *Wagner/Schwenk* [13] show that two third of the largest German companies, the DAX-100, take taxes into account in capital budgeting. Two third of the DAX-100 companies taking taxes into account take depreciation allowances into account; other accruals are usually neglected.

Even though companies use a very simplified model for tax planning, accruals other than depreciation allowances do have an effect on the tax burden of companies. *Schanz/Schanz* [8] show that inventory valuation and provisions mostly affect the tax base and therefore the tax burden of companies. The analysis is based on German companies of the manufacturing, construction, transport, wholesale and retail trade industries, and the services sector.

We have seen that the integration of taxes into decision making is important. Nevertheless, we argue that it is important not to overestimate the effect of taxes. Often, people are heavily interested in saving taxes. They follow tax saving strategies to such an extent that they do not realize that they loose more money than they save. In those cases investors focus solely on tax minimization. However, they do not keep in mind that the aims of tax minimization and maximizing after-tax wealth are often different. Tax minimization as technically derived in (1.2) and illustrated in Fig. 1.4 depends on the assumption that investment or financing decisions already took place. Therefore, accruals resulting from initial costs cannot be influenced any more.

Example 3.4 demonstrates the consequences of pure tax minimization. In the example, the objective of tax minimization is pursued without considering that pre-tax cash flows are also influenced. In our examples, the net present value of cash flows is highly negative and cannot be outweighed by the tax savings.

Example 3.4. Who Really Paid for the Reconstruction of East Germany!

The following case is an example for nonrational behavior by taxpayers that was carried out just because of tax saving reasons. *Kiesewetter* et al. [3] explain who really paid for the East German "boom".

After the German reunification in 1990, supply of residential property in East Germany was short and existing property was in pretty poor shape. To improve the situation, the Federal Government of Germany promoted the construction industry and reconstruction of existing residential property with broad additional tax benefits. As a result, the generous tax benefits caused a construction boom in the mid-1990s in East Germany. Beside the tax benefits, the reconstruction of East Germany is still financed by a solidarity surcharge of 5.5% on the personal and corporate income tax liability.

Investments in residential property located in East Germany acquired between December 31st, 1990 and January 1st, 1997 were treated preferentially for tax purposes due to the Assisted Area Act. The purpose of the Act was to assure a claim of an initial depreciation amount of 50% of the initial cost for privately held residential property in the year of completion. The remaining fraction of 50% of initial cost has to be depreciated with a rate of 1% over the remaining 50 years.

Due to extensive migration from East Germany to West Germany after the reunification, massive construction resulted in an oversupply of residential property. Vacancy has been rising, and property prices and rents have been falling since then. As a result, investment in residential property in East Germany after the reunification has turned out to be a financial disaster in most cases.

What happened? Because generous tax benefits were granted by the government, investors were solely focused on fast depreciation that results in a higher post-tax net present value due to earlier tax savings. Other important influences, such as the possible amount of rents that could be earned, were neglected. Investments were still carried out when it was clear, that population would not be high enough for all the empty residential property. The intention of investors was to produce losses that could be offset from other positive income to reduce tax liability.

So the objective of tax minimization instead of maximizing after-tax cash flows was fulfilled. Tax planning – taking both taxes and nontax considerations into account – would reveal negative after-tax net present values because house prices and rents fell heavily.

3.2.2 Discussion of Assumptions

In the previous section we presented the Standard Model. The model is quite popular and builds the basis for many analyses. Nevertheless, the model is based on restricting assumptions we have to be aware of:

(a) The tax base is simplified.
(b) The rate is assumed to be constant.
(c) Taxes other than profit income or corporate taxes are ignored.
(d) Tax loss offset rules are ignored. An immediate full loss offset is assumed.
(e) The investment is equity-financed.
(f) The investment is carried out in the legal form of a sole proprietorship or a partnership.
(g) The credit interest rate equals the debit interest rate.
(h) The investment and the alternative financial investment are assumed to be risk-free.

Let's have a look at the different assumptions. Right now, we need them in order to have a simple instrument for revealing tax distortions and calculating after-tax net present values.[5]

(a) We discussed the restrictions of a simplified tax base definition in the last section. Our tax base refers to a profit tax or an income tax.[6]
(b) We discussed the restrictions of a constant tax rate in the last section. Usually, progressive tax rate functions are applied. Even if a marginal tax rate is used, changes of the marginal tax rate might occur over time.
(c) Tax liability is reduced to income tax. Typically, countries levy personal income taxes and corporate income taxes. Income tax in the Standard Model is assumed to reflect income tax on all possible levels (e.g., foreign tax and domestic tax, tax on corporate level and personal level). Other kinds of taxes are ignored. Examples are property taxes and wealth taxes, estate and gift taxes or value-added taxes and sales taxes.

    Why do we ignore other types of taxes? There are two reasons. First, income taxes play the most important role in business decisions. In most countries, a very large proportion of an investor's tax burden decreases upon income taxes (*Oestreicher/Reister/Spengel* [7], p. 8). Other types of taxes affect the investor's decisions to a smaller extent. Value-added taxes (VAT) or sales taxes contribute

[5] Some assumptions are discussed critically later in this book. See Chap. 7.

[6] For a tax base discussion see also Sect. 6.1 on p. 215.

to a large extent to the tax revenue in many countries;[7] but they are designed as transit items which are passed-through to the final consumer. Assuming that VAT or sales taxes are passed-through to the consumer, they do not affect investment or financing decisions (*Caspersen/Metcalf* [2], p. 731).

(d) Without explicitly mentioning it, the Standard Model assumes a full immediate loss offset. If the tax base is negative and a loss occurs

$$TB_t = CF_t - D_t < 0, \tag{3.4}$$

we assume that an immediate tax refund

$$\tau \times TB_t \tag{3.5}$$

is granted. This assumption is unrealistic because fiscal authorities would levy a tax liability of zero and the taxpayer would be able to deduct the loss from the next year's taxable profit. Nevertheless, the simplified assumption is used in the Standard Model because it allows to calculate one year's tax base without taking the other year's tax bases into account. The assumption will be removed in Sect. 7.4.

In some circumstances, the assumption of an immediate loss offset meets reality and can be justified. Assume that the project which is evaluated is carried out by a running company. The company has considerably high profits from other projects. Now, the new project generates losses. The new project's losses can be offset from the current profits of the company. What is the consequence? The current tax liability of the company is reduced by the tax rate times the loss

$$\tau \times TB_t. \tag{3.6}$$

This reduction is caused by the new project and, therefore, needs to be allocated to the new project. Allocating the tax saving to the new project equals considering a tax refund exactly as it is done in the Standard Model.

Thus, the integration of rules dealing with loss offset restrictions into the Standard Model is only necessary when no other profits are available to offset losses occurring from the new project under consideration.

(e) The Standard Model ignores debt financing. The investment is equity financed. Therefore, taking a loan and paying interest can be omitted. Chapter 9 of this book introduces the effect of taxes on financing decisions.

(f) We have not yet talked about different legal forms of companies. Investments can be carried out by an individual, a sole proprietorship or a partnership, or through corporations. A characteristic of corporations is double taxation of their profits. First, profits are taxed on the corporate level, and second, dividends are taxed when they are distributed. The Standard Model does not cover these two levels and thus does not fit to corporations. By contrast, income taxes of sole

---

[7] See Sect. 4.2.

proprietorships and partnerships – as so-called pass-through entities – are levied only once. This is represented in the Standard Model. The Standard Model for corporations will be derived in Sect. 6.7.

(g) In the denominator of the Standard Model formula, we discount the investment's net cash flows at the interest rate i. This assumption is taken from the *NPV* model without taxes. The interest rate i indicates the opportunity cost of capital of the investor. It reflects the implicit assumption of a perfect capital market.[8] Interest rates for borrowing and lending are identical. The interest rate combines the interest rate of the optimal alternative investment, the borrowing rate, and the marginal rate of substitution of the investor. This is an unrealistic assumption in a world without taxes, but it is even more unrealistic when we take taxes into account. Even if we know the investor's correct interest rate before taxes i, the after-tax interest rate i^τ depends on its taxation which depends on the specific situation, e.g., the country.

So far, we applied $i^\tau = i \times (1 - \tau)$ as the after-tax discount rate. This implies that the financial investment's earnings (or the expenditures in case of borrowing) are completely liable to tax (deductible). This is not always the case as Table 3.1 shows: In many tax systems, borrowing and lending is taxed asymmetrically. For example, interest may be tax exempt, see case (1) in Table 3.1. This is the case for specific bonds in the United States (*Scholes* et al. [12], p. 76). Typically, interest on private consumption loans is not tax deductible at all (2). In both cases, even after taxes the interest rate

$$i^\tau = i \tag{3.7}$$

is used for discounting the after-tax net cash flows.

Full taxation of interest income takes place for most interest bearing products in the United States or in France (3). Full tax deductibility of interest is known worldwide if a loan is taken for financing business investments (4). In both situations the correct after-tax interest rate is

$$i^\tau = i \times (1 - \tau). \tag{3.8}$$

Nevertheless, there are exemptions. In Germany, interest paid on business loans is only partially tax deductible under certain conditions (6). Partial tax liability of interest income is also known. E.g., in Germany and Austria, interest

Table 3.1 After-tax interest rates

Discount rate i^τ	Credit interest rate	Debit interest rate
$i^\tau = i$	(1) Tax-exempt	(2) Not deductible
$i^\tau = i \times (1 - \tau)$	(3) Fully taxed	(4) Fully deductible
$i^\tau = i \times (1 - \tau^{flat})$	(5) Taxed at a flat, reduced rate	(6) Partially tax deductible

Source: Based on *Wagner* [15], p. 457.

[8] See Sect. 2.5.2.

earned is taxed at a reduced flat rate (5). Under those circumstances a mixture of full tax liability and no tax liability of interest income reflects reality. In case of interest expenses, a mixture of full tax deductibility and denied tax deductibility is given. Then the correct after-tax interest rate is

$$i^{\tau} = i \times (1 - \tau^{flat}). \tag{3.9}$$

(h) The assumption of a risk-free investment is taken from the *NPV* formula without taxes. We assume that the initial investment and the generated cash flows are certain and known before the investment decision is made. Correspondingly, there is no uncertainty concerning the constant interest rate and the constant tax rate. In this book we will stick to the assumption of certainty.[9]

3.3 Other Post-Tax Decision Criteria

The Standard Model aims at deriving the after-tax net present value of an investment. This is realized by taking taxes into account in both the numerator and the denominator of the net present value formula.

All other decision criteria discussed in the previous chapter can be extended similarly. In the following sections, we derive the after-tax formulas for the decision criteria present value, net future value, and future value, present value of an annuity, capital recovery factor, internal rate of return, and modified internal rate of return (Baldwin rate of return). We use the expressions "after-tax" and "post-tax" synonymously, as well as the expressions "before-tax" and "pre-tax".

3.3.1 Post-Tax Present Value

The post-tax present value (PV_t^{τ}) is defined as the sum of discounted post-tax cash flows $CF_{t+1}^{\tau}, \ldots, CF_n^{\tau}$ at time t. This gives:

$$PV_t^{\tau} = \sum_{j=t+1}^{n} \frac{CF_j^{\tau}}{(1+i^{\tau})^{j-t}} = \sum_{j=t+1}^{n} \frac{CF_j - T_j}{(1+i \times (1-\tau))^{j-t}}. \tag{3.10}$$

Present value in $t = 0$ accounts for

$$PV_0^{\tau} = \sum_{j=1}^{n} \frac{CF_j^{\tau}}{(1+i^{\tau})^j} = NPV^{\tau} + I_0 \tag{3.11}$$

which is equivalent to NPV^{τ} plus initial investment I_0.

[9] Uncertainty is discussed in detail in *Kruschwitz/Löffler* [5].

Example 3.5. Post-Tax Present Value

Let's use the assumptions of Ex. 2.2 on p.14. The investor faces a real investment opportunity with a cash flow vector of $CF = (-100; -30; 50; 70; 90)$ for $t = 0, \ldots, 4$. The interest rate before taxes is $i = 5\%$. The tax rate is $\tau = 50\%$ both on profits of the project and on interest income. Thus, the after-tax interest rate amounts to $i^\tau = 5\% \times (1 - 0.5) = 2.5\%$. The initial investment of $I_0 = 100$ is depreciated over $n = 4$ years. Yearly depreciation is $D_t = 25$. We assume that an immediate tax refund takes place in case of losses.

PV_t^τ accounts for

$$PV_4^\tau = 0$$

$$PV_3^\tau = \frac{90 - 0.5 \times (90 - 25)}{1.025} = 56.10$$

$$PV_2^\tau = \frac{70 - 0.5 \times (70 - 25)}{1.025} + \frac{90 - 0.5 \times (90 - 25)}{1.025^2} = 101.07$$

$$PV_1^\tau = \frac{50 - 0.5 \times (50 - 25)}{1.025} + \frac{70 - 0.5 \times (70 - 25)}{1.025^2} + \frac{90 - 0.5 \times (90 - 25)}{1.025^3} = 135.19$$

$$PV_0^\tau = \frac{-30 - 0.5 \times (-30 - 25)}{1.025} + \frac{50 - 0.5 \times (50 - 25)}{1.025^2} + \frac{70 - 0.5 \times (70 - 25)}{1.025^3} + \frac{90 - 0.5 \times (90 - 25)}{1.025^4} = 129.45.$$

The NPV^τ of the project equals the after-tax present value of year $t = 0$ minus the initial investment $NPV^\tau = PV_0^\tau - I_0 = 129.45 - 100 = 29.45$.

3.3.2 Post-Tax Net Future Value and Post-Tax Future Value

Post-tax net future value (NFV^τ) is defined as compounded after-tax cash flows to time horizon n. NFV^τ is

$$NFV^\tau = \sum_{t=0}^{n} CF_t^\tau \times (1 + i^\tau)^{n-t} \tag{3.12}$$

which is equivalent to

$$NFV^\tau = NPV^\tau \times (1 + i^\tau)^n, \tag{3.13}$$

using (3.1) to calculate the NPV^τ. The compounded initial investment I_0 is subtracted from the after-tax net future value. Thus, we sum up cash flows from $t = 0$.

As in the pre-tax case, NFV^{τ} follows the same decision rules as NPV^{τ}. If positive, invest, if negative, do not invest, if zero, be indifferent.

Example 3.6. Post-Tax Net Future Value

Using the assumptions of Ex. 3.5 on p. 91, NFV^{τ} accounts for $NFV^{\tau} = 29.45 \times (1+0.025)^4 = 32.51$.

The post-tax future value (FV^{τ}) is defined as the compounded post-tax present value PV_0^{τ}

$$FV^{\tau} = PV_0^{\tau} \times (1+i^{\tau})^n = (NPV^{\tau} + I_0) \times (1+i^{\tau})^n$$
$$= \sum_{t=1}^{n} CF_t^{\tau} \times (1+i^{\tau})^{n-t} = \sum_{t=1}^{n} (CF_t - T_t) \times (1+i \times (1-\tau))^{n-t}. \quad (3.14)$$

FV^{τ} itself is not applicable for decision making, because no comparison with an alternative investment is made. However, it can serve as a decision criterion, if the difference to the post-tax future value of the alternative investment is derived. The after-tax future value of the alternative financial investment is the initial investment compounded at the after-tax interest rate $I_0 \times (1+i^{\tau})^n$

$$\Delta FV^{\tau} = FV^{\tau} - I_0 \times (1+i^{\tau})^n = PV_0^{\tau} \times (1+i^{\tau})^n - I_0 \times (1+i^{\tau})^n = NFV^{\tau}. \quad (3.15)$$

The difference in future values equals the after-tax net future value NFV^{τ}.

Example 3.7. Post-Tax Future Value

Using the assumptions of Ex. 3.5 on p. 91, we get for FV^{τ} and ΔFV^{τ}

$$FV^{\tau} = PV_0^{\tau} \times (1+i^{\tau})^n = 129.45 \times (1+0.025)^4 = 142.89$$
$$\Delta FV^{\tau} = 142.89 - I_0 \times (1+i^{\tau})^n = 142.89 - 100 \times (1.025)^4 = 32.51.$$

If we do not know the PV_0^{τ} yet, we can derive the after-tax future value on the basis of a financial plan.

t	0	1	2	3	4
Cash flows CF_t	–100.00	–30.00	50.00	70.00	90.00
Depreciation D_t		25.00	25.00	25.00	25.00
Tax base TB_t		–55.00	25.00	45.00	65.00
Tax liability T_t		27.50	12.50	22.50	32.50
CF_t^{τ}	–100.00	–2.50	37.50	47.50	57.50

The tax base is calculated by taking the cash flows less depreciation. The tax liability is the product of the tax base and the tax rate. After-tax cash flows CF_t^τ consist of cash flows before taxes less tax liability. Compounding the after-tax cash flows CF_t^τ, we receive the after-tax future value FV^τ

$$FV^\tau = \sum_{t=1}^{n} CF_t^\tau \times (1 + i^\tau)^{n-t} = -2.50 \times 1.025^3 + 37.50 \times 1.025^2 + 47.50 \times 1.025^1 + 57.50 = 142.89.$$

Instead of compounding net cash flows, we can integrate the capital market investment (financial investment FI) in the financial plan.

t	0	1	2	3	4
Cash flows CF_t	−100.00	−30.00	50.00	70.00	90.00
Depreciation D_t		25.00	25.00	25.00	25.00
Financial investment FI_t	0	−2.50	34.94	83.31	142.89
$i \times FI_{t-1}$		0	−0.13	1.75	4.17
Tax base TB_t		−55.00	24.88	46.75	69.17
Tax liability T_t		27.50	12.44	23.37	34.58
CF_t^τ	−100.00	−2.50	37.44	48.37	59.58

We assume that the credit interest rate equals the debit interest rate. The positive or negative net cash flows at the end of each period are reinvested at the capital market and yield or cost interest i before taxes. Interest income is fully taxed while interest payments are fully tax deductible.

The tax base consists of the pre-tax cash flows, the depreciation, and the interest income/expense ($i \times FI_{t-1}$). Net cash flows are derived by adding pre-tax cash flows and interest income/expenses and subtracting tax payments. Financial investment of period t is calculated by adding previous year's financial investment to current net cash flows. At $t = n = 4$ financial investment is the after-tax future value $FV^\tau = 142.89$.

As FV^τ is an absolute decision criterion with $FV^\tau = 142.89$, we cannot evaluate the profitability of the real investment using this information exclusively. As we know that we can generate an alternative after-tax rate of return of 2.5% while investing in a financial investment, post-tax future value of our financial investment is $100 \times 1.025^4 = 110.38$. Now, we have two comparable post-tax future values. As the after-tax future value of our real investment option is greater than that of the financial investment, the real investment is carried out.

3.3.3 Post-Tax Present Value of an Annuity

The after-tax present value of an annuity in arrears ($PVAR^{\tau}$) is

$$PVAR^{\tau} = \frac{(q^{\tau})^n - 1}{i^{\tau} \times (q^{\tau})^n}. \tag{3.16}$$

Now, suppose an infinite annuity ($n \to \infty$). Then (3.16) simplifies to

$$\lim_{n\to\infty} \frac{(q^{\tau})^n - 1}{i^{\tau} \times (q^{\tau})^n} = \lim_{n\to\infty} \frac{1 - (q^{\tau})^{-n}}{i^{\tau}} = \frac{1}{i^{\tau}} = \frac{1}{i \times (1-\tau)}. \tag{3.17}$$

The after-tax future value of an annuity equals the after-tax present value of an annuity multiplied by $(1 + i \times (1 - \tau))^n = (q^{\tau})^n$ and amounts to

$$FVAR^{\tau} = \frac{(q^{\tau})^n - 1}{i^{\tau} \times (q^{\tau})^n} \times (q^{\tau})^n = \frac{(q^{\tau})^n - 1}{i^{\tau}}. \tag{3.18}$$

The post-tax present value of an annuity is based on cash payments in arrears. In contrast to this, the after-tax present value factor of an annuity in advance ($PVAD^{\tau}$) takes cash payments at the beginning of the year into account

$$PVAD^{\tau} = \frac{(q^{\tau})^n - 1}{i^{\tau} \times (q^{\tau})^{n-1}}. \tag{3.19}$$

The future value factor of an annuity in advance ($FVAD^{\tau}$) is determined by:

$$FVAD^{\tau} = \frac{(q^{\tau})^n - 1}{i^{\tau} \times (q^{\tau})^{-1}}. \tag{3.20}$$

Figure 3.1 summarizes the post-tax annuity factors derived.

3.3.4 Post-Tax Capital Recovery Factor

The reverse case to the after-tax present value of an annuity derived in the previous section is the after-tax annuity (ANN^{τ}) of a given NPV^{τ}. In this case the post-tax annuity in arrears is given by:

$$ANN^{\tau} = NPV^{\tau} \times \frac{1}{PVAR^{\tau}} = NPV^{\tau} \times \frac{i^{\tau} \times (q^{\tau})^n}{(q^{\tau})^n - 1}, \tag{3.21}$$

where

$$CRF^{\tau} = \frac{1}{PVAR^{\tau}} = \frac{i^{\tau} \times (q^{\tau})^n}{(q^{\tau})^n - 1} \tag{3.22}$$

is called post-tax capital recovery factor (CRF^{τ}).

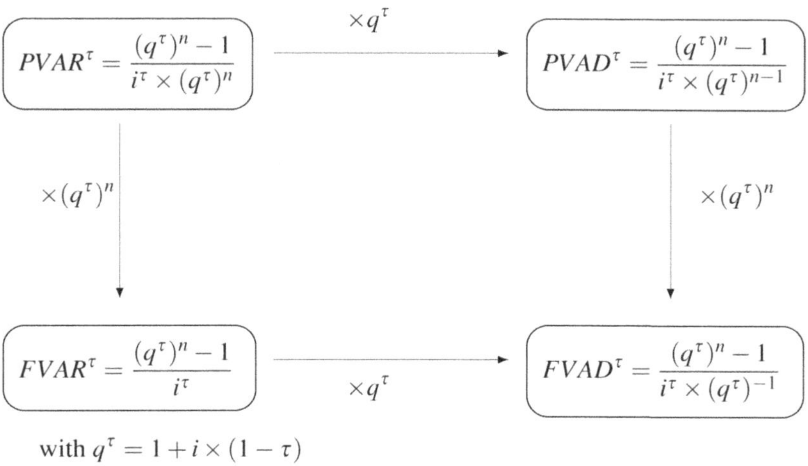

Fig. 3.1 Post-tax annuity-square

Example 3.8. Post-Tax Capital Recovery Factor

Using the assumptions of Ex. 3.5 on p. 91, we get NPV^τ of 29.45. Transforming that NPV^τ into an annuity in arrears would result in

$$ANN^\tau = 29.45 \times \frac{0.025 \times 1.025^4}{1.025^4 - 1} = 7.83. \tag{3.23}$$

3.3.5 *Post-Tax Internal Rate of Return*

The post-tax internal rate of return $i^{*,\tau}$ is the post-tax return i^τ for which the post-tax net present value of cash flows is equal to zero.

$$NPV^\tau = -I_0 + \sum_{t=1}^{n} \frac{CF_t^\tau}{(1+i^\tau)^t} \stackrel{!}{=} 0 \quad \Leftrightarrow \quad i^{*,\tau} = i^\tau \left| \sum_{t=1}^{n} \frac{CF_t^\tau}{(1+i^{*,\tau})^t} - I_0 = 0 \right. . \tag{3.24}$$

For any $i^\tau < i^{*,\tau}$, NPV^τ is positive; for $i^\tau > i^{*,\tau}$, NPV^τ is negative and if $i^\tau = i^{*,\tau}$ there is indifference. In summary

$$i^\tau \begin{Bmatrix} > \\ = \\ < \end{Bmatrix} i^{*,\tau} \Leftrightarrow NPV^\tau \begin{Bmatrix} < \\ = \\ > \end{Bmatrix} 0.$$

Problems with using the internal rate of return as decision criterion remain comparable to the pre-tax case which we discussed in Sect. 2.4.2. Therefore, we will focus on the other after-tax decision criteria discussed in this chapter.

3.3.6 *Post-Tax Modified Internal Rate of Return (Post-Tax Baldwin Rate of Return)*

The post-tax Baldwin rate of return (also called post-tax modified internal rate of return) can be used to evaluate the profitability of an investment because it overcomes the problems of the internal rate of return.[10] Now, we focus on the Baldwin formula with only one initial investment spent at the beginning of the project in $t = 0$.

Our calculation is based on the after-tax future value according to (3.14).

The after-tax Baldwin rate of return $r^{B,\tau}$ is defined as the geometrical average after-tax rate of return of the initial investment

$$I_0 \times (1 + r^{B,\tau})^n = FV^\tau. \tag{3.25}$$

If (3.25) is solved for $r^{B,\tau}$ as the post-tax Baldwin rate of return, we get

$$r^{B,\tau} = \sqrt[n]{\frac{FV^\tau}{I_0}} - 1. \tag{3.26}$$

The decision rule is as follows: For any $i^\tau < r^{B,\tau}$, NPV^τ is positive; for $i^\tau > r^{B,\tau}$, NPV^τ is negative. In summary

$$NPV^\tau \begin{Bmatrix} > \\ = \\ < \end{Bmatrix} 0 \Leftrightarrow r^{B,\tau} \begin{Bmatrix} > \\ = \\ < \end{Bmatrix} i^\tau.$$

The after-tax Baldwin rate of return typically is smaller compared to the Baldwin rate of return before taxes. Nevertheless, this does not necessarily mean that the profitability has decreased due to taxes, because one has to compare the after-tax Baldwin rate of return to the after-tax interest rate. If interest income is taxable then the after-tax interest rate is also less than the interest rate before taxes.

As in the pre-tax case, the results of our standard decision criterion net present value (invest, do not invest, indifferent) lead to the same results when the Baldwin rate of return is used as a decision criterion. Again, this is only true, if the expected useful life n, the after-tax capital market interest rate i^τ, and the initial investment I_0 of the investment alternatives are the same. If there are different expected useful

[10] See the discussion in Sects. 2.4.2 and 2.4.4.

lives, interest rates or initial investments, decisions according to the net present value criterion and the Baldwin rate of return can differ. In those cases, adjustments have to be made in order to make the projects comparable. The proceeding is as described in Sect. 2.4.4.

Example 3.9. Post-Tax Baldwin Rate of Return

Using the assumptions of Ex. 3.5 on p. 91, we get FV^τ of 142.89. Transforming that FV^τ into the post-tax Baldwin rate of return results in

$$r^{B,\tau} = \sqrt[n]{\frac{FV^\tau}{I_0}} - 1 = \sqrt[4]{\frac{142.89}{100}} - 1 = 9.33\%.$$

3.4 The Income Tax Paradox

Taxes are fees charged by the government. Individuals and corporations regard them as an expense, and they have to pay them without receiving a service in return. But sometimes, tax payments cause a positive effect: Despite paying taxes, the after-tax-value of an investment increases! This effect is known as "income tax paradox".[11]

3.4.1 Occurrence of the Income Tax Paradox

The income tax paradox occurs when the post-tax net present value NPV^τ is larger than the pre-tax net present value NPV. This effect is caused by differing tax treatments of the investment project in the numerator and the alternative investment in the denominator. The alternative investment is a capital market investment, where interest income is fully or partially taxed on a cash flow basis. On the contrary, the real investment project in the numerator is taxed on a profit basis instead of a cash flow basis. These different definitions of the tax bases may lead to a preferential treatment of the real investment which causes the tax paradox.

Example 3.10. The Income Tax Paradox Part I

Consider a real investment alternative that requires acquisition costs of $I_0 = 3{,}000$. Choosing that real investment alternative generates a future cash flow structure of

[11] See *Schneider* [10], *Schneider* [11], p. 246, *König/Wosnitza* [4], p. 33, and *Schanz/Schanz* [9].

t	0	1	2	3
CF_t	-3,000	1,050	1,150	1,450

Applying an interest rate of $i = 10\%$, the net present value before taxes results in

$$NPV = -3{,}000 + \frac{1{,}050}{1.1} + \frac{1{,}150}{1.1^2} + \frac{1{,}450}{1.1^3} = -5.63.$$

Because the net present value before taxes is negative, the investor is advised to choose the alternative financial investment and not to carry out the real investment.

Now, taxation is implemented. It is assumed that $\tau = 50\%$ and that both the real investment and the financial investment are equally taxed at the full marginal tax rate. In that case the discount rate is calculated with $i^\tau = 10\% \times (1 - 0.5) = 5\%$. We assume straight-line depreciation ($D_t = \frac{I_0}{n} = \frac{3{,}000}{3} = 1{,}000$). Thus, the cash flows after taxation are calculated as:

t	0	1	2	3
CF_t	-3,000	1,050	1,150	1,450
D_t		1,000	1,000	1,000
TB_t		50	150	450
T_t		25	75	225
CF_t^τ	-3,000	1,025	1,075	1,225

Therefore, NPV^τ results in

$$NPV^\tau = -3{,}000 + \frac{1{,}025}{1.05} + \frac{1{,}075}{1.05^2} + \frac{1{,}225}{1.05^3} = 9.45.$$

Surprisingly, the after-tax net present value is positive which advises the investor to carry out the real investment. This is amazing because we stated at the very beginning of this book that the net present value is nothing else than an additional consumption compared to the financial investment alternative. However, the explanation for the occurrence of an income tax paradox is quite simple. NPV^τ is just an indicator for additional consumption possibilities compared to the alternative financial investment and does not state anything about absolute consumption. Now, compared to the pre-tax case, if taxes are considered they reduce cash flows of real- and financial investment as well. So it seems to be clear that there are cases where preferential taxation of real investments occurs.

On a graphical basis we can find out if a tax paradox occurs for all possible tax rates. Net present value functions before taxes always run parallel to the axis of abscissae because the net present value before taxes does not depend on taxation. The income tax paradox can be found in the interval where $NPV^{\tau} > NPV$ is true.

Example 3.11. The Income Tax Paradox Part II

Based on the assumptions of Ex. 3.10, Fig. 3.2 depicts the net present value before and after taxes in dependence of the tax rate τ. The net present value function before taxes is independent from τ and, therefore, parallel to the axis of abscissae. The income tax paradox can be found in the overall interval $\tau \in]0, 1]$. In this interval it is true that $NPV^{\tau} > NPV$.

First, the net present value after taxes increases if the tax rate increases. Formally, it is true that $\frac{\partial NPV^{\tau}(\tau)}{\partial \tau} > 0$. If the tax rate increases, the advantage of the deductibility of depreciation allowances increases, because it is deducted from the tax base which is taxed at increasing tax rates.

At $\tau = 58.62\%$ the net present value after taxes reaches its maximum and decreases if the tax rate increases from that point, meaning $\frac{\partial NPV^{\tau}(\tau)}{\partial \tau} < 0$. From the point of $\tau = 58.62\%$ the net present value after taxes decreases if the tax rate increases. The advantage of the deductibility of depreciation allowances still increases, but it is weaker compared to the effect of a reduced discounting rate. At $\tau = 0\%$, the discount rate is 10%, at $\tau = 80\%$, the discount rate is reduced to 2%. With an increasing tax rate, the weight of the early cash flows in $t = 1$ is reduced while the weight of the cash flows in $t = 2$, and especially in $t = 3$, increases.

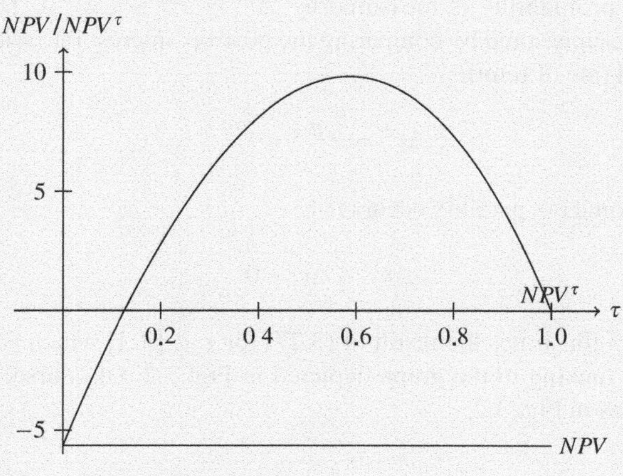

Fig. 3.2 The income tax paradox

If the tax rate reaches 100%, the interest rate after taxes becomes 0%. At the same time if $\tau = 100\%$, cash flows exceeding depreciation are collected by the government in total. In that case the numerator of the net present value formula consists of the depreciation that is discounted at a rate of $i^\tau = 0$ and therefore equals the initial cost of the investment

$$NPV^\tau = -3{,}000 + \frac{1{,}000}{1} + \frac{1{,}000}{1^2} + \frac{1{,}000}{1^3} = 0.$$

Hence, the net present value after taxes become zero.

Of course, the same effect can be found if other decision criteria are used, e.g., the modified rate of return. If we take the cash flow stream from Ex. 3.10, the pre-tax modified rate of return is

$$r^B = \sqrt[3]{\frac{(1{,}050 \times q^2 + 1{,}150 \times q + 1{,}450)}{3{,}000}} - 1$$
$$= 0.099.$$

Using (3.26), the post-tax modified rate of return is

$$r^{B,\tau} = \sqrt[3]{\begin{matrix}[(1{,}050 - \tau \times 50) \times (q^\tau)^2 + (1{,}150 - \tau \times 150) \times q^\tau \\ +(1{,}450 - \tau \times 450)] \times 3{,}000^{-1}\end{matrix}} - 1$$
$$= 0.051.$$

The pre-tax profitability is measured by $\Delta r = r^B - i > 0$. The post-tax profitability is measured by comparing the post-tax interest rate with the post-tax modified rate of return

$$\Delta r^\tau = r^{B,\tau} - i^\tau.$$

Now, an income tax paradox occurs if

$$\Delta r^\tau - \Delta r > 0. \tag{3.27}$$

Figure 3.3 illustrates the result of (3.27) for $\tau \in [0, 1]$ which is equivalent for decision making to the graph depicted in Fig. 3.2. Of course, we get the same graph as in Fig. 3.2.

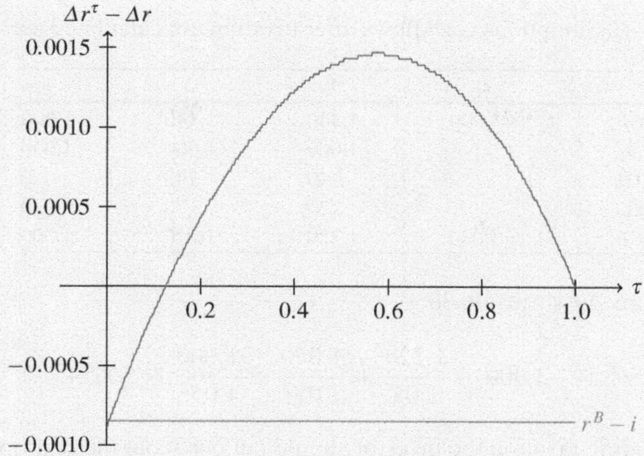

Fig. 3.3 The income tax paradox based on the modified rate of return

The occurrence of the income tax paradox increases the necessity for tax planning in order to avoid wrong investment decisions.

Remember: Investment decisions that are profitable (unprofitable) on a pre-tax basis can be unprofitable (profitable) because of the taxation of the corresponding income. An optimal investment decision can only be made by taking taxes into account.

Example 3.12. No Tax Paradox Occurs

Now, consider a real investment alternative that requires acquisition costs of $I_0 = 3{,}000$ and a certain future cash flow structure of

t	0	1	2	3
CF_t	-3,000	1,440	1,140	1,000

The net present value before taxes by applying an interest rate of $i = 10\%$ is

$$NPV = -3{,}000 + \frac{1{,}440}{1.1} + \frac{1{,}140}{1.1^2} + \frac{1{,}000}{1.1^3} = 2.55.$$

Net present value before taxes is positive and therefore, the investor is advised to prefer the real investment option to the financial investment alternative.

Now, taxation is implemented. It is assumed that $\tau = 50\%$ and that real investment and financial investment are equally treated in terms of the marginal tax rate. The discount rate is calculated with $i^\tau = 10\% \times (1-0.5) = 5\%$. We assume straight-line depreciation ($D_t = \frac{I_0}{n} = \frac{3{,}000}{3} = 1{,}000$).

Under these assumptions cash flows after taxation are calculated as:

t	0	1	2	3
CF_t	-3,000	1,440	1,140	1,000
D_t		1,000	1,000	1,000
TB_t		440	140	0
T_t		220	70	0
CF_t^τ	-3,000	1,220	1,070	1,000

Therefore, NPV^τ results in

$$NPV^\tau = -3{,}000 + \frac{1{,}220}{1.05} + \frac{1{,}070}{1.05^2} + \frac{1{,}000}{1.05^3} = -3.74. \quad (3.28)$$

After including taxation the investor should not carry out the real investment alternative.

Figure 3.4 shows the net present value after taxes of (3.28) in dependence of the marginal tax rate. The net present value after taxes is lower than the pre-tax net present value within the whole interval $\tau \in]0, 1]$.

First, the net present value after taxes decreases if the marginal tax rate increases $\left(\frac{\partial NPV^\tau(\tau)}{\partial \tau} < 0\right)$. The reason for that is because the marginal tax rate increases the disadvantage of the deferral of the depreciation increases. At a marginal tax rate of $\tau = 59.03\%$ the net present value after taxes reaches its minimum. From that point on the net present value after taxes increases if the marginal tax rate increases $\left(\frac{\partial NPV^\tau(\tau)}{\partial \tau} > 0\right)$. From that point on if the marginal tax rate increases the discount rate after taxes decreases and outweighs the disadvantage of the deferral of the depreciation.

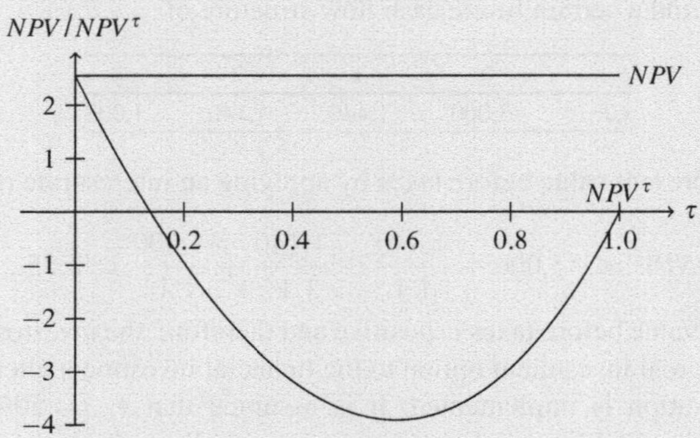

Fig. 3.4 No income tax paradox occurs within the whole interval $\tau \in]0, 1]$

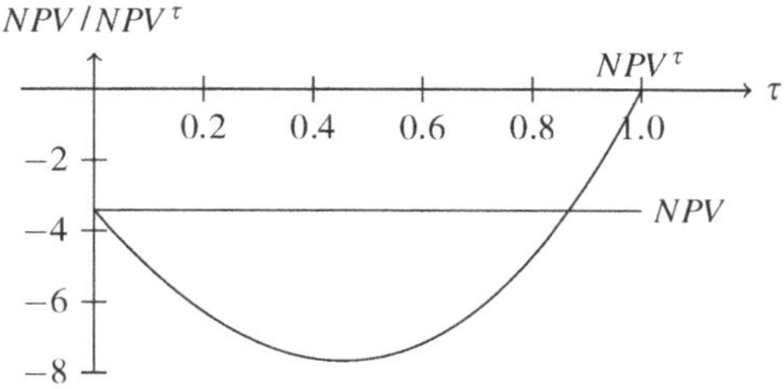

Fig. 3.5 Income tax paradox does not apply to the whole interval $\tau \in]0, 1]$

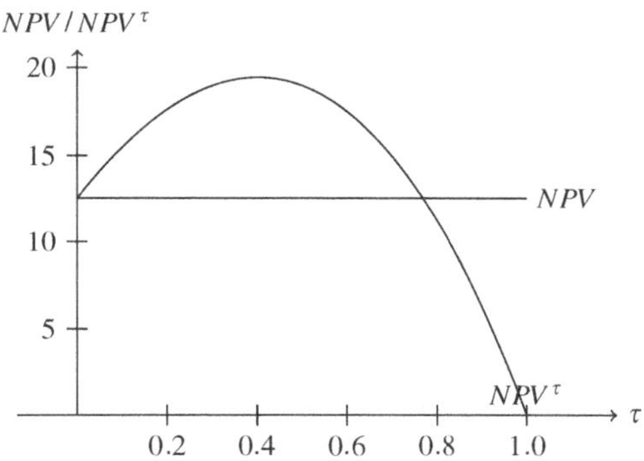

Fig. 3.6 Income tax paradox does not apply to the whole interval $\tau \in]0, 1]$

However, the income tax paradox does not have to apply to the whole interval $\tau \in]0, 1]$. Figure 3.5 is an example showing that the post-tax net present value first is below the pre-tax net present value and then overstates the pre-tax net present value. The cash flow stream assumed c.p. is

t	0	1	2	3
CF_t	–3,000	1,445	1,150	975

Figure 3.6 shows the corresponding case, where the net present value after taxes first overstates the pre-tax net present value and then is below the pre-tax net present value. In that case a cash flow stream c.p. of

t	0	1	2	3
CF_t	–3,000	1,070	1,150	1,450

is assumed.

Summary: The income tax paradox describes the curious effect that the post-tax net present value overstates the pre-tax net present value. This result seems to be surprising because we derived that the net present value states the additional consumption possibilities compared to the alternative financial investment. But why do consumption possibilities increase after taxation is taken into account although cash has to be paid to the tax authorities?

The answer is quite simple. First, the net present value represents a decision criterion that evaluates the investment opportunity relatively to the alternative financial investment. The result that the post-tax net present value overstates the pre-tax present value therefore just implies that the relative consumption possibilities might rise if taxation is included. However, nothing is stated in regard to absolute consumption possibilities. Second, if taxation is included, both the real investment (numerator) and the financial investment (denominator) are subject to taxation. Thus, the numerator and the denominator are reduced by taxation. The result in terms of the net present value depends on the fact that the real investment and the financial investment are not taxed neutrally because there is an accrued tax base applicable for real investments while the financial investment is taxed on a cash basis.[12]

3.4.2 Reason for Occurrence of the Income Tax Paradox

The formal condition that must hold for the occurrence of an income tax paradox is that the present value of depreciation is greater than the present value of economic depreciation.

Example 3.13. Reason for the Occurrence of the Income Tax Paradox

Based on Ex. 3.10, we compare the present value of tax depreciations and economic depreciations. In both cases the present value is calculated by using the after-tax interest rate. The formal condition – that the present value of depreciation has to be greater than the present value of economic depreciation – is derived in Sect. 5.4 on p. 206.

Present values evolve to

$$PV_0 = \frac{1{,}450}{1.1^3} + \frac{1{,}150}{1.1^2} + \frac{1{,}050}{1.1} = 2{,}994.37$$
$$PV_1 = \frac{1{,}450}{1.1^2} + \frac{1{,}150}{1.1} = 2{,}243.80$$
$$PV_2 = \frac{1{,}450}{1.1} = 1{,}318.18$$
$$PV_3 = 0.$$

[12] Neutral tax systems are discussed in Chap. 5.

After calculating the present values, we can easily derive economic depreciations

$$\begin{aligned} ED_1 &= 2{,}994.37 - 2{,}243.80 = 750.57 \\ ED_2 &= 2{,}243.80 - 1{,}318.18 = 925.62 \\ ED_3 &= 1{,}318.18 - 0 = 1{,}318.18. \end{aligned}$$

The present value of the depreciation PV^D accounts for

$$PV^D = 1{,}000 \times \frac{(1+0.05)^3 - 1}{0.05 \times (1+0.05)^3} = 2{,}723.25. \quad (3.29)$$

Notice that the present value of the depreciation is calculated using the after-tax discount rate.

The present value of the economic depreciation PV^{ED} – discounted at the after-tax rate – results in

$$PV^{ED} = \frac{750.57}{1.05} + \frac{925.62}{1.05^2} + \frac{1{,}318.18}{1.05^3} = 2{,}693.09.$$

As $PV^D > PV^{ED}$, the tax paradox occurs.

In Ex. 3.12, the present values amount to

$$\begin{aligned} PV_0 &= \frac{1{,}000}{1.1^3} + \frac{1{,}140}{1.1^2} + \frac{1{,}440}{1.1} = 3{,}002.55 \\ PV_1 &= \frac{1{,}000}{1.1^2} + \frac{1{,}140}{1.1} = 1{,}862.81 \\ PV_2 &= \frac{1{,}000}{1.1} = 909.09 \\ PV_3 &= 0. \end{aligned}$$

Now, the economic depreciation is derived as:

$$\begin{aligned} ED_1 &= 3{,}002.55 - 1{,}862.81 = 1{,}139.74 \\ ED_2 &= 1{,}862.81 - 909.09 = 953.72 \\ ED_3 &= 909.09 - 0 = 909.09. \end{aligned}$$

The present value of the depreciation PV^D accounts for

$$PV^D = 1{,}000 \times \frac{(1+0.05)^3 - 1}{0.05 \times (1+0.05)^3} = 2{,}723.25$$

and does not differ from (3.29), because the allocation of the total depreciation has not changed because straight-line depreciation is applied again. The present value of the economic depreciation is

$$PV^{ED} = \frac{1{,}139.74}{1.05} + \frac{953.72}{1.05^2} + \frac{909.09}{1.05^3} = 2{,}735.82$$

and overstates the present value of tax depreciation.

As $PV^{ED} > PV^{D}$, no tax paradox occurs and the net present value before taxes exceeds the after-tax net present value.

3.5 Types of Tax Effects

An investment's net present value after taxes may differ from the net present value before taxes. What causes this effect? Basically, three different types of tax effects that influence investment and financing decisions can be distinguished: These are (1) tax rate effects, (2) tax base effects, and (3) timing effects (see *Wagner* [15], pp. 454–456).

3.5.1 Tax Rate Effects

A tax rate effect occurs if different tax rates are applied to the same (comprehensive) tax base. As a result, a taxpayer has the incentive to increase the income stream which is taxed at a lower rate.

We distinguish between tax rate effects due to

1. Different types of income
2. Progressive tax rates
3. International differences in tax levels

1. Different types of income:
   Most countries define different types of income and apply different tax rates to their specific tax bases. This is often done to influence taxpayers' behavior or to mitigate double taxation. For example, capital income is very mobile compared to income from employment. An individual can easily shift his bank account abroad, but it is more costly and laborious to move and work abroad. Many countries react to this disparity and reduce tax rates on capital income, e.g., interest income. Another reason can be found in the double taxation – from an economic perspective[13] – of some types of income. Countries usually define a reduced tax rate on dividends because corporations' profits have been taxed at the company level.

[13] See the discussion in Sect. 6.6.2 on p. 232.

Example 3.14. Tax Rate Effects

In the United States, capital gains are taxed at a reduced flat tax rate. Ordinary income is taxed at a higher progressive income tax rate. An investor tries to declare his income as capital gains as opposed to ordinary income.

2. Progressive tax rates:
   Often, countries define progressive tax rates.[14] Taxpayers can profit from tax progression in two ways. They can either shift income to a year where their income is expected to be lower or they can shift income to relatives with less taxable income, e.g., shifting of income from parents to their children. Parents can donate a bank account to their children who in turn have to declare the corresponding interest as their income.

Example 3.15. Tax Rate Effects

Assume a country with one progressive tax rate function for all types of income. The simple tax rate function is as follows: 10% taxes for income between 0 and € 50,000, and 30% taxes for income above € 50,000. Now, there is a taxpayer who retires this year. His current income is € 100,000, and his yearly pension will be € 10,000. He thinks about selling his share in a company now or next year. The capital gain will be € 10,000. Selling it now will lead to an additional tax liability of $T = 0.3 \times 10{,}000 = 3{,}000$. Waiting until next year will reduce the tax payment to $T = 0.1 \times 10{,}000 = 1{,}000$. But be careful: Here we are also facing timing effects. They will be explained in the next section.

3. International differences in tax levels:
   Countries use their fiscal sovereignty to define different tax rates. Companies engaged in more than one country can try to shift income from high-tax countries to low-tax countries. One way is to declare very high or very low transfer prices for intracompany transactions.

Tax rates serve as an important signal for the total tax burden and their influence is usually over estimated (*Blaufus* et al. [1]).

3.5.2 *Tax Base Effects*

A tax base effect might occur when income elements may be included or excluded from the tax base. There are several reasons, why income can be tax exempt. Let us discuss three important tax base effects:

[14] Examples are given in Sect. 4.3 on p. 141.

1. Tax law excludes income from tax base,
2. Fiscal authorities are not able to control income,
3. Loss carry forwards are lost.

Income can be tax exempt, because tax law excludes it from the tax base. An example we often find is capital gains taxation. Capital gains realized by individuals from selling stocks or assets held for a certain minimum period are often tax exempt.

Tax exemption also results because fiscal authorities are not able to check where income is generated, for example in case of neighborly help.

Example 3.16. Tax Base Effects

If a neighbor helps gardening, his service will not be taxed. In contrast, if a gardener is employed, his service will be taxable. Once, the tax base includes the service, once it excludes the service.

A further tax base effect might occur due to loss offset rules because tax authorities do not grant immediate tax refunds in case of taxable losses.[15] Instead, a loss carry forward is generated. The loss carry forward reduces the tax base in the following years. Most countries apply a time restriction for offsetting loss carry forwards. If loss carry forwards get lost, a tax base effect will occur because the tax base of the investment increases.

When we talk about a tax base effect, we have to take the sum of tax bases of an investment into account. Deferral of a tax base component to the next year causes a timing effect, not a tax base effect.

3.5.3 *Timing Effects*

Timing effects occur if income is shifted from one period to another. This can be realized by deferring taxable income or by accelerating taxable expenses.

Example 3.17. Timing Effects

An investor is planning to depreciate an asset over 4 years. His tax advisor tells him that the asset can be requalified to be depreciated over just 3 years. Thus, depreciation is accelerated. Assume an investment of $I_0 = 100$, a tax rate of $\tau = 0.5$, and an interest rate before taxes of $i = 0.1$. Cash flows generated by the investment are $CF = (40; 40; 40; 40)$, the yearly tax base amounts to $TB_t = 40 - 25 = 15$ if depreciation takes place over 4 years.

[15] This effect will be explained in detail in Sect. 7.4.

It is $TB = (6.67; 6.67; 6.67; 40)$ if the asset is depreciated over 3 years.The interest rate after taxes is $i^\tau = i \times (1 - \tau) = 0.05$. Because of the timing effect the investor saves

$$\text{Saving} = \sum_{t=1}^{4} \frac{0.5 \times 15}{1.05^t} - \left[\sum_{t=1}^{3} \frac{0.5 \times 6.67}{1.05^t} + \frac{0.5 \times 40}{1.05^4} \right] = 26.59 - 25.54 = 1.05.$$

3.5.4 Comparison of Tax Effects

Tax rate effects, tax base effects, and timing effects influence investment decisions. But the importance of the effects differs. Typically, a tax base effect dominates a tax rate effect, and both dominate timing effects. This ranking may differ if we face a very high inflation compared to very small tax rate differences, for example. Let's get back to Ex. 3.17.

Example 3.18. Comparison of Tax Effects

Tax rate effect: We continue our previous example. The investment of $I_0 = 100$ is depreciated over 4 years, the interest rate before taxes is $i = 0.1$. Cash flows generated by the investment are $CF = (40; 40; 40; 40)$, the yearly tax base amounts to $TB_t = 40 - 25 = 15$. Now, the tax advisor proposes to move to a country with a tax rate of $\tau = 0.3$ instead of $\tau = 0.5$. The interest rate after taxes increases to $i^\tau = i \times (1 - \tau) = 0.07$. The saving due to this tax rate effect is

$$\text{Saving} = \sum_{t=1}^{4} \frac{0.5 \times 15}{1.05^t} - \sum_{t=1}^{4} \frac{0.3 \times 15}{1.07^t} = 26.59 - 15.24 = 11.35.$$

The tax rate effect influences both the tax payments of the real investment and the discount rate. The saving is much larger compared to the reduction of the taxable useful life by 1 year.

Tax base effect: The taxpayer decides not to move. He stays in his home country. His tax advisor figures out that the investment is environment-friendly and, therefore, is tax exempt since the last tax reform. The profits are excluded from the tax base. The saving is

$$\text{Saving} = \sum_{t=1}^{4} \frac{0.5 \times 15}{1.05^t} - 0 = 26.59 - 0 = 26.59.$$

Often, taxpayers face opposing tax effects. Deferring tax payments reduces the net present value of the tax burden, but the taxpayer might face a different tax rate.

Deferring income recognition is always profitable as long as tax rates are constant or declining over time. If they increase, the tax rate effect must be balanced against the timing effect.

Example 3.19. Tax Rate Effect and Timing Effect

Suppose an investor can choose between a tax payment $T_0 = 100$ now or a tax payment $T_1 = 120$ next year for profit he realizes by carrying out this investment. Next year's tax payment is higher because the taxpayer's salary increases and he lives in a country with progressive tax rates. At which interest rate will the delaying of the tax payments become unfavorable? Assume that interest income is tax exempt.

$$100 \stackrel{!}{=} \frac{120}{(1+i)} \quad \rightarrow \quad i = \frac{120}{100} - 1 = 0.20.$$

If the interest rate exceeds 0.20, it will be advantageous to defer income recognition, because the favorable timing effect (advantage) prevails the unfavorable tax rate effect.

3.6 Marginal and Average Tax Rates

Depending on the type of decision setting an investor is faced, he has to take either marginal tax rates or average tax rates into account.

The marginal tax rate is defined as the rate of tax applied to the last unit (Euro, e.g.) added to the tax base (taxable income). For example, the income you earn from investments is added to your income from all other sources. As a result, each additional Euro of investment income is taxed at the highest rate applicable to your total income. The marginal tax rate is calculated as derivative with respect to the tax base

$$\frac{\partial T(Tax\,Base)}{\partial Tax\,Base}.$$

The marginal tax rate is relevant when deciding on additional income.

Example 3.20. Marginal Tax Rate

An employee earns € 100,000. He lives in Germany where a progressive tax rate function is applied. He has to pay taxes amounting to $T = 0.42 \times 100{,}000 - 8{,}172 = 33{,}828$. His current marginal tax rate is $\frac{\partial T(Tax\,Base)}{\partial Tax\,Base} = 0.42$. He thinks about applying for an additional part-time job where he can earn

€ 10,000. The additional tax payment would be $0.42 \times 10{,}000 = 4{,}200$. The taxpayer has to take the marginal tax rate of 0.42 into account.

The average tax rate is calculated by dividing total income taxes paid by total tax base

$$\frac{T(Tax\,Base)}{Tax\,Base}.$$

The average tax rate incorporates taxes paid from the first to the last unit of the tax base so it will be less than the marginal rate, although a person's average and marginal tax rate will be close to equal for higher-income earners.

The average tax rate is important when investors decide between investing in different countries. Independent of the concrete tax rate functions and the marginal tax rates, an investor has to compare average tax rates of different countries to decide where to invest. This method can only be chosen if nontax factors are identical.

Example 3.21. Average Tax Rate

The average tax rate of the employee in the previous example is

$$\frac{T(Tax\,Base)}{Tax\,Base} = \frac{33{,}828}{100{,}000} = 0.34$$

which is below the marginal tax rate of 0.42.

If a tax rate is flat, the marginal tax rate always equals the average tax rate. Graphical examples for marginal and average tax rates are depicted in Sect. 4.3.

3.7 Fisher–Hirshleifer Model and Taxes

The following explanations are an extension to Sect. 2.5.2 on p. 49. We discuss the impact on consumption behavior by introducing a comprehensive tax system. As in the Standard Model, the tax base consists of cash flows less depreciation.

3.7.1 Taxation of Real Investments and Financial Investments

In Sect. 2.5 we derived the proof for practicability of the net present value criterion through the Fisher-Separation. But we have not taken taxation into account. Figure 3.7 shows the influence on the optimal initial investment I_0^*, if solely real investments are taxed. If tax authorities participate in the cash flow returns of the initial investment, the transformation function or the internal rate of return after-tax

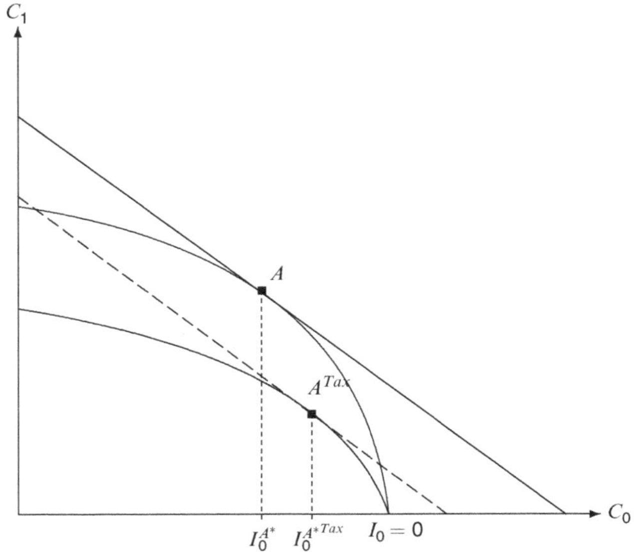

Fig. 3.7 Taxation of real investments

payments to the tax authorities would be smaller than before taxation. As the return on financial investments is not taxed at all in that example, the optimal initial investment after taxation is determined by a parallel translation of the financial market line until it is tangent to the transformation curve after taxation. Remember, the origin of initial investments is where the transformation curve meets the axis of abscissae. Therefore, the optimal initial investment after taxation is below the optimal initial investment in the case of absence of taxation.

Now, consider the case where taxation applies to both real and financial investments. That case is illustrated in Fig. 3.8. If interest is taxed at a proportional tax rate of τ, the return after taxation would be

$$i^{\tau} = i \times (1 - \tau).$$

Then, the slope of the financial market line after taxation is less steep than without taxation

$$\begin{aligned} 1 + i &> 1 + i \times (1 - \tau) \\ i &> i \times (1 - \tau). \end{aligned}$$

The result shown in Fig. 3.8 seems to be contrary to intuition because in that case, taxation causes a higher initial investment and therefore a higher net present value than without taxation (the dashed line representing the financial market line under consideration of taxes meets the axis of abscissae further right than the line without

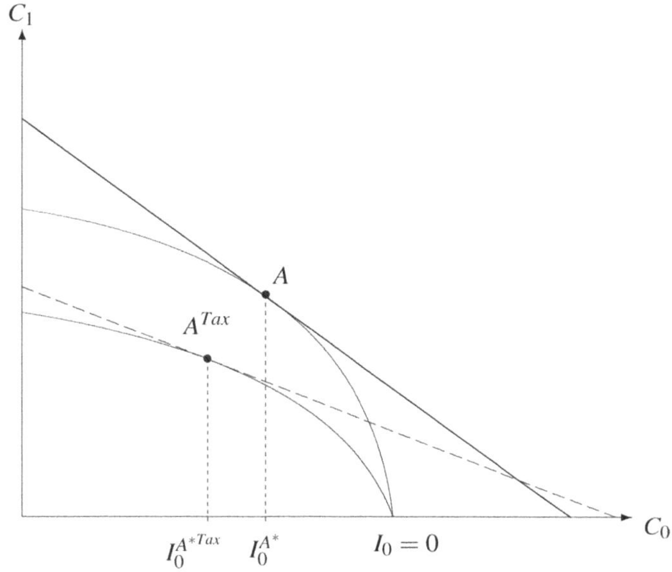

Fig. 3.8 Taxation of both real and financial investments

taxation). However, because the net present value is a relative decision criterion comparing the real investment and the alternative financial investment and both types of investments are taxed, taxation can cause rising or falling net present values. This phenomenon is also called the tax paradox. The tax paradox has been discussed in Sect. 3.4 on p. 97.

Depending on the characteristics of the investments, the initial investment and therefore the net present values can increase or decrease because of taxation.

Example 3.22. Optimal Consumption Bundle in Case of Taxes

In the following, we want to extend Ex. 2.25 on p. 60. The individual is still endowed with $W_0 = 100$ and utility function is still assumed to be

$$U(C_0, C_1) = C_0^2 \times C_1.$$

However, now the fiscal authority imposes taxes on real investment returns of $\tau = 40\%$. Interest is tax exempt. The real investment function is hence adjusted to

$$f(I_0) = 15 \times \sqrt{I_0} - \tau \times (15 \times \sqrt{I_0} - I_0).$$

It is assumed that there is no money left for consumption at the end of $t=1$. The Lagrangian function taking the adjusted real investment function into account is

$$\mathscr{L}(C_0, C_1, F_0, \lambda) = C_0^2 \times C_1 + \lambda \times \Big[15 \times \sqrt{(W_0 - C_0 - F_0)}$$
$$- \tau \times (15 \times \sqrt{(W_0 - C_0 - F_0)} - (W_0 - C_0 - F_0))$$
$$+ F_0 \times (1 + i) - C_1 \Big]$$

with $W_0 - C_0 - F_0 = I_0$. The partial derivatives with respect to C_0, C_1, F_0, and λ are

$$\frac{\partial \mathscr{L}}{\partial C_0} = 2 \times C_0 \times C_1 - \lambda \times \left[\frac{7.5 \times (1-\tau)}{\sqrt{(W_0 - C_0 - F_0)}} + \tau\right] = 0 \quad (3.30)$$

$$\frac{\partial \mathscr{L}}{\partial C_1} = C_0^2 - \lambda = 0 \quad (3.31)$$

$$\frac{\partial \mathscr{L}}{\partial F_0} = -\lambda \times \left[\frac{7.5 \times (1-\tau)}{\sqrt{(W_0 - C_0 - F_0)}} + \tau - (1+i)\right] = 0 \quad (3.32)$$

$$\frac{\partial \mathscr{L}}{\partial \lambda} = \Big[15 \times \sqrt{(W_0 - C_0 - F_0)} \times (1-\tau)$$
$$+ \tau \times (W_0 - C_0 - F_0) + F_0 \times (1+i) - C_1 \Big] = 0. \quad (3.33)$$

Solving (3.30) and (3.31) for λ and setting equal we get

$$\frac{2 \times C_0 \times C_1}{\frac{7.5 \times (1-\tau)}{\sqrt{(W_0 - C_0 - F_0)}} + \tau} = C_0^2. \quad (3.34)$$

Solving (3.34) for C_1 gives

$$C_1 = \frac{C_0 \times \left(\frac{7.5 \times (1-\tau)}{\sqrt{(W_0 - C_0 - F_0)}} + \tau\right)}{2}. \quad (3.35)$$

For $\lambda > 0$ we can solve (3.32) for F_0 and get

$$F_0 = W_0 - C_0 - \left(\frac{7.5 \times (1-\tau)}{(1+i) - \tau}\right)^2. \quad (3.36)$$

We insert (3.36) in (3.35) and insert the result in (3.33) and solve for C_0

$$C_0 = \frac{15 \times \frac{7.5\times(1-\tau)}{(1+i)-\tau} \times (1-\tau) + \tau \times \left(\frac{7.5\times(1-\tau)}{(1+i)-\tau}\right)^2 + \frac{\left(W_0 - \left(\frac{7.5\times(1-\tau)}{(1+i)-\tau}\right)^2\right)}{(1+i)^{-1}}}{(1+i) + \frac{(1+i)}{2}}.$$

With $i = 0.2$, $\tau = 0.4$, and $W_0 = 100$, C_0 is

$$C_0 = 80.73. \tag{3.37}$$

We insert (3.37) in (3.36) and get

$$F_0 = 100 - 80.73 - \left(\frac{7.5 \times (1-0.4)}{1.2-0.4}\right)^2 = -12.37. \tag{3.38}$$

Obviously, the individual is still in a situation where money is borrowed in $t = 0$. Now, we get C_1 by inserting (3.37) and (3.38) in (3.35)

$$C_1 = \frac{80.73 \times \left(\frac{7.5\times(1-0.4)}{\sqrt{(100.00-80.73+12.37)}} + 0.4\right)}{2} = 31.64. \tag{3.39}$$

Real investment in $t = 0$ is

$$I_0 = W_0 - C_0 - F_0 = 100 - 80.73 + 12.37 = 48.44. \tag{3.40}$$

Net present value of the real investment is

$$\begin{aligned} NPV &= -I_0 + \frac{f(I_0) - \tau \times (f(I_0) - I_0)}{(1+i)} \\ &= -31.64 + \frac{15 \times \sqrt{31.64} - 0.4 \times (15 \times \sqrt{31.64} - 31.64)}{1.2} \\ &= 21.09. \end{aligned}$$

The result of the present example compared with the result of Ex. 2.25 illustrated in Fig. 2.23 on p. 63 (dashed lines) is illustrated in Fig. 3.9.

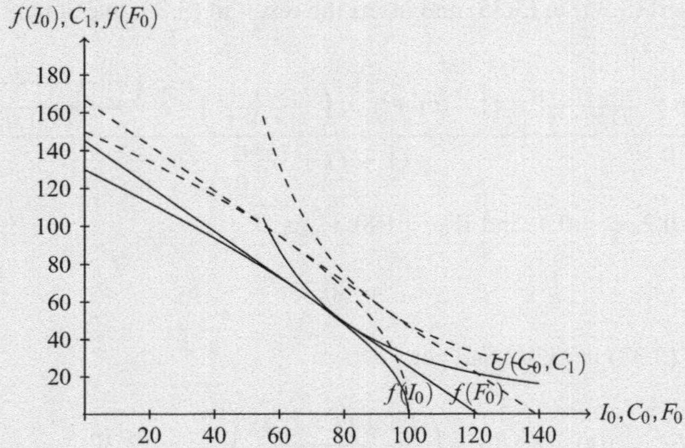

Fig. 3.9 Optimal consumption bundle if taxes on real investments are imposed

3.7.2 The Impact of Taxation and Debt Financing on Intertemporal Consumption Behavior

We can use the interrelations of variables used in the Fisher–Hirshleifer Model for conducting an analysis of debt financed transfers from governments to taxpayers.

Starting in 2008, we faced a considerable economic crisis. During the crisis governments all over the world raised funds in order to stabilize the economy. However, to be able to raise funds of this magnitude, governments have to finance this funds with credits that have to be paid back in the future. In this section, using a simple microeconomic model, we want to show the effect of a leveraged demand oriented economic policy if the individuals assume that in the future, the authorities will pay back the credit through higher tax rates.

We assume income today to be E_0 whereas income tomorrow is assumed to be E_1. Further we assume an intertemporal utility function with C_0 and C_1 (consumption today vs. consumption tomorrow) as our decision variables. The utility function is assumed to be represented by:

$$U(C_0, C_1) = \ln C_0 + \frac{\ln C_1}{1+\rho},$$

where ρ represents the time preference rate ($0 \leq \rho \leq 1$). The greater the time preference rate, the more the individual is willing to consume today instead of tomorrow. The individual can borrow and lend at the market interest rate of i to an unlimited extent.

The intertemporal budget constraint with savings of S_0 is defined as:

$$E_0 = C_0 + S_0 \tag{3.41}$$

with

$$S_0 \times (1 + i) = S_1. \tag{3.42}$$

In $t = 0$ the individual can break down his income into consumption or saving. If he saves money in $t = 0$ there will be S_1 available for consumption in $t = 1$. Therefore, consumption tomorrow consists of income in $t = 1$ and the saved money from $t = 0$ including interest

$$C_1 = E_1 + S_1. \tag{3.43}$$

Combining (3.41), (3.42), and (3.43) we get the budget constraint

$$0 \geq E_1 + (1 + i) \times \underbrace{(E_0 - C_0)}_{S_0} - C_1. \tag{3.44}$$

We derive the Lagrangian function

$$\mathcal{L}(C_0, C_1, \lambda) = \ln C_0 + \frac{\ln C_1}{1 + \rho} + \lambda \times [E_1 + (1 + i) \times (E_0 - C_0) - C_1].$$

The partial derivatives evolve to

$$\frac{\partial \mathcal{L}}{\partial C_0} = \frac{1}{C_0} - \lambda \times (1 + i) \stackrel{!}{=} 0 \tag{3.45}$$

$$\frac{\partial \mathcal{L}}{\partial C_1} = \frac{1}{C_1 \times (1 + \rho)} - \lambda \stackrel{!}{=} 0 \tag{3.46}$$

$$\frac{\partial \mathcal{L}}{\partial \lambda} = E_1 + (1 + i) \times (E_0 - C_0) - C_1 \stackrel{!}{=} 0. \tag{3.47}$$

Because we assume that the individual has consumed its whole wealth by the end of tomorrow, the constraint binds and hence $\lambda^* \neq 0$. If we solve (3.45) and (3.46) for λ we get

$$\frac{1}{C_0 \times (1 + i)} = \lambda \tag{3.48}$$

$$\frac{1}{C_1 \times (1 + \rho)} = \lambda. \tag{3.49}$$

Equalizing (3.48) and (3.49) and solving for C_1 results in

$$C_0 \times (1+i) = C_1 \times (1+\rho)$$

$$\Rightarrow \quad C_1 = \frac{C_0 \times (1+i)}{(1+\rho)}. \tag{3.50}$$

Inserting (3.50) in (3.47) and solving for C_0 gives

$$C_0 = \left[\frac{E_1}{(1+i)} + E_0\right] \times \frac{1+\rho}{2+\rho}. \tag{3.51}$$

Now suppose, the government launches a fund to stimulate demand in $t = 0$ by credit. That credit is assumed to be a money transfer in $t = 0$. However, the transfer has to be payed back by a flat rate income tax in the future ($t = 1$). Because of the income transfer in $t = 0$, the individual's income in $t = 0$ increases to

$$E_0^I = E_0 + \text{Transfer} \tag{3.52}$$

with E_0' as income in $t = 0$ after receiving transfer payments. If the transfer in $t = 0$ is financed by an equal amount of liability L, we have

$$\text{Transfer} = L. \tag{3.53}$$

The required additional tax revenue T in $t = 1$ is assumed to be

$$T = (1+i) \times L. \tag{3.54}$$

If Transfer $= L$, (3.52) can be written as:

$$E_0' = E_0 + L. \tag{3.55}$$

If the individual has to pay taxes in $t = 1$, its income tomorrow decreases to

$$E_1' = E_1 - (1+i) \times L. \tag{3.56}$$

Now, inserting (3.55) and (3.56) in (3.51) gives

$$C_0 = \left[\frac{E_1 - (1+i) \times L}{(1+i)} + E_0 + L\right] \times \frac{1+\rho}{2+\rho}$$

$$= \left[\frac{E_1}{(1+i)} + E_0\right] \times \frac{1+\rho}{2+\rho}. \tag{3.57}$$

As (3.57) is equal to (3.51), the debt financed fund to stimulate demand has no effect. The individual expects the lower income tomorrow and is not willing to adjust its consumption in $t = 0$.

Example 3.23. Consumption Behavior if Higher Taxes are Anticipated

Suppose an individual who has determined its intertemporal utility function as:

$$U(C_0, C_1) = \ln C_0 + \frac{\ln C_1}{1+i}.$$

In $t = 0$ the individual earns € 100 and in $t = 1$ earnings are € 120. It is assumed that everything is consumed by the end of $t = 1$. Time preference and interest rate are equivalent and $i = 10\%$.

To compute optimal consumption over time, we have to maximize the utility function with respect to the constraint derived in (3.44)

$$\max_{C_0, C_1} \quad U(C_0, C_1)$$

$$\text{s.t.} \quad C_1 = E_1 + (1+i) \times (E_0 - C_0).$$

The Lagrangian function then is

$$\mathcal{L}(C_0, C_1, \lambda) = \ln C_0 + \frac{\ln C_1}{1+i} + \lambda \times [E_1 + (1+i) \times (E_0 - C_0) - C_1].$$

The partial derivatives evolve to

$$\frac{\partial \mathcal{L}}{\partial C_0} = \frac{1}{C_0} - \lambda \times (1+i) \stackrel{!}{=} 0 \tag{3.58}$$

$$\frac{\partial \mathcal{L}}{\partial C_1} = \frac{1}{C_1 \times (1+i)} - \lambda \stackrel{!}{=} 0 \tag{3.59}$$

$$\frac{\partial \mathcal{L}}{\partial \lambda} = E_1 + (1+i) \times (E_0 - C_0) - C_1 \stackrel{!}{=} 0. \tag{3.60}$$

If we solve (3.58) and (3.59) for λ, set the result equal and solve for C_1 we get

$$C_1 = \frac{C_0 \times (1+i)}{(1+i)} = C_0. \tag{3.61}$$

If we insert (3.61) in (3.60) we get for C_0 and C_1

$$C_0 = \frac{E_1 + E_0 \times (1+i)}{2+i}$$

$$C_0 = \left[\frac{E_1}{1+i} + E_0\right] \times \left[\frac{1+i}{2+i}\right] \tag{3.62}$$

$$= \left[\frac{120}{1+0.1} + 100\right] \times \left[\frac{1+0.1}{2+0.1}\right]$$
$$= 109.52$$
$$C_1 = 109.52.$$

Now suppose, in $t = 0$ the individual gets child benefits amounting to €20. However, the individual knows about the budgeting problems of the government and knows that the benefits have to be debt financed. Hence, the individual anticipates, that in near future ($t = 1$) the government has to pay back debt including interest which amounts to €20×1.1 =€22. That amount is collected as a surcharge tax from the taxpayers. What happens to the consumption behavior of the individual in $t = 0$?

Let's adjust (3.62) to the situation described. Then we get

$$C_0 = \left[\frac{E_1 - 22}{1+i} + E_0 + 20\right] \times \left[\frac{1+i}{2+i}\right]$$
$$= \left[\frac{120 - 22}{1+0.1} + 100 + 20\right] \times \left[\frac{1+0.1}{2+0.1}\right]$$
$$= 109.52.$$

Consumption behavior does not change.

3.8 Maximizing Withdrawals or Future Value

This section deals with an extension of the type of decisions discussed in Sect. 2.6. As we already know, maximizing future value and maximizing, e.g., a constant stream of withdrawals might be contrary objectives if the borrowing and the lending rates differ from each other. In the pre-tax case, if the borrowing and the lending rated are equivalent, maximizing future value and maximizing an, e.g., constant stream of withdrawals will lead to the same result in terms of net present value. However, if the borrowing and the lending rate differ, even in the pre-tax case realizing a given stream of withdrawals and maximizing future value might be contrary objectives. In the post-tax case, even if the borrowing and the lending rates are equivalent, we might have cases where maximizing, e.g., a constant stream of withdrawals will lead to another result than maximizing future value (e.g., different real investment opportunities are profitable).

Suppose an investor wants to maximize his consumption at different points of time or maximize the future value, respectively. We assume the investor (taxpayer) to be a sole proprietor. This fits to the assumptions of our Standard Model. He is striving to maximize different consumption ambitions as follows:

1. Maximize the future value in $t = 3$; equity is 90,000. The cash flows are reinvested in a financial investment. Interest income is fully taxed.
2. Maximize the future value in $t = 3$; equity is 90,000. The after-tax cash flows are withdrawn and reinvested in a private financial investment that is taxed by applying a reduced flat tax.
3. Maximize the withdrawal in $t = 0$; equity is 90,000. The consumption will be prefinanced by borrowing money from the bank. Interest on this debt is not tax deductible.
4. Maximize the withdrawal in $t = 0$; equity is 90,000. The prefinancing of the consumption will be carried out by withdrawals. The sole proprietor takes a commercial loan. Interest on this debt is tax deductible.
5. Maximize the withdrawal in $t = 2$; equity is 60,000. In $t = 0$, the sole proprietor takes a commercial loan. Interest on this debt is tax deductible. The cash flows in $t = 1$ are reinvested in a financial investment, whereas the interest income is taxed using a reduced flat tax. In $t = 2$, the sole proprietor borrows money from his bank to finance his private consumption. Interest on this debt is not tax deductible.

The marginal income tax rate is supposed to be $\tau = 50\%$. The reduced flat tax is $\tau^{flat} = 25\%$. In each period cash inflows are equal to taxable revenues. Straight-line depreciation is applied over 3 years and the interest rate is $i = 10\%$. The real investment project has the following certain cash flow structure

t	0	1	2	3
CF_t	–90,000	44,000	50,000	60,000

1. In the first situation, the investor maximizes the future value in $t = 3$. Funds of equity (contribution to capital) are 90,000. At the end of each period cash flows after taxes are reinvested in a financial investment that yields 10%. Capital income is taxed at a marginal rate of 50%.
   The following financial plan mirrors the first situation. The first three rows are assigned to the real investment project. Notice, that the tax base and the tax liability solely include variables resulting from the real investment project. All other rows (except the last one) deal with the financial reinvestment. $CF_t^{\tau,real}$ is the post-tax cash flow of the real investment.

t	0	1	2	3
CF_t	–90,000	44,000	50,000	60,000
D_t		30,000	30,000	30,000
$TB_t = CF_t - D_t$		14,000	20,000	30,000
$T_t = \tau \times TB_t$		7,000	10,000	15,000
$CF_t^{\tau,real}$		37,000	40,000	45,000
reinvestment in $t = 1$		–37,000	37,000	
thereof interest			3,700	
thereof taxes = $\tau \times$ interest			1,850	
reinvestment in $t = 2$			–78,850	78,850
thereof interest				7,885
thereof taxes = $\tau \times$ interest				3,943
W_t	–90,000	0	0	127,792

Post-tax net present value is

$$NPV^{\tau} = -90{,}000 + \frac{0}{1.05} + \frac{0}{1.05^2} + \frac{127{,}792}{1.05^3} = 20{,}392.$$

2. The second situation is equivalent to the first situation except the taxation of capital income. Capital income is now assumed to be taxed at a flat rate of $\tau^{flat} = 25\%$. Of course, in this case future value is expected to increase. This is shown in the following table. Notice the numbers of the first five rows do not change compared to situation no. 1.

t	0	1	2	3
CF_t	–90,000	44,000	50,000	60,000
D_t		30,000	30,000	30,000
$TB_t = CF_t - D_t$		14,000	20,000	30,000
$T_t = \tau \times TB_t$		7,000	10,000	15,000
$CF_t^{\tau,real}$		37,000	40,000	45,000
reinvestment in $t = 1$		–37,000	37,000	
thereof interest			3,700	
thereof taxes = $\tau^{flat} \times$ interest			925	
reinvestment in $t = 2$			–79,775	79,775
thereof interest				7,978
thereof taxes = $\tau^{flat} \times$ interest				1,994
W_t	–90,000	0	0	130,759

Post-tax net present value is

$$NPV^{\tau} = -90{,}000 + \frac{0}{1.075} + \frac{0}{1.075^2} + \frac{130{,}759}{1.075^3} = 15{,}255.$$

3. The third situation demands maximization of withdrawals in $t = 0$. Consumption will be prefinanced by borrowing money from the bank. Pre-tax borrowing and lending rates are equivalent. However, interest on debt is assumed to be not tax deductible. Debt is assumed to be paid back as soon as possible. A flat tax rate of $\tau^{flat} = 25\%$ on interest income is applied.
To compute the maximum amount for consumption in $t = 0$ we have to solve the problem by backward induction. The withdrawal we can realize in $t = 0$ must be financed by a loan. From $t = 1$ to $t = 3$, the after-tax cash flows from our project must be sufficient to finance the loan and to pay interest on the loan. Here, interest income is not tax deductible, therefore the after-tax interest rate equals the before-tax interest rate of 0.1. We can calculate our maximum withdrawal

$$W_0 = \frac{37{,}000}{1.1} + \frac{40{,}000}{1.1^2} + \frac{45{,}000}{1.1^3} = 100{,}504.$$

In $t = 1$, interest is 10,050 and amortization is $CF_t^{\tau,real}$ minus interest payments $37{,}000 - 10{,}050 = 26{,}950$. In $t = 1$ remaining debt is 73,554, in $t = 2$ it is 40,909 and in $t = 3$ it is exactly 0.

t	0	1	2	3
CF_t	–90,000	44,000	50,000	60,000
D_t		30,000	30,000	30,000
$TB_t = CF_t - D_t$		14,000	20,000	30,000
$T_t = \tau \times TB_t$		7,000	10,000	15,000
$CF_t^{\tau,real}$		37,000	40,000	45,000
loan in $t = 0$	100,504			
thereof interest		–10,050		
thereof taxes (tax refund)		0		
amortization		–26,950		
loan in $t = 1$		73,554		
thereof interest			–7,355	
thereof taxes (tax refund)			0	
amortization			–32,645	
loan in $t = 2$			40,909	
thereof interest				–4,091
thereof taxes (tax refund)				0
amortization				–40,909
W_t	100,504	0	0	0

Alternatively, we can calculate the maximum withdrawal by looking at the periods separately when we apply backward induction. Let's start with $t = 2$. In $t = 2$ maximum loan is restricted to maximum amortization in $t = 3$ plus the interest due on the loan from $t = 2$. In $t = 3$ maximum cash for amortization and interest is

$$CF_3 - T_3 = 60{,}000 - 15{,}000 = 45{,}000.$$

Again, the first five rows remain unchanged. If the amount of 45,000 is split up into amortization and interest we get

$$\begin{aligned} \text{amortization}_3 = \text{loan}_2 &= \frac{CF_3 - T_3}{(1+i)} = \frac{45{,}000}{1.1} = 40{,}909 \qquad (3.63)\\ \text{interest} &= \text{amortization}_3 \times i = 40{,}909 \times 0.1 = 4{,}091. \end{aligned}$$

Now consider $t = 1$. At the end of $t = 2$ the loan is restricted to 40,909. In $t = 1$ hence, the loan is restricted to after-tax cash flow from the real investment project plus loan in $t = 2$. The loan in $t = 1$ is

$$\begin{aligned} \text{loan}_1 &= \frac{CF_2 - T_2 + \text{loan}_2}{(1+i)} \qquad (3.64)\\ &= \frac{50{,}000 - 10{,}000 + 40{,}909}{1.1} = 73{,}554. \end{aligned}$$

Amortization and interest in $t = 2$ is

$$\begin{aligned} \text{amortization}_2 &= \text{loan}_1 - \text{loan}_2 = 73{,}554 - 40{,}909 = 32{,}645\\ \text{interest}_2 &= \text{loan}_1 \times i = 73{,}554 \times 0.1 = 7{,}355. \end{aligned}$$

From the perspective of $t = 1$, computation of maximum loan in $t = 0$ goes along the computation of maximum loan in $t = 1$. Using (3.64) analogous, we get

$$\text{loan}_0 = \frac{44{,}000 - 7{,}000 + 73{,}554}{1.1} = 100{,}504.$$

The post-tax net present value is $NPV^\tau = -90{,}000 + 100{,}504 = 10{,}504$ and represents additional consumption in terms of withdrawals compared to the alternative financial investment. The post-tax net present value can be separated into the post-tax net present value of the real investment and the post-tax net present value of the loan. Applying the flat tax rate, post-tax net present value of our real investment is

$$NPV^{\tau,\text{real}} = -90{,}000 + \frac{37{,}000}{1.075} + \frac{40{,}000}{1.075^2} + \frac{45{,}000}{1.075^3} = 15{,}255.$$

The post-tax net present value of the loan is

$$NPV^{\tau,\text{loan}} = +100{,}504 - \frac{37{,}000}{1.075} - \frac{40{,}000}{1.075^2} - \frac{45{,}000}{1.075^3} = -4{,}751.$$

We get

$$NPV^\tau = NPV^{\tau,\text{real}} + NPV^{\tau,\text{loan}} = 15{,}255 - 4{,}751 = 10{,}504.$$

Now, you certainly wonder why the cash flow structure of the loan equals the opposite sign of the cash flow structure of the real investment. Consider $t = 1$, interest on debt plus amortization amounts to –10,050 plus –26,950 which gives $CF_1^{\tau,real} = -37{,}000$. For all other periods, the negative cash flow of the loan is equivalent to post-tax cash flows of the real investment. Cash flow after taxes from the real investment are transformed into a loan.

4. The fourth situation is equivalent to the third situation except for tax deductible interest payments on debt. Now, the investor takes a commercial loan that leads to tax deductible interest on debt. Debt is paid back as soon as possible. Because deductibility of interest on debt leads to tax refunds, in $t = 0$ the maximum loan is expected to increase compared to the previous situation.
We can compute the maximum loan in $t = 0$ by using the post-tax interest rate. The maximum loan in $t = 0$ is

$$PV^{\tau} = \frac{37{,}000}{1.05} + \frac{40{,}000}{1.05^2} + \frac{45{,}000}{1.05^3} = 110{,}392,$$

which exceeds the present value in situation 3. The following table contains the financial plan if interest on debt is deductible. BV^L represents the book value of the liability and CF_t^{τ} are the post-tax cash flows in t that are equivalent to amortization$_t$.

t	0	1	2	3
CF_t	–90,000	44,000	50,000	60,000
D_t		30,000	30,000	30,000
BV_t^L	110,392	78,911	42,856	0
amortization$_t$		–31,481	–36,055	–42,857
interest on debt$_t$		–11,039	–7,891	–4,286
$TB_t = CF_t - D_t -$interest on debt$_t$		2,961	12,109	25,714
$T_t = \tau \times TB_t$		1,480	6,054	12,857
CF_t^{τ}		31,481	36,055	42,857
W_t	110,392	0	0	0

Let's consider the computation of the net present value again. Recall, we apply a flat tax rate on capital income. Hence, post-tax net present value of our real investment is just

$$NPV^{\tau,\text{real}} = -90{,}000 + \frac{37{,}000}{1.075} + \frac{40{,}000}{1.075^2} + \frac{45{,}000}{1.075^3} = 15{,}255.$$

However, if we take the post-tax net present value of the loan into account

$$NPV^{\tau,\text{loan}} = 110{,}392 - \frac{37{,}000}{1.075} - \frac{40{,}000}{1.075^2} - \frac{45{,}000}{1.075^3} = 5{,}137,$$

we get

$$NPV^{\tau} = NPV^{\tau,\text{real}} + NPV^{\tau,\text{loan}} = 15{,}255 + 5{,}137 = 20{,}392.$$

Consider $t = 1$, interest on debt and amortization amount to $-11{,}039$ and $-31{,}481$. Moreover, the tax refund resulting from tax deductible interest on debt is $0.5 \times 11{,}039 = 5{,}520$. Altogether we get

$$-11{,}039 - 31{,}481 + 5{,}520 = 37{,}000.$$

For all other periods, the negative cash flows of the loan are equivalent to the post-tax cash flows of the real investment. Cash flows after taxes from the real investment are transformed into a loan.

Of course, we can derive the solution by applying backward induction as well. The financial plan is computed analogously to situation no. 3. We get

t	0	1	2	3
CF_t	–90,000	44,000	50,000	60,000
D_t		30,000	30,000	30,000
$TB_t = CF_t - D_t$		14,000	20,000	30,000
$T_t = \tau \times TB_t$		7,000	10,000	15,000
$CF_t^{\tau,real}$		37,000	40,000	45,000
loan in $t = 0$	110,392			
thereof interest		–11,039		
thereof taxes (tax refund)		–5,520		
amortization		25,961		
loan in $t = 1$		78,912		
thereof interest			–7,891	
thereof taxes (tax refund)			–3,946	
amortization			–36,054	
loan in $t = 2$			42,857	
thereof interest				–4,286
thereof taxes (tax refund)				–2,143
amortization				42,857
W_t	110,392	0	0	0

5. The fifth situation deals with the maximization of withdrawals in $t = 2$. Now, available funds of equity (contribution to capital) are 60,000. The investor takes out a commercial loan in $t = 0$. The interest on this debt is tax deductible. It is assumed that the loan from $t = 0$ is amortized as soon as possible. In $t = 1$ cash flows after taxes are reinvested in a financial investment, whereas the interest income is taxed at a flat rate of $\tau^{flat} = 25\%$. In $t = 2$, the sole proprietor borrows money from his bank to finance his private consumption. The interest on that debt is not tax deductible.

The following table reflects situation no. 5. In $t = 1$, interest due to the loan in $t = 0$ is paid and a tax refund of 1,500 is granted. Cash flow after taxes amounts to 5,500. They are reinvested in a financial investment yielding 10%. Interest on the financial investment is taxed at the flat rate of τ^{flat} in $t = 2$. In $t = 2$ the maximum loan for consumption is already known from (3.63). As a result, maximum withdrawal in $t = 2$ is

$$\begin{aligned} W_2 &= CF_2 - T_2 + FI_1 + i \times FI_1 \times (1 - \tau^{flat}) + \text{loan}_2 \\ &= 50{,}000 - 10{,}000 + 5{,}500 + 413 + 40{,}909 = 86{,}822, \end{aligned}$$

where FI stands for financial investment.

t	0	1	2	3
CF_t	–90,000	44,000	50,000	60,000
D_t		30,000	30,000	30,000
$TB_t = CF_t - D_t$		14,000	20,000	30,000
$T_t = \tau \times TB_t$		7,000	10,000	15,000
$CF_t^{\tau,real}$		37,000	40,000	45,000
loan in $t = 0$ for investment	30,000			
amortization		–30,000		
thereof interest		–3,000		
thereof taxes (tax refund)		–1,500		
reinvestment in $t = 1$ (FI_1)		–5,500	5,500	
thereof interest			550	
thereof taxes			138	
loan in $t = 2$ for consumption			40,909	
amortization				–40,909
thereof interest				–4,091
thereof taxes (tax refund)				0
W_t	0	0	86,821	0

Now, what does the post-tax net present value account for? To compute the post tax net present value, we have to determine the post-tax net present value of the

1. Loan for investment in $t = 0$,
2. Equity financed real investment,
3. Loan for consumption in $t = 2$.

Post-tax net present value of the loan for investment in $t = 0$ is

$$NPV^{\tau,\text{loan},t=0} = +30{,}000 - \frac{30{,}000 + 3{,}000 - 1{,}500}{1.075} = 698.$$

Post-tax net present value of the real investment is

$$NPV^{\tau,\text{real}} = -90{,}000 + \frac{37{,}000}{1.075} + \frac{40{,}000}{1.075^2} + \frac{45{,}000}{1.075^3} = 15{,}255.$$

Finally, post-tax net present value of the loan for consumption is

$$NPV^{\tau,\text{loan},t=2} = \frac{40{,}909}{1.075^2} - \frac{40{,}909 + 4{,}091}{1.075^3} = -823.$$

Hence, total post-tax net present value is

$$\begin{aligned} NPV^{\tau} &= NPV^{\tau,\text{loan},t=0} + NPV^{\tau,\text{real}} + NPV^{\tau,\text{loan},t=2} \\ &= 698 + 15{,}255 - 823 = 15{,}130. \end{aligned}$$

Of course, if withdrawals are discounted we will get the same result. Notice, in this case we have to use the fraction of the acquisition costs that are financed by equity.

$$NPV^{\tau} = -60{,}000 + \frac{86{,}822}{1.075^2} = 15{,}130.$$

Compared to Ex. 2.26 on p. 65, possible distortions in the present example are exclusively caused by taxation. Borrowing and lending rates are equal. However, tax deductibility, taxes on interest income and tax refunds of interest on debt differ and lead to distortions.

Questions

3.1. Why does conventional taxation of income not meet the requirement for a tax system that taxes the individual's objective? Which tax base elements can be distinguished in the Standard Model?

3.2. Why must investors take taxes into account in investment decision settings?

3.3. Explain the integration of taxation into the decision criteria of single- and multiperiod investment decisions using adequate models.

3.4. Discuss the main assumptions of the Standard Model. Make suggestions how the Standard Model can be adjusted to remove some of these assumptions.

3.5. Describe the different tax treatment of real investments and financial investments.

3.6. How does the net present value after taxes change if c.p.

(a) The acquisition costs I_0 increase,
(b) The interest rate i decreases,
(c) The level of cash flows decreases,
(d) The useful life n increases?

3.7. Give examples for different credit and debit interest rates after taxes.

3.8. Based on examples from your home country, explain tax effects due to tax rate-, tax base-, or timing effects, respectively.

3.9. Are there specific types of decision settings where tax minimization or minimization of present value of tax liability should not be applied, respectively?

3.10. Explain the following terms and formally derive their interdependency:

(a) Tax minimization,
(b) Maximizing present value of tax liability,
(c) Maximizing net present value after taxes,
(d) Maximizing present value of expenses,
(e) Maximizing profits after taxes.

3.11. What kind of problems are in the focus of tax consulting? Why?

3.12. Explain possible differences between tax planning models – and resulting impacts based on the planning approach – and results based on empirical investigations.

3.13. Discuss advantages and disadvantages of using marginal and average income tax rates to evaluate the profitability of an investment.

3.14. Provide an example covering three periods where

(a) $NPV^{\tau} < NPV$.
(b) $NPV^{\tau} > NPV$.
(c) $NPV^{\tau} = NPV$.

3.15. What happens to the optimal initial investment in the Hirshleifer Model, if $i = \rho$ and (a) exclusively real investments are taxed, (b) exclusively financial investments are taxed, (c) both real and financial investments are taxed, and (d) i and ρ are taxed at different rates with a proportional tax rate, respectively?

3.16. Graphically derive the tax paradox using the Fisher–Hirshleifer Model.

3.17. Explain why debt financed stimulation of demand might not affect today's behavior of consumption.

3.18. What are the main assumptions for equivalence of realizing a given stream of withdrawals and maximizing future value? Explain how borrowing and lending rates as well as taxes distort investment decisions.

Exercises

Solutions are provided starting on p. 391.

3.19. Evaluating Profitability After Taxes

Suppose there are two mutually exclusive real investment alternatives A and B and an alternative financial investment.

$SUM^{\tau,A}, SUM^{\tau,B}$:	not discounted sum of future cash flows after taxes
$NPV^{\tau,A-B}$:	net present value of the difference investment $A - B$ after taxes
NPV^{A}, NPV^{B} :	net present value before taxes
$NPV^{\tau,A}, NPV^{\tau,B}$:	net present value after taxes
$PV^{D,A}, PV^{D,B}$:	present value of depreciation
$PV^{ED,A}, PV^{ED,B}$:	present value of economic depreciation

If the investors' general objective is maximizing future value after taxes, what investment alternative will be carried out (A, B, or the alternative financial investment *FI*; if there is not enough information to make a decision, place a cross at "?").

	A	B	FI	?
1. $NPV^{A} > NPV^{B} > 0$				
2. $NPV^{A} > NPV^{B} > 0$ and $NPV^{\tau,A} > NPV^{\tau,B}$				
3. $NPV^{A} < NPV^{B} < 0$ and $NPV^{\tau,A} > NPV^{\tau,B} > 0$				
4. $NPV^{\tau,A} > NPV^{B} > 0$				
5. $NPV^{\tau,A} < NPV^{\tau,B} < 0$				
6. $NPV^{\tau,A} > SUM^{\tau,B} > 0$				
7. $NPV^{\tau,A-B} > 0$				
8. $NPV^{A} < NPV^{B} < 0$ and $PV^{D,A} > PV^{ED,A}$ and $NPV^{\tau,B} < 0$				
9. $NPV^{A} > NPV^{B} > 0$ and $PV^{D,A} < PV^{ED,A}$ and				
10. $PV^{D,B} < PV^{ED,B}$				

3.20. Standard Model

Assume a real investment opportunity with acquisition costs of $I_0 = 120{,}000$ and the following stream of certain future cash flows:

t	0	1	2	3	4
CF_t	–120,000	20,000	35,000	50,000	65,000

The lending rate is $i = 10\%$ and the constant marginal income tax rate is $\tau = 35\%$. Moreover, straight-line depreciation is applied.

(a) Cash flows after taxes are withdrawn at the end of each period. Compute the before-tax and after-tax net present value.

(b) In $t = 1, 2, 3$ no cash is withdrawn. Total cash after-taxes is withdrawn in $t = 4$. Compute the after-tax future value if reinvestment on the company level yields $i = 10\%$, too.

(c) Consider $t = 1$. Due to an assumed immediate full loss offset, what type of investment is this? Why?

3.21. Standard Model and Depreciation

Assume the following acquisition costs and certain future cash flows of a real investment project:

t	0	1	2	3
CF_t	–300.00	110.00	121.00	133.10

Suppose the capital market rate to be $i = 10\%$ and the constant marginal tax rate to be $\tau = 40\%$. Cash flows after taxes are withdrawn at the end of each period.

(a) Suppose the following seven different depreciation plans and compute post-tax net present values. Discuss your results. Do you know any real investment projects that qualify for the given depreciation plan characteristics?

	A	B	C	D	E	F	G
D_1	300	200	150	100	50	0	0
D_2	0	100	100	100	100	100	0
D_3	0	0	50	100	150	200	300

(b) What will happen to the post-tax net present value if economic depreciation is assumed for tax purposes?

(c) According to (b), what will happen if $\tau = 50\%$?

3.22. Standard Model and Income Tax Paradox

An investor is offered two mutual exclusive real investment opportunities A and B. Acquisition costs of each project amount to $I_0 = 1{,}000$. Certain future cash flow streams of the two investments can be derived from the following table:

t	0	1	2	3	4
CF_t^A	–1,000	600	250	250	250
CF_t^B	–1,000	350	350	350	350

Borrowing and lending rates are assumed to be $i = 10\%$. Further, straight-line depreciation is applied and the investor withdraws all cash after taxes at the end of each period.

(a) Compute the pre-tax net present value of both projects in case of cash flows after taxes are withdrawn at the end of each period.

(b) Now, complete the following table and discuss your results.

	$NPV^{\tau,A}$	$NPV^{\tau,B}$
$\tau = 0\%$		
$\tau = 10\%$		
$\tau = 20\%$		
$\tau = 30\%$		
$\tau = 40\%$		
$\tau = 50\%$		
$\tau = 60\%$		
$\tau = 100\%$		

3.23. Standard Model and Income Tax Paradox

Assume a real investment project with acquisition costs of $I_0 = 102{,}000$. Straight-line depreciation is applied, the investor withdraws all cash after taxes at the end of each period and the lending rate is $i = 10\%$. Certain future cash flow stream of the investment can be derived from the following table

t	0	1	2	3	4
CF_t	–102,000	23,600	27,300	36,500	43,100

(a) Complete the following table in case cash flows after taxes are withdrawn at the end of each period.

	NPV^{τ}
$\tau = 0\%$	
$\tau = 10\%$	
$\tau = 20\%$	
$\tau = 30\%$	
$\tau = 40\%$	
$\tau = 50\%$	
$\tau = 60\%$	
$\tau = 100\%$	

(b) What marginal tax rate does the government at least have to introduce to make sure that the real investment project is carried out?

3.24. Maximizing Withdrawals

An investor is endowed with funds of an equity of €800,000. Moreover, she can reinvest annual cash flows after taxes in a financial investment yielding $i = 10\%$. Borrowing and lending rates are equivalent. Her marginal income tax rate on business income is $\tau = 50\%$. Interest on debt for consumption purposes is not tax deductible. The investor is offered the following real investment project (straight-line depreciation):

t	0	1	2	3	4
$CF_t^{outflow}$	–800,000				
CF_t^{inflow}		300,000	400,000	500,000	600,000

(a) The investor wants to maximize the withdrawal in $t = 4$. Capital income is taxed at $\tau = 50\%$. Compute the post-tax net present value.
(b) Again, the investor wants to maximize the withdrawal in $t = 4$. But now capital income is taxed at a flat rate of $\tau^{flat} = 25\%$. Compute the post-tax net present value.
(c) The investor wants to maximize the withdrawal in $t = 2$. Capital income is taxed at a flat rate of $\tau^{flat} = 25\%$ and interest on debt is not tax deductible. Compute the post-tax net present value.

3.25. Maximizing Withdrawals or Future Value

An investor is offered two investments, A and B. Acquisition costs are financed by equity. The projects promise the following certain future cash flows:

t	0	1	2	3
CF_t^A	–120,000	50,000	55,000	107,000
CF_t^B	–120,000	69,000	69,000	69,000

The borrowing and lending rate is $i = 10\%$. The marginal income tax rate is $\tau = 40\%$. Capital income is taxed at a flat rate of $\tau^{flat} = 25\%$. Moreover, straight-line depreciation is applied.

(a) Determine the pre-tax net present value for both investments.
(b) Determine the post-tax future value and post-tax net present value in case cash flows after taxes are reinvested at the end of each period. Which investment is carried out?
(c) Now, the investor wants to withdraw €55,000 in $t = 1$ as well as in $t=2$. Interest on debt for consumption purposes is not tax deductible. Which investment is the investor supposed to carry out? Discuss your result.

3.26. Marginal Tax Rates and Average Tax Rates

(a) Take the German progressive tax rate function from Table 4.3 on p. 142 and compute the first derivative with respect to the tax base (*TB* or *Income*). What is the marginal tax rate for the first taxable Euro ($TB = 8{,}004$)?
(b) Suppose Holger's taxable income from his job as a business analyst is €45,000. Compute the marginal and average income tax rate. Holger gets an additional consulting job offered that pays him another €5,000. Will Holger accept the job if he wants to have at least an increase in income after taxes of €3,500?

3.27. Fisher–Hirshleifer Model

Suppose two investors A and B with an initial endowment of $W_0 = 200$. They face the following utility functions

$$U^A(C_0, C_1) = C_0^3 \times C_1$$
$$U^B(C_0, C_1) = C_0 \times C_1^3.$$

The pre-tax real investment function is

$$f(I_0) = 20 \times \sqrt{I_0}.$$

The marginal tax rate on cash flow less depreciation is $\tau = 30\%$. It is assumed that all cash is consumed by the end of $t = 1$.

(a) Derive the real investment function after taxes in case the tax base is calculated as cash flow less straight-line depreciation.
(b) Derive the transformation curve.
(c) Determine optimal C_0, C_1, I_0, and F_0 for both investors in case the borrowing and lending rate is $i = 10\%$ and only real investments are subject to tax. Determine the net present value for both investors. Compare your results with the results of Exercise 2.46 on p. 75.
(d) What will happen to optimal C_0, C_1, and the utility level for investor A if interest is taxed at the same rate at that real investments is taxed?

References

1. Blaufus, K., Bob, J., Hundsdoerfer, J., Kiesewetter, D., Weimann, J.: It's All About Tax Rates. An Empirical Study of Tax Perception. arqus Discussion Papers in Quantitative Tax Research No. 106, www.arqus.info (2009)
2. Caspersen, E., Metcalf, G.: Is a value added tax regressive? annual versus lifetime incidence measures. Nat. Tax J. **47**(4), 731–746 (1994)
3. Kiesewetter, D., Benseman, T., Schönemann, K.: Who has really paid for the Reconstruction of East Germany? Expected and Realized Returns on Real Estate Investments in East and West Germany in the 1990s. Business Res. 11–37 (2009)
4. König, R., Wosnitza, M.: Betriebswirtschaftliche Steuerplanungs- und Steuerwirkungslehre. Physica-Verlag, Heidelberg (2004)
5. Kruschwitz, L., Löffler, A.: Discounted Cash Flow: A Theory of the Valuation of Firms. Wiley, Chichester (2005)
6. Kruschwitz, L.: Investitionsrechnung. 12th edn. Walter de Gruyter, Berlin, New York (2009)
7. Oestreicher, A., Reister, T., Spengel, C.: Common Corporate Tax Base (CCTB) and Effective Tax Burdens in the EU Member States. ZEW Discussion Paper No. 09-026 (2009)
8. Schanz, D., Schanz, S.: Finding a new corporate tax base after the abolishment of the one-book system in eu member states. Eur. Account. Rev. **19**(2), 311–341 (2010)
9. Schanz, D., Schanz, S.: The income tax paradox. Intertax **38**(3), 167–169 (2010)
10. Schneider, D.: Korrekturen zum Einfluss der Besteuerung auf die Investition. Zeitschrift für betriebswirtschaftliche Forschung **21**, 297–325 (1969)

11. Schneider, D.: Investition, Finanzierung, Besteuerung. 7th edn. Gabler, Wiesbaden (1992)
12. Scholes, M.S., Wolfson, M.A., Erickson, M., Maydew, E.L., Shevlin, T.: Taxes and Business Strategy. A Planning Approach. 4th edn. Prentice Hall, Upper Saddle River (2009)
13. Wagner, F.W., Schwenk, A.: Empirische Steuerwirkungen als Grundlage einer Reform der Gewinnbesteuerung - Ergebnisse aus den DAX 100-Unternehmen. In: Schwaiger, M., Harhoff, D. (eds.) Empirie und Betriebswirtschaft, pp. 373–398, Stuttgart (2003)
14. Wagner, F.W., Dirrigl, H.: Die Steuerplanung der Unternehmung. Gustav Fischer Verlag, Stuttgart (1980)
15. Wagner, F.W., Besteuerung. In: Bitz, M., Domsch, M., Ewert, R., Wagner, F.W. (eds.) Vahlens Kompendium der Betriebswirtschaftslehre, vol. 2, 5th edn., pp. 407–477, München (2005)

Chapter 4
Tax Facts

Abstract In this chapter, we present basic tax law information which build the basis for the examples throughout the book. First, we show which types of taxes contribute to the tax revenue in various countries and we show which taxpayers contribute to national income tax revenue based on information from Germany and the United States. Second, we explain progressive tax rate functions for individual income taxes as well as corporate income tax rate functions in both countries. For OECD countries we present marginal tax rates. The definitions of income tax bases are presented briefly. Treatment of capital income typically deviates from other income types; therefore, we explain taxation of capital income separately. We refer to national tax codes as from 2010.

4.1 Types of Taxes

Different national tax authorities levy different types of taxes. The names of the taxes differ among countries as well as the specific design of the tax systems, but most taxes can be classified as taxes on income, profits and capital gains, taxes on property, and taxes on goods and services.

Figure 4.1 depicts the 2006 tax revenues of OECD countries. It shows, that taxes on income, profits, and capital gains as well as taxes on goods and services contribute to a very large extent to national tax revenues. As taxes on goods and services are often considered as transit items which are passed through to final consumers, they affect investment and financing decisions less than profit taxes. Therefore, we omit taxes on goods and services such as sales taxes in this book and focus on profit taxes.

With the exception of Mexico, individual and corporate taxes on income, profits and capital gains are accountable for around 50% of national tax revenues. Very often the focus is on individual income taxes. In the following, we will use the expressions "individual income tax" and "personal income tax" as synonyms.

D. Schanz and S. Schanz, *Business Taxation and Financial Decisions*,
DOI 10.1007/978-3-642-03284-4_4,

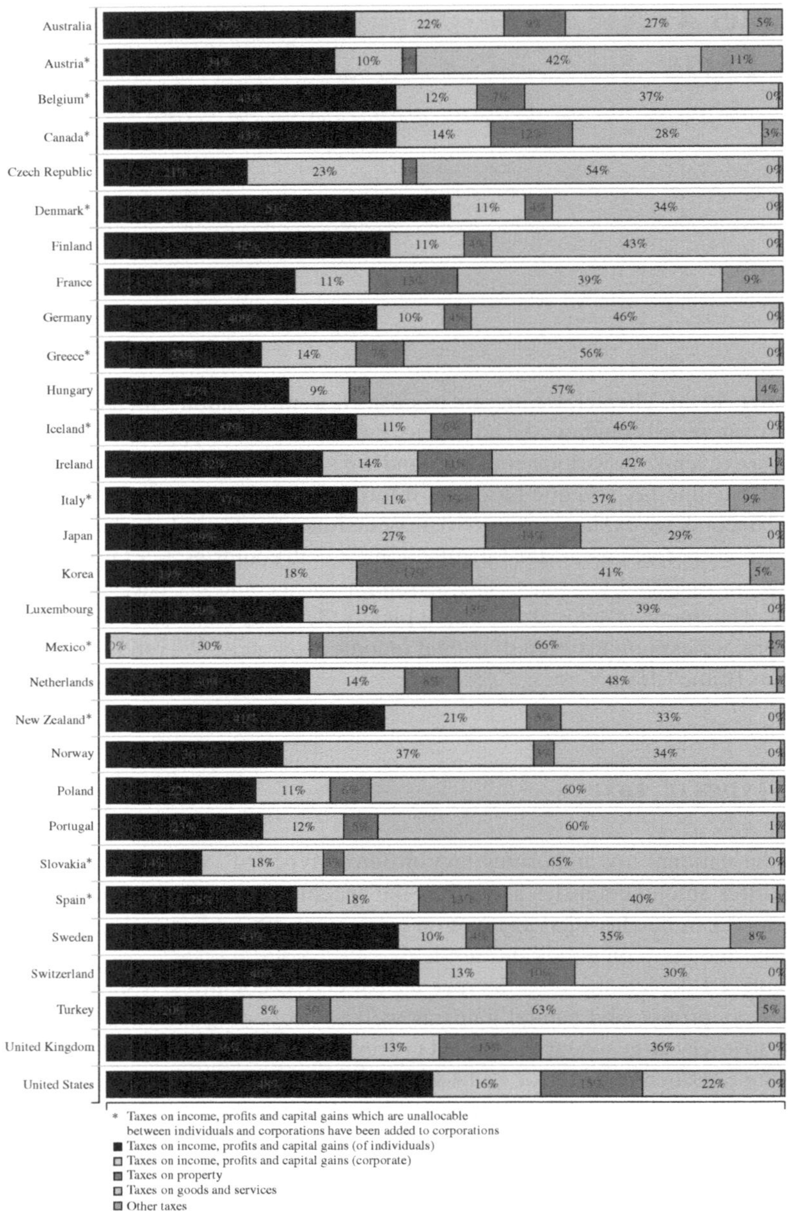

Fig. 4.1 Tax revenue of OECD countries as percentage of total tax revenue 2006. Source: OECD Revenue Statistics 1965–2006 (2007), pp. 134–223

4.2 Distribution of Individual Income Tax Burden

Focusing on individual income taxes, it is worth to take a look at *who* is burdened with the tax. Let us first look at the example of Germany. Official statistics tell us that out of the population of around 82 million people only 27 million or one third pay individual income taxes. In those statistics, married couples filing jointly count as one person. In Fig. 4.2, these 27 million people represent 100% of total taxpayers who account for 100% of the individual income tax revenue.

We see that the distribution of the tax burden is nonlinear. Instead, very few people contribute to a large part of the tax revenue. About 5% of the taxpayers with the highest income account for around 39% of the income tax revenue. The 0.1% taxpayers with the highest income pay 9% of the German individual income taxes. About 50% of the taxpayers contribute to more than 92% of the tax revenue while the other half of the taxpayers contribute to 8% only. More numbers are given in Table 4.1.

This distribution of the tax payments shows very well how unequally distributed taxpayers' contributions are to the personal income tax revenue in Germany. The distribution is even more unequal in the United States. Figure 4.3 compares the distribution to the personal income tax revenues of the two countries.

In the US, approximately 5% of the taxpayers with the highest income account for around 55% of the income tax revenue. The approximately 0.1% taxpayers with the highest income pay 21% of the US individual income taxes. About 50% of the taxpayers contribute to 92% of the tax revenue while the other half of the taxpayers contribute to 8% only. More numbers are given in Table 4.2.

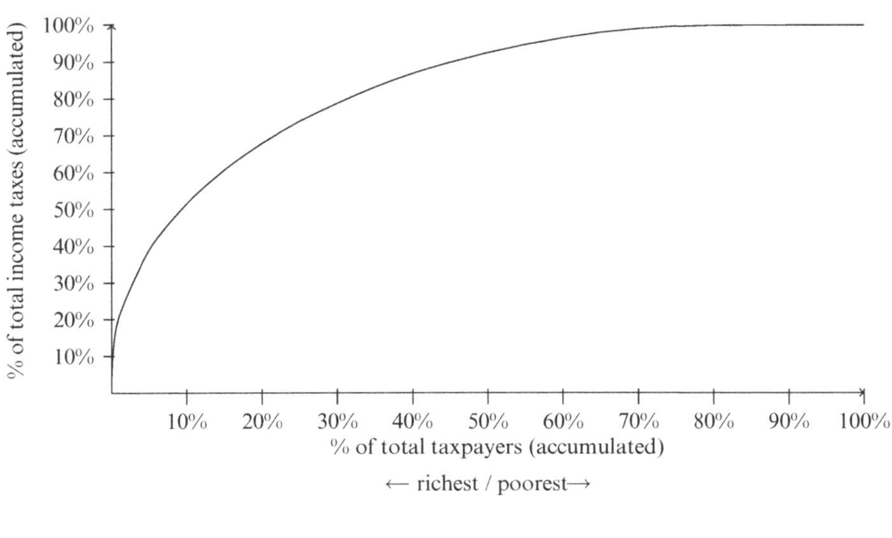

Fig. 4.2 Contribution to personal income tax revenue 2002 in Germany. Source: Based on Statistisches Bundesamt, Finanzen und Steuern, Fachserie 14 Reihe 7.1.1, 2006, p. 7

Table 4.1 Contribution to personal income tax revenue 2002 in Germany

Accumulated % of taxpayers	Sum of income ≥ … €	Accumulated % of income taxes
0.1%	533,133	8.7%
1%	161,925	20.9%
5%	84,265	38.9%
10%	65,127	51.4%
15%	55,238	60.6%
20%	48,469	67.8%
25%	43,229	73.8%
30%	38,933	78.8%
35%	35,291	83.1%
40%	32,187	86.8%
45%	29,481	89.8%
50%	27,001	92.4%
55%	24,615	94.6%
60%	22,235	96.4%
65%	19,701	97.9%
70%	16,977	98.9%
75%	14,118	99.6%
80%	11,155	99.9%
90%	5,115	100.0%
100%	0	100.0%

Source: Statistisches Bundesamt, Finanzen, und Steuern, Fachserie 14 Reihe 7.1.1, 2006, p. 7.

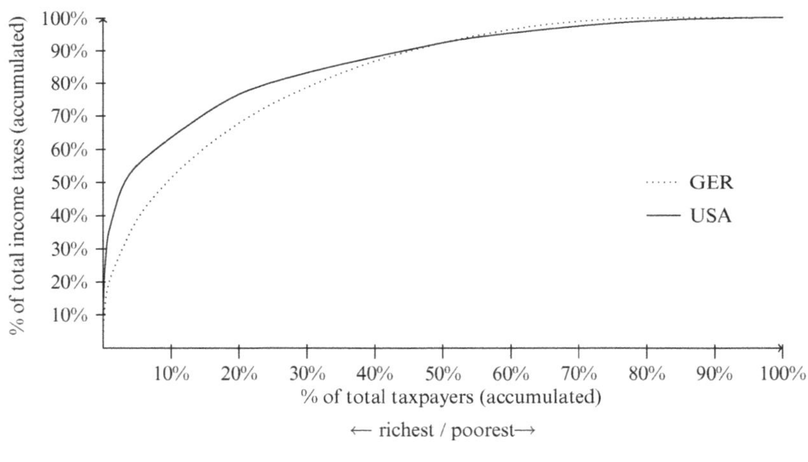

Fig. 4.3 Contribution to personal income tax revenue 2002 in Germany and 2007 in the United States. Sources: Statistisches Bundesamt, Finanzen und Steuern, Fachserie 14 Reihe 7.1.1, 2006, p. 7 (Germany) and Department of the Treasury Internal Revenue Service, Individual Income Tax Returns 2007, Publication 1304 (Rev. 07-2009), Table 1.1 Selected Income and Tax Items, by Size and Accumulated Size of Adjusted Gross Income, Tax Year 2007, p. 31 (US)

Table 4.2 Contribution to personal income tax revenue 2007 in the US

Accumulated % of taxpayers	Sum of income $\geq \ldots$ \$	Accumulated % of income taxes
0.02%	10,000,000	9.94%
0.05%	5,000,000	13.87%
0.16%	2,000,000	20.83%
0.23%	1,500,000	23.46%
0.41%	1,000,000	27.79%
1.08%	500,000	37.04%
4.70%	200,000	54.64%
18.60%	100,000	75.14%
30.60%	75,000	83.55%
49.63%	50,000	92.24%
59.75%	40,000	95.24%
71.67%	30,000	97.74%
77.64%	25,000	98.65%
83.72%	20,000	99.31%
89.64%	15,000	99.73%
95.63%	10,000	99.93%
99.04%	5,000	99.98%
100.00%	2,500	99.99%
100.00%	1	99.99%
100.00%	No adjusted gross income	100.00%

Source: Department of the Treasury Internal Revenue Service, Individual Income Tax Returns 2007, Publication 1304 (Rev. 07-2009), Table 1.1 Selected Income and Tax Items, by Size and Accumulated Size of Adjusted Gross Income, Tax Year 2007, p. 31.

4.3 Income Tax Rates

Why is the tax burden unequally distributed? On the one hand, it is due to a nonuniform distribution of income before taxes, but on the other hand this effect is caused by nonlinear tax rates. We have to distinguish between individual income taxes and corporate income taxes. Very often, corporate income taxes are designed as flat tax rates, whereas individual income taxes follow a progressive tax rate function. But we can find exceptions to both principles.

Let's have a closer look at the individual income tax rates and corporate income tax rates in Germany and the United States.

4.3.1 Individual Income Tax Rates

In the following individual income tax rates in Germany and the United States are presented. Of course, to compare the tax burden of Germany and the United States you have to take the tax rates and the tax base into account. E.g., tax rates in the United States might be lower than in Germany, however, Germany might have a lower tax base.

Table 4.3 Individual income tax rates in Germany 2010

Income in € from ... to ...	Tax in €	
0 – 8,004	0	
8,005 – 13,469	$(912.17 \times y + 1{,}400) \times y$	$y = \frac{Income - 8{,}004}{10{,}000}$
13,470 – 52,881	$(228.74 \times z + 2{,}397) \times z + 1{,}038$	$z = \frac{Income - 13{,}469}{10{,}000}$
52,882 – 250,730	$0.42 \times Income - 8{,}172$	
> 250,731	$0.45 \times Income - 15{,}694$	

4.3.1.1 Germany

Germany applies a progressive income tax rate function (§ 32a EStG). The tax rates for single taxpayers are defined in Table 4.3.

To calculate the income tax burden, one has to find the appropriate row of Table 4.3 according to the income. Only the formula in this row is relevant for deriving the absolute tax payment. If the income is € 8,004 or less, tax payment is zero.

In Germany, some allowances are granted. For example, a lump-sum allowance for income from employment of € 920 (§ 9a EStG) and a lump-sum allowance for capital income of € 801 (§ 20 (9) EStG). We do not integrate those allowances in our models.

Example 4.1. German Individual Income Tax

Frederick's income is € 50,000. The income is between € 13,470 and € 52,881. Therefore, the formula $(228.74 \times z + 2{,}397) \times z + 1{,}038$, $z = \frac{Income - 13{,}469}{10{,}000}$ is relevant to derive the tax burden. First, Frederick has to calculate z. It is

$$z = \frac{50{,}000 - 13{,}469}{10{,}000} = 3.6531.$$

Frederick inserts z into the tax formula. His tax burden T is

$$T = (228.74 \times 3.6531 + 2{,}397) \times 3.6531 + 1{,}038 = 12{,}847.05.$$

The individual income tax increases with higher income. For lower income, the slope increases. In the upper two tax brackets, the slope is flat. The marginal and average tax rates are depicted in Fig. 4.4. They are calculated as explained in Sect. 3.6.

The tax rate function as presented in Table 4.3 applies to single taxpayers. Single taxpayers are singles or spouses who decide to file separately. Spouses have a second

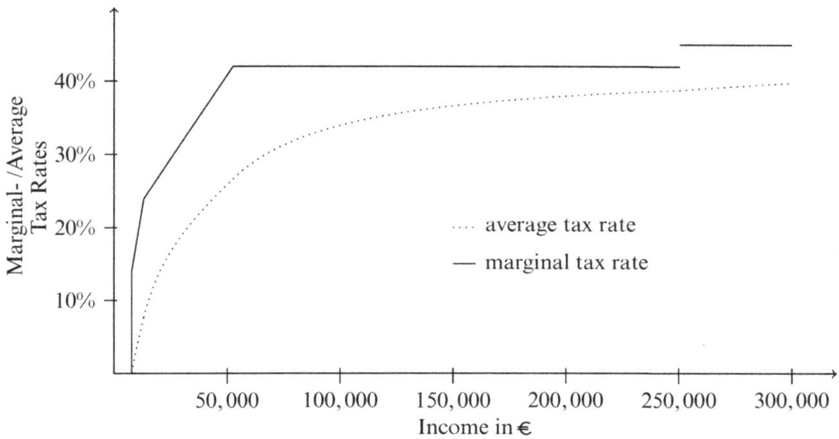

Fig. 4.4 Marginal and average individual income tax rates in Germany

option: They can choose to file jointly (§ 26b EStG). If married couples file jointly, they add their incomes, apply the tax rate function as defined for singles to half of their combined income, and multiply the tax liability by two. The splitting method is advantageous when the spouses' income differ. In this case the couple profits from a lower progression.

Example 4.2. German Splitting Method

Matthew's income is € 50,000. His wife Martha works as a freelancer and had an unsuccessful year. Her income was € 10,000. Should they file separately or jointly?

Filing separately, Matthew pays € 12,847.05 taxes as calculated in Ex. 4.1. Martha's income is between € 8,005 and € 13,469. Therefore, the formula $(912.17 \times y + 1{,}400) \times y$, $y = \frac{Income - 8{,}004}{10{,}000}$ is relevant to derive her tax burden. She calculates

$$y = \frac{10{,}000 - 8{,}004}{10{,}000} = 0.1996.$$

Inserting y yields the tax burden T

$$T = (912.17 \times 0.1996 + 1{,}400) \times 0.1996 = 315.78.$$

Adding up their tax payments yields a total tax of € 12,847.05 + € 315.78 = € 13,162.83.

Filing jointly and applying the splitting method, they add their income to € 60,000. Half of it, € 30,000, is used to calculate the income tax according to the income tax rate function. The income is between € 13,470 and € 52,881. Therefore, the formula $(228.74 \times z + 2{,}397) \times z + 1{,}038$, $z = \frac{Income - 13{,}469}{10{,}000}$ is relevant to derive the tax burden. The couple calculates

$$z = \frac{30{,}000 - 13{,}469}{10{,}000} = 1.6531.$$

Inserting z yields a tax burden T of

$$T = (228.74 \times 1.6531 + 2{,}397) \times 1.6531 + 1{,}038 = 5{,}625.57.$$

Doubling the tax yields the total tax of € 5,625.57 × 2 = € 11,251.14. The couple saves € 13,162.83–€ 11,251.14 = € 1,911.69 by filing jointly.

Currently, Germany levies an additional surcharge on the individual income tax. The so-called solidarity surcharge is 5.5% of the tax payment of the individual income tax and the corporate income tax. It has been implemented in order to finance the German reunification. As we ignore surcharges and other taxes than income taxes we will neglect the solidarity surcharge in the following.

4.3.1.2 United States

In the United States, taxes are paid on three levels: Federal taxes, state taxes, and city/county taxes. As state taxes and city or county taxes vary heavily, we will ignore them in this book and focus on federal taxes only.

The United States define their federal individual income tax brackets in the Internal Revenue Code (IRC), title 26, subtitle A, Chap. 1, subchapter A, part I, sec. 1. There are four different classifications for tax payers: Single, married filing jointly, married filing separately, and head of household. For each group, separate tax brackets are defined for ordinary income. The tax brackets for singles are described later and in Fig. 4.5.

Table 4.4 has to be interpreted differently in comparison to the German tax rate: The taxpayer has to add up all tax payments calculated on the basis of the different tax brackets up to his amount of income. For singles, a standard deduction of $5,700 is granted. The standard deduction is not available for nonresident aliens. This tax-free amount is not included in the tax rate definition. Instead, the standard deduction is subtracted from the income before finding the appropriate tax bracket the taxpayer is in. The taxpayer may prove higher itemized deductions instead of the standard deduction.

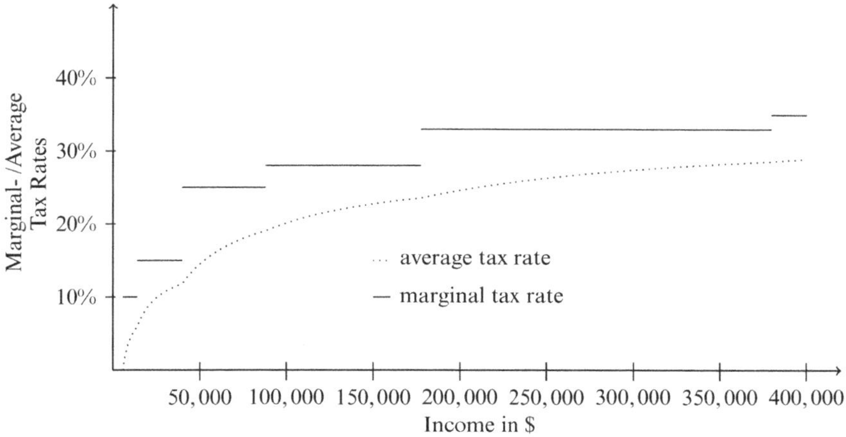

Fig. 4.5 Marginal and average individual income tax rates in the United States

Table 4.4 Individual income tax rates in the United States 2010

Income in $ from ... to ...			Tax in %
0	–	8,375	10
8,375	–	34,000	15
34,000	–	82,400	25
82,400	–	171,850	28
171,850	–	373,650	33
	>	373,650	35

Example 4.3. United States Individual Income Tax

Sara's income is $50,000. After deducting the standard deduction of $5,700 it is $44,300. This amount is between $34,000 and $82,400. Therefore, Sara is in the 25% tax bracket. The tax payments from the first to the third tax brackets have to be added up. Sara adds

$$\begin{aligned} T &= 8{,}375 \times 0.1 + (34{,}000 - 8{,}375) \times 0.15 + (44{,}300 - 34{,}000) \times 0.25 \\ &= 8{,}375 \times 0.1 + 25{,}625 \times 0.15 + 10{,}300 \times 0.25 = 7{,}256.25. \end{aligned}$$

Sara's tax burden T is $7,256.25.

Figure 4.5 depicts the marginal and average individual income tax rates in the United States. They are calculated as explained in Sect. 3.6. Compared to Germany, you see a saltus in the marginal tax rate when a new tax bracket is reached. The average tax rate curve is always below the marginal tax rate function.

4.3.1.3 OECD Countries

Individual income tax rates of OECD countries are listed in Table 4.5. The numbers in the first column describe top marginal individual income taxes on the federal level. Numbers in the second column combine both federal and local income taxes and surcharges.

Table 4.5 Top marginal individual income tax rates and combined top marginal individual income tax rates of OECD countries 2010

Country	Top marginal individual income tax rate (in %)	Combined top marginal individual income tax rate (in %)
Australia	45.00	45.00
Austria	50.00	50.00
Belgium	50.00	53.00
Canada	29.00	46.40
Chile	40.00	40.00
Czech Republic	15.00	15.00
Denmark	51.50	51.50
Finland	30.00	49.10
France	40.00	45.80
Germany	45.00	47.48
Greece	40.00	40.00
Hungary	36.00	40.00
Iceland	33.00	33.00
Ireland	41.00	47.00
Italy	43.00	44.15
Japan	40.00	50.00
Korea	35.00	38.50
Luxembourg	38.00	38.95
Mexico	30.00	30.00
Netherlands	52.00	52.00
New Zealand	37.00	37.00
Norway	28.00	40.00
Poland	32.00	32.00
Portugal	42.00	42.00
Slovakia	19.00	19.00
Spain	43.00	43.00
Sweden	25.00	56.60
Switzerland	11.50	39.97
Turkey	35.00	35.00
United Kingdom	50.00	50.00
United States	35.00	43.20

Combined tax rates include both federal and (average) local taxes as well as surcharges.

Source: Based on OECD, www.oecd.org/ctp/taxdatabase, Table I.1., April 10 2010; Bundesministerium der Finanzen, Die wichtigsten Steuern im internationalen Vergleich 2009; www.deloitte.com/dits; www.taxsummaries.pwc.com.

4.3.2 Corporate Income Tax Rates

In most countries, corporate income taxes are designed as flat taxes with a flat tax rate. We find an exception in the United States, where the tax rates increase with higher income.

4.3.2.1 Germany

Germany's flat corporate tax rate is 15% (§ 23 KStG). In addition, a local business tax is levied on business profits which are defined differently compared to the corporate tax base. We do not focus on the differences here. The local business tax is calculated by multiplying 0.035 with a local multiplier which is set by municipalities. The average local multiplier is 4.29. Assuming a multiplier of 4.29, the combined tax rate is

$$0.035 \times 4.29 = 0.15015.$$

Therefore, the total tax burden on corporate profits approximately is

$$0.15 + 0.15 = 0.30.$$

4.3.2.2 United States

The United States define their federal corporate income tax brackets in the Internal Revenue Code (IRC), title 26, subtitle A, Chap. 1, subchapter A, part II, sec. 11. There are four tax brackets as described in Table 4.6. Again, this table only covers federal taxes. State taxes and city/county taxes which might be levied additionally vary heavily and will be omitted in the following.

As known from the individual income tax in the United States, you add up the tax payment of the different tax brackets to calculate the tax burden. Companies with an income of more than $10 million pay 35% taxes on the income exceeding $10 million. There is no standard deduction available for corporations.

For reasons of simplicity, most textbooks and practitioners use a 35% corporate tax rate in their calculations and ignore the steps below.

Table 4.6 Individual corporate tax rates in the United States 2010

Income in $ from ... to ...	Tax in %
0 – 50,000	15
50,000 – 75,000	25
75,000 – 10,000,000	34
> 10,000,000	35

4.3.2.3 OECD Countries

Corporate tax rates of OECD countries are listed in Table 4.7. The numbers in the first column describe federal corporate income tax rates. Numbers in the second column combine both federal and local corporate income taxes and surcharges.

Table 4.7 Corporate tax rates and combined corporate tax rates of OECD countries 2010

Country	Federal corporate income tax rate (in %)	Combined corporate income tax rate (in %)
Australia	30.00	30.00
Austria	25.00	25.00
Belgium	33.00	33.99
Canada	19.00	33.00
Chile	17.00	17.00
Czech Republic	19.00	19.00
Denmark	25.00	25.00
Finland	26.00	26.00
France	33.33	34.43
Germany	15.00	29.83
Greece	24.00	24.00
Hungary	16.00	19.00
Iceland	18.00	18.00
Ireland	12.50	12.50
Italy	27.50	31.40
Japan	30.00	41.00
Korea	22.00	24.50
Luxembourg	21.84	28.59
Mexico	30.00	30.00
Netherlands	25.50	25.50
New Zealand	30.00	30.00
Norway	28.00	28.00
Poland	19.00	19.00
Portugal	25.00	26.50
Slovakia	19.00	19.00
Spain	30.00	30.00
Sweden	26.30	26.30
Switzerland	8.50	21.17
Turkey	20.00	20.00
United Kingdom	28.00	28.00
United States	35.00	39.10

Combined tax rates include both federal and (average) local taxes as well as surcharges. In Belgium, the effective tax rate can be substantially reduced by an allowance for corporate equity (ACE tax).

Source: Based on OECD, www.oecd.org/ctp/taxdatabase, Table II.1., April 10 2010; Bundesministerium der Finanzen, Die wichtigsten Steuern im internationalen Vergleich 2009; www.deloitte.com/dits; www.taxsummaries.pwc.com.

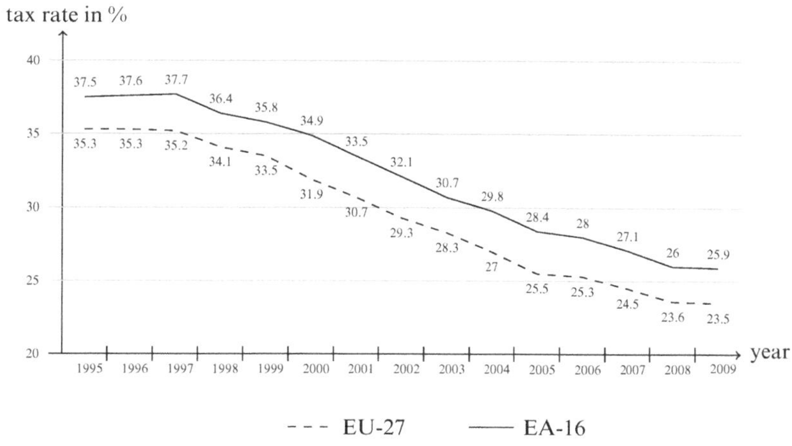

Fig. 4.6 Corporate tax rates in the European Union 1995–2009. Source: Based on European Commission, Taxation trends in the European Union, 2009, p. 104. *EU*: European Union; *EA*: Euro-Area

Due to globalization, there is an ongoing tax competition between countries. The competition is especially intense with regard to mobile factors such as capital income and business income. This can be seen when we look at the development of corporate tax rates over the last 15 years in Fig. 4.6.

4.4 Income Tax Bases

The tax bases are defined in national tax codes. The details differ heavily among countries.

Usually, countries define different tax baskets or types of income to determine the individual income tax and separately define tax bases for these baskets. Corporate income is typically not subdivided into different baskets. Determination of business income will be discussed in Chap. 6.

4.4.1 Germany

In Germany, there are seven different income baskets defined in the German Income Tax Code (§ 2 (1) EStG). The income baskets are shown in Table 4.8.

Table 4.8 Income baskets in the German individual income tax code

Income from
1. Agriculture and forestry (§13 EStG)
2. Business income (§15 EStG)
3. Income from self-employment (§18 EStG)
4. Income from employment (§19 EStG)
5. Investment income / capital income (§20 EStG)
6. Income from renting and leasing (§21 EStG)
7. Other income (§22 EStG)

4.4.2 United States

In contrast to Germany, the United States do not define separate income baskets. Instead, Art. 61 IRC states that "gross income means all income from whatever source derived".

For specific purposes, e.g., foreign tax credits (FTC), there are two types of income baskets relevant (Art 904 IRC). "Passive income" includes dividends, interest, rents, royalties, etc., while the "general category income" includes all remaining income types. Up to 2006, taxpayers had to differentiate between nine different FTC basket limitations.

4.5 Taxation of Capital Income

In many countries, capital income is taxed differently from other income baskets. Therefore, we deal with the taxation of capital income in a separate section. Typically, a flat tax is levied on capital income. Progressive tax rate functions as discussed before apply to ordinary income only.

4.5.1 Germany

In Germany, the progressive tax rate function is applied to ordinary income. Capital income such as dividends, interest income, and certain capital gains is taxed differently.

After a major tax reform in 2008, the current rules are applied since January 1st 2009. Interest and dividends of privately held financial assets are attributed to capital income (§ 20 (1) no. 1, 7 EStG). Capital gains on shares are also defined as capital income (§ 20 (2) no. 1 EStG) and are taxed independent of the holding period. Dividends, capital gains (if share in corporation is $<1\%$), and interest income are taxed at a reduced flat rate of 25% (§ 32d (6) EStG, so-called "Abgeltungsteuer").

If the average tax rate of the taxpayer is below 25%, the progressive tax rate structure is applied (§ 32d (6) EStG).

Thus, financial investments will be taxed lower than real investments because of the introduction of the flat (rate) tax. This increases the necessary pre-tax return on real investments in comparison to financial investments (*Kiesewetter/Lachmund* [6]). Capital gains of privately held stakes are taxed according to § 17 EStG, if the stake in subscribed capital of the corporation is >1% at any one time within the last 5 years. In these cases 60% of the capital gain is taxed at the personal income tax rate (§ 3 no. 40 c) EStG, so-called "Teileinkünfteverfahren").

With regard to capital gains from shares, there is a "grandfathering-rule": Capital gains on shares bought before 2009 will be tax-exempt if they are sold after a holding period of 1 year. Before the tax reform 2008, realized capital gains were tax exempt, if the shares were held for more than 1 year (speculative period) and the share in common stock of a company was less than 1%.

We explained that if the average tax rate of the taxpayer is below 25%, the progressive tax rate structure is applied. But how can we decide in our tax planning models, whether applying the progressive tax rate on capital income is advantageous?

To calculate the advantage tax treatment of capital income, you compare the average tax rate on capital income to the flat tax of 25%. First, you have to separate capital income from other baskets of income. You always assume that capital income is earned in addition to other income. Therefore, the highest marginal tax rate is applied on capital income.

You derive the tax payment due on total income including capital income if the progressive tax rate function is applied. Then you calculate the tax payment due on other income only. You divide the difference by your capital income which yields the average tax rate on capital income. If this average tax rate is below 25% then applying the progressive tax rate function is correct and you ignore the flat tax of 25%. If it is higher, you apply the flat tax on capital income. If income is quite low in a more-period model, you will have to do the optimization year by year.

Example 4.4. Taxation of Capital Income

Assume your salary is € 13,000 and your interest income is € 3,000. Therefore, your total income is € 16,000. According to the German progressive income tax rate function, you are in the third tax bracket, because your income is between € 13,470 and € 52,881 (see Table 4.3 on p. 142). You calculate

$$z = \frac{Income - 13{,}469}{10{,}000} = \frac{16{,}000 - 13{,}469}{10{,}000} = 0.2531.$$

You insert z

$$T = (228.74 \times z + 2{,}397) \times z + 1{,}038$$
$$= (228.74 \times 0.2531 + 2{,}397) \times 0.2531 + 1{,}038 = 1{,}659.$$

You perform the same calculation for your other income of € 13,000 only. Now, you are in the second tax bracket, because your income is between € 8,005 and € 13,469. You calculate

$$y = \frac{Income - 8{,}004}{10{,}000} = \frac{13{,}000 - 8{,}004}{10{,}000} = 0.4996.$$

You insert y

$$T = (912.17 \times y + 1{,}400) \times y = (912.17 \times 0.4996 + 1{,}400) \times 0.4996 = 927.$$

The difference between the two tax liabilities is

$$\Delta T = 1{,}659 - 927 = 732,$$

the average tax rate on capital income is $\frac{732}{3{,}000} = 24.4\%$ which is below 25%. Therefore, the progressive tax rate is applied on total income. Total tax payment is € 1,659 as calculated earlier.

A second possibility to figure out which tax treatment of capital income is advantageous is to compare tax payments in both cases without referring to the average tax rate.

Example 4.5. Taxation of Capital Income

Let's get back to Ex. 4.4.

Tax on total income including salary and capital income was calculated as $T = 1{,}659$. Tax liability on salary only was $T = 927$. Now you have to add the flat tax due on capital income

$$T(\text{capital income}) = 0.25 \times 3{,}000 = 750.$$

Total tax payment in this case is

$$T = 927 + 750 = 1{,}677.$$

1,677 is higher than 1,659; therefore, applying the progressive tax rate function on total income is chosen.

4.5.2 United States

In the United States, the progressive tax rate structure is applied to ordinary income. Capital gains and dividends are taxed at a reduced flat rate of usually 15%. In the US, capital gains include both gains on shares and on real estate. For taxpayers in income tax brackets higher than 15%, dividends are taxed at 15%. The Tax Increase Prevention and Reconciliation Act of 2006 (TIPRA) reduced the tax rate to 0% from 2008 through 2010 for taxpayers in the 10% and 15% tax brackets. The maximum tax rate on long-term capital gains (defined as gains on assets held for more than 1 year) was reduced from 20% to 15%. The TIPRA reduced the tax rate to 0% from 2008 through 2010 for taxpayers in the 10% and 15% tax brackets.

4.5.3 OECD Countries

Dividend tax rates of OECD countries are listed in Table 4.9. Very often, those tax rates include dividends and other types of capital income like interest income and capital gains, but the rules are not consistent over countries. Therefore, we focus on dividend tax rates only. A detailed explanation of how corporate tax systems work and how dividend taxes are integrated, is given in Sect. 6.6.

Table 4.9 Dividend tax rates of OECD countries 2010. Tax rates include local taxes and surcharges

Country	Tax rate on dividend income (in %)
Australia	23.60
Austria	25.00
Belgium	25.00
Canada	23.10
Chile	40.00
Czech Republic	15.00
Denmark	45.00
Finland	28.00
France	30.10
Germany	26.40
Greece	10.00
Hungary	25.00
Iceland	10.00
Ireland	47.00
Italy	12.50
Japan	10.00
Korea	29.30
Luxembourg	38.95
Mexico	0.00

(Continued)

Table 4.9 (Continued)

Country	Tax rate on dividend income (in %)
Netherlands	25.00
New Zealand	11.40
Norway	28.00
Poland	19.00
Portugal	20.00
Slovakia	0.00
Spain	18.00
Sweden	30.00
Switzerland	39.97
Turkey	17.50
United Kingdom	25.00
United States	17.30

Source: Based on OECD, www.oecd.org/ctp/taxdatabase, Table II.4., April 10 2010; Bundesministerium der Finanzen, Die wichtigsten Steuern im internationalen Vergleich 2009; www.deloitte.com/dits; www.taxsummaries.pwc.com.

Questions

4.1. Describe which type of taxes contribute to national tax revenues in OECD countries.

4.2. Do low-income earners or high-income earners contribute the most to income tax revenue in Germany?

4.3. Do low-income earners or high-income earners contribute the most to income tax revenue in the United States?

4.4. Why do so many people pay no income tax at all? Provide different explanations. Is this fair? Discuss!

4.5. Why is a corporate income tax typically designed as a constant tax rate?

4.6. Why do income tax rates typically increase?

4.7. How does the German income tax splitting method work for married couples? Is it always advantageous to file jointly?

4.8. Why is tax law so complicated? Can you think of benefits resulting from this complexity?

Exercises

Solutions are provided starting on p. 393.

4.9. German Individual Income Tax
Calculate the German income tax for an income of

(a) € 8,000,
(b) € 12,000,
(c) € 20,000,
(d) € 50,000,
(e) € 300,000.

4.10. Marginal and Average Tax Rates
Calculate marginal and average tax rates for an income of

(a) € 8,000,
(b) € 12,000,
(c) € 20,000,
(d) € 50,000,
(e) € 300,000,

in Germany. Please be aware that tax payments are not rounded to calculate the marginal tax rates.

4.11. German Splitting Method
Assume a married couple. She earns € 80,000 while her husband earns € 30,000 per year. How much does the couple save filing jointly compared to filing separately?

4.12. German Splitting Method
What is the maximum tax saving a married couple can realize when they file jointly?

4.13. US Individual Income Tax
Calculate the United States income tax for an income of

(a) $8,000,
(b) $12,000,
(c) $20,000,
(d) $50,000,
(e) $300,000.

4.14. Marginal and Average Tax Rates
Calculate marginal and average tax rates for an income of

(a) $8,000,
(b) $12,000,
(c) $20,000,

(d) $50,000,
(e) $300,000,

in the United States.

4.15. Taxation of Capital Income
You work and live in Germany. Your yearly salary is € 10,000. In addition, you earn € 1,000 interest income. Is it more advantageous to pay 25% flat tax on capital income or to apply the progressive income tax rate function on total income including capital income?

4.16. Taxation of Capital Income
You work and live in Germany. Your yearly salary is € 30,000. In addition, you earn € 1,000 interest income. Is it more advantageous to pay 25% flat tax on capital income or to apply the progressive income tax rate function on total income including capital income? Does an increase in your salary change your result?

Additional Sources

Most national tax books are available in the national language. But because of increasing international business activities, more English literature is coming into the market.

German tax details can be found in *Amann* [1], and *Djanani* et al. [3], for example. *Amann* [1] describes both national and cross-border regulations in detail, but the book is quite old and readers must check for changes in tax law. The second edition will be published in 2011.

The US federal income tax system is introduced by *Chirelstein* [2]. He describes the income concept in detail. In contrast to this book, *Scholes* et al. [8] touch tax law only shortly; the focus is on integrating taxes into business strategies.

A good UK introduction is given by *Miller/Oats* [7].

Many books compare different national tax rules. *Endres* [4] provides information about corporate taxable income in Member States of the European Union. The book is very well structured and specific information can be easily found. For each income item, *Endres* [4] explains IFRS rules first, followed by a list of tax accounting rules of the EU Member states.

All tax law books share one problem: Shortly after their appearance, the content becomes out of date. Continuous tax reforms make up-to-date books nearly impossible. This forces readers to be very careful with what they read. You always have to doublecheck with current tax codes whether the content is still correct.

Up-to-date information can be found on the internet. The Organisation for Economic Co-operation and Development (OECD) compares tax systems, tax rates, and selected items across their members on www.oecd.org/ctp/taxdatabase.

The International Bureau of Fiscal Documentation (IBFD) collects country tax information and cross-border tax expertise. The price for a 1-year access is € 1,730 ($2,250). A seven day trial access is possible. IBFD publishes an international tax glossary (*IBFD* [5]). They explain and define more than 2,000 tax terms.

The Big-4 auditing and tax companies provide basic tax information on their homepages free of charge.

PricewaterhouseCoopers offers a well-structured website www.taxsummaries.pwc.com. You find information about corporate taxes and individual taxes for 130 countries. You have to register free of charge to be able to use the site.

Deloitte provides "Deloitte International Tax Source" (www.deloitte.com/dits), a tool with detailed information for single countries as well as overviews such as tax-rate matrices. The website includes information about current and historic corporate income tax rates, indirect tax rates, domestic and treaty withholding tax rates, and comparative data on holding companies and transfer pricing policies.

KPMG's information on the website is rather basic (www.kpmg.com/Global/en/IssuesAndInsights/ArticlesPublications/Documents/Individual-Income-Tax-Rates-Survey-2009.pdf). A short document covering 87 countries compares marginal personal income tax rates, effective income tax rates, and social security rates and provides brief country-specific information. In contrast, their books (including CD-ROMs) "Global Corporate Tax Handbook", "Global Individual Tax Handbook" and "European Tax Handbook" – presented by *IBFD* – provide a well-structured and detailed basis for gaining tax knowledge about many countries. The "Global Corporate Tax Handbook" covers 97 countries and gives an introduction to corporate income tax, information about groups of companies, other taxes on income, taxes on payroll, taxes on capital, international aspects, anti-avoidance rules, value added taxes, and indirect taxes. Students should check if the books are available at the university libraries, because prices are between € 200 and € 330 each and books are updated each year.

Ernst & Young publish detailed information about 145 countries free of charge under www.ey.com/Publication/vwLUAssets/Global_Corporate_Tax_Guide_2009/$FILE/WWCT_2009.pdf. The document is 1,182 pages long. Information about each country include taxes on corporate income and gains, determination of trading income, other significant taxes and treaty withholding tax rates.

The website www.eiu.com by the Economist Intelligence Unit provides analyses and forecasts on more than 200 countries and six key industries. The analyses do not only cover general and political country information, but also overviews about personal and corporate taxes. Country-specific articles of the Economist Intelligence Unit are also available at most Universities via the database EBSCOhost.

But even when using the online sources you have to check carefully the current date of the publications.

The list of books and websites is far away from being complete. Instead, it provides a good starting basis for readers who want to learn more about tax law details of specific countries.

References

1. Amann, R. (ed.): German Tax Guide. Kluwer Law International, The Hague (2001)
2. Chirelstein, M.A.: Federal Income Taxation, 10th edn. Foundation Press, New York (2005)
3. Djanani, C., Brähler, G., Lösel, C.: German Income Tax. Verlag Recht und Wirtschaft, Frankfurt a.M. (2007)
4. Endres, D. (ed.): The Determination of Corporate Taxable Income in the EU Member States. Kluwer Law International, Alphen aan den Rijn (2007)
5. International Bureau of Fiscal Documentation: International Tax Glossary, 6th edn. IBFD Publications, Amsterdam (2009)
6. Kiesewetter, D., Lachmund, A.: Wirkungen einer Abgeltungsteuer auf Investitionsentscheidungen und Kapitalstruktur von Unternehmen. Die Betriebswirtschaft 395–411 (2004)
7. Miller, A., Oats, L.: Principles of International Taxation, 2nd edn. Tottel Publishing, Amsterdam (2009)
8. Scholes, M.S., Wolfson, M.A., Erickson, M., Maydew, E.L., Shevlin, T.: Taxes and Business Strategy. A Planning Approach. 4th edn., Prentice Hall, Upper Saddle River (2009)

Chapter 5
Neutral Income Tax Systems

Abstract In this chapter we introduce the idea of neutrality as a superior objective of tax systems. We illustrate common models of neutral taxation and discuss critically how they are and can be implemented in practice. The models discussed are the cash flow tax, the allowance for corporate equity tax and the Johansson/Samuelson tax. After studying this chapter you will know why neutral taxation is essential from an efficient macroeconomic perspective and from an investor's perspective. You are able to distinguish different types of neutral tax systems and you are able to evaluate their relevance in practice.

5.1 Introduction

The previous chapters show clearly that taxation effects investment decisions. Tax effects appear necessarily and affect decisions by accident or are the result of conscious planned fiscal policy. Without consideration of taxation, individuals might make incorrect decisions and carry out suboptimal investment alternatives. Hence, tax effects force investors to take taxation into account when they make decisions. However, taking taxation into account generates costs (e.g., for human resources) which cannot be intended from an efficient macroeconomic perspective. Decision neutrality is the systematic absence of tax effects.

Why is the absence of tax effects desirable? The ideal of neutral tax systems is that investment and financing decisions are not influenced by taxation at all. Moreover, a suboptimal level of investment is avoided. In a macroeconomic perspective, the efficient allocation of resources (capital, human resources) is not distorted by taxation. No tax-driven allocation of investment funds from more productive to less productive assets are found. There is no excess burden. At the individual investor's perspective, there are no tax-planning costs. Under a neutral tax system, even ignoring taxes in the tax-planning process leads to correct investment decisions (see *Schneider* [18], p. 206, *König/Wosnitza* [13], p. 139, and *Wagner* [22], p. 416). In summary, levying a neutral tax would not distort investment decisions at all.

D. Schanz and S. Schanz, *Business Taxation and Financial Decisions*,
DOI 10.1007/978-3-642-03284-4_5,

5.1.1 Subtypes of Decision Neutrality

Decision neutrality can be split up in several special alternative terms of neutrality. In the following, we briefly describe what is meant by

1. Neutrality of legal forms,
2. Neutrality of company size,
3. Sector neutrality,
4. Investment neutrality,
5. Financing neutrality,
6. Neutrality concerning working and spare-time decisions,
7. Consumption neutrality,
8. Neutrality of allocations of earnings.

Neutrality of legal forms means that the optimal legal form (corporation, sole proprietorship/partnership or hybrid form) is not affected by taxation. However, neutrality of legal forms usually will not hold true in real-world tax systems because of different taxation of sole proprietorships/partnerships and corporations.

Neutrality of company size means that taxation is independent of the level of tax bases, e.g., profits. This condition generally does not hold true if tax allowances exist or if tax accounting is connected to income levels. An example for such a dependency are loss carry forwards restricted to absolute amounts. Small companies profit from those rules, while big companies can only offset a limited amount.

Sector neutrality means that income is taxed equally over all industries (e.g., such as trade, traffic, consumer industry). This demand is usually diluted by specific conditions for the farming and forestry industry. But even between other sections without specific tax rules, there is no tax neutrality. The reason lies in depreciation rules. Tax depreciation allowances typically differ from economic depreciation. Therefore, sectors with high levels of assets are treated differently compared to sectors where investments in assets are less important, for example the services sector.

One of the most important neutrality demands is investment neutrality. It states that the ranking order of all investment alternatives according to their profitability before and after taxes does not change. E.g., if the ranking of net present values of the investment alternatives A, B, and C before consideration of taxation is $B > A > C$, the same order must be true after taking taxes into account and comparing the after-tax net present values.[1] Financing neutrality means that investment decisions are not affected by their financial structure (equity or debt financing or hybrids). However, different tax treatment of borrowing and lending (usually reduced tax rates for lending – e.g., flat rate tax in Germany and Austria – , whereas interest on debt is fully deductible).

Neutrality concerning working and spare-time decisions means that the decision of an individual that disposes over a fixed amount of hours per day to offer its manpower or to be lazy (spare time) is not affected by taxation. This condition will

[1] See Sect. 3.2.1, starting on p. 80, for an example.

only hold if a poll tax is implemented. In that case no matter what the individual does, it always has to pay a fixed amount of taxes. However, a poll tax is socially and politically not desired and realizable.

Consumption neutrality demands that taxation does not affect the decision to consume today or tomorrow. This condition does not hold because interest is usually taxed. This causes immediate consumption of free funds to be more attractive instead of saving them. Moreover, tax systems are dynamic and generally change every year so that nobody knows about future tax rates and tax bases.

The last postulate of neutrality deals with the neutrality of allocation of earnings. I.e., withdrawal/contribution to equity or distribution of dividends/retaining earnings is not affected by taxation. However, allocation of earnings is typically taxed differently.

5.1.2 Classification of Neutral Tax Systems

Tax systems that do not affect decisions, i.e., decisions made on a pre-tax basis would not be revised if taxation is integrated into the decision model, meet the conditions of investment neutrality. Tax systems meeting those conditions can be separated into two categories: Tax systems that do not affect decisions at all and tax systems that tax the overall objective of the individual (cash flows) (see *Schneider* [18] and *König/Wosnitza* [13]).

5.1.2.1 Tax Systems that do not Affect Decisions at all

Tax systems in which decisions are not affected by taxation mean that taxation is independent of the overall objective – maximizing cash flows after taxes. In this case assignment of taxes to single decisions is not possible, because the tax is charged no matter how many decision settings there are and no matter what volume they cover. A tax system that meets this requirement is, e.g., a poll tax.[2]

Actually, there are some examples of poll taxes in practice or at least features of such a tax. First, there is an example that took place in ancient Egypt. The tax system was connected to the water level of the river Nile. The annual flooding of the Nile was measured by special stairs and pillars. According to the water level, authorities calculated the possible crop yield. No matter what the crop yield actually was, the owner of the fields had to pay a fixed amount of taxes imposed by the authorities.

The second example took place during the administration of Margaret Thatcher in Great Britain at the end of the 80s and the beginning of the 90s. The implemented poll tax was designed as a community charge. However, the political pressure caused the administration to abolish that onerous kind of taxation.

---

[2] See *Smith* [19].

Example 5.1. The British Poll Tax Disaster

The local property tax (better known as "the rates") was the sole source of local taxation for the British local government until 1989. The tax was imposed on both residential and nonresidential property. The apparent inequity due to the large variety of tax bases all over the country resulted in a proposal of the national government to replace the residential property tax by a flat rate community charge – known as poll tax.[3] The poll tax was supposed to be paid by all adults living in a jurisdiction. The proposal was claimed by Margaret Thatcher as the "flagship" for her new administration since she won the 1987 election. Firstly introduced in Scotland in 1989, the poll tax was introduced in Wales and England in 1990. The implementation caused widespread public demonstrations over the country, civil unrest expressed by riots in central London, and extensive nonpayment. The facts that led to the abolishment in 1991 were

1. 36% of entries on the community charge register changed in the first year in rural areas. In inner London the rate accounted for 55%.
2. The 1991 Census of Population indicated the first drop in population in the United Kingdom since 1801.
3. Reluctance among many citizens to register in spite of heavy fines.
4. The administrative costs of collecting local taxes rose from £200 million to £605 million in the first year (increased costs of court actions and debt recovery, and the shortfall in revenue arising from nonpayment are excluded).

A third example can be found in the Netherlands. The tax reform act 2001 implemented a tax on presumptive returns of financial investments. No matter what the return of a specific financial investment is, the individual has to pay taxes on a return of 4% defined by the government.

Example 5.2. The Fundamental Tax Reform in the Netherlands

In 2001 the Netherland's government replaced the actual realization-based capital gains tax by a presumptive capital income tax which is in fact a net wealth tax.[4] Capital income is taxed on the basis of an expected (ex-ante) investment return. The personal capital income, represented by the return of personally held assets like deposits, stocks and bonds, is defined as 4% of the value of these assets, regardless of the actual returns. Levying a statutory tax rate of 30% results in an actual net wealth tax rate of $4\% \times 30\% = 1.2\%$.

[3] The example is based on *Smith* [19].

[4] The fundamental change is described in detail by *Cnossen/Bovenberg* [4].

E.g., if an individual owns bonds amounting to let's say €50,000, $50{,}000 \times 0.04 \times 0.3 = 600$ taxes have to be paid. Now suppose the actual yield is 6%. In this case the individual would be better off because taxes are just levied on 4%. However, if the individual faces losses or a low return, he is penalized twice. First, because of the losses or small return generated by the assets, and second, by tax authorities that collect 4% × 30% of the assets.

Example 5.3. Poll Tax and Intertemporal Consumption Neutrality

The following model is derived from the results of Sect. 2.5.2 starting on p. 49. Assume an individual maximizing his consumption utility U within a two-period setting with a fixed tax T in $t = 1$. Hence, the optimization problem can be described as:

$$\begin{aligned} &\max U\,(C_0, C_1)\\ \text{s.t. } &C_0 = W_0 - F_0 - I_0 \\ &C_1 = (1+i) \times F_0 + f(I_0) - T, \end{aligned} \tag{5.1}$$

where C denotes consumption, W_0 represents the initial endowment, F_0 the financial investment yielding interest i, I_0 the real investment, and $f(I_0)$ is the real investment function. In $t = 0$, the part of the initial endowment that is not invested in the real or financial investment can be consumed. In $t = 1$, consumption is restricted to the return of the real and financial investment less taxes. Now, the individual has to decide how much to invest in $t = 0$ in order to maximize his overall utility.

The Lagrangian function derived from (5.1) is determined as:

$$\begin{aligned} \mathcal{L}(C_0, C_1, F_0, \lambda) = U(C_0, C_1) + \lambda \times (&f[W_0 - C_0 - F_0] \\ &+ F_0 \times (1+i) - T - C_1), \end{aligned}$$

where $W_0 - C_0 - F_0 = I_0$. The partial derivatives then account for

$$\begin{aligned} \frac{\partial L}{\partial C_0} &= \frac{\partial U}{\partial C_0} + \lambda \times \frac{df}{dI_0} \times \frac{\partial I_0}{\partial C_0} = \frac{\partial U}{\partial C_0} - \lambda \times \frac{df}{dI_0} = 0 \\ \frac{\partial L}{\partial C_1} &= \frac{\partial U}{\partial C_1} - \lambda = 0 \\ \frac{\partial L}{\partial F_0} &= \lambda \times \left(\frac{df}{dI_0} \times \frac{\partial I_0}{\partial F_0} + (1+i) \right) = 0. \end{aligned} \tag{5.2}$$

Because of nonsaturation, the condition binds and hence $\lambda^* \neq 0$. While $\frac{\partial I_0}{\partial F_0} = -1$, (5.2) is reduced to

$$\frac{df}{dI_0} = 1 + i. \tag{5.3}$$

The optimal consumption bundle is not affected by T. Therefore, taxation cannot be assigned to the investment object. Equation (5.3) states the known condition to maximize the net present value. Remember the net present value that is defined as:

$$NPV(I_0) = -I_0 + \frac{f(I_0)}{1+i}. \tag{5.4}$$

The first derivative gives

$$\frac{dNPV(I_0)}{dI_0} = -1 + \frac{\frac{df(I_0)}{dI_0}}{1+i} = 0 \quad \Leftrightarrow \quad \frac{df(I_0)}{dI_0} = 1 + i. \tag{5.5}$$

The simple model shows that a poll tax does not affect the optimal consumption bundle and hence, does not affect consumption decisions.

5.1.2.2 Tax Systems that Tax the Overall Objective of Individuals

Tax systems that tax cash flows or economic income as the overall objective of an individual are

(a) Cash flow taxes,
(b) Allowance for corporate equity taxes and the
(c) Johannsson/Samuelson tax.

Again, we have to define what the objective of an individual is. As it is assumed that individuals strive to maximize their consumption utility, it is easy to derive that cash flows after taxes are the objective. The individual is able to transform cash (after taxes) into consumption utility if he buys consumer goods with the available after-tax cash flow. Hence, profit maximization cannot be the target because profits usually consist of accruals and cash flows.

Taxation of the investors' objectives (economic income and consumption) is the most important design principle of tax systems. This is implemented in some important income tax baskets in many countries worldwide

1. Employment income,
2. Capital income,
3. VAT (value added tax).

If cash flows after taxes are to be maximized, income taxation of an employee can be considered as neutral. The reason for this is that income consists almost exclusively of cash components. Accruals do not play an important role. Maybe there is a small amount of depreciation of a laptop or some lump sum deductions for the way to work, however, that does not play the main role. The same is true for capital income. Usually, no accrual occur. A VAT is normally imposed on revenue. Because revenue is based on cash (if receivables and withdrawals of assets are neglected), a VAT can be considered as a neutral tax.

Tax planning (meaning taking taxes into account in decision making) is necessary for all other kinds of income, when taxation of the investor's target is not realized. Due to accruals this is especially true for business income.

In the following sections, we discuss the three neutral tax systems that tax the investor's objective and give – if possible – examples for use in practice.

5.1.3 Taxing the Objective

Before introducing neutral tax systems, we need to derive the conditions to get the the objective of an individuals taxed in effect.

We already know that maximizing the net present value automatically maximizes consumption utility of the individual (remember Fisher's separation in Sect. 2.5 starting on p. 36). Now, by levying a tax proportional to the investor's objective guarantees that the before-tax ranking of investment projects according to their net present values remains unaffected by taxation. Knowing this characteristic, we can use the net present value to prove the "ranking order neutrality" of a tax system that taxes the objective. The feature of investment neutrality can be described by:

$$NPV^{\tau} = f(NPV), \tag{5.6}$$

where $f(\cdot)$ has to hold the following characteristics

1. $f(\cdot)$ is strictly monotonically increasing: $\frac{df(\cdot)}{dNPV} > 0$
2. $f(0) = 0$.

This implies that, the net present value after taxes must be a transformation of the pre-tax net present value. Then, for investment alternatives (a), (b), (c), (d), and (e), with net present values before taxes of

$$NPV(a) < 0 = NPV(b) < NPV(c) < NPV(d) = NPV(e) \tag{5.7}$$

the following conditions hold

$$\begin{aligned} f[NPV(a)] < 0 &= f[NPV(b)] < f[NPV(c)] < f[NPV(d)] = f[NPV(e)] \\ &\Leftrightarrow \\ NPV^{\tau}(a) < 0 &= NPV^{\tau}(b) < NPV^{\tau}(c) < NPV^{\tau}(d) = NPV^{\tau}(e). \end{aligned}$$

5.2 Cash Flow Tax

Tax systems that tax an investor's objective were firstly introduced by *E. Cary Brown*.[5] Let's first have a look at his development of the cash flow tax.

5.2.1 Preliminary Thoughts of Brown

Brown [3] summarized the existence of taxes as:[6]

> They reduce the disposable income of some income recipients, decrease their consumption expenditures, and, indirectly, may reduce the level of investment.

Moreover, he states that considering a system of economic-life depreciation – meaning the allocation of historical costs over the economic-life time of the initial investment in whatever manner – investment incentives are more adversely affected the longer the economic life-cycle of the investment is. The reason for this is that allocating the historical costs over the economic life of an asset for tax reasons causes the present value of the depreciation expense to differ from the acquisition costs I_0. Formally, this is described as:

$$I_0 \neq \sum_{t=1}^{n} \frac{D_t}{(1+i)^t}. \tag{5.8}$$

If straight-line depreciation is assumed, the present value of future depreciation PV^D can be calculated as:

$$PV^D = \frac{I_0}{n} \times \frac{(1+i)^n - 1}{i \times (1+i)^n} = D \times PVAR \tag{5.9}$$

that is the present value of an annuity in arrears of the constant depreciation over time.

Example 5.4. Present Value of Depreciation

Assume acquisition costs of $I_0 = 1{,}000$, an economic life-time of $n = 4$ periods and an interest rate of $i = 6\%$. The present value of future expenditures represented by depreciation then accounts for

$$PV^D = \frac{1{,}000}{4} \times \frac{(1+0.06)^4 - 1}{0.06 \times (1+0.06)^4} = 866.28.$$

[5] See *Brown* [3].

[6] *Brown* [3], p. 300.

Table 5.1 Present value of straight-line depreciation of historical cost over the economic life of an asset of € 1

Economic life	Annual deduction	Present value of depreciation discounted at rate of interest of			
		2%	4%	6%	10%
(1)	(2)	(3)	(4)	(5)	(6)
2	50%	97.1%	94.3%	91.7%	86.8%
5	20%	94.3%	89.0%	84.2%	75.8%
10	10%	89.8%	81.1%	73.6%	61.4%
20	5%	81.8%	68.0%	57.3%	42.6%
40	2.5%	68.4%	49.5%	37.6%	24.4%
50	2%	62.8%	43.0%	31.5%	19.8%

The present value of depreciation is $\frac{PV^D}{I_0} = \frac{866.28}{1{,}000} = 86.63\%$ of the initial acquisition costs.

It is obvious that the longer the economic life is, there are more periods over which the depreciation has to be allocated resulting in a lower present value of depreciation. Table 5.1 shows the percentage of present value of depreciation in relation to the initial acquisition costs if straight-line depreciation is applied.[7] Use (5.9) with $I_0 = 1$ to reconstruct the values. The difference between initial investment and present value of future expenses becomes significant if residential property is considered. Suppose you have to depreciate residential property over a period of 50 years, facing a certain interest rate of about 10% during that period. In this case the percentage of depreciation in relation to the initial investment would be 19.8%. Facing these results, *Brown* states:[8]

> It becomes clear why the tax reduces investment incentives: It stems from the failure of the present worth of the tax rebates from depreciation to reduce cost of the asset by an amount proportionate to the rate of tax.

Example 5.5. Brown's Approach to Evaluate the Profitability of Investments

Consider the following stream of cash flows

t	0	1	2	3	4	5
CF_t	–4,000.00	898.00	901.00	900.00	949.00	982.00

[7] See *Brown* [3], p. 306.

[8] *Brown* [3], p. 305.

If the interest rate is supposed to be $i = 5\%$, the net present value before taxes will be $NPV \approx 0$. Hence, we face a marginal investment alternative, because we are indifferent between the real investment and the alternative financial investment. Now assume that the government imposes a tax of $\tau = 50\%$. If straight-line depreciation is applied, the annual tax saving evolving from deducting depreciation from taxable income will be $\tau \times \frac{I_0}{n} = 0.5 \times \frac{4{,}000}{5} = 400$. Therefore, the present value of future tax savings due to depreciation $PV^{D,\tau}$ accounts for

$$PV^{D,\tau} = 400 \times \frac{(1 + 0.025)^5 - 1}{0.025 \times (1 + 0.025)^5} = 1{,}858.33.$$

The tax reduction to the amount of 1,858.33 decreases the initial investment payout to $I_0^\tau = 4{,}000.00 - 1{,}858.33 = 2{,}141.67$. Now, consider the present value of the net receipts.

t	0	1	2	3	4	5
CF_t		898.00	901.00	900.00	949.00	982.00
T_t		449.00	450.50	450.00	474.50	491.00
CF_t^τ		449.00	450.50	450.00	474.50	491.00
PV_0^τ	2,148.56					

Hence, the present value of future receipts is $PV^\tau = 2{,}148.56$. Now, acquisition costs after taxes are $I_0^\tau = 2{,}141.67$. However, net receipts after taxation account for $PV^\tau = 2{,}148.56$. This is greater than the acquisition costs after taxes. Thus, the investment should be carried out. Net present value in that case gives $NPV^\tau = -2{,}141.67 + 2{,}148.56 = 6.89$.

Using the Standard Model, we receive the same result, for sure. Let's have a look at the financial plan

t	0	1	2	3	4	5
CF_t	−4, 000.00	898.00	901.00	900.00	949.00	982.00
D_t		800.00	800.00	800.00	800.00	800.00
TB_t		98.00	101.00	100.00	149.00	182.00
T_t		49.00	50.50	50.00	74.50	91.00
CF_t^τ		849.00	850.50	850.00	874.50	891.00
NPV^τ	6.89					

5.2.2 The Model

As a result of his findings, *Brown* developed the taxation of cash flows that holds the characteristic of taxing an individual's objectives because no accruals occur for tax reasons. In this case, the tax base consists solely of cash components. Tax payments of the period T_t result in

$$T_t = \tau \times (CIF_t - COF_t),$$

where *CIF* and *COF* denote cash inflow and cash outflow, respectively. Hence, fiscal authorities participate in all future cash inflows. However, they also take part in the initial investment I_0. Moreover, tax authorities will pay for any losses of the company at the same rate as income is taxed. However, one of the main attributes of cash flow taxation is the immediate depreciation of the acquisition costs.

Calculating the net present value after taxes NPV^τ of an investment alternative under consideration of the cash flow tax gives

$$\begin{aligned} NPV^\tau &= -I_0 \times (1-\tau) + \sum_{t=1}^{n} \frac{CIF_t - COF_t - \tau \times (CIF_t - COF_t)}{(1+i)^t} \\ &= (1-\tau) \times \sum_{t=0}^{n} \frac{CIF_t - COF_t}{(1+i)^t}. \end{aligned} \tag{5.10}$$

It is easy to see that the net present value after taxes is a linear transformation of the net present value before taxes.

$$NPV^\tau = NPV \times (1-\tau).$$

The overall conditions to ensure neutrality are satisfied

$$\frac{df(NPV)}{dNPV} = 1 - \tau > 0$$
$$f(0) = 0.$$

One specific characteristic of a cash flow tax interest is tax exempt. The postulate of neutrality must also be true for the fixed rate financial investment which represents our standard alternative investment option. Under a cash flow tax system, basically, on the one hand, lending money means an initial investment that is tax deductible for the lender, on the other hand, borrowing money leads to a taxable cash inflow. However, at the time when the money is paid back the whole amount including interest would be subject to tax (or tax deductible for the borrower). Hence, the after-tax return in case of lending money is $I_0 \times (1+i) \times (1-\tau)$. Now look at a one-period model to see what happens if investing money was deductible and the money payback including interest was subject to tax

$$\begin{aligned} i^\tau &= \frac{-(1-\tau)\times I_0 + I_0 \times (1+i)\times(1-\tau)}{(1-\tau)\times I_0} \\ &= \frac{-I_0 + I_0 \times (1+i)}{I_0} \\ &= \frac{I_0 \times (1+i-1)}{I_0} \\ i^\tau &= i\,. \end{aligned} \tag{5.11}$$

Equation (5.11) shows that after-tax cash flows are discounted at the pre-tax interest rate i (*Wagner* [22], p. 481). The tax exemption of interest can be explained with the immediate deductibility of the initial investment. Immediate deductibility comes along with overall taxable future cash flows. As immediate deductibility implies that the whole depreciation potential is already depleted in $t = 0$, there is no depreciation in the future. If the initial investment is immediately tax deductible and future cash flows are fully taxed, we can calculate the after-tax return as after-tax cash flow after investing (numerator) over post-tax investment, see (5.11). We see that the after-tax return equals the interest before taxes. In a consumption-based tax system, the alternative financial investment is not taxed.

Tax exemption of interest payments can also be interpreted as an administrative simplification because tax exemption of interest payments is easier to handle than immediate deductibility of financial investments combined with taxation of payouts from financial investments.

Example 5.6. Taxation of the Financial Investment Alternative under a Cash Flow Tax

Neutral taxation of the underlying investment alternative also demands neutral taxation of the financial investment alternative. Taking a financial investment into consideration, we will show why it is an administrative simplification not to tax interest yields. Suppose a financial investment of $I_0 = 1{,}000$ yielding $i = 10\%$, $n = 4$, and $\tau = 40\%$.

First, let's consider taxation of interest. According to the characteristics of the cash flow tax, acquisition costs even in the case of financial investments can be written off for tax purposes immediately. But receiving equity in $t = n$ leads to full taxable income. Hence, we get after-tax receipts of

t	0	1	2	3	4
CF_t	−1,000	100	100	100	1,100
T_t	−400	40	40	40	440
CF_t^τ	−600	60	60	60	660

Taking the pre-tax interest rate for discounting, we get the result of $NPV^\tau = 0$.

Second, financial investment is not taxed. If interest yields are not taxed at all, the investment payout cannot be written off and cash receipts in $t = n$ are not taxed, correspondingly.

t	0	1	2	3	4
CF_t	−1,000	100	100	100	1,100
T_t	0	0	0	0	0
CF_t^τ	−1,000	100	100	100	1,100

Taking the pre-tax interest rate for discounting again, we also get again $NPV^\tau = 0$. Therefore, taxing financial investments or not taxing them makes no difference. When fiscal authorities omit taxing them, no exception is granted. Instead, this is just an administrative simplification.

Please notice that the NPV^τ of our financial investment alternative always is zero in case the discount rate equals the interest rate.

In practice, lending money is not tax deductible. Correspondingly, repayments are not subject to tax. However, interest is subject to tax. Taking the assumptions from above and $\tau = 40\%$, NPV^τ is calculated as:

t	0	1	2	3	4
CF_t	−1,000	100	100	100	1,100
T_t		40	40	40	40
CF_t^τ	−1,000	60	60	60	1,060
NPV^τ	0,00				

This financial plan refers to an income tax system instead of a cash flow tax system. Remember, the discount rate in this case is $i^\tau = 10\% \times (1 - 40\%) = 6\%$. This calculation demonstrates that financial investments yielding a fixed interest rate are neutrally taxed, even under an otherwise non-neutral income tax system.

Example 5.7. Cash Flow Tax

Suppose there is a sole proprietorship and the sole proprietor makes a contribution to capital of € 1,000 in $t = 0$. The money is used to buy a machine immediately ($I_0 = 1{,}000$). The certain future cash flow stream is assumed to be

t	0	1	2	3	4
CF_t	−1,000	460	360	260	220

At the end of each period, the investor withdraws all cash flows after taxes. The marginal tax rate is assumed to be $\tau = 30\%$, the interest rate accounts for $i = 8\%$. Based on these assumptions, net present value before taxation is

$$NPV = -1{,}000 + \frac{460}{1.08} + \frac{360}{1.08^2} + \frac{260}{1.08^3} + \frac{220}{1.08^4} = 102.67. \tag{5.12}$$

Using a financial plan, cash flows after taxes are

t	0	1	2	3	4
CF_t	−1,000	460	360	260	220
TB_t	−1,000	460	360	260	220
T_t	−300	138	108	78	66
CF_t^τ	−700	322	252	182	154

Discounting after-tax cash flows CF_t^τ, net present value after taxes gives

$$NPV^\tau = -700 + \frac{322}{1.08} + \frac{252}{1.08^2} + \frac{182}{1.08^3} + \frac{154}{1.08^4}$$
$$= 71.87 = (1 - \tau) \times NPV.$$

To make the cash flow tax more transparent, we want to look at the journal entries. Accounting takes place as under currently implemented (comprehensive) income tax systems.

(a) Accounting records (Debit account Dr, Credit account Cr) in $t = 0$ are

1. Contribution to capital:

Dr	cash account	1,000			
			Cr	equity	1,000

2. Buying the machine:

Dr	plant & equipment	1,000			
			Cr	cash account	1,000

3. Immediate initial depreciation of the machine:

Dr	depreciation	1,000			
			Cr	plant & equipment	1,000

4. Tax payment:

Dr	cash account	300			
			Cr	tax revenue	300

5. Withdrawal of net cash flows (equivalent to the tax refund):

Dr	equity	300			
			Cr	cash account	300

Further steps:

6. Closing journal entries of asset accounts and liability accounts does not apply because the balance equals zero for each account.
7. Closing journal entries of the tax and depreciation accounts to the profit and loss account (P&L):

Dr	tax revenue	300			
	P&L	1,000			
			Cr	P&L	300
				depreciation	1,000

8. Closing the profit and loss account to the equity account:

Dr	equity	700			
			Cr	P&L	700

9. Closing the equity account to the final balance sheet is not necessary, because balance of the equity account is equal to zero.

Selected accounts:

P&L

depreciation	1,000	tax expense	300
		loss (equity)	*700*

Equity

cash	300	plant & equipment	1,000
P&L	700		
balance sheet	*0*		
total	*1,000*	*total*	1,000

Final balance sheet (t = 0,1,2,3)

plant & equipment	0	equity	0
bank (cash)	0		
total assets	*0*	*total equity and liabilities*	*0*

(b) Accounting records in $t = 1$:

1. Revenue:

Dr	cash account	460			
			Cr	sales revenue	460

2. Tax payments:

Dr	tax expense	138			
			Cr	cash account	138

3. Withdrawal of all cash flows left:

Dr	equity	322			
			Cr	cash account	322

4. Closing:

Dr	sales revenue	460			
	P&L	138			
	P&L	322			
	equity	322			
			Cr	P&L	460
				tax expense	138
				equity	322
				P&L	322

(c) Accounting records in $t = 2, 3, 4$ are analogous to records in $t = 1$.

5.2.3 *Integration of a Cash Flow Tax into the Fisher–Hirshleifer Model*

We refer to the Fisher–Hirshleifer Model and integrate a cash flow tax.

Example 5.8. Cash Flow Tax and the Fisher–Hirshleifer Model

The following example is based on the pre-tax example discussed in Ex. 2.25 on p. 60. An investor owns $W_0 = 100$ in $t = 0$. The utility function is

$$U(C_0, C_1) = C_0^2 \times C_1.$$

The pre-tax real investment function is

$$f(I_0) = 15 \times \sqrt{I_0}$$

whereas in case of a cash flow tax, the post-tax real investment function is

$$f^{\tau}(I_0) = 15 \times \sqrt{I_0} \times (1 - \tau).$$

It is assumed that there is no money left for consumption at the end of $t = 1$. According to (2.57) on p. 59 there are two restrictions to consider. First, consumption in $t = 1$ has to be equivalent to the return of the real investment after taxes plus the return of the financial investment which might be negative. Hence, the first restriction is

$$C_1 = f^{\tau}(I_0) + F_0 \times (1 + i).$$

The second restriction deals with the amount that is invested in the real investment. That amount is restricted to initial wealth less consumption in $t = 0$ less positive or plus negative financial investment in $t = 0$. Because we assumed a cash flow tax, initial costs are immediately deductible which leads to a tax refund of $I_0 \times \tau$. Hence, the restriction in $t = 0$ is

$$\begin{aligned} I_0 \times (1 - \tau) &= W_0 - C_0 - F_0 \\ I_0 &= \frac{W_0 - C_0 - F_0}{(1 - \tau)}. \end{aligned}$$

We have to maximize the Lagrangian function with respect to C_0, C_1, and F_0. We get

$$\mathcal{L}(C_0, C_1, F_0, \lambda) = C_0^2 \times C_1 + \lambda \times \left[15 \times \sqrt{\frac{(W_0 - C_0 - F_0)}{(1-\tau)}} \times (1-\tau) \right.$$
$$\left. + F_0 \times (1+i) - C_1 \right].$$

Notice, interest is tax exempt in case of a cash flow tax system. The partial derivatives with respect to C_0, C_1, F_0, and λ are

$$\frac{\partial \mathcal{L}}{\partial C_0} = 2 \times C_0 \times C_1 - \lambda \times \frac{7.5}{\sqrt{\frac{(W_0-C_0-F_0)}{(1-\tau)}}} \stackrel{!}{=} 0 \tag{5.13}$$

$$\frac{\partial \mathcal{L}}{\partial C_1} = C_0^2 - \lambda \stackrel{!}{=} 0 \tag{5.14}$$

$$\frac{\partial \mathcal{L}}{\partial F_0} = \lambda \times \left[-\frac{7.5}{\sqrt{\frac{(W_0-C_0-F_0)}{(1-\tau)}}} + (1+i) \right] \stackrel{!}{=} 0 \tag{5.15}$$

$$\frac{\partial \mathcal{L}}{\partial \lambda} = 15 \times \sqrt{\frac{(W_0-C_0-F_0)}{(1-\tau)}} \times (1-\tau) + F_0 \times (1+i) - C_1 \stackrel{!}{=} 0. \tag{5.16}$$

Solving (5.13) and (5.14) for λ and setting equal we get

$$\frac{2 \times C_0 \times C_1}{\frac{7.5}{\sqrt{\frac{(W_0-C_0-F_0)}{(1-\tau)}}}} = C_0^2. \tag{5.17}$$

Solving (5.17) for C_1 gives

$$C_1 = \frac{C_0}{2} \times \frac{7.5}{\sqrt{\frac{(W_0-C_0-F_0)}{(1-\tau)}}}. \tag{5.18}$$

For $\lambda > 0$ we can solve (5.15) for F_0 and get

$$F_0 = W_0 - C_0 - \left(\frac{7.5}{(1+i)} \right)^2 \times (1-\tau). \tag{5.19}$$

We insert (5.18) and (5.19) in (5.16) and solve for C_0

$$C_0 = \frac{15 \times (1-\tau) \times \frac{7.5}{(1+i)} + \left(W_0 - \left(\frac{7.5}{(1+i)} \right)^2 \times (1-\tau) \right) \times (1+i)}{(1+i) + \frac{(1+i)}{2}}.$$

With $i = 0.2$, $\tau = 30\%$, and $W_0 = 100$, C_0 is

$$C_0 = 84.90. \tag{5.20}$$

We insert (5.20) in (5.19) and get

$$F_0 = 100 - 84.90 - \left(\frac{7.5}{1.2}\right)^2 \times (1 - \tau) = -12.24. \tag{5.21}$$

Obviously, the individual is in a situation where money is borrowed in $t = 0$. Now, we calculate C_1 by inserting (5.20) and (5.21) in (5.18)

$$C_1 = \frac{84.90}{2} \times \frac{7.5}{\sqrt{\frac{(100-84.90+12.24)}{(1-0.3)}}} = 50.94. \tag{5.22}$$

In $t = 0$ real investment is

$$I_0 = \frac{W_0 - C_0 - F_0}{(1 - \tau)} = \frac{100 - 84.90 + 12.24}{(1 - 0.3)} = 39.06. \tag{5.23}$$

Notice, in $t = 0$ the real investment does not change because of taxation. In the pre-tax case we get the same amount for I_0.

The post-tax net present value of the real investment is

$$\begin{aligned} NPV^\tau &= -I_0 \times (1 - \tau) + \frac{f^\tau(I_0)}{(1 + i)} \\ &= -39.06 \times (1 - 0.3) + \frac{15 \times \sqrt{39.06} \times (1 - 0.3)}{1.2} = 27.34 \end{aligned}$$

which is

$$\begin{aligned} NPV^\tau &= NPV \times (1 - \tau) \\ &= 39.06 \times (1 - 0.3) \\ &= 27.34. \end{aligned}$$

5.2.4 *Excursus: Deductibility of Taxes in a Cash Flow Tax System*

The tax base in cash flow based system consists solely of cash elements and, hence, the overall objective of an investor – the potential of consumption – is taxed. However, if we assume cash outflow to be a negative element reducing the investor's objective, what about taxes themselves? Because taxes have to be paid to tax authorities, they represent cash outflow for investors, too. But if we look at our formal description of the cash flow tax in (5.10), we realize that taxes are not being deducted at all.

If taxes are deductible for tax purposes, tax T_t is computed as:

$$T_t = \tau \times (CF_t - T_t) \tag{5.24}$$

with the statutory tax rate τ. Solving for T_t gives

$$T_t = \frac{\tau}{1+\tau} \times CF_t.$$

If τ^{eff} represents the effective tax rate and if CF_t is scaled to 1 ($CF_t = 1$), we get

$$\tau^{eff} = \frac{\tau}{1+\tau}. \tag{5.25}$$

Post-tax net present value now is determined as:

$$NPV^{\tau} = -I_0 + \sum_{t=1}^{n} \frac{CF_t - \tau^{eff} \times CF_t}{(1+i)^t}. \tag{5.26}$$

If τ stays constant over time, τ^{eff} does so, too. In this case, (5.26) simplifies to

$$\begin{aligned} NPV^{\tau} &= -I_0 + (1-\tau^{eff}) \times \sum_{t=1}^{n} \frac{CF_t}{(1+i)^t} \\ &\Leftrightarrow \\ NPV^{\tau} &= (1-\tau^{eff}) \times NPV, \end{aligned} \tag{5.27}$$

where

$$NPV = \sum_{t=0}^{n} \frac{CF_t}{(1+i)^t}.$$

The post-tax net present value still remains a linear transformation of the pre-tax net present value and is neutral – in terms of distorting investment decisions – , too.

Example 5.9. Cash Flow Tax in Case Taxes are Deductible

Suppose the cash flow stream used in Ex. 5.7. Further assume $i = 8\%$ and $\tau = 25\%$. The effective tax rate accounts to

$$\tau^{eff} = \frac{0.25}{1+0.25} = 0.2.$$

First, we want to show what happens to the financial alternative investment. Of course, NPV^τ has to be zero. How can we achieve this? The following financial plan contains the computation of NPV^τ.

t	0	1	2	3	4
$CF_t = TB_t$	−1,000	80	80	80	1,080
$T_t = \tau^{eff} \times CF_t$	−200	16	16	16	216
CF_t^τ	−800	64	64	64	864
NPV^τ	0				

Consider $t = 1$, for example. T_1 gives $CF_0 \times \tau^{eff} = 0.2 \times 80 = 16$. Based on (5.24), the tax is computed as $T_1 = 0.25 \times (80 - 16) = 16$. Results are always equivalent, whether (5.24) or a formula based on the effective tax rate is used.

If the post-tax cash flow stream is discounted at the pre-tax interest rate, we will get the known result $NPV = NPV^\tau = 0$.

Computing the post-tax net present value for the real investment goes along the computation of post-tax net present value for the financial investment. The subsequent financial plan demonstrates the calculation of the post-tax net present value.

t	0	1	2	3	4
$CF_t = TB_t$	−1,000	460	360	260	220
$T_t = \tau^{eff} \times CF_t$	−200	92	72	52	44
CF_t^τ	−800	368	288	208	176
NPV^τ	82.14				

Remember, the pre-tax net present value of 102.67 is determined in (5.12). Now, the post-tax NPV^τ gives

$$NPV^\tau = (1 - 0.2) \times 102.67 = 82.14.$$

5.2.5 Problems of Implementing a Cash Flow Based Tax System

If a cash flow tax is implemented, tax authorities will face several problems. First, it is an unusual design of an accounting system. Therefore, practitioners have to be made familiar with a new system. A rollout might last years. Second, tax revenues could be quite volatile, because the tax base solely consists of cash components. In years where lots of investments are carried out, tax revenue would fall significantly. In contrast to a cash flow tax system, current income tax systems provide equally distributed depreciation allowances and therefore tax bases and revenues are being smoothed. Third, the cash flow tax is vulnerable to abuse, because fake bills also lead to an immediate tax refund. Value added tax systems that allow an input tax reduction are confronted with the same problems. Fourth, cross-border taxation can cause problems. Purchase of fixed assets in high-tax countries and shifting them to low-tax countries diminishes national tax revenue.

One further argument that might negatively affect the decision of implementing a cash flow based tax system, is the transition period. When the new cash flow tax base is first applied, there are assets that have not enjoyed immediate write-off yet, however, future cash flows generated by these assets are comprehensively subject to tax. On the contrary, assets bought after the tax reform are immediately deductible. One might argue that all assets enjoy an immediate write-off of their current book values when the new system is implemented. This option might jeopardize national tax revenues if no step-by-step deductibility is granted in the transition process.

5.2.6 Flows of Funds

This section deals with the categorization of flows of funds. The neutral cash flow tax is also known as taxation of the flow-of-funds base. Cash flows arise in different sections of a company. Table 5.2 suggests how cash flows might be categorized.

This categorization was first proposed by the *Meade Committee* [14]. First, there are cash inflows – marked with the superscript *in* – and cash outflows – marked with the superscript *out*. Second, we distinguish cash flow elements assigned to real items (R), financial items (F), share items (S), and tax items (T).

Cash flow elements of real items are purchases and sales of goods, services, and fixed assets. Changes in cash on account of financial transactions – e.g., changes in debtor's or creditor's positions – including changes in holding of shares in foreign corporate bodies and yields based on these shares, are represented by F elements. Dividend payments and transactions in domestic corporate shares are covered by S items. Taxes paid and tax refunds are considered as T elements.

Implementing a cash flow tax leaves a broad scope in designing the tax system, because several types of cash flow taxes are known. The most common categories are the R-base cash flow tax as defined by *Brown* [3], the R+F-base cash flow tax and the S-base cash flow tax defined by the *Meade Committee* [14].

5.2.6.1 An R-Base Cash Flow Tax

The R-base cash flow tax grants an immediate write-off of real investments. Financial assets are considered as not existent for tax purposes. Thus, the company's investment decisions concerning financial investments are not distorted by taxation at all. Neither borrowing or lending and amortization, respectively, nor yields or interest payments on debt are taxed or deductible for tax purposes.

Table 5.2 Corporate flow of funds

Inflows		Outflows	
Real items			
R_1^{in}	Sale of produce	R_1^{out}	Purchase of materials
R_2^{in}	Sale of services	R_2^{out}	Wages, salaries and purchase of other services
R_3^{in}	Sale of fixed assets	R_3^{out}	Purchase of fixed assets
R^{in}		R^{out}	
Financial items other than shares of domestic corporate bodies			
F_1^{in}	Increase in creditors	F_1^{out}	Decrease in creditors
F_2^{in}	Decrease in debtors	F_2^{out}	Increase in debtors
F_3^{in}	Increase in overdraft	F_3^{out}	Decrease in overdraft
F_4^{in}	Decrease in cash balance	F_4^{out}	Increase in cash balance
F_5^{in}	Increase in other borrowing	F_5^{out}	Decrease in other borrowing
F_6^{in}	Decrease in other lending	F_6^{out}	Increase in other lending
F_7^{in}	Interest received	F_7^{out}	Interest paid
F_8^{in}	Decrease in holding of shares in foreign corporate bodies	F_8^{out}	Increase in holding of shares in foreign corporate bodies
F^{in}		F^{out}	
Share items of domestic corporate bodies			
S_1^{in}	Increase in own shares issued	S_1^{out}	Decrease in own shares issued
S_2^{in}	Decrease in holding of shares in other domestic corporate bodies	S_2^{out}	Increase in holding of shares in other domestic corporate bodies
S_3^{in}	Dividends received from other domestic corporate bodies	S_3^{out}	Dividends paid
S^{in}		S^{out}	
Tax items			
T^{in}	Tax refund	T^{out}	Tax paid
$R^{in} + F^{in} + S^{in} + T^{in} =$ Total inflows	$\Leftrightarrow$	$R^{out} + F^{out} + S^{out} + T^{out} =$ Total outflows	

Source: Based on *Meade Committee* [14], p. 231.

An R-base cash flow tax is the one described in (5.10). Returns of real investments are fully taxable and initial costs are immediately deductible. Further, a pre-tax discount rate is used, suggesting no tax on financial investments. As stated earlier, the tax system can be interpreted as tax authorities acquiring a stake in the company to the amount of immediate tax refund due to the immediate write-off. The stake the government wishes to have, therefore can be managed by the level of the tax rate. The greater the tax rate, the greater the stake, and the greater the stake on future returns.

One substantial lack of an R-base cash flow system – beside the general problems of a cash flow based taxation discussed earlier – is the perceived inequality in the taxation of industry sectors. As financial institutions do not have any R elements, but solely fully tax deductible F elements, no taxes are levied on financial institutions.

5.2.6.2 An (R+F)-Base Cash Flow Tax

An (R+F)-base cash flow tax does not distinct between elements of real and financial items. In this case, the excess of interest payments received and interest paid on debt is subject to tax. Companies have to pay taxes on interest payments received, however, interest payments on debt then are fully deductible. Referring to Table 5.2, our new tax base would be defined as:

$$TB = \left[(R^{in} + F^{in}) - (R^{out} + F^{out})\right].$$

5.2.6.3 An S-Base Cash Flow Tax

If we consider cash flow items of Table 5.2, we will see that net cash inflows and outflows of real and financial items have to be equal to net cash inflows and outflows of share and tax items. I.e., the net of cash in- and outflows are distributed between shareholders and the tax authority. We already defined that the government is a stakeholder in the company on the occasion of a cash flow tax. Formally, the condition must satisfy

$$(R^{in} + F^{in}) - (R^{out} + F^{out}) = (S^{out} - S^{in}) + (T^{out} - T^{in}).$$

Remember our statement at the very beginning of this book on p. 8, where we defined the company as being nothing else than an investment vehicle. Now, it should be clear why future cash flow returns are split up between the government and the investor. Under the S-base tax, transactions within the corporate sector are not taxable and only transactions between shareholders and corporations are subject to tax.[9] Dividends and withdrawals are fully taxable on the shareholder's level. Figure 5.1 illustrates the functionality of an S-base cash flow tax.

Compared to an R-base or (R+F)-base cash flow tax, an S-base cash flow tax seems favorable, because documentation requirements and compliance costs are lower.

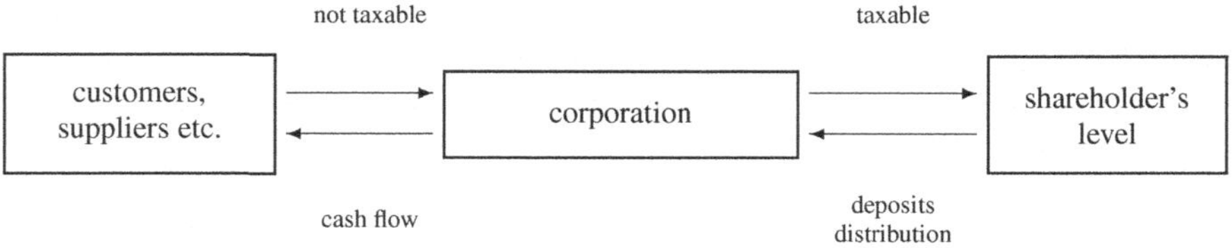

Fig. 5.1 Functionality of an S-base cash flow tax
Source: Based on *Knirsch/Niemann* [12], p. 105.

[9] See *Knirsch/Niemann* [12].

5.3 Allowance for Corporate Equity Tax (ACE Tax)

Knowing the main problems of a cash flow tax, we need to seek for a neutral tax system that can be implemented without changing the complete legal framework. The allowance for corporate equity tax (ACE tax) solves this problem. The ACE tax was developed by *Boadway/Bruce* [2].

5.3.1 The Model

In Germany, the allowance for corporate equity tax was introduced by *Wenger* [23]. Simultaneously, it was introduced to the international scientific community by *Boadway/Bruce* [2].

The ACE tax is an interest-adjusted income tax system that taxes the economic value added (EVA) instead of profits. Only returns that exceed the opportunity costs of capital are included in the tax base. This tax base is also known as "pure profit", "residual income", "economic profit", "economic income", or "economic rent". As it is only a transformation of the cash flow tax, it is a consumption-based tax system. The design of the present (tax or financial) accounting system remains unchanged, no matter if IFRS, US-GAAP, or local GAAP are used. In contrast to the cash flow tax, assets are depreciated over time. Problems arising because of accruals are remedied by means of the well-known Preinreich–Lücke Theorem.[10] The Preinreich–Lücke Theorem states that the present value PV of residual income equals the present value of cash flows

$$PV(\text{residual income}) = PV(\text{cash flow}) \tag{5.28}$$

as far as the congruence principle holds true. The principle states that the sum of residual profits has to be equivalent to the sum of cash flows over time.

If income according to IFRS, US-GAAP, or local GAAP is reduced by the interest on the fixed capital of the preceding year $t-1$ then present value of this adjusted income will equal the present value of cash flows ($= NPV$).

Example 5.10. The Preinreich–Lücke Theorem

Assume the following cash flow stream

t	0	1	2	3	4
CF_t	$-1,000.00$	300.00	400.00	500.00	600.00

[10] See *Preinreich* [15].

The interest rate is assumed to be $i = 5\%$. The pre-tax net present value gives

$$NPV = -1{,}000 + \frac{300}{1.05} + \frac{400}{1.05^2} + \frac{500}{1.05^3} + \frac{600}{1.05^4} = 574.07.$$

Taking the Preinreich–Lücke Theorem into account, the net present value of the residual income (RI) has to be equal to the net present value. The residual income is calculated as profits (P) less imputed interest (II) based on the fixed capital of the previous period (F_{t-1}).

$$RI_t = P_t - i \times F_{t-1}, \tag{5.29}$$

where F_{t-1} is the difference of the sum of profits up to $t-1$ less cash flows up to $t-1$. F_{t-1} is calculated as:

$$F_{t-1} = \sum_{k=0}^{t-1} P_k - \sum_{k=0}^{t-1} (CIF_k - COF_k), \tag{5.30}$$

with $F_{-1} = 0$. Assuming straight-line depreciation ($D_t = \frac{I_0}{n} = 250$), the following financial plan is derived:

t	0	1	2	3	4
CF_t	−1,000.00	300.00	400.00	500.00	600.00
D_t		250.00	250.00	250.00	250.00
P_t		50.00	150.00	250.00	350.00
F_t	1,000.00	750.00	500.00	250.00	0.00
$i \times F_{t-1}$		50.00	37.50	25.00	12.50
RI_t		0.00	112.50	225.00	337.50
$RI_t \times q^{-t}$		0.00	102.04	194.36	277.66
$PVRI$	574.07				

Fixed assets in $t = 1$ are calculated according to (5.30). In this example, the value of fixed assets is always equivalent to the book value of the assets bought in $t = 0$. The present value of the residual income ($PVRI$) equals the net present value of the investment

$$PVRI = \frac{0.00}{1.05} + \frac{112.50}{1.05^2} + \frac{225.00}{1.05^3} + \frac{337.50}{1.05^4} = 574.07.$$

Note that the result is independent of the allocation of the initial costs over the economic life-time. Assume depreciation to be $D_1 = 400$ and $D_t = D_{t-1} - 100$ for $t = 2, 3, 4$. Then we get

t	0	1	2	3	4
CF_t	−1,000.00	300.00	400.00	500.00	600.00
D_t		400.00	300.00	200.00	100.00
P_t		−100.00	100.00	300.00	500.00
F_t	1,000.00	600.00	300.00	100.00	0.00
$i \times F_{t-1}$		50.00	30.00	15.00	5.00
RI_t		−150.00	70.00	285.00	495.00
$RI_t \times q^{-t}$		−142.86	63.49	246.19	407.24
$PVRI$	574.07				

And again, the present value of the residual income equals the net present value.

Calculating the net present value in case of the allowance for corporate equity tax ($NPV^{\tau,ACE}$), we get

$$\begin{aligned} NPV^{\tau,ACE} &= \sum_{t=0}^{n}\left(CF_t - \tau \times \left(\underbrace{P_t - i \times F_{t-1}}_{EVA}\right)\right) \times q^{-t} \\ &= \sum_{t=0}^{n}\left(CF_t - \tau \times \left(\underbrace{CF_t + (F_t - F_{t-1})}_{P_t} - i \times F_{t-1}\right)\right) \times q^{-t} \\ &= \sum_{t=0}^{n} CF_t \times q^{-t} - \tau \times \sum_{t=0}^{n} (CF_t + (F_t - F_{t-1} \times (1+i))) \times q^{-t} \\ &= NPV - \tau \times NPV \\ &= (1-\tau) \times NPV. \end{aligned} \tag{5.31}$$

The proof for (5.31) will be given later. In case of the ACE tax, the tax base is defined as the economic value added which is calculated as operating profit P_t less imputed interest on the fixed capital of the previous period ($i \times F_{t-1}$). The result shows that the $NPV^{\tau,ACE}$ is also a linear transformation of the net present value before taxes. The result of (5.31) also proves that the ACE tax is nothing else than a cash flow tax. In other words, the schedule of depreciation allowances does not affect post-tax net present value. Because the schedule of depreciation allowances is irrelevant, an immediate write-off might also be possible, which is the case at a flow-of-funds base for taxation or cash flow taxation. Again, interpreting the result leads to the insight that in a cash flow tax system and an ACE tax system, total investment is taxed. Even though tax is levied annually, the present value of tax due to the investment project only reflects tax on the total present value of economic profits.

Fixed capital at the end of $t-1$ (F_{t-1}) is defined as fixed capital at the beginning of t consisting of all cash outflows which have not yet been recognized as expenses (EXP) plus all recognized earnings (ER) up to that period not being cash inflows. Technically, F_{t-1} can be described as:

$$\begin{aligned} F_{t-1} &= \sum_{k=0}^{t-1}(COF_k - EXP_k) + \sum_{k=0}^{t-1}(ER_k - CIF_k) \\ &= \sum_{k=0}^{t-1}(ER_k - EXP_k) - \sum_{k=0}^{t-1}(CIF_k - COF_k) \\ &= \sum_{k=0}^{t-1} P_k - \sum_{k=0}^{t-1} CF_k \\ &\text{with} \quad F_{-1} = 0, F_n = 0. \end{aligned}$$

It still has to be proved that $P_t = CF_t + (F_t - F_{t-1})$. The change in fixed capital is

$$\begin{aligned} F_t - F_{t-1} &= \sum_{k=0}^{t} P^k - \sum_{k=0}^{t} CF^k - \sum_{k=0}^{t-1} P^k + \sum_{k=0}^{t-1} CF^k = P_t - CF_t \\ &\Leftrightarrow \\ P_t &= CF_t + (F_t - F_{t-1}). \end{aligned}$$

We want to prove the following equation used in (5.31)

$$\sum_{t=0}^{n}(CF_t + (F_t - F_{t-1} \times (1+i))) \times q^{-t} = \sum_{t=0}^{n} CF_t \times q^{-t} = NPV.$$

Proof.

$$\begin{aligned} &\sum_{t=0}^{n}(CF_t + (F_t - F_{t-1} \times (1+i))) \times q^{-t} \\ &\quad = \sum_{t=0}^{n} CF_t \times q^{-t} - (1+i) \times \sum_{t=0}^{n} F_{t-1} \times q^{-t} + \sum_{t=0}^{n} F_t \times q^{-t} \\ &\quad \text{with } F_{-1} = 0; F_n = 0 \\ &\quad = \sum_{t=0}^{n} CF_t \times q^{-t} - (1+i) \times \sum_{t=1}^{n+1} F_{t-1} \times q^{-t} + \sum_{t=0}^{n} F_t \times q^{-t} \end{aligned}$$

$$= \sum_{t=0}^{n} CF_t \times q^{-t} - \sum_{t=1}^{n+1} F_{t-1} \times q^{-(t-1)} + \sum_{t=0}^{n} F_t \times q^{-t}$$

$$= \sum_{t=0}^{n} CF_t \times q^{-t} - \sum_{t=0}^{n} F_t \times q^{-t} + \sum_{t=0}^{n} F_t \times q^{-t}$$

$$= \sum_{t=0}^{n} CF_t \times q^{-t} = NPV.$$

□

Example 5.11. ACE Tax

This example is based on Ex. 5.7 on p. 171. There is a sole proprietorship and the proprietor makes a contribution to capital of € 1,000 in $t = 0$. The money is used to buy a machine immediately ($I_0 = 1{,}000$). The future cash flow is:

t	0	1	2	3	4
CF_t	−1,000	460	360	260	220

At the end of each period, the investor withdraws all cash after taxes. The marginal tax rate is assumed to be $\tau = 30\%$, the interest rate accounts for $i = 8\%$. Moreover, straight-line depreciation is assumed. At first, an immediate full loss offset is assumed. According to these assumptions, using a financial plan, after-tax cash flows at the end of each period are

t	0	1	2	3	4
CF_t	−1,000	460	360	260	220
D_t		250	250	250	250
P_t		210	110	10	−30
F_{t-1}		1,000	750	500	250
$i \times F_{t-1}$		80	60	40	20
TB_t		130	50	−30	−50
T_t		39	15	−9	−15
CF_t^τ	−1,000	421	345	269	235

$$NPV^{\tau,ACE} = -1{,}000 + \frac{421}{1.08} + \frac{345}{1.08^2} + \frac{269}{1.08^3} + \frac{235}{1.08^4}$$
$$= 71.87 = (1-\tau) \times NPV.$$

The fixed capital of the previous period accounts for

$$F_{t-1} = \sum_{k=0}^{t-1} P_k - \sum_{k=0}^{t-1} CF_k$$

$$F_0 = 0 - [-1{,}000] = 1{,}000$$

$$F_1 = 0 + 210 - [-1{,}000 + 460] = 750$$

$$F_2 = 0 + 210 + 110 - [-1{,}000 + 460 + 360] = 500$$

$$F_3 = 0 + 210 + 110 + 10 - [-1{,}000 + 460 + 360 + 260] = 250$$

$$F_4 = 0 + 210 + 110 + 10 - 30 - [-1{,}000 + 460 + 360 + 260 + 220] = 0.$$

(a) Accounting records in $t = 0$:
1. Contribution to capital:

Dr	cash account	1,000			
			Cr	equity	1,000

2. Buying the machine:

Dr	plant & equipment	1,000			
			Cr	cash account	1,000

(b) Accounting records in $t = 1$:
1. Sales:

Dr	cash account	460			
			Cr	sales revenue	460

2. Depreciation of the machine:

Dr	depreciation	250			
			Cr	plant & equipment	250

3. Imputed interest:

Dr	imputed interest	80			
			Cr	equity	80

4. Taxes are paid:

Dr	tax expense	39			
			Cr	cash account	39

(c) Closings entries at $t = 1$:

1. Closing plant & equipment which amounts to initial cost less depreciation in $t = 1$:

Dr	balance sheet	750			
			Cr	plant & equipment	750

2. Closing the sales revenue account to the profit and loss account:

Dr	revenue	460			
			Cr	P&L	460

3. Closing the depreciation account to the profit and loss account:

Dr	P&L	250			
			Cr	depreciation	250

4. Closing the tax expense account to the profit and loss account:

Dr	P&L	39			
			Cr	tax expense	39

5. Closing the imputed interest account to the profit and loss account:

Dr	P&L	80			
			Cr	imputed interest	80

6. Closing the profit and loss account to the equity account:

Dr	P&L	91			
			Cr	equity	91

7. Withdrawal of all cash flow after taxes:

Dr	equity	421			
			Cr	cash account	421

Imputed interest in the annual statement:

P&L

depreciation	250	revenue	460
tax expense	39		
imputed interest	80		
profit (equity)	*91*		

Equity

cash account	421	plant & equipment	1,000
		imputed interest	80
		P&L	91
balance sheet	*750*		

In contrast to a pure cash flow tax system, the items' values at the final balance sheet may deviate from zero.

Final balance sheet (t = 1)

plant & equipment	750	equity	750
bank (cash)	0		
total assets	*750*	*total equity and liabilities*	*750*

As you can see, equity at the end of $t = 1$ is equivalent to F_1.

Example 5.12. ACE Tax with Loss Offset Restrictions

This example is based on Ex. 5.11. However, now depreciation in $t = 1$ is assumed to be 70% of the initial investment, $0.7 \times 1{,}000 = 700$. The remaining book value is straight-line depreciated over the economic life-time.

Moreover, we cancel the assumption of an immediate full loss offset for tax purposes.[11] In the following, we assume an unlimited loss carry forward LCF_t with no time restriction. This means that no tax refund is granted in case of losses. If losses occur, the tax liability is zero. The loss is carried forward and can be offset in the following periods. Loss offsets LO_t are deductible to the amount of future adjusted gross income AGI_t. AGI_t stands for adjusted

[11] Loss offset restrictions are discussed in more detail in Sect. 7.4 beginning on p. 275.

gross income and represents the taxable income TB_t before consideration of a loss offset

$$AGI_t = CF_t - D_t - i \times F_{t-1}.$$

t	0	1	2	3	4
CF_t	−1,000.00	460.00	360.00	260.00	220.00
D_t		700.00	100.00	100.00	100.00
P_t		−240.00	260.00	160.00	120.00
F_{t-1}		1,000.00	620.00	309.60	100.00
$i \times F_{t-1}$		80.00	49.60	24.77	8.00
AGI_t		−320.00	210.40	135.23	112.00
LCF_t		320.00	109.60		
LO_t			210.40	109.60	
TB_t		0.00	0.00	25.63	112.00
T_t		0.00	0.00	7.69	33.60
CF_t^τ	−1,000.00	460.00	360.00	252.31	186.40

$$\begin{aligned} NPV^{\tau,ACE} &= -1{,}000.00 + \frac{460.00}{1.08} + \frac{360.00}{1.08^2} + \frac{252.31}{1.08^3} + \frac{186.40}{1.08^4} \\ &= 71.87 = (1-\tau) \times NPV. \end{aligned}$$

The variable loss carry forward LCF_t consists of the loss carry forward of the previous period less negative AGI_t less the deductible loss offset LO_t

$$LCF_t = LCF_{t-1} - \min\{AGI_t; 0\} - LO_t.$$

The deductible loss offset is restricted to positive AGI_t on the one hand, and the loss carry forward on the other hand.

$$LO_t = \min\{LCF_{t-1}; \max\{AGI_t; 0\}\}.$$

The general problem is to calculate the fixed capital in case of losses. Let's have a look at $t = 1$. Fixed capital in $t = 1$ accounts for

$$F_1 = 0 - 240 + 320 - [-1{,}000 + 460] = 620.$$

Why is the amount of 320 added? The reason for this is quite simple. As the negative adjusted gross income has not yet been relevant for taxation, the investor has an asset of $LCF_1 = 320$ which increases his fixed capital.

Let's have a look at the final balance sheet in $t = 1$.

Final balance sheet (t = 1)

plant & equipment	300	equity	620
loss carry forward	320		
total assets	*620*	*total equity and liabilities*	*620*

Total equity equals $F_1 = 620$.

Now consider $t = 2$. F_2 is calculated as:

$$F_2 = 0 - 240 + 320 + (260 - 210.40) - [-1{,}000 + 460 + 360] = 309.60.$$

Operating profits in $t = 2$ account for $P_2 = 260$. However, part of the loss from $t = 1$ carried over to $t = 2$ is deducted in $t = 2$. This amount causes tax expenses, reduces the value of assets and therefore the fixed capital of the period. Fixed capital in $t = 3$ is

$$\begin{aligned} F_3 &= 0 - 240 + 320 + (260 - 210.40) + (160 - 109.60) \\ &\quad -[-1{,}000 + 460 + 360 + 260] \\ &= 100. \end{aligned}$$

$$\begin{aligned} F_4 &= 0 - 240 + 320 + (260 - 210.40) + (160 - 109.60) + 120 \\ &\quad -[-1{,}000 + 460 + 360 + 260 + 220] \\ &= 0. \end{aligned}$$

Based on these results, we can define F_{t-1} in case of loss offset restrictions as:

$$F_{t-1} = \sum_{k=0}^{t-1} P_k - \sum_{k=0}^{t-1} \min\{AGI_k; 0\} - \sum_{k=0}^{t-1} LO_k - \sum_{k=0}^{t-1} CF_k.$$

Example 5.13. ACE Tax and Provisions

This example is based on Ex. 5.11. Other than in Ex. 5.12, we still assume a full loss offset. Consider that the investor claims a provision (*PRO*) in $t = 2$ amounting to $PRO_2 = 40$ that is tax deductible. However, in $t = 4$ the provision will be released and therefore taxed.

t	0	1	2	3	4
CF_t	$-1,000.00$	460.00	360.00	260.00	220.00
D_t		250.00	250.00	250.00	250.00
PRO_t			-40.00		40.00
P_t		210.00	70.00	10.00	10.00
F_{t-1}		1,000.00	750.00	460.00	210.00
$i \times F_{t-1}$		80.00	60.00	36.80	16.80
TB_t		130.00	10.00	-26.80	-6.80
T_t		39.00	3.00	-8.04	-2.04
CF_t^τ	$-1,000.00$	421.00	357.00	268.04	222.04

The net present value is not affected by the provision. Again, it accounts for

$$\begin{aligned} NPV^{\tau,ACE} &= -1{,}000.00 + \frac{421.00}{1.08} + \frac{357.00}{1.08^2} + \frac{268.04}{1.08^3} + \frac{222.04}{1.08^4} \\ &= 71.87 = (1-\tau) \times NPV. \end{aligned}$$

The provision affects fixed capital in $t = 2$. Fixed capital decreases according to the amount of the provision. Hence, the imputed interest in $t = 3, 4$ is lower compared to Ex. 5.11.

Example 5.14. Equity and Debt Financing

This example is designed to show that opportunities for arbitrage between shareholder level and company level are reduced in a world with an ACE tax. The financial structure of an investment project – and hence the financial structure of the company – is not affected by taxation.

Suppose a shareholder holding 100% of the shares of a company that is endowed with € 1,000 of equity. The funds are used to buy nondepreciable assets. Now, the investor decides to carry out an additional investment with acquisition costs of $I_0 = 500$. For reasons of simplification, we assume again that the asset cannot be depreciated. Assuming an ACE tax, he has to decide between increasing capital stock or giving a shareholder loan to finance the acquisition costs.

In the case of increasing equity, he deposits cash of € 500. At the end of the year, profits of 200 arise from all investments made. Before dividend payout, the two balance sheets are given as:

Balance sheet opening

assets	1,000	equity	1,500
cash account	500		
total assets	*1,500*	*total equity and liabilities*	*1,500*

Balance sheet closing			
assets	1,500	equity	1,500
cash account	200	profit	200
total assets	*1,700*	*total equity and liabilities*	*1,700*

In the case of a shareholder loan, it is assumed that the interest rate of the loan equals the rate of allowance for corporate equity $i = 10\%$. At the beginning of the period, the investor also transfers €500. However, at the end of the year, the profit after interest is reduced by the interest on the loan of $500 \times 10\% = 50$. The balance sheets are:

Balance sheet opening			
assets	1,000	equity	1,000
cash account	500	debt	500
total assets	*1,500*	*total equity and liabilities*	*1,500*

Balance sheet closing			
assets	1,500	equity	1,000
cash account	150	profit	150
		debt	500
total assets	*1,650*	*total equity and liabilities*	*1,650*

Now, we assume a tax rate of 40% on the corporate level and 20% on the personal level. And moreover, if dividends and interest are tax exempt – which is a characteristic of an ACE tax – the overall tax burden is

	equity financing	*debt financing*
profit	200	150
equity	1,500	1,000
imputed interest	150	100
tax base	50	50
tax	20	20

As we can see, it does not matter if the investment project is financed by equity or debt. However, we see where problems might arise in practice. The example presented only holds true if the interest rate on the loan is equal to the imputed interest rate. But the problem of different lending and borrowing rates also exists in tax systems where no imputed interest is deductible.

The ACE tax differs from the cash flow tax because of the tax deductible expenses. In our standard case, deductible (noncash) expenses are $D_t + i \times F_{t-1}$ under the ACE tax, whereas the cash flow tax allows immediate depreciation. However, because of $\sum_{t=1}^{n}(D_t + i \times F_{t-1}) \times q^{-t} = I_0$, present values of deductions are equivalent. Therefore, investment neutrality of the ACE tax can be traced back to the cash flow tax. Compared to cash flow taxation, tax deductions under the ACE tax occur later.

5.3.2 Comparison of the ACE Tax with the Cash Flow Tax

Table 5.3 summarizes and compares important features of the two neutral tax systems "cash flow tax" and "allowance for corporate equity tax".

Table 5.3 Comparison of cash flow tax and ACE tax

	Cash flow tax	ACE tax
Taxation of target value?	Yes	Yes
Existence of accruals?	No	Irrelevance of accounting rules causing accruals
Taxation of financial assets	Immediate deductibility of all financial investments, full tax liability of investment including return; result: tax exemption of interest	Tax exemption of interest amounting to the capital market interest rate, full tax liability of exceeding interest
Impact on the investment's *NPV*	Linear transformation of the pre-tax *NPV* to the amount of $(1 - \tau)$	Linear transformation of the pre-tax *NPV* to the amount of $(1 - \tau)$
Problems in case of inflation?	None, because assets are immediately deducted → no need to allocate historical costs over the economic life	None, as tax exemption of the capital market interest rate is given, which includes a component of inflation
Relation to traditional tax accounting	Cash flow tax is realized regarding salaries and wages	Accrual accounting (with current rules), but with additional ACE
Problems with cross-border business operations?	Problem of abuse in case of business relocations, because immediate tax refunds are granted	None

5.3.3 Experiences with the ACE Tax in Practice

Several countries are applying an ACE tax or a variation of the ACE tax for business income. Later we describe selected examples. Other countries currently experiencing ACE taxes are Denmark, Sweden, Finland, and Brazil. The names for the ACE tax variations and for the imputed interest vary across countries.

Example 5.15. ACE Tax in Practice

A first approach to an ACE tax in practice based on the work of *Boadway/Bruce* [2] was described by *Devereux/Freeman* [5]. In practice, an ACE tax on corporate profits only makes sense if the tax system as a whole – including personal taxation – fulfills the conditions of investment neutrality.

ACE Tax in Croatia

After declaring its independence in 1991, Croatia implemented a new administration and had to think about a new tax system. German tax researchers *Gerd Rose*, *Franz W. Wagner*, and *Ekkehard Wenger* designed and implemented an ACE tax in Croatia in 1996.

The arguments toward an ACE based taxation in Croatia were[12]

1. No difficult depreciation rules are needed because the pattern of depreciation does not affect the present value of the profit tax payments (shown earlier).
2. No inflation adjustments are needed because there is no distortion as in conventional historical cost accounting systems. An important feature since Croatia experienced high inflation in the early 1990s.
3. Because an ACE tax provides symmetric taxation of debt and equity financing, no thin capitalization rules are needed to prevent companies from artificially designing their financial structure to minimize taxes.

The imputed interest rate (protective interest rate) increases from a 5% level in 1998 up to 11.2% in 2001. The increase to 11.2% was due to recession in Croatia. At that time the risk free interest rates varied between 10% and 15%.

Arguments of critics were

1. Overvalued companies benefit from excessive protected interest rate deductions.
2. International complications will arise if double tax treaties are not existent and foreign countries tax foreign-source income from Croatia applying a tax credit instead of exempting the foreign-source income.
3. Substantial complexity in practice resulting in significant extra effort in computing the tax base.
4. Loss of tax revenue by one third (due to recession).
5. Problems defining the correct protective interest rate.

---

[12] See *Keen/King* [10].

Because of political pressure, the Croatian ACE tax was abolished in 2001. One problem was the necessity of high statutory tax rates in case of an ACE tax. The underlying problem was that an ACE tax base is smaller compared to common income tax bases due to deduction of the imputed interest. To realize the same tax revenue, countries applying the ACE tax have to apply higher statutory tax rates. This causes no real problem, because the tax liability is not increasing, but the signaling function of statutory tax rates is important. Therefore, Croatia as a small country in a competitive environment decided to abolish the ACE tax. However, a positive judgement was provided by the International Monetary Fund (IMF).

ACE Tax Elements in Austria

From 2000 to 2004, Austria's tax system provided an allowance for an increase in equity for both new subscriptions of capital and retained earnings (Eigenkapitalzuwachsverzinsung). The main target of this "equity tax shield provision" was to generate an impact on the capital structure of firms. It was expected that introducing tax shields for equity and not only for debt would stimulate equity financing. Interest payments were still deductible. The applicable interest rate for fictitious interest deduction was fixed by the Austrian Minister of Finance. The rate corresponded to the average of secondary market yields for all issuers of the Austrian bond market during the year. In detail, the notional rates were 4.9% in 2000, 6.2% in 2001, 5.5% in 2002, 4.9% in 2003, and 4.23% in 2004.[13]

In 2005, the Austrian ACE tax was abolished. In comparison to a real ACE tax, allowing deduction of imputed interest on incremental equity rather than total equity worked less well.

ACE Characteristics in Italy

Lasting from 1997 to 2003, the Italian ACE system was restricted to notional interest on equity that was subscribed or retained after the tax reform in 1997.[14] The main feature of the Italian ACE system was a notional interest that qualified for a reduced corporate income tax rate rather than a deduction. In 2000, postreform new equity was decided to count 120% for notional interest computation, in order to move toward a system that qualifies total equity for notional interest. In 2001, the step-up was temporarily raised to 140% before it was cut back to 100%. Despite those restrictions, corporate income

[13] See *Frühwirth/Kobialka* [6], p. 7.
[14] See *Klemm* [11].

tax clearly qualified for a neutral ACE tax. Empirical studies show that due to the implemented ACE characteristics, leverage decreased as expected.[15]

Notional Interest Deduction in Belgium

As from 2007 (income 2006), corporations in Belgium are allowed to deduct a fictitious interest on equity from taxable profits.[16] As a characteristic of an ACE tax, there is an annual deduction from taxable income up to an amount equal to the interest they would have paid on equity in case of long-term debt financing. The rate of the "Notional Interest Deduction" is determined every year on the basis of the average interest rate for 10-year Belgian Government bonds. For year 2006-income, the rate was fixed at 3.442%.

The main objectives of the Belgian Government are

1. A reduction of the effective corporate tax rate and a corresponding higher after-tax return on investments,
2. Stimulation of capital intensive investments,
3. Opportunities for equity-funded, intercompany financing.

The "Notional Interest Deduction" is calculated on the basis of the equity as stated in the company's balance sheet according to Belgian accounting principles. However, adjustments have to be made, e.g., eliminating the net book value of the company's holding.

Norway's Elements of an ACE Tax

As effective of January 1, 2006 Norway implemented an ACE tax on share returns.[17] Personal tax is only levied on the equity premium, e.g., returns on shares exceeding the after-tax rate of return of government bonds. The imputed return – so-called Rate-of-Return-Allowance (RRA) – can be deducted from the shareholders income. If a fraction of profit is retained and hence the RRA might exceed dividends, the unutilized part can be carried forward. The following example illustrates how the Norwegian ACE tax works.

---

[15] See *Staderini* [21].

[16] See *Gérard* [8] and *Gérard* [7] for more details.

[17] See *Sørensen* [20] and *Alstadsæter/Fjærli* [1] as sources.

t	0	1	2
Equity (injection)	10,000	10,200	10,000
Profit after corporate income tax		500	510
Dividend		300	710
Retained earnings		200	
RRA (5% of equity)		500	510
Unutilized RRA carried forward		200	
Total RRA			710
Taxable dividend		0	0

Suppose in $t = 0$, a contribution to capital of Norwegian Krones (NOK) 10,000 occurs. The after-tax interest rate of government bonds as well the after-tax rate of return on corporate level is assumed to be 5%. Hence, in $t = 1$ profits after tax account for NOK 500. Now, if dividends amounting to NOK 300 are distributed, NOK 200 are retained and equity will increase by this amount. Because RRA is NOK 500 and dividends only are NOK 300, an unutilized RRA of NOK 200 is carried forward. No dividends are subject to tax in $t = 1$.

As equity is NOK 10,200 at the end of $t = 1$, profits after corporate taxes as well as RRA in $t = 2$ are NOK 10,200 $\times$ 0.05 = NOK 510. If all profits are distributed at the end of $t = 2$, basically dividends and retained earnings of NOK 710 will be subject to tax. However, RRA from $t = 1$ plus remaining RRA from $t = 2$ account for NOK 710, too. Again, dividends are not taxed.

5.3.4 Adjustments to Cash Flow Taxation Using Basic Elements of an ACE Tax

Compared with a traditional R-base tax, the S-base tax reduces the likelihood of tax fraud significantly, because tax reimbursement cannot occur if a modified version of an S-base tax is applied. Under the traditional S-base tax introduced by the *Meade Committee* [14] capital raised by shareholders leads to immediate tax reimbursements. This problem can be avoided, if deposits do not qualify for an immediate tax relief. Rather, deposits by shareholders should be subject to an allowance for shareholder equity that can be subtracted from future distributions or realized capital gains.[18]

[18] See *Knirsch/Niemann* [12], p. 108.

Example 5.16. Deferred Shareholder Tax

Building on the assumptions in Ex. 5.11 on p. 187 ($\tau = 30\%$ and $i = 8$), we assume an S-base cash flow tax as described in Sect. 5.2.6.3. However, it is additionally assumed that capital endowment is not tax deductible immediately according to the adjusted S-base tax developed by *Knirsch/Niemann* [12]. Cash flows are distributed immediately to the shareholder. Distributions (withdrawals) ($Dist_t$) to the shareholder are taxable if distribution exceeds compounded endowment or the equity account in $t-1$. Formally, the equity account EA at the end of t is calculated as capital endowment in t (CE_t) plus the compounded equity account after distribution from $t-1$ less the distribution in t

$$EA_t = \max\{(1+i) \times EA_{t-1} - Dist_t; 0\} \text{ in } t > 0,$$
$$EA_0 = CE_0.$$

Then the tax base is calculated as:

$$TB_t = \max\{Dist_t - EA_{t-1} \times (1+i); 0\}.$$

Using a financial plan and assuming the described adjusted S-base cash flow tax, post-tax NPV gives

t	0	1	2	3	4
$CF_t = Dist_t$		460.00	360.00	260.00	220.00
CE_t	1,000.00				
EA_t	1,000.00	620.00	309.60	74.37	0.00
TB_t		0.00	0.00	0.00	139.68
T_t		0.00	0.00	0.00	41.90
CF_t^τ	−1,000.00	460.00	360.00	260.00	178.10
NPV_t^τ	71.87				

$$NPV^\tau = -1{,}000 + \frac{460.00}{1.08} + \frac{360.00}{1.08^2} + \frac{260.00}{1.08^3} + \frac{178.10}{1.08^4}$$
$$= 71.87 = (1-\tau) \times NPV.$$

The same idea can be applied to an R-base cash flow tax. One common problem of an R-base cash flow tax are fluctuating tax revenues for the government. Especially, in periods with high-investment expenditure, negative tax revenues might occur. This problem could be solved by implementing loss offset restrictions. However, in case of loss carry forwards, the compounded value of the losses is deductible in future periods. Basically, the result is the same as for the deferred shareholder tax described earlier.

Example 5.17. Adjusted R-base Tax

Apply the same assumptions concerning tax rate, cash flow stream, and interest rate as in Ex. 5.16. If we consider an R-base cash flow tax, initial costs will be immediately tax deductible and hence result in a tax refund. However, if we assume initial costs to be compoundable loss carry forwards, the loss carry forward is defined as:

$$LCF_t = LCF_{t-1} \times (1 + i) - \min\{CF_t; 0\} - LO_t,$$

where $LCF_{-1} = 0$. Loss offset is calculated as:

$$LO_t = \min\{LCF_{t-1} \times (1 + i); \max\{CF_t; 0\}\}.$$

Based on these assumptions, the post-tax net present value gives

t	0	1	2	3	4
CF_t	−1,000.00	460.00	360.00	260.00	220.00
LCF_t	1,000.00	620.00	309.60	74.37	0.00
LO_t		460.00	360.00	260.00	80.32
TB_t	0.00	0.00	0.00	0.00	139.68
T_t		0.00	0.00	0.00	41.90
CF_t^τ		460.00	360.00	260.00	178.10
NPV_t^τ	71.87				

Note, the result $NPV_t^\tau = 71.87$ is the same as in Ex. 5.16.

5.4 Johansson/Samuelson Tax

The previous sections discuss neutral tax systems that provide a tax exempt interest yield up to the capital market interest ($i^\tau = i$). But does a neutral tax system exist in which returns on real and financial investments are fully taxable? In this case, the discount rate would not be $i^\tau = i$ as for the cash flow tax and the ACE tax, but $i^\tau = i \times (1 - \tau)$ implying that the discount rate after taxes is applied. These conditions are true in case the "true economic profit" is taxed. This concept is also known as the Johansson/Samuelson tax.[19] The "economic concept of income" was described in Sect. 2.3.2. Deducting economic depreciation for tax purposes leads to

[19] See *Samuelson* [16] and *Johansson* [9].

a taxation of the "true economic profit". The resulting tax base is the yield based on the present value of the previous period which in turn is the economic profit.

The economic profit EP_t can be interpreted as the return on the investment's value in each period. The value of the investment is calculated as discounted future cash flows and is already known as present value PV_t. The return is calculated based on the capital market interest rate i. The tax base equals $i \times PV_{t-1}$. Therefore, the Johansson/Samuelson income concept deviates fundamentally from traditional income concepts. Income concepts we know in business practice are backward oriented, while the Johannson/Samuelson tax is based on future cash flows.

Let's derive why the Johansson/Samuelson tax works. The condition that must hold true in order to get a neutral tax system in which the discount rate after taxes is applied, is the level invariance of the target value before and after taxation. Hence

$$NPV = NPV^{\tau}. \tag{5.32}$$

To meet condition (5.32), the real investment has to be taxed equivalent to the alternative financial investment, implying numerator and denominator of the net present value formula have to be reduced by the same factor.

$$\frac{CF_t}{(1+i)^t} \quad \text{evolves to} \quad \frac{(1-\tau) \times CF_t}{(1+i \times (1-\tau))^t}.$$

The condition for equivalence of pre-tax and post-tax net present value, therefore, is

$$\begin{aligned} NPV &= NPV^{\tau} \\ -I_0 + \sum_{t=1}^{n} \frac{CF_t}{(1+i)^t} &= -I_0 + \sum_{t=1}^{n} \frac{CF_t - \tau \times (CF_t - D_t)}{(1+i \times (1-\tau))^t}. \end{aligned} \tag{5.33}$$

Considering the left and right-hand side of (5.33), the sole problem to meet this condition is depreciation. What does D_t account for? If we subtract post-tax net present value from pre-tax net present value, we must get zero

$$\Delta NPV^{\tau} = NPV - NPV^{\tau} \stackrel{!}{=} 0.$$

Then we get

$$\begin{aligned} \Delta NPV^{\tau} &= \sum_{t=1}^{n} CF_t \times q^{-t} - \sum_{t=1}^{n} [CF_t - \tau \times (CF_t - D_t)] \times (q^{\tau})^{-t} \\ &= \sum_{t=1}^{n} CF_t \times (q^{-t} - (q^{\tau})^{-t}) + \tau \times \sum_{t=1}^{n} (CF_t - D_t) \times (q^{\tau})^{-t} \\ &\qquad \text{factoring out } -q^{-t} \end{aligned}$$

$$= -\sum_{t=1}^{n} CF_t \times q^{-t} \times \left(\left(\frac{q}{q^{\tau}} \right)^t - 1 \right)$$

$$+ \tau \times \sum_{t=1}^{n} (CF_t - D_t) \times (q^{\tau})^{-t} \qquad \text{expand with } \left(1 - \frac{q^{\tau}}{q}\right)$$

$$= -\left(1 - \frac{q^{\tau}}{q}\right) \times \sum_{t=1}^{n} CF_t \times q^{-t} \times \left(\frac{\left(\frac{q}{q^{\tau}}\right)^t - 1}{1 - \frac{q^{\tau}}{q}} \right)$$

$$+ \tau \times \sum_{t=1}^{n} (CF_t - D_t) \times (q^{\tau})^{-t}. \tag{5.34}$$

Now

$$\left(\frac{\left(\frac{q}{q^{\tau}}\right)^t - 1}{1 - \frac{q^{\tau}}{q}} \right)$$

looks similar to the present value factor of an annuity in arrears.[20] Therefore, we use the derivation of the present value factor of an annuity in arrears to get a simplification. If we start with

$$\sum_{k=1}^{t} \alpha^k = \psi = \alpha^1 + \alpha^2 + \alpha^3 + \ldots + \alpha^{t-1} + \alpha^t, \tag{5.35}$$

we get

$$\alpha^{-1} \times \psi = 1 + \alpha^1 + \alpha^2 + \ldots + \alpha^{t-2} + \alpha^{t-1} \tag{5.36}$$

by multiplying (5.35) with α^{-1}. Now subtracting (5.36) from (5.35) and solving for ψ gives

$$\psi - \alpha^{-1} \times \psi = \alpha^t - 1$$
$$\psi \times (1 - \alpha^{-1}) = \alpha^t - 1$$
$$\psi = \frac{\alpha^t - 1}{1 - \alpha^{-1}}.$$

We define

$$\alpha = \frac{q}{q^{\tau}}.$$

[20] See Sect. 2.4 on p. 19.

Consider (5.34). If

$$\left(\frac{\left(\frac{q}{q^{\tau}}\right)^{t}-1}{1-\frac{q^{\tau}}{q}}\right)$$

is replaced by

$$\sum_{k=1}^{t}\left(\frac{q}{q^{\tau}}\right)^{k}$$

we get

$$\begin{aligned}
\Delta NPV^{\tau} &= -\left(1-\frac{q^{\tau}}{q}\right)\times\sum_{t=1}^{n}CF_t\times q^{-t}\times\sum_{k=1}^{t}\left(\frac{q}{q^{\tau}}\right)^{k}+\tau\times\sum_{t=1}^{n}(CF_t-D_t)\times(q^{\tau})^{-t}\\
&= -\left(1-\frac{q^{\tau}}{q}\right)\times\sum_{t=1}^{n}\sum_{k=1}^{t}CF_t\times q^{-t+k}\times(q^{\tau})^{-k}+\tau\times\sum_{t=1}^{n}(CF_t-D_t)\times(q^{\tau})^{-t}\\
&= -(q-q^{\tau})\times\sum_{t=1}^{n}\sum_{k=1}^{t}CF_t\times q^{-t+k-1}\times(q^{\tau})^{-k}+\tau\times\sum_{t=1}^{n}(CF_t-D_t)\times(q^{\tau})^{-t}\\
&= -(q-q^{\tau})\times\sum_{k=1}^{n}\sum_{t=1}^{k}CF_k\times q^{-k+t-1}\times(q^{\tau})^{-t}+\tau\times\sum_{t=1}^{n}(CF_t-D_t)\times(q^{\tau})^{-t}\\
&= -(q-q^{\tau})\times\sum_{t=1}^{n}\sum_{k=t}^{n}CF_k\times q^{-k+t-1}\times(q^{\tau})^{-t}+\tau\times\sum_{t=1}^{n}(CF_t-D_t)\times(q^{\tau})^{-t}.
\end{aligned} \tag{5.37}$$

From (2.3) on p. 15 we know that

$$PV_{t-1}=\sum_{k=t}^{n}CF_k\times q^{-k+t-1}.$$

Moreover, we can transform $(q-q^{\tau})$ to $i\times\tau$. Implementing in (5.37) results in

$$\Delta NPV^{\tau}\overset{!}{=}0=\quad -i\times\tau\times\sum_{t=1}^{n}PV_{t-1}\times(q^{\tau})^{-t}+\tau\times\sum_{t=1}^{n}(CF_t-D_t)\times(q^{\tau})^{-t}. \tag{5.38}$$

We can derive

$$i\times PV_{t-1}=CF_t-ED_t \tag{5.39}$$

from (2.6), (2.7) and (2.8). (5.39) used for (5.38) results in

$$\tau \times \sum_{t=1}^{n}(CF_t - D_t) \times (q^\tau)^{-t} = \tau \times \sum_{t=1}^{n}(CF_t - ED_t) \times (q^\tau)^{-t}$$

$$\sum_{t=1}^{n}(CF_t - D_t) \times (q^\tau)^{-t} = \sum_{t=1}^{n}(CF_t - ED_t) \times (q^\tau)^{-t}$$

$$\sum_{t=1}^{n} D_t \times (q^\tau)^{-t} = \sum_{t=1}^{n} ED_t \times (q^\tau)^{-t}. \qquad (5.40)$$

Equation (5.40) shows that the present value of the depreciation of the initial acquisition costs over the economic life of the asset equals the present value of the economic depreciation. If this condition is true, we get $NPV = NPV^\tau$. However, this condition will only be met if τ stays constant over time. There is one exception. If τ varies over time, condition (5.40) is true in case depreciation equals economic depreciation in each period

$$D_t = ED_t \quad \forall t = 1, \ldots, T.$$

Example 5.18. Johansson/Samuelson Tax

Let's step back to the assumptions made in Ex. 5.7 on p. 171. The stream of cash flows is assumed to be

t	0	1	2	3	4
CF_t	−1,000.00	460.00	360.00	260.00	220.00

The tax rate is $\tau = 50\%$ and the interest rate accounts for $i = 8\%$. Hence, the discount rate after taxes is

$$i^\tau = 8\% \times (1 - 0.5) = 4\%.$$

Using a financial plan, cash flows after taxes CF_t^τ result in

t	0	1	2	3	4
CF_t	−1,000.00	460.00	360.00	260.00	220.00
PV_t	1,102.67	730.88	429.36	203.70	0.00
ED_t		371.79	301.53	225.65	203.70
$TB_t = EP_t$		88.21	58.47	34.35	16.30
T_t		44.11	29.24	17.17	8.15
CF_t^τ		415.89	330.76	242.83	211.85

To calculate present values, we have to use the pre-tax discount rate.

$$NPV^{\tau} = -1{,}000 + \frac{415.89}{1.04} + \frac{330.76}{1.04^2} + \frac{242.83}{1.04^3} + \frac{211.85}{1.04^4} = 102.67 = NPV.$$

The neutrality condition would still be met if the constant tax rate was, e.g., $\tau = 35\%$ and $i^{\tau} = 8\% \times (1 - 0.35) = 5.2\%$.

t	0	1	2	3	4
CF_t	−1,000.00	460.00	360.00	260.00	220.00
PV_t	1,102.67	730.88	429.36	203.70	0.00
ED_t		371.79	301.53	225.65	203.70
$TB_t = EP_t$		88.21	58.47	34.35	16.30
T_t		30.87	20.46	12.02	5.70
CF_t^{τ}		429.13	339.54	247.98	214.30

$$NPV^{\tau} = -1{,}000 + \frac{429.13}{1.052} + \frac{339.54}{1.052^2} + \frac{247.98}{1.052^3} + \frac{214.30}{1.052^4} = 102.67 = NPV.$$

Now, we know how the Johansson/Samuelson tax works. If the economic profit builds the tax base in a comprehensive income tax where business profits and interest income is taxed, the tax system will be neutral. Comparing this neutral tax system to current real tax systems, we understand why they are non-neutral and we understand why a tax paradox can occur. The most simple form of a model that reflects real tax systems is the Standard Model, which we discussed in Sect. 3.2 on p. 80. We already discussed an example of non-neutrality using the Standard Model without naming it: This was Ex. 3.10 on p. 97 which demonstrated the occurrence of a tax paradox.

In Sect. 3.4 we promised to formally derive the conditions that have to met that a tax paradox can occur. The condition for a tax paradox is that post-tax net present value exceeds pre-tax net present value. If the after-tax net present value has to be greater than the pre-tax present value for all tax rates in order to get an income tax paradox then formally the following condition will have to be met

$$\Delta NPV = NPV - NPV^{\tau} < 0. \tag{5.41}$$

Now (5.41) reminds us of the condition of (5.32) on p. 202. The same proof as for condition (5.32) is applicable for (5.41).[21] As a result, we get the condition corresponding to (5.40)

[21] See also *Schanz/Schanz* [17].

$$\sum_{t=1}^{n} D_t \times (q^\tau)^{-t} > \sum_{t=1}^{n} ED_t \times (q^\tau)^{-t}. \tag{5.42}$$

That is, the present value of the depreciation – discounted with the post-tax interest rate – has to be greater than the present value of the economic depreciation. In this case the tax paradox occurs, because depreciation allowances are more advantageous than under a neutral tax system. The condition in (5.42) only is true if the tax rate does not vary over time. However, there is one exception: If depreciation equals economic depreciation, the condition of (5.42) will also be true when the tax rates vary over time. In the case of $\Delta NPV = NPV - NPV^\tau > 0$, we get analogously

$$\sum_{t=1}^{n} D_t \times (q^\tau)^{-t} < \sum_{t=1}^{n} ED_t \times (q^\tau)^{-t}.$$

Questions

5.1. What different types of neutrality can be distinguished? Do these types of neutrality occur in your home country? Why? Why not?

5.2. Derive characteristics to categorize neutral tax systems into two main different types.

5.3. Why is a poll tax politically not desired? What were the main problems of the British Poll Tax?

5.4. Under what circumstances are taxes negligible in decision making?

5.5. Show in a formal way, why a cash flow tax does not affect the pre and post-tax rank order of the profitability of investments.

5.6. Can an income tax paradox occur in a cash flow tax system? Why?

5.7. How does the cash flow tax influence (a) the net present value, (b) the rate of return of investment projects?

5.8. What is the reason for using the pre-tax discount rate in case of a cash flow tax? What is meant by administrative simplification as a justification for applying the pre-tax discount rate?

5.9. Explain formally why tax exemption of interest and immediate write-off of financial investments is equivalent.

5.10. Does tax exemption of interest payments under a cash flow tax violate the condition of equal taxation of real and financial investments?

5.11. Discuss main differences between the cash flow tax and the ACE tax.

5.12. Using an own four-period example, explain why current depreciation can be applied under an ACE tax.

5.13. Explain equivalence of a cash flow tax and an ACE tax based on examples where (a) provisions, (b) deferred income, and (c) inventories are considered.

5.14. What problems do occur under a cash flow tax concerning (a) cross-border movements of individuals and (b) the end of life of individuals?

5.15. What similar problems exist in conventional (comprehensive income) tax systems and cash flow tax systems?

5.16. What changes would occur if a cash flow tax was implemented in your home country concerning (a) determination of labor income, (b) determination of income for small and medium-sized companies, and (c) determination of income according to financial accounting rules?

5.17. Assume a cash flow tax. How would (a) the exchange of assets between companies and (b) noncash benefits of employees be treated for tax purposes?

5.18. Considering investment and consumption decisions, what are the differences between conventional income tax systems and VAT systems, respectively?

5.19. What is the main problem of an R-base cash flow tax?

5.20. Why is the government called a "stakeholder" to private investments in case of a cash flow tax system?

5.21. What is meant by Preinreich–Lücke Theorem? Explain the theorem using an own four-period example.

5.22. Give a substantial explanation why taxing the economic profit leads to investment neutrality (Johansson/Samuelson tax).

5.23. Explain why there is no substantial difference between the cash flow tax and the ACE tax.

5.24. Regarding the taxation of economic profits, what is the level of depreciation in case of neutrality if an investment with infinite cash flows is taken into account?

5.25. Explain the difference between the cash flow tax and the ACE tax with regard to bank deposits with common interest.

5.26. Discuss the advantages and the disadvantages of an ACE tax in practice compared to a cash flow tax and taxation of economic profit (Johansson/Samuelson tax).

5.27. What kind of taxation is neutral regarding (a) work time/leisure time decisions, (b) choice of time of consumption and (c) investment decisions?

5.28. Why do tax systems usually tax an individual's objective?

5.29. Explain why on the one hand taxation of labor income usually can be characterized as taxation of an individual's objective and on the other hand taxation of income according to financial accounting does not fulfill the requirement to tax an individual's objective.

5.30. Who might be interested in implementing a decision neutral tax system? Why?

5.31. What tasks of tax accountants would be obsolete, what fields would remain in an environment of neutral taxation?

Exercises

Solutions are provided starting on p. 394.

5.32. Cash Flow Tax and Fisher–Hirshleifer Model

Suppose two investors A and B with an initial endowment of $W_0 = 200$ each, that face the following utility functions

$$U^A(C_0, C_1) = C_0^3 \times C_1$$
$$U^B(C_0, C_1) = C_0 \times C_1^3.$$

The pre-tax real investment function is

$$f(I_0) = 20 \times \sqrt{I_0}.$$

It is assumed that total cash is consumed by the end of $t = 1$. The lending and borrowing rate is $i = 10\%$ and $\tau = 30\%$. Determine the post-tax real investment function in case of a cash flow tax. Determine optimal C_0, C_1, I_0, F_0, and NPV^τ for both investors, in case a cash flow tax is applied. Compare your results with the results of Exercise 2.46 from p. 75.

5.33. Cash Flow Tax and ACE Tax

You are an entrepreneur and endowed with equity of €250,000. A real investment alternative generating the following cash flow stream is given

t	0	1	2	3	4	5
CF_t	–250,000	80,000	112,500	150,000	180,000	200,000

Applying the straight-line method, acquisition costs are spread over a period of 5 years. The interest rate is supposed to be 9%. Your marginal tax rate is 45%. Interest income is taxed by applying a flat tax of 25%. Please assume that after-tax cash flows are withdrawn at the end of each period.

(a) Calculate the before-tax net present value and the modified rate of return. Which investment is carried out?
(b) Now, determine the after-tax net present value.
(c) What does the after-tax net present value amount to in case of a cash flow tax with a tax rate of 45%?
(d) Compute the modified rate of return based on the assumptions in (c).
(e) Now, imagine you are resident in a country where an allowance for corporate equity tax system (ACE) with a tax rate of 45% is applied. Set up the complete financial plan for the investment alternative above and calculate the after-tax net present value. This financial plan must at least include the fixed capital in each period as well as the resulting tax base for this tax system. Please explain in your own words why an ACE tax simply is a transformation of a cash flow tax (a mathematic derivation is not required).
(f) In case of a consumption-based tax system, it does not matter whether the financial investment is taxed or not. Please demonstrate and explain this statement.

5.34. ACE Tax and Losses

Assume the following pre-tax cash flow stream of a real investment alternative

t	0	1	2	3
CF_t	–900,000	200,000	700,000	800,000

The interest rate is be 5%. The marginal tax rate for real and financial investment income is 30%. Moreover, straight-line depreciation is applied.

(a) Determine the pre-tax net present value.
(b) Determine the post-tax net present value, in case an ACE tax with immediate full loss offset is applied.
(c) In $t = 2$, a provision of €200,000 is deducted for tax purposes and released in $t = 3$ to the same amount. A full immediate loss offset is applied. Determine the post-tax net present value in case of an ACE tax.
(d) Use the same assumptions as in (c), however, restricted loss offset rules are applied. Losses are deductible up to the positive amount of adjusted gross income. Losses that cannot be deducted due to this restriction are carried over to the following periods with no time restriction. Determine the post-tax net present value.

5.35. Adjusted Cash Flow Tax

Suppose $\tau = 40\%$, $i = 6\%$ and the following stream of cash flows.

t	0	1	2	3	4
$CF_t = W_t$	–1,200	–200	400	600	800

Cash flows equal withdrawals in each period.

(a) Determine the pre-tax net present value.

(b) Assume an S-base cash flow tax as described in Sect. 5.2.6.3. Remember, capital endowments are not tax deductible immediately. Total cash is distributed immediately. Distributions (withdrawals) to the owner are taxable, in case distribution exceeds compounded contribution to capital. Calculate the post-tax net present value.

(c) Now, assume an adjusted R-base cash flow tax. Remember, negative cash flows result in a compounded loss carry forward. Loss offset is restricted to positive cash flows in t and the compounded loss carry forward from the previous period ($LCF_{-1} = 0$). Calculate the post-tax net present value.

5.36. ACE Tax and Cash Flow Tax

An investor has the opportunity to carry out a real investment. Acquisition costs in $t = 0$ are $I_0 = 900{,}000$ and future certain cash flows before taxes are $CF_t = 500{,}000$, $CF_2 = 200{,}000$, and $CF_3 = 500{,}000$. Both, borrowing and lending rates are $i = 10\%$; the marginal tax rate is $\tau = 50\%$. Cash flows after taxes are withdrawn at the end of each period.

(a) Determine the post-tax net present value in case of a cash flow tax.

(b) Determine the post-tax net present value in case of an ACE tax, if

- straight-line depreciation and
- immediate full loss offsets

are assumed.

(c) Now again assume an ACE tax and determine the post-tax net present value, if

- a special depreciation of 60% of initial costs can be claimed in $t = 1$; in $t = 2, 3$ depreciation is 20% annually,
- immediate full loss offsets, and
- no withdrawals in $t = 1, 2$ and maximum withdrawal in $t = 3$

are assumed.

(d) Determine the post-tax net present value in case of an ACE tax, if

- straight-line depreciation,
- immediate full loss offsets,
- no withdrawals in $t = 1, 2$ and maximum withdrawal in $t = 3$,
- a tax deductible provision of € 100,000 is claimed in $t = 2$ and released to the same amount in $t = 3$

are assumed.

(e) Now determine the post-tax net present value with the "Standard Model" assuming

- straight-line depreciation,
- immediate full loss offsets, and
- withdrawal of post-tax cash flow at the end of each year.

(f) Provide accounting records in $t = 2$ for (b)–(e).

(g) Explain the differences between the post-tax net present values in (b) and (e).

5.37. Johansson/Samuelson Tax

Suppose $\tau = 35\%$, $i = 4\%$ and a cash flow stream of

t	0	1	2	3	4
CF_t	–1,600	500	200	700	400

Cash flows after taxes at the end of each period are withdrawn.

(a) Determine the pre-tax net present value.
(b) Determine the post-tax net present value under a Johansson/Samuelson tax.
(c) Considering (b), what will happen, if τ changes to $\tau = 50\%$? Determine the corresponding financial plan.

References

1. Alstadsæter, A., Fjærli, E.: Neutral Taxation of Shareholder Income? Corporate Response to an Announced Dividend Tax. CESifo Working Paper No. 2530 (2009)
2. Boadway, R., Bruce, N.: A general proposition on the design of a neutral business tax. J. Public Econ. **24**(2), 231–239 (1984)
3. Brown, C.E.: Business-income taxation and investment incentives. In: Metzler, L.A. (ed.), Income, Employment, and Public Policy: Essays in Honor of Alvin H. Hansen, pp. 300–316, W.W. Norton & Co., New York (1948)
4. Cnossen, S., Bovenberg, L.: Fundamental tax reform in the Netherlands. Int. Tax Public Finance **8**(4), 471–484 (2001)
5. Devereux, M.P., Freeman, H.: A general neutral profits tax. Fiscal Stud. **12**(3), 1–15 (1991)
6. Frühwirth, M., Kobialka, M.: Do Equity Tax Shields Reduce Leverage? The Austrian Case. Working Paper Vienna University (2008)
7. Gérard, M.: Belgium moves to dual allowance for corporate equity. Eur. Tax. 156–162 (2006)
8. Gérard, M.: A closer look at Belgium's notional interest deduction. Tax Notes Int. **41**(5), 449–453 (2006a)
9. Johansson, S.-E.: Income taxes and investment decisions. Swedish J. Econ. **71**(2), 104–110 (1969)
10. Keen, M., King, J.: The croatian profit tax: an ACE in practice. Fiscal Stud. **23**(3), 401–418 (2002)
11. Klemm, A.: Allowances for corporate equity in practice. CESifo Econ. Stud. **53**(2), 229–262 (2007)
12. Knirsch, D., Niemann, R.: Deferred shareholder taxation – implementing a neutral business tax in the European Union. Account. Eur. **5**(2), 101–125 (2008)
13. König, R., Wosnitza, M.: Betriebswirtschaftliche Steuerplanungs- und Steuerwirkungslehre. Physica-Verlag, Heidelberg (2004)
14. Meade C. (ed.): The Structure and Reform of Direct Taxation. Report of a Committee chaired by Professor J. E. Meade, George Allen&Unwin, London (1978)
15. Preinreich, G.A.D.: Valuation and amortization. Account. Rev. **12**, 209–226 (2004)
16. Samuelson, P.A.: Tax deductibility of economic depreciation to insure invariant valuations. J. Political Econ. **72**, 604–606 (1964)
17. Schanz, D., Schanz, S.: The income tax paradox. Intertax **38**(3), 167–169 (2010)
18. Schneider, D.: Investition, Finanzierung, Besteuerung. 7th edn. Gabler, Wiesbaden (1992)
19. Smith, P.: Lessons from the British poll tax disaster. Nat. Tax J. **44**(2), 421–436 (1991)
20. Sørensen, P.B.: Neutral taxation of shareholder income. Int. Tax Public Finance **12**(6), 777–801 (2005)

21. Staderini, A.: Tax reforms to influence corporate financial policy: the case of the Italian business tax reform of 1997 – 1998. Banca, d'Italia, Working Paper No. 423. (2001)
22. Wagner, F.W., Besteuerung. In: Bitz, M., Domsch, M., Ewert, R., Wagner, F.W. (eds.) Vahlens Kompendium der Betriebswirtschaftslehre, vol. 2, 5th edn., pp. 407–477, München (2005)
23. Wenger, E.: Gleichmässigkeit der Besteuerung von Arbeits- und Vermögenseinkünften. FinanzArchiv **40**, 207–252 (1983)

Chapter 6
Introduction to Business Taxation

Abstract This chapter deals with taxation of different legal entities. In detail taxation of sole proprietorships and partnerships on the one hand and corporations on the other hand are explained. We show how tax bases are defined, describe one-book and two-book accounting systems and further discuss advantages and disadvantages of the existing accounting systems. Moreover, we show how different types of corporate tax systems work and provide examples how countries apply the corporate tax systems discussed. Further, we discuss avoidance mechanism of triple taxation. After explaining the legal framework for corporations, we present a Standard Model for corporations taking taxes into account. In particular, we discuss the cases of financing the initial investment by retained earnings or new equity. Concerning distribution policies, we investigate immediate dividend distribution and retention of cash flows.

6.1 Tax Base Determination for Business Income

Companies are taxed depending on their legal form (*König/Maßbaum/Sureth* [7]). Owners of partnerships and sole proprietorships usually are subject to personal income tax. Corporations are subject to corporate income taxes; their shareholders are subject to personal income taxes on dividends and capital gains. Thus, corporate profits are usually taxed twice. But the latter tax can be deferred, because it is only due when profits are distributed or shares are sold. If the corporation retains earnings, there will be no personal income tax due.

Independent of the legal form, business *profits* are taxed instead of cash flows: Taxable income is a noncash number. Tax reporting of business income is generally based on accrual accounting according to local GAAP. Thus, the tax base is determined as a comprehensive income tax. This broad tax base definition includes capital income. This kind of tax system is also called Schanz–Haig–Simons tax (see *Schanz* [8]). Usually, some exceptions are made for small and medium-sized enterprises (SME), because of disproportional financial accounting and tax accounting costs. The tax base for SME is often based on cash or modified cash bases (no immediate write-off of assets). However, taxable income might also be determined as a percentage of turnover gross income as for example in Portugal or Hungary.

D. Schanz and S. Schanz, *Business Taxation and Financial Decisions*,
DOI 10.1007/978-3-642-03284-4_6,

In Germany, the firm's taxable income (business income) is usually determined by applying the accrual basis of accounting, where the change in assets and liabilities is subject to taxation. The taxable income of the companies is determined not only by tax law but also by the German commercial code (local German GAAP; Handelsgesetzbuch (HGB)). This is due to the dependence principle (Massgeblichkeitsprinzip), which links a company's individual financial income and taxable income. Apart from some exceptions, financial accounting determines taxable income. Vice versa, tax rules are mostly valid for financial statements. This tight relation between the two external accounting systems is called "one-book system".

In countries with a very loose or no connection between tax accounting and financial accounting, the system is denoted as "two-book system". One example are the United States. In the US, companies face two separate sets of rules for tax and financial reporting. The Internal Revenue Code (IRC) states that

> Taxable income shall be computed under the method of accounting on the basis of which the taxpayer regularly computes his income in keeping his books (§ 446).

Nevertheless, tax accounting and financial accounting heavily differ in the US. The only exception is the valuation of inventory. For valuation purposes, the lifo-method (last in first out) has to be applied for financial accounting in case it is applied for tax accounting. The effect of this conformity rule was examined in detail. *Dopuch/Pincus* [3] and *Dhaliwal/Frankel/Trezevant* [2] find that there is a tax induced motivation in choosing the valuation method (lifo or fifo (first in first out)). However, *Shackelford/Shevlin* [10] find ambiguous results. The use of a two-book accounting system has been discussed critically during the past years. In the context of famous accounting scandals, such as Enron[1] and WorldCom, supporters of book-tax-conformity argued that they could have been prevented, if a one-book system had been used. Enron, on the one hand, reported high financial US-GAAP earnings over many years – which were used as an approximation for future earnings by investors – while, on the other hand, taxable income was negative.

It's common sense that financial accounting targets other addressees and pursues other objectives than tax accounting does. Addressees of financial accounting include shareholders, potential investors, and creditors. Hence, the objectives of financial accounting are to provide information that is useful for a wide range of users in making economic decisions, e.g., IFRS, and to restrict distribution of capital, e.g., German GAAP. The only addressee of tax accounting is the government, and the only purpose of tax accounting is to provide a litigable taxable basis.

Example 6.1. Success and Collapse of Enron

In 1985, Enron was founded by its later chief executive officer (CEO) Kenneth Lay resulting from a merger of two American gas pipeline operators. In the 1990s, Enron had – due to a market deregulation leading to the possibility for utilities to choose their energy supplier – glittering success. Sales of Enron's capital and trade division increased from $10 million in 1994 to $4 billion in

[1] For a summary of an insider see *Cruver* [1]. See also *Stiglitz* [11], pp. 241–268.

1997. Enron's total revenue reached $40.1 billion in 1999 and was boosted up to $100 billion by 2000.

Enron was praised for its innovative risk management derivatives. Proudness of its dexterity was unlimited which led even to the announcement of having invented "weather derivatives". This resulted in an almost complete transformation of Enron as an energy company to a financial institution, trading with financial derivatives as well as energy contracts.

At the beginning of its downturn, media attested Enron an arrogant and overambitious management that tried to reach a self-committed annual growth in earnings of 15%.

In August 2001, after being in charge of the business of Enron for less than a half a year, CEO Jeffrey Skilling left the company. Kenneth Lay became CEO again. In October 2001, Enron's credit rating was downgraded from Moody's and Fitch leading almost immediately to additional payments to debtholders to the amount of $3.9 billion due to a clause in debt contracts. On just one day in October 2001, market capitalization of Enron fell by 19%. In November 2001, Enron's top management got rid of their Enron shares selling over $1 billion of shares to other investors. On December 2, 2001 Enron filed for Chap. 11 bankruptcy. A couple of days before, $55 million were paid to five hundred people to stay at Enron for at least 90 more days. The payments also were called "The 90 day retention bonus". On January 10, 2002, an Enron share was worth $0.67. In summer 2000 a share was worth more than $100.

As a result of Enron's bankruptcy, Enron's auditor Arthur Anderson disappeared from the auditing market. Since then, the market for auditing is shared by the "big four", not any more by the "big five". An Enron insider summarized Enron's policy as[2]

> (...) keep the public confused, keep reality off the books, and keep the auditors on your side.

What triggered the bankruptcy? Basically, it was Enron's financial reporting behavior that led to this spectacular scandal. Here are some examples:

- Profits that never occurred were reported,
- Restatement of accounts (which triggered an investigation by the SEC (Securities & Exchange Commission)) that reduced profits by about $600 million[3],

Year	Reduced income	Increased debt
1997	$97 million	$711 million
1998	$113 million	$561 million
1999	$250 million	$685 million
2000	$132 million	$628 million

[2] *Cruver* [1], p. 180.
[3] See *Cruver* [1], p. 163.

- To keep its earnings per share (EPS) on an (increasing) high level, Enron soured debt out in so-called special purpose entities (SPE) which did not have to be consolidated. This resulted in a "cleaned" balance sheet (liabilities were hidden),
- Incorrect use of market to market accounting; assets were over-evaluated.

Incentives for illegally boosting those accounting numbers would have been much lower under a one-book system, because they would have been accompanied by enormous tax payments.

6.2 Evaluation of One-Book Accounting Systems

Now the question arises why a litigable tax base should be derived from accounting profits. The supporters deriving the tax base from accounting profits and hence the supporters of implementing a dependency principle particularly argue that the dependency principle leads to

1. Low costs of disclosure and tax compliance costs,
2. Restrictions of the possibilities to lower taxable income with a corresponding increase of accounting profits,
3. Simplification of accounting rules due to the reduction of legal standards for both groups of addressees (of financial accounting and tax accounting) and
4. A decrease of tax evasion.

Opponents of the dependency principle complain

1. The loss of information for the capital market due to distorted reported profits because of adjustment of financial accounting for tax accounting purposes, and
2. The lack of insurance that uniform one-book accounting leads to fewer adjustments for tax saving purposes than two-book accounting systems. This concern is based on the fact that even under one-book accounting systems, tax accounting and financial accounting never are 100% identical; typically, several adjustments are made.

In the following, we discuss the advantages and disadvantages brought forward by supporters and opponents of the dependency principle.

6.2.1 Low Tax Compliance Costs

Low tax costs and simplification of accounting play an important role when designing a tax system, because costs of tax systems are categorized as "social waste" and hence cannot be neglected. Costs of tax systems can be separated in tax filing

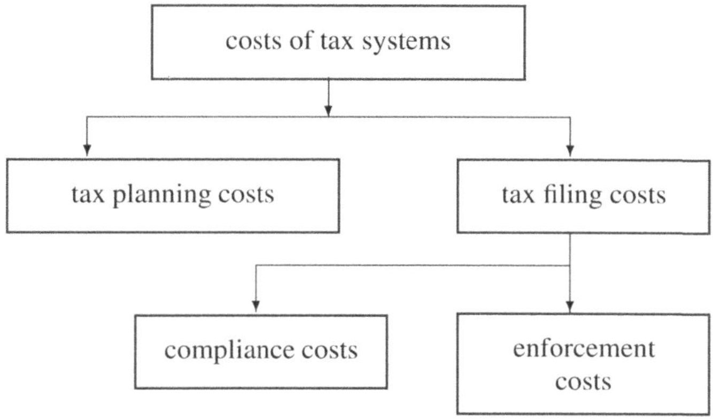

Fig. 6.1 Tax costs
Source: Based on *Wagner* [12]

costs and tax planning costs. For fiscal authorities, tax filing costs are enforcement costs (costs of imposition). On the taxpayer's level, tax filing costs occur in form of compliance costs. A summary of a tax system's costs is provided in Fig. 6.1.

Compliance costs might occur because of the time and money needed to file the tax return (opportunity cost). Money in order to determine the tax base might be spent for internal or external resources. Internal resources are, e.g., human resources of the internal tax division. External resources are tax consultants or the auditing industry. However, external resources might also be legal (court) expenses and attorneys' fees due to disputes with fiscal authorities.

On the level of fiscal authorities, tax filing costs occur because of enforcement costs that are necessary to supervise tax evasion of taxpayers.

The advantage of low compliance costs under a one-book system seems to be more clear, if, at first, existing separate accounting systems of financial accounting and tax accounting – as, e.g., in the US – are considered. In the US, taxes on income are levied without specifying in detail what exactly is meant by "income". It is, therefore, up to courts and fiscal authorities to define what income does include and what income does not include. It is clear that tax law is influenced by judges to a greater extent than in countries where income is defined very detailed (e.g., in Germany). At the same time, construction of tax law by judges causes immense costs for courts and lawyers. In total, tax filing costs will be lower if the dependency principle is applied and financial accounting rules are precise enough.

However, cost savings due to the implementation of a dependency principle might not only occur regarding external services, but also regarding internal resources, because redundancy might be avoided.

An international index of conflict sensitivity of implemented tax accounting does not exist. In Germany and Austria, there are some studies that try to develop a measure based on court decisions as an indicator for conflict sensitivity of the implemented tax systems. However, statements whether the principle of dependency leads to fewer conflict situations between taxpayers and fiscal authorities are missing.

6.2.2 Distorted Reported Profits

While the requirement of financial accounting is to make the impossible possible, that is to determine the "real", the "true profit" and to suggest a "true and fair view", the result of tax accounting must be a justiciable tax base, "an artificial structure" or an artificial assessment period. On the one hand, financial accounting must be future-oriented and therefore has to provide adequate evaluation figures that provide shareholders and potential investors with sufficient information to meet their concerns. On the other hand, tax accounting is past-oriented and restricted to the concerned year of assessment. If those different requirements – just because of a principle of dependency – are mixed, necessarily a tug of war arises about reporting the "true profit", as a pretended objective of financial accounting, and a desirable low tax base.

As a result, the two accounting frameworks are not "robust against any pollution" because of integration of legal settings, that originally should serve to reach objectives of the other accounting setting, respectively.

The US delegate Lloyd Doggett summarizes that tug of war intuitively as:[4]

> When investors hear only of rosy earnings while at tax time Uncle Sam only hears of regrets and red ink, something is very wrong.

The conflicting aims result in a compromise that leads to carrying out possibly available electives in financial accounting – affecting profits – exclusively due to interests in tax accounting (lowest present value of tax payments). However, such results are in conflict with the information concerns of the shareholders.

Due to the "deformed" financial accounting settings because of tax accounting interests, addressees potentially resume distorted conclusions that lead to wrong forecasts of cash flows if forecasting takes place on the basis of accounting profits. However, it is questionable if a complete separation of the two accounting systems leads to an improvement of the predictive ability of financial accounting profits.

In fact, there is no conflict in case of complete separation, but it might be presumed that because of this latitude the incentive rises to "gloss up" financial statement information. That might lead to an over-optimistic – if not even consciously too profitable – presentation of financial statement data.

Concerning this problem, *Hanlon* [5] finds, that periods where companies report huge differences between financial accounting profit and taxable income, reported accounting profit is a worse predictor for the level of profits than in the case of small differences between profit and income. Moreover, according to her investigations, huge differences between profit and income represent a "red flag" for investors in a way that in case of increasing differences investors expect future profits to be lower.

In the academic community, Enron and Worldcom are used to investigate the dependency between financial profit and taxable income empirically. Many authors

---

[4] Cited in *Hanlon* [5], p. 138.

find a constant divergence of profits and taxable income. Two main reasons were identified:

1. There is an increase in earnings management
2. Possibility of tax evasion arose due to globalized business.

In the early 1980s and especially in the 1990s, there was an increased reporting of high accounting profits with correspondingly low taxable income. The Wall Street Journal from January 29, 2003 states:

> Currently it is almost impossible to know a firm's tax bill by looking at its financial statements, and thus it is impossible to figure out what actual profits are. Profits reported to the IRS, where firms have less discretion in making calculations, are considered to be closer to the truth, but they are confidential and unavailable to investors. Book profits and tax profits can be wildly different – a divergence, by the way, that increased markedly in the 1990s.

This development results in an adjustment of the alternative minimum tax (AMT) to the accounting profit. Using that loophole, a partial principle of dependency was implemented in the US. If accounting profit exceeds the tax base of the AMT, a fraction of the difference is subject to tax.

However, the intensive discussion of advantages and disadvantages of the one-book accounting and the two-book accounting as a relationship between profit and taxable income leads to the result, that in the US, the current two-book accounting is maintained. The main reason for that decision is that the two-book accounting leads to a "pollution" of financial accounting because of tax driven targets. In that case, financial accounting does not reflect an adequate basis in order to forecast profits and therefore leads to misinterpretation by its addressees.

6.3 Relationship Between Tax Accounting and Financial Accounting in EU Member States

Many countries' tax systems lie in between the two extremes of one-book accounting and two-book accounting. Tax accounting and financial accounting are somehow linked together, but accounting profits and taxable profits are – even if a one-book accounting systems is applied – far away from being identical. An overview over the relationships in the EU Member States is presented in Table 6.1. The table shows whether the EU Member State adopts a one-book system or a two-book system. As a result, 22 of 27 countries prefer a one-book system, whereas just five countries do not. But even though they are classified as countries with one-book systems, adjustments always have to be made for tax purposes.

An interesting development is the adoption of IFRS rules for countries with a one-book accounting system. In that case, the linkage between financial accounting and tax accounting means, that IFRS rules affect taxation. If that is true, countries would accept that tax revenue indirectly depends on the decisions of an external private institution. Table 6.2 shows, that 9 countries of 27 adopt IFRS rules for

Table 6.1 Relationship of financial accounting and tax accounting in EU member states

Country	One-book system?	Country	One-book system?
Austria	Yes	Latvia	Yes
Belgium	Yes	Lithuania	Yes
Bulgaria	Yes	Luxembourg	Yes
Cyprus	Yes	Malta	Yes
Czech Republic	Yes	Netherlands	No
Denmark	No	Portugal	Yes
Estonia	No	Romania	Yes
Finland	Yes	Slovakia	Yes
France	Yes	Slovenia	Yes
Germany	Yes	Spain	Yes
Greece	Yes	Sweden	Yes
Hungary	Yes	Poland	No
Ireland	No	United Kingdom	Yes
Italy	Yes		

Table 6.2 Application of IFRS in some EU member states

Country	Application
Czech Republic	The Czech Accounting Standards must still be followed.
Cyprus	Accounting profit is based on IFRS, for tax purposes adjustments must be made.
France	Since January 2005 French GAAP is in line with IFRS, French GAAP is the basis for taxation.
Greece	Differences between IFRS and Greek GAAP must be adjusted for tax purposes.
Malta	IFRS are mandatory for financial purposes. For tax purposes financial profit must be modified, however, the IFRS are the basis for the determination of taxable income.
Portugal	Portuguese companies have an option to use the IFRS in the annual accounts. However, for tax purposes the Portuguese Accounting Standards must still be followed.
Slovakia	Selected companies must prepare their financial statements according to IFRS; therefore, IFRS are also applicable for tax purposes. However, in determining the taxable income adjustment must be made.
Slovenia	The application of IFRS for tax purposes is allowed.
United Kingdom	Financial accounting is based on the regulations of IFRS, therefore the rules of tax accounting are also based on the IFRS. However, tax adjustments must be made.

Source: *Endres* et al. [4], p. 26.

single closing. However, even if countries adopt IFRS rules, tax base is just affected indirectly because several adjustments have to be made.[5] There is no country that adopts IFRS without adjustments for tax purposes.

[5] See *Endres* et al. [4], p. 26.

sole proprietorships/partnerships	*corporations*
→ only one level of taxation → there is no distinction between the business entity level and the individual level → withdrawal of money from the business entity level causes no taxation	1. level: business level → taxation of taxable income on the level of the corporation → corporate income tax 2. level: individual level → taxation of dividends received → income tax

Fig. 6.2 Taxation of sole proprietorships/partnerships and corporations

6.4 Principles of Business Taxation for Different Legal Entities

Figure 6.2 shows the main characteristics of taxation of sole proprietorships or partnerships and corporations. Sole proprietorships and partnerships are "pass-through" entities which means that financial transactions between the company and the owner does not affect taxation. Withdrawals do not increase the tax base on the one hand, on the other hand capital contributions do not reduce the tax base.

Corporate income is actually taxed on two levels. First, corporate income is due to corporate income tax on the business level. This is because corporations are legal persons and subject to corporate income tax, not to personal income tax.

Cash after taxes on corporate level, however, is not ready for consumption for the owner. There has to be a dividend payout (cash distribution) before shareholders are able to consume. Corporations usually cannot just distribute what they want. Distribution is restricted to profits and retained earnings. If the shareholder receives cash from his corporate business entity, fiscal authorities usually access that cash flow a second time for taxation, hence the second level tax.

6.5 Taxation of Partnerships and Sole Proprietorships

Now, we look at the legal entity of sole proprietorships and partnerships as so-called "pass through" entities for tax purposes. Income is not taxed at the company level. Instead, income earned by the entity is passed through to be taxed at the personal level of the owners.

In Germany, owners of partnerships and sole proprietorships are subject to personal income tax "Einkommensteuer" (ESt). They also pay local business tax "Gewerbesteuer" (GewSt), but an allowance for the local business tax is granted with regard to the personal income tax which has the aim to compensate for the additional local business tax. Therefore, we neglect local business taxes in the following and solely take the individual income tax into account.

In the United States, owners of partnerships, limited partnerships, and sole proprietorships are subject to personal income tax. Shareholders of subtitle S corporations are taxed like owners of partnerships if the condition of a maximum of 75 shareholders is fulfilled (§ 1361 IRC).

As owners of partnerships and sole proprietorships pay individual income taxes on business profits independent of the profit distribution, the influence of taxes on their investment decisions can be determined on the basis of the "Standard Model" which was presented in Sect. 3.2.

Example 6.2. Standard Model for Sole Proprietorships and Partnerships

The Standard Model for sole proprietorships or partnerships, respectively, is quite simple to introduce. That is because it goes along with the "Standard Model" developed in Sect. 3.2 starting on p. 80.

Suppose Rainer wants to manufacture shoes in the legal framework of a small sole proprietorship. He wants to specialize on manual production and hires six employees who are supposed to keep the business running. His target customers are basically well situated business women and since economy runs well, future looks well in terms of profit (and cash flows). The initial investment necessary to construct the manufacturing hall and necessary factory and office equipment is $I_0 = 340,000$. The cash flow stream is predicted for sure for the following 4 years as:

t	0	1	2	3	4
CF_t	–340,000.00	90,000.00	100,000.00	130,000.00	90,000.00

The initial investment is straight-line depreciated over Rainer's time horizon of 4 years. His individual marginal income tax is $\tau^p = 35\%$. The alternative financial investments promise a before-tax return of 6%. At the end of each period, Rainer withdraws an amount of € 50,000 (W_t) to be able to cover his costs of living.

As the following financial plan states, there is no big difference between the Standard Model for sole proprietorships or partnerships and the basic Standard Model presented in Chap. 3. The only difference are the withdrawals W_t. However, withdrawals do not affect the tax base T_t. They just reduce the financial investment in t.

t	0	1	2	3	4
CF_t	–340,000.00	90,000.00	100,000.00	130,000.00	90,000.00
D_t		85,000.00	85,000.00	85,000.00	85,000.00
W_t		50,000.00	50,000.00	50,000.00	50,000.00
IP_t		0.00	2,295.00	5,069.51	9,122.22
FI_t		38,250.00	84,491.75	152,036.93	196,216.37
TB_t		5,000.00	17,295.00	50,069.51	14,122.22
T_t		1,750.00	6,053.25	17,524.33	4,942.78
CF_t^τ	–340,000.00	38,250.00	46,241.75	67,545.18	44,179.44

NPV^{τ} for Rainer's investment now consists of the net present value of the withdrawals up to $t = 4$ and the present value of the financial investment at the end of $t = 4$.

$$\begin{aligned} NPV^{\tau} &= -340,000.00 + 50,000.00 \times \frac{1.039^4 - 1}{0.039 \times 1.039^4} + \frac{196,216.37}{1.039^4} \\ &= -340,000 + 181,923.31 + 168,373.23 \\ &= 10,296.54. \end{aligned}$$

Rainer is advised to carry out the shoe manufacturing.

As sole proprietorships and partnerships are no independent legal entities, contracts between the companies and their owners are not recognized for tax purposes. This is relevant for payments from the company to their owners, for example in case of loans given to the partnership or employment of owners. As a consequence of the transparency principle, interest paid on a loan given by the owner or salary paid to an owner who works within a partnership cannot be deducted from the tax base. In addition, interest income will not be recognized as capital income. Instead, it is requalified as business income or ordinary income. The most important consequence in Germany is that the progressive tax rate instead of a reduced tax rate on interest income has to be applied, if the alternative financial investment is carried out as a business asset.

6.6 Taxation of Corporations

In contrast to partnerships, corporations are legal entities where shareholders face limited liability. Legally these firms are regarded as independent legal entities. Economically, these firms can be regarded as investment vehicles of their owners.[6] Usually, income of corporations is taxed twice: First, at the level of the corporation (corporate level or business level); second, at the level of the shareholders (personal level).

There are different types of corporate tax systems and different methods of integrating corporate and personal income taxes applied worldwide. In many countries, double taxation is mitigated at least partially. Possible corporate tax systems are:

1. Taxation exclusively at the level of the firm,
2. Classical tax system,
3. Classical tax system with shareholder relief elements,
4. Partial or full imputation system,
5. Partnership method (full integration).

[6] See Fig. 1.2 on p. 8.

6.6.1 *Types of Corporate Tax Systems*

In the following, we describe five different types of corporate tax systems using illustrative examples to clarify the way the systems work. Moreover, we provide examples for countries applying the corporate tax systems discussed.

6.6.1.1 Taxation Exclusively at the Level of the Firm

Corporations are subject to corporate income tax. Distributed dividends are not taxed at the owner's level.

Example 6.3. Taxation Exclusively at the Corporate Level

Assume the profit of the corporation P^c is equal to before-tax cash flows on corporate level CF^c and also represents the tax base on corporate level TB^c and accounts for € 100. The corporate income tax rate is supposed to be $\tau^c = 35\%$. The total accumulated tax burden of the corporate level and the owner's level is

corporate level		Profit before tax ($CF^c = TB$)	100.00
	–	Corporate income tax ($T^c = \tau^c \times TB^c$)	35.00
	=	Profit after corporate income tax ($CF^{\tau,c}$)	65.00
owner's level		Dividend income (Div)	65.00
	–	Owner's personal income tax ($T^p = \tau^p \times Div$)	0.00
	=	Dividend after taxes	65.00
		Total tax burden on corporate profit	35.00

Further variables used:

Div: distributed cash flow (dividend)
τ^p: personal marginal tax rate of the owner
T^c : tax liability on corporate level
T^p : tax liability on the personal level of the owner

Note that the dividend after taxes represents the income after taxes in case of investment in a corporation.

Example 6.4. Countries with Taxation Exclusively at the Corporate Level

Countries that apply a uniform corporate income tax are, e.g., Estonia, Latvia, Cyprus, and Slovakia. Those countries levy taxes only at the level of the corporation. Dividends are tax-free at the level of the owner.

Table 6.3 Selected countries where taxation is reduced to the corporate level

Country	Corporate level[a]	Owner's level
Cyprus	10%	0%
Estonia	0% in case of retained earnings; else 21%	0%
Latvia	15%	0%
Slovakia	19%	0%

[a]Nominal tax rate without surcharges or local business tax

The Estonian corporate tax system has an additional distinctive feature: Retained earnings are totally tax exempt. Only when profits are distributed, a 21% corporate income tax is levied on the corporate level; there are no additional shareholder taxes. Table 6.3 summarizes the selected countries that apply a uniform corporate income tax.

6.6.1.2 Classical Tax System

In a classical tax system, taxation takes place first at the level of the corporation and second at the level of the owner. Dividends are taxed by applying the owner's regular income tax rate. The classical tax system allows unrelieved double taxation and does not apply a reduced tax rate on dividends.

Example 6.5. Classical Tax System

Suppose, the cash equivalent profit on corporate level to be € 100. The corporate income tax rate stays at $\tau^c = 35\%$ and the personal marginal income tax rate of the owner is $\tau^p = 40\%$.

corporate level		Profit before tax ($CF^c = TB^c$)	100.00
	–	Corporate income tax ($T^c = \tau^c \times TB^c$)	35.00
	=	Profit after corporate income tax ($CF^{\tau,c}$)	65.00
owner's level		Dividend income (Div)	65.00
	–	Owner's personal income tax ($T^p = \tau^p \times Div$)	26.00
	=	Dividend after taxes	39.00
		Total tax burden on corporate profit	61.00

In this case, the total tax burden amounts to € 61 meaning that the effective tax rate taking both levels of taxation into account is 61%.

Example 6.6. Countries that Apply a Classical Corporate Tax System

Examples for classical corporate tax systems are the United States until 2002, Ireland and Switzerland. In addition to the corporate income tax, shareholders pay personal income taxes on distributed profits.

Let's look at an example for Switzerland

corporate level		Profit before tax ($CF^c = TB^c$)	100.00
	–	Corporate income tax ($T^c = \tau^c \times TB^c$)	25.00
	=	Profit after corporate income tax ($CF^{\tau,c}$)	75.00
owner's level		Dividend income (Div)	75.00
	–	Owner's personal income tax ($T^p = \tau^p \times Div$)	21.75
	=	Dividend after taxes	53.25
		Total tax burden on corporate profit	46.75

In our simplified example, the tax rate on the corporate level is assumed to be 25%, the one on the personal level is 29%. In Switzerland, both tax rates depend on the canton and the municipality of the corporation and the owner and can differ heavily. We assume the mentioned tax rates to cover the taxes levied on the federal, the cantonal, and the municipal level. In this examples, we neglect net wealth taxes.

Based on those assumptions, the corporate income tax of 25% is levied on the profit of € 100. We assume that enough cash is available to distribute the after-tax profit of € 75 to the shareholders. On the shareholder level, the dividend is added to the ordinary income of the shareholder and taxes are due according to the progressive tax rate function. There is no relief for capital income. The personal income tax amounts to € 75 × 29% = € 21.75. Total taxes paid on the profit amount to € 46.75. The shareholder keeps € 53.25 profit after personal and corporate income taxes.

In Table 6.4, we provide countries adopting a pure classical corporate tax system. Swiss tax rates deviate from our example, because Table 6.4 neglects cantonal and municipal taxes.

Table 6.4 Selected countries that apply a pure classical corporate tax system (without reduced rate on shareholder's level)

Country	Corporate level[a]	Owner's level
Czech Republic	19%	Dividends are completely taxable
Ireland	12.5%	Dividends are completely taxable
Switzerland	8.5%	Dividends are completely taxable

[a]Nominal tax rate without surcharges or local business tax

Classical tax systems are more common in countries with tax rates below international average tax rates.

6.6.1.3 Classical Tax System with Shareholder Relief Elements

In shareholder relief tax systems, taxation takes place at the level of the corporation and at the level of the owner. But there is some relief on dividend income, either by a reduced tax rate or by taxing only a fraction of the dividends by applying the regular rate.

Shareholder relief systems cause moderated double taxation. The total tax burden may be higher or lower than on an ordinary income which is only subject to personal income taxation.

Example 6.7. Classical Tax System with Shareholder Relief

The following example reflects the tax burden in the United States. The US top marginal corporate tax rate of 35% is levied on the profit of $100. We neglect additional state or city/county taxes. Dividend distribution is $65. The tax rate on capital income on the personal level is 15% only. The tax burden amounts to 15%× $65 = $9.75. The sum of taxes is $44.75; the dividend after both types of taxes is $55.25.

This example reveals how applying a reduced tax rate on dividends reduces the overall tax burden. Levying the top marginal personal tax rate of 35% instead of 15% would result in an income tax payment of $22.75 instead of $9.75. In this case, far less than half of the profit would reach the shareholder: Only $42.25 instead of $55.25 would be the profit after both taxes.

corporate level		Profit before tax ($CF^c = TB^c$)	100.00
	–	Corporate income tax ($T^c = \tau^c \times TB^c$)	35.00
	=	Profit after corporate income tax ($CF^{\tau,c}$)	65.00
owner's level		Dividend income (Div)	65.00
	–	Owner's personal income tax ($T^p = \tau^p \times Div$)	9.75
	=	Dividend after taxes	55.25
		Total tax burden on corporate profit	44.75

The effective tax rate compared to the classical system is reduced to 44.75%.

Example 6.8. Countries that Adopt a Classical System with Shareholder Relief

Classical corporate tax systems with shareholder relief are very common nowadays. Examples are Austria, Germany, or the United States. In Austria, a flat tax of 25% is applied on dividends, while the top marginal income tax rate is 50%. In the US, a flat tax of 15% is applied on dividends, while the top marginal income tax rate is 35%. In Germany, a flat tax of 25% is applied on dividends, while the top marginal income tax rate is 45%. In those three countries, the tax rates on dividends are even below these mentioned rates if the taxpayers are in low tax brackets. Please note that tax rates in this chapter are federal tax rates excluding local taxes and surcharges.

A summary of countries that apply a corporate income tax system with shareholder relief elements – resulting basically in a reduced personal tax rate – is displayed in Table 6.5.

Table 6.5 Selected countries that apply a classical corporate tax system with shareholder relief elements

Country	Corporate level[a]	Owner's level
Austria	25%	Flat tax of 25% or half average income tax rate if dividends are assessed
Belgium	33%	Flat tax of 25% / option for assessment
Bulgaria	10%	Flat tax of 5%
Denmark	25%	Flat tax of 28% / if dividends exceed 46,700 Danish Krones (102,600 Danish Krones) 43% (45%)
Finland	26%	Listed corporations: 30% tax exempt and 25% witholding tax on the remaining 70%; other corporations: 9% of share (up to € 90,000) tax exempt, exceeding amount: 28% withholding tax on 70%
France	33.33%	Flat tax of 30.1% or assessment of 60% of the dividends
Germany	15%	Flat tax of 25% / option for assessment
Greece	24%	10%
Hungary	16%	Listed companies: tax rate of 10%; otherwise: 25% if dividend does not exceed 30% of share of equity, 35% of exceeding amount
Italy	27.5%	Flat tax of 12.5%
Lithuania	15%	Flat tax of 15%
Luxembourg	21.84%	50% of dividends are tax exempt
Netherlands	25.5%	25% on dividends if share exceeds 5%; otherwise income tax of 30% of a notional return
Norway	28%	Dividends up to a fraction of the acquisitions costs are tax exempt
Poland	19%	Flat tax of 19%
Portugal	25%	Flat tax of 20% or option to assess dividends with 50% tax exemption
Romania	16%	Flat tax of 16%
Spain	30%	18% tax rate on dividends; no other option
Sweden	26.3%	30% tax rate on dividends; no other option
United States	35%[b]	15% tax rate on dividends

[a]Nominal tax rate without surcharges or local business tax

[b]Progressive tax with tax rates of 15%, 25%, and 34%

6.6.1.4 Partial or Full Imputation System

In corporate tax systems with imputation, corporate income tax is levied on a firm's profit and dividends are fully taxable at the owner's (shareholder's) level. So far there is no difference between the imputation system and the classical system. However, applying the imputation system, shareholders receive a tax credit which corresponds to

1. The full amount of corporate income tax which has been paid on the part of the profit that is distributed as dividend (full imputation).
2. Some part of corporate income tax which has been paid on the part of the profit that is distributed as dividend (partial imputation).

Shareholders have to declare the dividend received plus the tax credit amount as income. As a result, distributed profits are subject only to personal income tax (full imputation) or to a mixed tax rate higher than the personal income tax rate (partial imputation).

In case of a 100% dividend payout, the full imputation system converts the corporate income tax to a partnership form of taxation. As a consequence, income is taxed at the personal income tax rate τ^p. In case of a partial dividend payout, retained earnings are taxed at the corporate rate τ^c. If $\tau^c < \tau^p$, there may be an advantage (timing effect) to retain earnings for shareholders in high tax brackets.

Example 6.9. Imputation System

If cash equivalent profit is € 100, corporate income tax rate $\tau^c = 35\%$ and the personal income tax rate of the owner $\tau^p = 40\%$, for a full imputation system where 100% of the corporate income tax is imputed and a partial imputation system, where an amount of 15% of the corporate income is imputed, the following dividends after taxes result

			Full Imputation	Partial Imputation
corporate level		Profit before tax ($CF^c = TB^c$)	100.00	100.00
	–	Corporate income tax ($T^c = \tau^c \times TB^c$)	35.00	35.00
	=	Profit after corporate income tax ($CF^{\tau,c}$)	65.00	65.00
	=	Dividend payment (Div)	65.00	65.00
	+	T^c imputed to shareholder	35.00	15.00
owner's level	=	Dividend income	100.00	80.00
	–	Owner's personal income tax ($T^p = \tau^p \times Div$)	40.00	32.00
	+	Tax credit	35.00	15.00
	–	Tax payment after offsetting the tax credit	5.00	17.00
	=	Dividend after taxes	60.00	48.00
		Total tax burden on corporate profit	40.00	52.00

Table 6.6 Selected countries with full or partial imputation system

Country	Corporate level[a]	Owner's level
1. Full imputation system		
Malta	35%	Corporate tax is credited. As a result, dividends are taxed with personal income tax
2. Partial imputation system		
Canada	19%	Tax base is dividend plus an increase of 45%; 11/18 of the increase are imputable
Japan	30%	Imputation of 5% or 10% of dividends
United Kingdom	28%	Tax base is dividend plus increase of 1/9 that is imputable

[a]Nominal tax rate without surcharges or local business tax

Note, that in the case of the full imputation system, the overall effective tax burden equals the shareholder's personal tax rate of $\tau^p = 40\%$. As a matter of fact, if the shareholder's personal tax rate is less than the corporate income tax rate levied on corporate profits, he gets a tax refund at the amount of the difference from tax authorities.

Countries that implemented a full or partial imputation system are displayed in Table 6.6.

6.6.1.5 Partnership Method (Full Integration)

Under the full integration method, all earnings (whether distributed or not) are attributed to shareholders just as if the corporation was a partnership. As a result, there is a full integration of the corporate taxation in the taxation of the owner. In this case, corporate income tax is irrelevant for decision reasons, that is because corporate income tax just serves as a withholding tax. At the owner's level, dividend income and capital gains (realized or unrealized) are taxed as personal income. In fact there is no income tax levied on the corporate level. The withholding tax just serves as a guarantee for fiscal authority – in terms of tax revenue – that dividends are filed. The full integration method hence results in the same effective tax rate taking personal and corporate level into account as in the case of the full imputation system.

6.6.2 Double Taxation

Corporations are legal entities that are artificial persons according to a jurist. Of course, corporations cannot make own decisions, however, for tax purposes, corporations are juristic persons that are subject to law. This is important to know in order to be able to distinguish between the juristic and the economic understanding of double taxation.

Taking the juristic understanding of double taxation, taxing the corporate entity with corporate income tax and the shareholder as an individual with personal income tax does not meet the criteria for double taxation, because corporation and individual are two separate "persons".

As we mentioned at the beginning of this book in Sect. 1.4 on p. 8, no matter what kind of legal body is used for investments, for economic understanding, companies are just used as investment vehicles. Taking that definition, all taxes that reduce cash flow up to the point where cash is available for consumption for the individual have to be added up no matter in what juristic scope they have to be paid. Now, it is clear that corporate income tax and personal income tax on top causes double taxation in an economic understanding.

6.6.3 Avoidance of Triple Taxation

As you have seen so far, double taxation of profits of corporations is common in many countries. However, usually, countries try to mitigate or avoid triple taxation of profits. Triple taxation might occur if corporations are held by other corporations and dividends are passed through different levels. If dividends are taxed at each level, so-called cascade effects occur.

Sometimes people perceive tax exemption of dividends and capital gains at the corporate level as loophole or inequitable advantage for corporations. Based on Fig. 6.3, we see that this is not the case, because the same profit will be taxed twice, on the first corporate level and on the individual level. Only a third or higher level of taxation is avoided, which has nothing to do with total tax exemption.

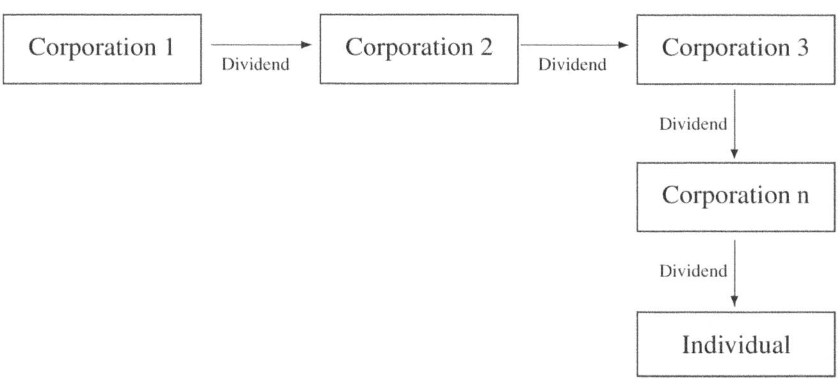

Fig. 6.3 Cascade effect

Example 6.10. Cascade Effect

1. Suppose an individual owns 100% of corporation C. Corporation C owns 100% of corporation B and corporation B again holds 100% of shares of corporation A. Corporation A distributes dividends of € 100 to corporation B, where the dividends are passed through to the individual.
2. Suppose a 100% exemption of dividends received at the corporate level.

The corporate income tax rate is assumed to be 25%, whereas the personal income tax rate on dividends received by the individual is 20%. The following table illustrates the difference if a triple taxation avoidance mechanism is implemented or not. The differences are shown between a system with no avoidance system and a system with 100% exemption of intercompany dividends. In the case of no avoidance of triple taxation, total tax burden sums up to 66.25%. The case of 100% exemption of dividends reduces total tax burden on both levels to 40%.

Let's have a look at the different corporate levels. Notice that there is no difference at the first level – at corporation A. Dividend payout to corporation B in both cases is € 75. Also dividend received for financial accounting purposes is € 75 at the level of corporation B. However, for tax purposes, the 100% exemption method deducts all dividends received lasting in a taxable income of € 0, whereas in the case of no avoidance of triple taxation financial accounting profit of € 75 is fully taxable, lasting in a corporate income tax liability of $0.25 \times 75 = € 18.75$. Corporation B now is able to distribute € 75 in case of 100% exemption and $€ 75 - € 18.75 = € 56.25$ in case of full double taxation. Treatment at the level of corporation C goes along the treatment at the level of corporation B. As you can see, distribution is cut through corporate income tax just in case of the first distribution (from corporation A to corporation B) and is not reduced in any case of further distribution, if 100% tax exemption is granted.

	No avoidance mechanism	*100% Exemption*
Corp. A		
taxable income	100.00	100.00
– corporate income tax	25.00	25.00
= dividend	75.00	75.00
Corp. B		
dividend received	75.00	75.00
taxable income	75.00	0.00
– corporate income tax	18.75	0.00
= dividend	56.25	75.00

	No avoidance mechanism	*100% Exemption*
Corp. C		
dividend received	56.25	75.00
taxable income	56.25	0.00
– corporate income tax	14.06	0.00
= dividend	42.19	75.00
Individual		
dividend received	42.19	75.00
– personal income tax	8.44	15.00
= net dividend	33.75	60.00
Total tax	*66.25*	*40.00*

The final distribution to the shareholder represented by an individual accounts for €75 in case of the 100% exemption and just €42.19 in case of the double taxation system. Tax liability on the owner's level accounts for €$42.19 \times 0.2 =$ €8.44 in case of full double (triple) taxation, which is less than in the case of full exemption €$75 \times 0.2 =$ €15.

Example 6.10 illustrates the effect of triple taxation, respectively, using the 100% exemption method as a tool for preventing triple taxation. However, to avoid triple taxation there are more existing avoidance mechanisms. Those can be separated in

1. Full exemption,
2. Partial exemption,
3. Tax credit.

Table 6.7 shows the different avoidance mechanism implemented in EU Member States.[7]

In Germany according to § 8b KStG (German Corporate Income Tax Code) corporations that receive dividends from other corporations only declare 5% of these dividends as taxable corporate income. About 95% of the dividends are tax exempt.

Table 6.7 Double taxation relief for intercompany dividends

Method of avoidance	Country
100% exemption	Austria, Cyprus, Czech Republic, Denmark, Estonia, Finland, Greece, Hungary, Ireland[a], Latvia, Lithuania, Luxembourg, Netherlands, Poland, Portugal, Slovakia, Slovenia, Sweden, United Kingdom[a]
95% exemption	Belgium, France, Germany, Italy
Tax credit	Ireland[b], Malta, Spain, United Kingdom[b]

[a] only for domestic dividends, [b] only for foreign dividends

[7] According to *Endres* et al. [4], p. 18.

Capital gains are 95% tax exempt, too. However, group taxation provides the possibility to even prevent taxation of 5% of received dividends from subsidiaries.

In the US, corporations are entitled to dividends received deduction (DRD) regarding their participation in other domestic US corporations. The DRD allows the firm to exempt a fraction of the dividends received from other corporations:

- Exemption of 70% in case of a participation of less than 20%.
- Exemption of 80% in case of a participation of more than 20%.
- Exemption of 100% in case of a participation of more than 80%.

There is no equivalent for capital gains at the corporate level.[8]

6.7 Standard Model for Corporations

In the following, we present a Standard Model for corporations (*Kiesewetter/ Dietrich* [6]). Other than in the Standard Model for sole proprietorships or partnerships, we have to take two levels of taxation into account. Basically, all taxes at all levels up to the point of possible consumption by the individual shareholder have to be taken into account. However, at first we use a short-sighted perspective, where only the corporate level is taken into account.

If τ^c represents the corporate income tax rate, periodic after-tax cash flows $CF_t^{\tau,c}$ at $t = 1, \ldots, n$ after taxes on the company level are defined as:

$$CF_t^{\tau,c} = CF_t^c - T_t^c = CF_t^c - \tau^c \times (CF_t^c - D_t) \quad \text{with} \quad \sum_{t=1}^{n} D_t = I_0.$$

D_t represents yearly depreciation of the initial investment I_0 and T^c denotes corporate tax payments. Net present value after taxes on company level $NPV^{\tau,c}$ is hence computed as:

$$NPV^{\tau,c} = -I_0 + \sum_{t=1}^{n} CF_t^c \times (q^{\tau,c})^{-t} \qquad \text{with} \qquad q^{\tau,c} = 1 + i \times (1 - \tau^c).$$

Notice that capital budgeting based on this $NPV^{\tau,c}$ does not necessarily maximize shareholder value. Taxes on both the corporate level and the personal level have to be taken into account. Additional assumptions for calculating $NPV^{\tau,p}$ are

1. One individual holds 100% of shares.
2. There is no change in the ownership structure during the planning horizon.
3. Investment I_0 is financed by retained earnings or new equity.
4. There is no debt financing.

---

[8] For information regarding the avoidance of full tax liability of capital gains, see *Scholes* et al. [9], p. 22.

5. There are positive tax bases and cash flows during the planning period.
6. The owner is subject to personal income tax as resident at the personal marginal income tax rate τ^p.
7. Equity is paid back at the latest at $t = n$.
8. The owner's alternative investment is a financial investment that yields the capital market interest rate i and is taxed at the owner's personal tax rate.
9. Opportunity cost of capital is $i^\tau = i \times (1 - \tau^p)$.

We cannot present the after-tax net present formula on the owner's level yet, because this formula depends on further assumptions concerning financing and distribution policy.

Because of the characteristics of the legal form of a corporation, dividend payout restrictions have to be considered. In many countries, dividend distributions of limited liability companies are restricted to financial accounting profits. This restriction is independent of how much money is available for distribution. The reason for the limitation is protection of creditors. In countries without those restrictions (United States and United Kingdom, e.g.), single bank contracts limit dividend distributions of limited liability companies. Contracts are often designed based on financial accounting figures. As a result, distributions are limited to financial accounting profits or similar numbers. Therefore, the following formulas fit to most countries worldwide.

Dividends are assumed to consist of distributions of current profits from real investments Div_t^P, of distributions of retained earnings Div_t^{RE}, and of distributions of interest on an internal financial investment Div_t^{FI}. Dividend payout from current after-tax profits is[9]

$$Div_t^P = \alpha \times P_t^\tau = \alpha \times (1 - \tau^c) \times (CF_t^c - D_t) \tag{6.1}$$

with $0 \leq \alpha \leq 1$, where α represents the dividend payout ratio

$$\alpha = \left\{ \begin{array}{l} 0 \text{ no distribution of profits} \\ 1 \text{ full distribution of profits} \end{array} \right\}. \tag{6.2}$$

Notice that P_t stands for profit before tax in time t and is defined as:

$$P_t = CF_t^c - D_t \tag{6.3}$$

and D_t is a (noncash equivalent) accrual representing depreciation allowances.

In the following, we are considering four cases. First, we separate between financing by retained earnings (cases A and B) and new equity (cases C and D). Second, we separate between retaining profits (cases A and C) and full distribution of profits (cases B and D) during the investment period. In cases A and C, no

[9] Remember, the term "profits" fits to financial accounting language and does not have to be necessarily equivalent to the term "taxable income" which belongs to the tax accounting framework.

distributions are assumed up to $t = n$, which leads to $Div_t = 0$ for $t = 1, \ldots, n-1$ (retention). Cases B and D deal with the maximum possible dividend distribution (immediate distribution), only restricted by financial accounting payout restrictions.

Hence, our four cases considered are

Case A: financing by retained earnings where profits are retained.
Case B: financing by retained earnings where profits are immediately distributed.
Case C: financing by new equity where profits are retained.
Case D: financing by new equity where profits are immediately distributed.

6.7.1 Financing by Retained Earnings

Opportunity cost for the shareholder in case of financing the initial real investment cost by retained earnings are

$$(1 - \tau^p) \times I_0. \tag{6.4}$$

The idea behind that is, that the owner is able to forgo distribution of retained earnings and reinvest the money in form of additional paid-in capital. However, due to our assumption that dividends are taxed on the personal level, the amount for reallocation is reduced by personal taxes and therefore by $\tau^p \times I_0$. Dividends after taxes on personal level are hence $I_0 - \tau^p \times I_0 = (1 - \tau^p) \times I_0$ as stated in (6.4). If retained earnings are not distributed, but reinvested at the corporate level, the investor's money available for consumption is only reduced by $I_0 \times (1 - \tau^p)$.

If the investment is financed by retained earnings, retained earnings can be distributed in addition to the annual profit whenever sufficient cash is available, that is if

$$CF_t^{\tau,c} \geq Div_t^P. \tag{6.5}$$

If retained earnings are taken for distributions (Div_t^{RE}), the distributed amount exceeds P_t^τ because of the noncash equivalent accrual D_t. The exceeding amount is defined as:

$$Div_t^{RE} = \alpha \times CF_t^{\tau,c} - Div_t^P. \tag{6.6}$$

Using (6.1) for Div_t^P, (6.6) changes to

$$\begin{aligned} Div_t^{RE} &= \alpha \times CF_t^{\tau,c} - \alpha \times P_t^\tau \\ &= \alpha \times (CF_t^c - \tau^c \times (CF_t^c - D_t)) - \alpha \times (1 - \tau^c) \times (CF_t^c - D_t) \\ &= \alpha \times D_t. \end{aligned} \tag{6.7}$$

Equation (6.7) states, that additional distribution on top of profits is equivalent to a fraction of the only accrual – depreciation in t.

After distributing Div_t^P and Div_t^{RE}, the remaining cash flow is invested at the capital market interest rate i on the corporate level. The financial investment FI_t is

$$FI_t = CF_t^{\tau,c} - Div_t^P - Div_t^{RE} + FI_{t-1} \times (1 + i \times (1 - \tau^c)). \tag{6.8}$$

If a fraction of the interest income is distributed as well, we get

$$Div_t^{FI} = \alpha \times i \times (1 - \tau^c) \times FI_{t-1}. \tag{6.9}$$

Finally, total dividend distribution corresponds to the sum of the three fractions ((6.1), (6.7), and (6.9)) of distribution

$$Div_t = Div_t^P + Div_t^{RE} + Div_t^{FI}. \tag{6.10}$$

The final distribution at time $t = n$ is

$$Div_n = CF_n^{\tau,c} + (1 + i \times (1 - \tau^c)) \times FI_{n-1}. \tag{6.11}$$

The after-tax NPV^τ from owner's perspective then gives

$$NPV^{\tau,p} = (1 - \tau^p) \times \left[-I_0 + \sum_{t=1}^{n} \frac{Div_t}{(1 + i \times (1 - \tau^p))^t} \right]. \tag{6.12}$$

The initial investment is diminished by τ^p. Again, as the investment is financed by retained earnings, the owner waives the possible distribution of I_0 in $t = 0$. Thus, he saves the tax payment of $\tau^p \times I_0$. Depending on the relation of the owner's marginal tax rate and the corporate tax rate, either maximum distribution of profits or maximum retention of profits until $t = n$ is favorable.

Now, all dividends distributed are taxed at the personal income tax rate of the owner. The reason is that retained earnings were used to finance the investment. There is no capital investment from outside the company, which could be distributed free of taxes.

Now, we distinguish retaining profits (case A) and distributing profits (case B).

6.7.1.1 Case A: Financing by Retained Earning where Profits are Retained

If profits are retained until $t = n$ then dividend payout ratio is $\alpha = 0$ and therefore $Div_t = 0$ for $0 \leq t < n$. Retained profits are invested in a financial investment on the corporate level. The financial investment FI_t is calculated as:

$$\begin{aligned}
FI_0 &= 0 \quad \text{(Assumption)} \\
FI_1 &= CF_1^{\tau,c} \\
FI_2 &= CF_2^{\tau,c} + (1 + i^{\tau,c}) \times FI_1 = CF_2^{\tau,c} + (1 + i^{\tau,c}) \times CF_1^{\tau,c} \\
FI_3 &= CF_3^{\tau,c} + (1 + i^{\tau,c}) \times FI_2 \\
&= CF_3^{\tau,c} + (1 + i^{\tau,c}) \times CF_2^{\tau,c} + (1 + i^{\tau,c})^2 \times CF_1^{\tau,c} \\
&\ldots \\
FI_n &= \sum_{t=1}^{n} CF_t^{\tau,c} \times (1 + i^{\tau,c})^{n-t},
\end{aligned}$$

where $i^{\tau,c}$ stands for $i \times (1 - \tau^c)$. The after-tax NPV^τ from the owner's perspective can then be derived as:

$$NPV^{\tau,p} = (1-\tau^p)\times\left[-I_0 + (1+i^{\tau,p})^{-n} \times \sum_{t=1}^{n} CF_t^{\tau,c} \times (1+i^{\tau,c})^{n-t}\right]. \quad (6.13)$$

Notice, the after-tax cash flows are compounded by the capital market rate after corporate income tax while distribution in $t = n$ is discounted at the capital market rate after personal income tax.

Example 6.11. Net Present Value if Profits are Retained

Referring to the German tax system 2010, $i = 5\%$, $\tau^c = 30\%$, and τ^p – as the tax rate paid on dividends and interest – equals in our case $\tau^p = \tau^{flat} = 25\%$. The after-tax interest rates on corporate and owner's level are

$$i^{\tau,c} = 0.05 \times (1 - 0.3) = 0.035$$
$$i^{\tau,p} = 0.05 \times (1 - 0.25) = 0.0375.$$

Remember, in Germany there is an option for assessing dividend income. The option is profitable if the individual progressive tax rate is below $\tau^{flat} = 25\%$. As we assume an individual marginal tax rate of $\tau^p = 45\%$, assessment is never profitable in this example.

Further, we use the straight-line depreciation method. Initial investment is supposed to be $I_0 = 120$. Expected useful life of our real investment alternative is three periods. Now suppose the following stream of cash flows

t	0	1	2	3
CF_t^c	–120.00	45.00	50.00	60.00

1. Net Present Value Before Taxes

   In the case of financing the initial investment by retained earnings, the dividend payout restriction does not bind. Profits and retained earnings are at least equal to the amount of cash flow available for distribution and hence could be distributed. However, we investigate the case were profits are retained. After-tax cash flow is hence reinvested in a financial investment on corporate level. FI_3 denotes financial investment at the end of year 3 just before the final dividend is distributed.

   At the end of $t = 3$, total cash available is distributed to the shareholder. We get (Table 6.8)

Table 6.8 Pre-tax *NPV*, reinvestment on corporate level

t	0	1	2	3
CF_t^c	−120.00	45.00	50.00	60.00
IP_t		0.00	2.25	4.86
FI_t		45.00	97.25	162.11
Div_t	−120.00	0.00	0.00	162.11
Div_t^{disc}	−120.00			140.04
NPV	20.04			

Table 6.9 Balance sheet, pre-tax case, assets

t	0	1	2	3
BV_t	120.00	80.00	40.00	0.00
FI_t	0.00	45.00	97.25	162.11
$ASSETS_t$	120.00	125.00	137.25	162.11

Div_t^{disc} is calculated as:

$$Div_t^{disc} = Div_t \times (1 + i)^{-t}.$$

Let's take financial accounting into account and see what happens in the balance sheet. Notice, we are still in the pre-tax case.
In the following tables, numbers in $t = 3$ refer to the end of year 3, one second before the final distribution of funds to the shareholder takes place. Table 6.9 represents the development of the asset accounts over time. The first row contains the book value (BV_t) of the real investment. Book value in t is defined as book value of the previous period less depreciation in t.

$$BV_t = BV_{t-1} - D_t.$$

Because we assumed straight-line depreciation, depreciation in t is

$$D_t = D = \frac{I_0}{n} = \frac{120}{3} = 40.$$

Total cash inflow in t is calculated as cash flow in terms of return of the real investment and interest payments resulting from the financial investment from the previous period, hence

$$CF_t^c + i \times FI_{t-1}.$$

Financial investment in $t = 0$ is assumed to be zero. Cash outflow in t is reduced to dividend payments. Cash available for financial investments in t is then

$$FI_t = FI_{t-1} \times (1 + i) + CF_t^c - Div_t.$$

Table 6.10 Balance sheet, pre-tax case, equity

t	0	1	2	3
RE_t	120.00	125.00	137.25	162.11
$EQUITY_t$	120.00	125.00	137.25	162.11

Assets in t as the sum of all asset accounts are

$$ASSETS_t = BV_t + FI_t. \tag{6.14}$$

Table 6.10 shows the development of equity over time in the pre-tax case. Retained earnings increase by annual profits P_t. Profits consist of revenue (cash flow) plus financial returns less depreciation

$$P_t = CF_t^c + i \times FI_{t-1} - D_t. \tag{6.15}$$

Based on that, the profits P_t are

$$P_1 = 45.00 + 0.00 - 40.00 = 5.00$$
$$P_3 = 50.00 + 0.05 \times 45.00 - 40.00 = 12.25$$
$$P_3 = 60.00 + 0.05 \times 97.25 - 40.00 = 24.86.$$

Because of our assumption to retain profits, dividend payout is zero, hence $Div_t^P = Div_t^{RE} = Div_t^{FI} = 0$. The equity account *retained earnings* is calculated as:

$$RE_t = RE_{t-1} + P_t,$$

where $RE_0 = 120$. Equity, therefore, consists solely of the balance account *retained earnings*.

2. Net Present Value After Taxes: Consideration of Corporate Level Exclusively

In Table 6.11, the post-tax financial plan, considering the corporate level exclusively, is displayed. In that case dividend payout restrictions are neglected. Here, there is no difference between retaining and distributing earnings, because personal level is assumed to be not existent. Investment evaluation goes, therefore, along the rules according to an investment decision in the framework of a sole proprietorship or partnership.

It is important to mention that the discount rate now is not the interest rate reduced by the owner's individual marginal tax rate but by the corporate tax rate. Hence, we have to use

$$i^{\tau,c} = 0.05 \times (1 - 0.3) = 0.035.$$

Table 6.11 Financial plan considering corporate level exclusively

t	0	1	2	3
CF_t^c	−120.00	45.00	50.00	60.00
D_t		40.00	40.00	40.00
TB_t		5.00	10.00	20.00
T_t		1.50	3.00	6.00
$CF_t^{\tau,c}$	−120.00	43.50	47.00	54.00
$CF_t^{\tau,c,disc}$	−120.00	42.03	43.88	48.70
$NPV^{\tau,c}$	14.61			

3. Net Present Value After Taxes: Taking Owner's Level into Account

We first consider the corporate level. After evolving asset and equity accounts as in the pre-tax case, we must have a look at the owner's level in order to calculate the will's consumption potential in terms of after-tax NPV. Table 6.12 illustrates the development of assets if corporate income tax is taken into consideration. Because there is assumed to be no dividend payment, financial investment in t consists of financial investment of the previous period plus after-tax cash flow in t

$$FI_t = FI_{t-1} + CF_t^{\tau,c}.$$

After-tax cash flow in t consists of cash flows of the real investment, the return of the financial investment less corporate income tax.

$$CF_t^{\tau,c} = CF_t^c + i \times FI_{t-1} - \tau^c \times (CF_t^c - D_t + i \times FI_{t-1}).$$

Assets are still the sum of financial investments in t and book value of the real investment.

Table 6.12 Balance sheet, post-tax case, assets

t	0	1	2	3
BV_t	120.00	80.00	40.00	0.00
FI_t	0.00	43.50	92.02	149.24
$ASSETS_t$	120.00	123.50	132.02	149.24

Table 6.13 shows the development of equity, if corporate income taxes are considered.

Retained earnings in t are calculated as:

$$RE_t = RE_{t-1} + P_t^{\tau}.$$

Remember that taxes represent expenses for financial accounting purposes (for tax accounting purposes, taxes are usually not deductible). Keeping that in mind, after-tax profit accounts for

Table 6.13 Balance sheet, post-tax case, equity

t	0	1	2	3
RE_t	120.00	123.50	132.02	149.24
$EQUITY_t$	120.00	123.50	132.02	149.24

Table 6.14 Financial plan from the owner's perspective

t	0	1	2	3
CF_t^c	−120.00	45.00	50.00	60.00
D_t		40.00	40.00	40.00
FI_t		43.50	92.02	149.24
IP_t		0.00	2.18	4.60
P_t		5.00	12.18	24.60
T_t		1.50	3.65	7.38
$CF_t^{\tau,c}$		43.50	48.52	57.22
$Div_t = CF_t^p$	−120.00	0.00	0.00	149.24
$\tau^{flat} \times Div_t$	−30.00	0.00	0.00	37.31
$CF_t^{\tau,p}$	−90.00	0.00	0.00	111.93
$CF_t^{\tau,p,disc}$	−90.00	0.00	0.00	100.23
$NPV^{\tau,p}$	10.23			

$$P_t^{\tau} = CF_t^c - D_t + i^c \times FI_{t-1} - \tau^c \times (CF_t^c - D_t + i^c \times FI_{t-1}).$$

Table 6.14 shows the calculation of the $NPV^{\tau,p}$ from the owner's perspective. Cash flow ready for consumption is equivalent to dividend received after personal income taxes – in our case after German flat tax rate of 25%. The amount of 149.24 is available for distribution, because it represents the financial investment at the end of the planning horizon. Over time, there is a transformation of the asset account represented by the initial real investment to the cash account or bank account. Please notice that other than in the case of the corporate perspective where the discount rate is represented by the interest rate less corporate income tax, now the interest rate is reduced by the personal income tax, in our case the flat tax.

$$i^{\tau,p} = i \times (1 - \tau^p) = 0.05 \times (1 - 0.25) = 0.0375.$$

In $t = 0$, there are opportunity costs of $I_0 \times (1 - \tau^{flat})$. That means, if retained earnings of 120 were distributed, the owner would just be able to reinvest 90 because of dividend taxation. That is why I_0 is 90 from the owner's perspective and not 120 as from the corporate's perspective.

Now, if you compare the $NPV^{\tau,p}$ from the owner's perspective as a result of Table 6.14 with the $NPV^{\tau,c}$ from the corporate's perspective using the result from Table 6.11, you can realize, that neglecting the owner's perspective might lead to carrying out unprofitable investment alternatives. That is because $NPV^{\tau,p} < NPV^{\tau,c}$. It's up to the corporate tax system and the relationship between the corporate income tax rate and the tax rate on distributed profits on the owner's level, if there are distortions when the owner's level is neglected for capital budgeting.

6.7.1.2 Case B: Financing by Retained Earnings where Profits are Immediately Distributed

In the case of financing the initial investment cost by retained earnings in our model, the restriction of limiting the distributed amount to the level of profits (dividend payout restriction) does not bind, because in addition to the profits, retained earnings can be distributed, too. Therefore, it is possible to distribute all cash flow after taxes and not an amount limited to the annual profit. If profits are distributed as early as possible, the dividend payout ratio is $\alpha = 1$ and, therefore, $Div_t = CF_t^{\tau,c}$ for $0 < t \leq n$. Hence, dividend payout is

$$Div_t = CF_t^{\tau,c} = CF_t^c - \tau^c \times (CF_t^c - D_t). \tag{6.16}$$

Because cash flow after taxes on corporate level is distributed completely, there is no financial investment at the corporate level. The after-tax $NPV^{\tau,p}$ from the owner's perspective then accounts for

$$NPV^{\tau,p} = (1 - \tau^p) \times \left[-I_0 + \sum_{t=1}^{n} CF_t^{\tau,c} \times (1 + i^{\tau,p})^{-t} \right]. \tag{6.17}$$

Financial investment occurs at the personal level of the owner. The best alternative investment is a financial investment taxed at t^p.

Example 6.12. Net Present Value if Profits are Distributed

Suppose the assumptions of Ex. 6.11. However, now the reverse case is assumed. All cash flows after corporate income taxes are distributed immediately.

1. Net Present Value Before Taxes

   We still face the case where initial investment is financed by retained earnings. Insofar dividend payout restriction does not bind. *NPV* before taxes is equal to Case A. According to Table 6.8, *NPV* is 20.04. The before-tax *NPV* is not distorted by dividend payout decisions. No matter if cash is distributed

Table 6.15 Available distribution in case of immediate maximum distribution

t	1	2	3
CF_t^c	45.00	50.00	60.00
D_t	40.00	40.00	40.00
P_t	5.00	10.00	20.00
Div_t^P	5.00	10.00	20.00
Div_t^{RE}	40.00	40.00	40.00
Div_t	45.00	50.00	60.00
RE_t	80.00	40.00	0

Table 6.16 Pre-tax NPV, immediate distribution

t	0	1	2	3
CF_t^c	−120.00	45.00	50.00	60.00
Div_t	−120.00	45.00	50.00	60.00
Div_t^{disc}	−120.00	42.86	45.35	51.83
NPV	20.04			

immediately or retained and distributed in $t = n$, NPV stays unaffected. Reinvesting free cash flow on the company's level up to $t = n$ and distribution in n is illustrated in Table 6.8. Immediate distribution is illustrated in Table 6.15.

The following table shows that P_t is always below CF_t^c. To be able to distribute CF_t^c, retained earnings of 40 each year have to be reversed.

All cash flow can be distributed to the shareholders. Because of that, the net present value before taxes on the corporate level as well of the owner's level then gives 20.04 (Table 6.16).

2. Net Present Value After Taxes: Consideration of Corporate Level Exclusively

   If the owner's level is neglected, the net present value from the company's perspective is equivalent to Case A. According to Table 6.11, $NPV^{\tau,c}$ is 14.61.

3. Net Present Value After Taxes: Taking Owner's Level into Account

   Table 6.17 shows the development of the asset accounts. In contrast to the assumption of retaining earnings (Table 6.12), dividend payout is equal to available cash flow after corporate income tax. As there is no financial investment, because all liquidity is distributed, after-tax cash flow in t gives

$$CF_t^{\tau,c} = CF_t^c - \tau^c \times (CF_t^c - D_t).$$

   It is easy to see that asset accounts are equivalent to the book value of the real investment because there is no liquidity left at the end of the year.

Table 6.17 Balance sheet, post-tax case, assets

t	0	1	2	3
BV_t	120.00	80.00	40.00	0.00
FI_t	0.00	0.00	0.00	0.00
$ASSETS_t$	120.00	80.00	40.00	0.00

Table 6.18 Balance sheet, post-tax case, equity

t	0	1	2	3
RE_t	120.00	80.00	40.00	0.00
$EQUITY_t$	120.00	80.00	40.00	0.00

Table 6.19 Financial plan from the owner's perspective

t	0	1	2	3
CF_t^c	−120.00	45.00	50.00	60.00
D_t		40.00	40.00	40.00
FI_t		0.00	0.00	0.00
P_t		5.00	10.00	20.00
T_t		1.50	3.00	6.00
$CF_t^{\tau,c}$	−120.00	43.50	47.00	54.00
Div_t^P		3.50	7.00	14.00
$+Div_t^{RE}$		40.00	40.00	40.00
$= Div_t$	−120.00	43.50	47.00	54.00
$\tau^{flat} \times Div_t$	−30.00	10.88	11.75	13.50
$CF_t^{\tau,p}$	−90.00	32.63	35.25	40.50
$CF_t^{\tau,p,disc}$	−90.00	31.45	32.75	36.27
$NPV^{\tau,p}$	10.46			

The financial plan shows, that all cash after corporate income tax is distributed. However, we now have to show that dividend payout restrictions do not bind, so that distribution of total cash after taxes is possible for legal reasons. Table 6.18 shows the development of equity in the case of immediate distribution of post-tax cash flow. First of all, you can see that the post-tax return of the financial investment is zero. This corresponds to the fact that that there is no financial investment, because all cash is distributed. Second, we have to justify the dividend payments. Notice that annual profits after taxes are not enough. Consider the first year. From Table 6.19 we know that there is a planned distribution of 43.50. However, the profit in $t = 1$ after taxes is just 3.50 as we can derive from Table 6.19. Now, for double entry bookkeeping, we need to distribute retained earnings to the amount of exactly the value of the depreciation to reach the desired amount for distribution of 43.50.

Notice that it would be possible to distribute the retained earnings in total. However, there would be not enough cash available for distribution.
Table 6.19 illustrates the financial plan at owner's level. Dividends after flat tax have to be discounted in order to get the post-tax $NPV^{\tau,p}$. Once more, the discount rate in this case is $i^{\tau,p} = 0.0375$.

6.7.1.3 Comparison of Retaining Earnings and Immediate Distribution

In the case of retaining earnings and distributing cash flow after taxes in $t = n$, the net present value from owner's perspective $NPV^{\tau,p}$ is – according to Table 6.14 – 10.23. If we take the result in Case B – where profits are distributed immediately – of 10.46 (Table 6.19), we realize that immediate distribution leads to a greater $NPV^{\tau,p}$. What's the reason for that result? The answer is quite simple and is caused by taxation of financial returns at different rates on the corporate level and the owner's level. In our example we have

$$i^{\tau,flat} = 0.05 \times (1 - 0.25) = 0.0375 > 0.035 = 0.05 \times (1 - 0.3) = i^{\tau,c}. \quad (6.18)$$

Financial return after taxes on corporate level is 3.5%, whereas it is 3.75% on the owner's level due to flat rate taxation of financial returns. Now, it is more profitable to reinvest money at the owner's level than on the corporate level due to a higher after-tax return on the owner's level.

For deciding between retention and distribution of profits, we can use the following decision rule

$$\begin{aligned} i^{\tau,p} &> i^{\tau,c} &\Rightarrow&\quad \text{immediate distribution is profitable} \\ i^{\tau,p} &< i^{\tau,c} &\Rightarrow&\quad \text{retaining earnings is profitable} \\ i^{\tau,p} &= i^{\tau,c} &\Rightarrow&\quad \text{indifference.} \end{aligned}$$

The third case, where $i^{\tau,p} = i^{\tau,c}$, exists in Austria. In Austria, the corporate income tax rate is 25% (there is no local business tax or any surcharge) as well as the flat tax for dividends and interest income.

Example 6.13. Explaining the Differences between Retention and Distribution

The difference of $NPV^{\tau,p}$ in case of retention (see Table 6.14) and in case of distribution (see Table 6.19) is computed as:

$$10.46 - 10.23 = 0.23.$$

The difference is caused by tax rate effects due to different after-tax rates of return on the company's level and the owner's level. In case of distribution, cash arrives earlier at the owner's level than in the case of retention. There, it is taxed at the smaller flat tax rate. The following table includes dividend received after flat rate tax on owner's level in the case of retention ($CF_t^{\tau,p,retention}$) and distribution ($CF_t^{\tau,p,distribution}$). Differences are displayed in the last row: $\Delta = CF_t^{\tau,p,distribution} - CF_t^{\tau,p,retention}$.

t	0	1	2	3
$CF_t^{\tau,p,distribution}$	-90.00	32.63	35.25	40.50
$CF_t^{\tau,p,retention}$	-90.00	0.00	0.00	111.93
Δ	0.00	32.63	35.25	-71.43

Now, the difference in terms of $NPV^{\tau,p}$ occurs, because in the case of distribution, the amounts of 32.63 in $t = 1$ and 35.25 are discounted at a greater rate (1.0375) than the received net return on the company level (1.035). Amounts received in $t = n$ cause no difference in terms of $NPV^{\tau,p}$. The difference in total can be computed as follows

$$\Delta = \underbrace{\frac{32.63}{1.0375} - \frac{32.63 \times 1.035^2}{1.0375^3}}_{\text{effect due to distribution in t=1}} + \underbrace{\frac{35.25}{1.0375^2} - \frac{35.25 \times 1.035}{1.0375^3}}_{\text{effect due to distribution in t=2}} = 0.23.$$

6.7.1.4 Lock-in-Effect and Clientele Effect

The result derived in the previous subsection can be taken to explain the so-called lock-in-effect. Suppose the rate of return before taxes is equal on both the company's level and the owner's level. Now, if the corporate income tax rate exceeds the personal tax rate ($i^{\tau,p} < i^{\tau,c}$), the owner is willing to reinvest cash flows after taxes on the company's level, because he can earn a higher net rate of return on financial investments. To maximize $NPV^{\tau,p}$, the money is locked in the company.

Now, assume that the corporation is not controlled to 100% by just one owner, but by hundreds or thousands of shareholders. In this situation, we usually face a listed corporation on the stock exchange. Further, assume that dividends are taxed at the personal marginal tax rate and the tax rate is formed progressively. In this case, there are surely shareholders that have a tax rate below the proportional marginal corporate income tax rate and there are additionally well-off shareholders who have individual marginal tax rates that exceed the corporate income tax rate by far. Of course, there might be also shareholders whose marginal tax rate just meets the corporate income tax rate. Taking our net rate of return, we have $i^{\tau,p} > i^{\tau,c}$ and $i^{\tau,p} < i^{\tau,c}$ and further $i^{\tau,p} = i^{\tau,c}$. For the management it is difficult to develop a dividend payout strategy that meets the expectations of all types of shareholders. Those shareholders for whom $i^{\tau,p} > i^{\tau,c}$ is true, are interested in immediate distribution of profits and do not prefer retention. Shareholders who are in the situation of $i^{\tau,p} < i^{\tau,c}$, do not prefer immediate distribution of profits for reinvestment on the personal level, but prefer retention. Those who are in the happy situation to be indifferent ($i^{\tau,p} = i^{\tau,c}$) between distribution and retention of profits, are likely the smallest fraction of shareholders.

Let's say rich shareholders face $i^{\tau,p} < i^{\tau,c}$ and the corporation decides to retain all profits, poor shareholders who are in the situation of $i^{\tau,p} > i^{\tau,c}$ are not willing to invest in that corporation. Therefore, the corporation attracts a clientele that is characterized by high taxable income and, therefore, rich individuals.

Now, you probably understand the problem of taking the individual level into account when evaluating investment alternatives. The more shareholders with different personal situations, the greater the problem of taking the personal level into account. However, if management surrenders taking the personal level into account, distortions are probably greater than using a notional marginal tax rate as a representative tax rate for all shareholders for distribution policy making.

6.7.2 *Financing by New Equity*

If initial investment costs are financed by new equity from the current owner, we assume an amount I_0 of new equity is raised from the current owner and will be returned to the owner at $t = n$. In comparison to the case where I_0 is financed by retained earnings, now the dividend payout restriction binds, because there are no retained earnings for distribution. Dividend payout is, hence, restricted to the annual profit after taxes. Of course, there is the possibility of annual reduction of share capital to simulate the same distribution as in the case of financing I_0 by retained earnings. However, that case is neglected.

6.7.2.1 Case C: Financing by New Equity where Profits are Retained

The after-tax $NPV^{\tau,p}$ from the owner's perspective is calculated as in case A (see (6.13)), however, without tax relief of $\tau^p \times I_0$. There is no deduction for tax purposes in case of an increase in share capital in $t = 0$. Correspondingly, there is no tax levied on the amounts received due to reduction of the share capital in $t = n$. If $FV^{\tau,c}$ represents the future value after taxes on the company's level in $t = n$, the after-tax $NPV^{\tau,p}$ is

$$NPV^{\tau,p} = -I_0 + (1 + i^{\tau,p})^{-n} \times [FV^{\tau,c} - \tau^p \times (FV^{\tau,c} - I_0)].$$

Notice that $FV^{\tau,c} - I_0$ represents accumulated retained earnings in $t = n$ that are subject to tax. We then get

$$NPV^{\tau,p} = -I_0 + (1 + i^{\tau,p})^{-n} \times \left[(1 - \tau^p) \times \left(\sum_{t=1}^{n} CF_t^{\tau,c} \times (1 + i^{\tau,c})^{n-t} \right) + \tau^p \times I_0 \right]. \quad (6.19)$$

Example 6.14. Financing with New Equity: Net Present Value if Profits are Retained

Suppose the assumptions of Ex. 6.11. If profits are retained until $t = n$ then dividend payout ratio is $\alpha = 0$ and, therefore, $Div_t = 0$ for $0 \leq t < n$. Retained profits are invested in a financial investment on the corporate level. *NPV* before taxes is not affected by source of financing. *NPV* is still the same as in the case of financing the initial investment by retained earnings (see Table 6.8.).

1. Net Present Value Before Taxes

   We now face the situation where dividend payout restrictions basically bind. However, in case of reinvesting cash flows on corporate level, payout restrictions are not considered. Because of equivalent returns on financial investment on corporate level and owner's level as well, the pre-tax *NPV* is unaffected concerning the source of funds for initial investment.
2. Net Present Value After Taxes: Consideration of Corporate Level Exclusively

   If the owner's level is neglected, the net present value from the company's perspective is equivalent to Case A. According to Table 6.11, $NPV^{\tau,c}$ is 14.61.
3. Net Present Value After Taxes: Taking Owner's Level into Account

   If the owner's level is neglected, $NPV^{\tau,c}$ is not affected compared to case A. Table 6.20 illustrates the development of the asset accounts in

Table 6.20 Balance sheet, post-tax case, assets

t	0	1	2	3
BV_t	120.00	80.00	40.00	0.00
FI_t	0.00	43.50	92.02	149.24
$ASSETS_t$	120.00	123.50	132.02	149.24

Table 6.21 Balance sheet, post-tax case, equity

t	0	1	2	3
APC_t	120.00	120.00	120.00	120.00
RE_t	0.00	3.50	12.02	29.24
$EQUITY_t$	120.00	123.50	132.02	149.24

Table 6.22 Financial plan from the owner's perspective

t	0	1	2	3
CF_t^c	−120.00	45.00	50.00	60.00
D_t		40.00	40.00	40.00
FI_t	0.00	43.50	92.02	149.24
IP_t		0.00	2.18	4.60
P_t		5.00	12.18	24.60
T_t		1.50	3.65	7.38
$CF_t^{\tau,c}$		43.50	48.52	57.22
Div_t		0.00	0.00	29.24
APC_t	−120.00	0.00	0.00	120.00
CF_t^p	−120.00	0.00	0.00	149.24
TB_t	0.00	0.00	0.00	29.24
$\tau^{flat} \times Div_t$	0.00	0.00	0.00	7.31
$CF_t^{\tau,p}$	−120.00	0.00	0.00	141.93
$CF_t^{\tau,p,disc}$	−120.00	0.00	0.00	127.09
$NPV^{\tau,p}$	7.09			

case of financing the initial investment cost with new equity. Table 6.20 corresponds to Table 6.12. There are no differences between financing by retained earnings and new equity on the asset side.
Table 6.21 shows the side of equity. The first row represents the additional paid-in capital APC_t that stays constant over time. The second row is represented by the accumulated retained earnings that are calculated as the retained earnings from the previous period plus profit in t.
Table 6.22 shows the handling of cash flows for tax purposes on the owner's level. Notice that in $t = 0$ additional paid-in capital is not tax deductible. However, it reduces the tax base in $t = n$. Cash flow in $t = n$ has to be discounted at $(1 + i^{\tau,flat}) = 1.0375$.

The net present value from the owner's perspective in case of new equity financing and retention is lower than in the case of retention of profits and financing by retained earnings ($NPV^{\tau,p}$ =10.23, see Table 6.14 on p. 244). The difference stems from the different taxable treatment of the two different sources of cash to finance the initial cost. In case of using retained earnings, opportunity costs are reduced at the amount of $\tau^{flat} \times I_0$ in $t = 0$, whereas in the case of equity financing, additional paid-in capital reduces the tax base in

$t = n$. To explain the differences, we have to calculate the timing effect of the different taxable treatment. We get

$$\tau^{flat} \times I_0 - \frac{\tau^{flat} \times I_0}{(1 + i^{\tau,flat})^3} = 30 - 26.86 = 3.14 \tag{6.20}$$

which explains the difference of $NPV^{\tau,p}$: $10.23 - 7.09 = 3.14$.

6.7.2.2 Case D: Financing by New Equity where Profits are Immediately Distributed

As the investment in $t = 0$ is financed by new equity, dividends are restricted to current after-tax profits. Cash flows above after-tax profits are invested on the corporate level. Distribution Div_t and the financial investment FI_t are calculated as:

$$\begin{aligned} Div_1 &= P_1^\tau = (1 - \tau^c) \times (CF_1^c - D_1) \\ FI_1 &= CF_1^{\tau,c} - Div_1 \\ &= CF_1^c - \tau^c \times (CF_1^c - D_1) - (1 - \tau^c) \times (CF_1^c - D_1) = D_1, \end{aligned}$$

$$\begin{aligned} Div_2 &= P_2^\tau + i^{\tau,c} \times FI_1 = (1 - \tau^c) \times (CF_2^c - D_2) + i^{\tau,c} \times FI_1, \\ FI_2 &= CF_2^{\tau,c} - Div_2 + (1 + i^{\tau,c}) \times FI_1 = D_1 + D_2. \\ &\dots \end{aligned}$$

Notice, that the financial investment equals the accumulated depreciation. At any time $0 < t \leq n$, we have

$$\begin{aligned} FI_t &= \sum_{j=1}^{t} D_j \qquad \text{and} \\ Div_t &= Div_t^p + Div_t^{FI} = P_t^\tau + i^{\tau,c} \times FI_{t-1}. \end{aligned}$$

In $t = n$ we get

$$FI_n = \sum_{j=1}^{n} D_j = I_0. \tag{6.21}$$

Those values refer to the moment just before distributing all funds to the shareholder. Afterward, financial investment at the corporate level is always zero.

At $t = n$, the profit P_n^τ and the financial investment are distributed. Capital of I_0 is refunded, respectively.

$$\begin{aligned} Div_n + I_0 &= CF_n^{\tau,c} + (1 + i^{\tau,c}) \times FI_{n-1} \\ &= P_n^\tau + i^{\tau,c} \times FI_{n-1} + D_n + FI_{n-1} \\ &= P_n^\tau + i^{\tau,c} \times FI_{n-1} + I_0. \end{aligned}$$

The after-tax $NPV^{\tau,p}$ from the owner's perspective is

$$NPV^{\tau,p} = -I_0 + I_0 \times (1 + i^{\tau,p})^{-n} + (1 - \tau^p) \times \sum_{t=1}^{n} Div_t \times (1 + i^{\tau,p})^{-t}$$

and hence

$$\begin{aligned} NPV^{\tau,p} &= -I_0 + I_0 \times (1 + i^{\tau,p})^{-n} \\ &\quad + (1 - \tau^p) \times \sum_{t=1}^{n} (P_t^\tau + i^{\tau,c} \times FI_{t-1}) \times (1 + i^{\tau,p})^{-t}. \end{aligned}$$

Example 6.15. Financing with New Equity: Net Present Value if Profits are Distributed

Suppose the assumptions of Ex. 6.11. However, now initial investment is financed by outside funds and we assume maximum immediate distribution of cash flows.

1. Net Present Value Before Taxes

   Because there are no retained earnings available for additional distribution dividend payout is restricted to annual profits. However, since the before-tax return on owner's level and corporate level is equivalent, the pre-tax *NPV* is not affected, which is illustrated in Table 6.23.

Table 6.23 Pre-tax *NPV*, annual distribution of profits

t	0	1	2	3
CF_t^c	−120.00	45.00	50.00	60.00
IP_t		0.00	2.00	4.00
FI_t		40.00	80.00	120.00
Div_t		5.00	12.00	24.00
APC_t	−120.00	0.00	0.00	120.00
CF_t^p	−120.00	5.00	12.00	144.00
$CF_t^{p,disc}$	−120.00	4.76	10.88	124.39
NPV	20.04			

2. Net Present Value After Taxes: Consideration of Corporate Level Exclusively

   If the owner's level is neglected, net present value from the company's perspective is still equivalent to Case A (see Table 6.11).

3. Net Present Value After Taxes: Taking Owner's Level into Account

   Table 6.24 illustrates the development of the asset accounts in case of financing the initial investment cost with new equity and immediate distribution of profits. Table 6.24 is different to Table 6.12, because despite immediate distribution of profits, there is a financial investment. That is due to the fact that distribution is limited to annual profits and not to available after-tax cash flows as in the case of financing by retained earnings.

Table 6.24 Balance sheet, post-tax case, assets

t	0	1	2	3
BV_t	120.00	80.00	40.00	0.00
FI_t	0.00	40.00	80.00	120.00
$ASSETS_t$	120.00	120.00	120.00	120.00

Table 6.25 Balance sheet, post-tax case, equity

t	0	1	2	3
APC_t	120.00	120.00	120.00	120.00
RE_t	0.00	0.00	0.00	0.00
$EQUITY_t$	120.00	120.00	120.00	120.00

Finally, Table 6.25 shows the net cash flow from the owner's perspective. Net present value in this case is $NPV^{\tau,p} = 7.12$. Cash outflow in terms of dividends meets the annual profit minus corporate taxes displayed in Table 6.26. Notice, that in the case considered, we have $Div_t^{FI} > 0$ in $t = 2, 3$ in contrast to cases A, B, and C.

Table 6.26 Financial plan from the owner's perspective

t	0	1	2	3
CF_t^c	−120.00	45.00	50.00	60.00
D_t		40.00	40.00	40.00
FI_t	0.00	40.00	80.00	120.00
IP_t		0.00	2.00	4.00
P_t	0.00	5.00	12.00	24.00
T_t	0.00	1.50	3.60	7.20
$CF_t^{\tau,c}$		43.50	48.40	56.80

(Continued)

Table 6.26 (Continued)

t	0	1	2	3
Div_t^P		3.50	7.00	14.00
$+Div_t^{FI}$		0.00	1.40	2.80
$= Div_t$		3.50	8.40	16.80
APC_t	−120.00	0.00	0.00	120.00
CF_t^P	−120.00	3.50	8.40	136.80
TB_t	0.00	3.50	8.40	16.80
$\tau^{flat} \times Div_t$	0.00	0.88	2.10	4.20
$CF_t^{\tau,p}$	−120.00	2.63	6.30	132.60
$CF_t^{\tau,p,disc}$	−120.00	2.53	5.85	118.74
$NPV^{\tau,p}$	7.12			

4. Comparing $NPV^{\tau,p}$ in Case of Immediate Distribution and Retention

You certainly recognized the difference of $NPV^{\tau,p}$ in case of immediate distribution and retention that is $7.12 - 7.09 = 0.03$. In the following Table 6.27, the annual differences of cash received by the owner in case of immediate distribution (Table 6.26) and retention (Table 6.22) is displayed and represented by Δ, respectively.

Table 6.27 Differences in cash flows in case of retention and immediate distribution

t	0	1	2	3
$CF_t^{\tau,p,distribution}$	−120.00	2.63	6.30	132.60
$CF_t^{\tau,p,retention}$	−120.00	0.00	0.00	141.93
Δ	0.00	2.63	6.30	−9.33

The difference results from the different after-tax return on financial investments on corporate level and owner's level. Explanation, therefore, goes along to explanation in Ex. 6.13 on p. 248.

$$\Delta = \underbrace{\frac{2.63}{1.0375} - \frac{2.63 \times 1.035^2}{1.0375^3}}_{\text{effect due to distribution in t = 1}} + \underbrace{\frac{6.30}{1.0375^2} - \frac{6.30 \times 1.035}{1.0375^3}}_{\text{effect due to distribution in t = 2}}$$
$$= 0.03.$$

5. Summary and Explanation of Differences

Table 6.28 shows the summary of $NPV^{\tau,p}$ of all four cases discussed. The differences of $NPV^{\tau,p}$ are described by Δ.

Table 6.28 Summary of $NPV^{\tau,p}$ and differences

	Financing by retained earnings		Equity financing	
	Retention	Distribution	Retention	Distribution
$NPV^{\tau,p}$	(A) 10.23	(B) 10.46	(C) 7.09	(D) 7.12
	Δ			
$\Delta : (B) - (A)$	0.23	for explanation see p. 248		
$\Delta : (C) - (D)$	0.03	for explanation see p. 256		
$\Delta : (A) - (C)$	3.14	for explanation see (6.20) on p. 253		
$\Delta : (A) - (D)$	3.11			
$\Delta : (B) - (C)$	3.37			
$\Delta : (B) - (D)$	3.34			

Three differences are left for explanation. Let's first consider the difference in $NPV^{\tau,p}$ of retention in case of financing by retained earnings and immediate distribution in case of equity financing ($\Delta = 3.11$). Now consider the difference of retention in case of financing by retained earnings and financing by new equity which is $\Delta = 3.14$. The difference to 3.11 is 0.03 which is exactly the difference between retention and immediate distribution in case of equity financing ($3.14 - 0.03 = 3.11$).

Explaining the following two differences is now straight forward. The difference between immediate distribution in case of financing by retained earnings and retention in case of equity financing is 3.37 which is exactly the difference between retention in case of financing by retained earnings and financing by new equity (3.14) plus the difference between retention and immediate distribution in case of financing by retained earnings (0.23). The difference between immediate payout in case of financing by retained earnings and financing by new equity is 3.34. This difference represents the sum of the difference of retention in case of financing by retained earnings and immediate payout in case of financing by new equity (3.11) and the difference between retention and immediate payout in case of financing by retained earnings (0.23).

6.7.3 Some Comments on the Assumptions of the Standard Model for Corporations

The Standard Model for corporations introduced in the previous section does not cover debt financing. Debt financing is discussed in Chap. 9. The treatment of a corporation as a legal person leads to the problem of hidden distribution of profits. The idea behind that is, that owners try to generate payout that is tax deductible on the corporate level. Remember that dividends are not deductible for tax purposes but so is interest on debt provided by the owner.

Another problem that we neglected is, that marginal tax rates on owner's level might vary because of taxable income. Additionally, there might be an option for assessment or flat rate taxation. In this case, dividend payout strategies might be very complex, in particular if loss offset restrictions are taken into account. In this case, $NPV^{\tau,p}$ has to be maximized over the annual amount of dividend payout or the option for assessment. In the case of modeling the option of assessment by using a binary variable (e.g., $1 =$ assessment, $0 =$ flat rate taxation), there are 2^n possibilities to carry out the elective.

Further, we assume constant marginal tax rates on owner's level during the planning horizon. In Chap. 7 we deal with the problem of changing marginal tax rates. Basically, it's not a problem to deal with changing marginal tax rates in case of the Standard Model for sole proprietorships or partnerships, however, because of explicit dividend taxation in the corporate model, changing marginal tax rates affect dividend payout strategies and makes the decision setting more complex.

Finally, taxes on corporate level are just represented by the nominal corporate income tax. Additionally, surcharges or local business taxes might have to be taken into account.

6.8 A Static Comparison of Partnerships and Corporations

Example 6.16 compares tax payments of partnerships and corporations.

Example 6.16. Comparison of Partnerships and Corporations

After completing their studies at WHU – Otto Beisheim School of Management, Mark and Oliver want to set up a company in the IT sector in Germany. Mark only wants to participate as a partner, whereas Oliver additionally will work as managing director. Oliver will receive a yearly salary for this function amounting to € 80,000. The residual profit will be split up and distributed equally. The yearly earnings before taxes (EBT) and before Oliver's salary will be € 400,000. Mark and Oliver have sufficient other income so that the marginal tax rate of $\tau^p = 45\%$ is applicable. Please assume that dividends, are taxed at a flat tax of $\tau^{flat} = 25\%$. The corporate tax rate is $\tau^c = 30\%$. Is it more profitable if the legal form of the company will be a corporation or a partnership? Compute the tax burden in each case!

Before presenting the answer, we have to remember that this example can be ranked as a static decision setting because we just take statutory tax rates into account on a 1-year basis. The focus is to show how income is taxed using different legal settings.

We first consider a partnership. Cash flow after taxes in case of choosing a partnership as a legal framework is calculated in Table 6.29. Starting with EBT, Oliver's salary is deductible for financial accounting purposes, however, it is taxed at his marginal income tax rate. Financial profit after salary is the basis for splitting profit between the two owners. No matter what Mark and Oliver do with the money, it represents taxable income and is subject to taxation. Taxable income is, hence, equal to EBT. Oliver has to pay taxes on €80,000 + €160,000 = €240,000 whereas Mark just pays taxes on €160,000. Considering the marginal tax rate of $\tau^p = 45\%$, the tax burden in total is €180,000 and cash flow after taxes in total is €220,000.

Table 6.29 Partnership

	$\sum$ €	*Mark* €	*Oliver* €
EBT	400,000		
Salary Oliver	80,000		80,000
	320,000		
Profit		160,000	160,000
Taxable income	400,000	160,000	240,000
Personal income taxes $\tau^p = 45\%$	180,000	72,000	108,000
Cash flow after taxes	220,000	88,000	132,000

Table 6.30 Corporation

	$\sum$ €	*Mark* €	*Oliver* €
EBT	400,000		
Salary Oliver	80,000		80,000
	320,000		
Corporate income tax $\tau^c = 30\%$	96,000		
Distributional profit	224,000		
Dividend	224,000	112,000	112,000
Tax on dividend $\tau^{flat} = 25\%$	56,000	28,000	28,000
Taxable income (without dividends)	80,000	0	80,000
Personal income tax $\tau^p = 45\%$	36,000	0	36,000
Cash flow after taxes	212,000	84,000	128,000

Now, consider the case where Mark and Oliver use a corporation for their investment which is illustrated in Table 6.30. As in the case of a partnership, Oliver's salary reduces profit, too, however, now profit after consideration of the salary is taxed at a rate of $\tau^c = 30\%$. Profit after taxes (€320,000 – €96,000 = €224,000) is ready for distribution and equals the taxable dividend on the level of Mark and Oliver. Oliver's salary is subject to tax $\tau^p = 45\%$ on his personal level. He has to pay income taxes of €36,000.

Cash flow after taxes in total is less than in the case of a partnership. Total tax burden is computed as the sum of corporate income tax, flat rate tax, and personal income tax (€ 96,000 + € 56,000 + € 36,000 = € 188,000).

This result is straight forward, because only nominal tax rates do play a role. In case of the framework of a corporation, we assumed immediate distribution. However, if profits are retained, the framework of a corporation becomes more profitable compared to a partnership. If retention is chosen, it is assumed that living cost can be financed by other sources of income. If there are no other sources of income, at least a fraction of annual profits must be assumed to be distributed so that the owners are able to finance their cost of living.

To calculate the nominal tax burden, we have to compare the marginal personal income tax rate of $\tau^p = 45\%$ in case of the partnership and the sum of the corporate income tax rate and taxation of dividends in case of the corporation (notice, taxation of salary is equivalent in both cases and can, therefore, be neglected). In the case of the corporation, the statutory tax burden is calculated as

$$0.3 + (1 - 0.3) \times 0.25 = 0.475$$

which is greater than $\tau^p = 0.45$.

Questions

6.1. What are the characteristics of a one-book system and a two-book system? Discuss advantages and disadvantages! What kind of system is used in your home country?

6.2. What problems do occur, if a country uses a one-book system and adopts IFRS for financial accounting purposes?

6.3. Explain the main differences in tax treatment of the legal entities sole proprietorship/partnership and corporation.

6.4. What kinds of corporate tax systems do you know? Which one is implemented in your home country? Provide an example for your home country where you compute the total tax on both levels in total.

6.5. Explain the differences between the economic and judicial sight on "double taxation".

6.6. What problem concerning taxes does occur if a corporation receives dividends from its subsidiary? How is this problem handled in your home country?

6.7. What do you have to take into account in addition to nominal corporate income tax rates in order to make tax burdens in different countries comparable?

6.8. Discuss the ability of governments to use nominal tax rates as a strategic option to attract investors. What tax matters and nontax matters do you have to take into consideration if you are evaluating countries as possible investment locations?

6.9. Discuss the assumptions of the Standard Model for corporations critically.

6.10. Explain in own words the main difference between financing the initial investment by retained earnings or new equity from the owner's perspective in case of corporations.

6.11. Why do dividend payout restrictions prevent optimal reallocation of capital?

6.12. What is meant by lock-in-effect? Does a lock-in-effect occur in your home country? Why?

6.13. Explain the term clientele effect. When does it occur?

6.14. Compare the decision calculus of an individual and a "corporation" concerning tax effects.

6.15. Why do we have an imperfect decision setting, if we neglect taxes on the owner's personal level?

6.16. Why might management of a listed publicly owned firm be forced to restrict tax consideration to the corporate level?

Exercises

Solutions are provided starting on p. 394.

6.17. Corporate Tax Systems

Suppose a corporation earns cash equal profits of 250. If the personal marginal income tax rate is not specified by tax law (e.g., in case of a progressive tax rate function), suppose τ^p to be 30%. Now compute

(a) Taxable dividend and
(b) Cash after total taxes on both corporate and personal level, respectively,

if profits are distributed totally considering a corporation in

1. Slovakia
2. Ireland
3. Austria
4. Malta
5. United Kingdom

and if nominal corporate tax rates are used.

6.18. Avoidance of Triple Taxation

Suppose the A-Corporation is located in Berlin and owns 100% of a subsidiary called B-Corporation which is located in Munich. Further, the C-Corporation is located in Hamburg and is controlled by 100% by the B-Corporation. Finally, Mr. Thatcher, who lives in Berlin, owns 100% of the stakes of A-Corporation. The cash equal corporate income of the C-Corporation is €250,000. If group taxation is neglected and if it is assumed that all cash is distributed, what amount – ready for consumption – is received by Mr. Thatcher? Suppose, only nominal corporate income taxes on the corporate level.

6.19. Standard Model for Corporations

Suppose the following cash flow stream on the corporate level

t	0	1	2	3
CF_t^c	–120.00	45.00	48.00	48.50

Assume further $i = 8\%$, a marginal corporate income tax rate of $\tau^c = 30\%$ and a flat tax rate on distributed dividends of $\tau^{flat} = 25\%$. Now determine for both initial financial alternatives, (a) financing by retained earnings and (b) financing by new equity

1. The net present value before taxes on corporate level,
2. The net present value before taxes from the owner's perspective,
3. The net present value after taxes neglecting the owner's level,
4. The net present value after taxes from the owner's perspective,

in case profits are distributed immediately or retained until $t = n$, respectively. Interpret your results concerning the after-tax cases. Should the investment be carried out? If so, under what assumptions of distribution? Explain the differences in after-tax net present values on the personal level ($NPV^{\tau,p}$) for all cases.

References

1. Cruver, B.: Enron—Anatomy of Greed—The Unshredded Truth from an Enron Insider. Arrow Books, London (2003)
2. Dhaliwal, D.S., Frankel, M., Trezevant, R.: The taxable and book income motivations for a LIFO layer liquidation. J. Account. Res. 278–289 (1994)
3. Dopuch, N., Pincus, M.: Evidence on the choice of inventory accounting methods: LIFO versus FIFO. J. Account. Res. 28–59 (1988)
4. Endres, D. (ed.): The Determination of Corporate Taxable Income in the EU Member States. Kluwer Law International, Alphen aan den Rijn (2007)
5. Hanlon, M.: The persistence and pricing of earnings, accruals, and cash flows when firms have large book-tax differences. Account. Rev. **80**(1), 137–166 (2005)

6. Kiesewetter, D., Dietrich, M.: Ein Standardmodell für Investitionsentscheidungen in Kapitalgesellschaften. Wirtschaftswissenschaftliches Studium 235–244 (2007)
7. König, R., Maßbaum, A., Sureth, C.: Besteuerung und Rechtsformwahl, 4th edn. Neue Wirtschafts-Briefe, Herne (2009)
8. Schanz, G. von: Der Einkommensbegriff und die Einkommensteuersätze. Finanzarchiv **13**, 1–87 (1896)
9. Scholes, M.S., Wolfson, M.A., Erickson, M., Maydew, E.L., Shevlin, T.: Taxes and Business Strategy. A Planning Approach. 4th edn., Prentice Hall, Upper Saddle River (2009)
10. Shackelford, D.A., Shevlin, T.: Empirical tax research. J. Account. Econ. **31**(1), 321–387 (2001)
11. Stiglitz, J.E.: The Roaring Nineties. W.W. Norton & Company Ltd., New York (2003)
12. Wagner, F. W.: Was bedeutet Steuervereinfachung wirklich? Perspektiven der Wirtschaftspolitik 19–33 (2006)

Chapter 7
Extensions of the Standard Model

Abstract The "Standard Model" for tax planning introduced in Chap. 3 is considerably simple. To adjust the model to reality, some rigorous assumptions will be removed in this section. For example, capital gains taxation will be integrated. One major focus to make our model more realistic is to introduce limited loss offset rules. Moreover, further adjustments to meet current law are discussed. After reading this chapter, you are able to evaluate investment alternatives by adjusting the "Standard Model" to basic tax law details applied in your home country.

7.1 Introduction

As we have operated in a very simplified world using our basic "Standard Model", we should remove some of our restricting assumptions and become more realistic. Our first step to get closer to reality is to remove the assumption of not taxing capital gains. Further adjustments discussed are real-world loss offset rules, adjustments to the tax base and uncertainty concerning predicted cash flow structures. A brief discussion about the discount rate closes this chapter.

Compared to our simple model, reality is much more complex. To file a tax return for a company you must consider at first thousands of pages of national tax code, guidelines, and comments. However, if you have clients with cross-border investments you also have to consider tax code, guidelines, and comments of the countries regarded. On top you have to consider double taxation agreements. You are never able to integrate all rules in detail in your decision criterion, but you have to determine the most important rules that cause main distortions.

You do not have to model tax law details that do not affect your investment decision. So you must integrate tax law details that are specific for the decision setting considered. If too many details are considered, tax planning costs (e.g., human resources) might overstate the advantage of choosing the right investment alternative.

D. Schanz and S. Schanz, *Business Taxation and Financial Decisions*,
DOI 10.1007/978-3-642-03284-4_7,

7.2 Taxing Capital Gains

The first extension of our simple model so far is to take taxation of capital gains into account. At this point we do not discuss sense or nonsense of taxing capital gains – especially taxing capital gains of financial investments – from an economic perspective.

Suppose, you purchased an asset and enjoyed reduction of your tax liability due to depreciation allowances. If you sell your asset (=liquidation), the selling price might be greater than the current book value which is defined as initial costs minus accumulated depreciations. This occurs often in cases where real property is sold that was purchased years ago. Before presenting an example, we first want to derive the extended net present value formula.

Tax base for capital gains CG is supposed to be the difference between current book value BV and selling price SP in $t = n$, hence the new tax base in n gives

$$TB_n = CF_n - D_n + \underbrace{SP_n - BV_n}_{CG_n},$$

where n ist the time horizon of the investment project.

Current book value in n is determined as acquisition cost I_0 less depreciation D claimed for tax purposes

$$BV_n = I_0 - \sum_{t=1}^{n} D_t. \tag{7.1}$$

We have to distinguish two cases:

1. Asset is sold after taxable useful life has expired: $n^* < n$,
2. Asset is sold before end of taxable useful life is reached: $n^* > n$.

In the first case $n^* < n$, depreciation ends before the asset is sold. Capital gain is therefore represented by the selling price because in that case book value is zero. There is no depreciation between the time of end of useful life n^* and time of liquidation n

$$D_t = 0 \quad \text{for} \quad n^* < t \leq n.$$

The tax base in $t = n^*, \ldots, n$ is, therefore, simplified to CF_t. The "Standard Model" is hence adjusted as follows

$$NPV^\tau = -I_0 + \sum_{t=1}^{n^*} [CF_t - \tau \times (CF_t - D_t)] \times (q^\tau)^{-t}$$

$$+ \sum_{t=n^*+1}^{n} (1-\tau) \times CF_t \times (q^\tau)^{-t} + (1-\tau) \times SP_n \times (q^\tau)^{-n}.$$

Now consider the second case, where $n^* > n$. In that case capital gain is represented by the difference of selling price and book value in n whereas book value is calculated according to (7.1). We get

$$NPV^\tau = -I_0 + \sum_{t=1}^{n} [CF_t - \tau \times (CF_t - D_t)] \times (q^\tau)^{-t} \\ + \left[SP_n - \tau \times \left(SP_n - I_0 + \sum_{t=1}^{n} D_t \right) \right] \times (q^\tau)^{-n}. \tag{7.2}$$

If selling price just equals book value in n and $SP_n > 0$, we have

$$NPV^\tau = -I_0 + \sum_{t=1}^{n} [CF_t - \tau \times (CF_t - D_t)] \times (q^\tau)^{-t} + SP_n \times (q^\tau)^{-n}. \tag{7.3}$$

If selling price equals book value and if selling price amounts to zero – $SP_n = BV_n = 0$ – ,(7.2) results in

$$NPV^\tau = -I_0 + \sum_{t=1}^{n} [CF_t - \tau \times (CF_t - D_t)] \times (q^\tau)^{-t} \tag{7.4}$$

which represents the formula for your "Standard Model" right away.

Example 7.1. Integrating Capital Gains into our Standard Model

Suppose you are in a situation to buy real property or not. You are endowed with funds with an equity of € 150,000 that are equivalent to the price for new real property offered by an estate agent. The property is considered as an investment for you, resulting in renting it to a third party. Annual rent as cash flow return of that property is supposed to be € 9,600. Legal depreciation has to be spread over 25 years. You already know that at the end of $n = 20$ you are finally going to sell the property in order to have enough funds to construct an own sweet home for you and your family. At that time you can realize € 35,000 for the asset. Interest rate is assumed to be $i = 4\%$ and your marginal tax rate is $\tau = 40\%$. Calculating the net present value without consideration of capital gains taxation leads to

$$NPV^\tau = -150{,}000 + \left[9{,}600 - 0.4 \times \left(9{,}600 - \frac{150{,}000}{25} \right) \right] \\ \times \frac{1.024^{20} - 1}{0.024 \times 1.024^{20}} + 35{,}000 \times 1.024^{-20} = 198.03.$$

As a result real investment is carried out.

Now, capital gains taxation is considered. To determine the capital gain that arises in $n = 20$ we need to calculate the current book value in n that is

$$BV_n = 150{,}000 - 20 \times \frac{150{,}000}{25} = 30{,}000.$$

Capital gain in n evolves to $CG_n = 35{,}000 - 30{,}000 = 5{,}000$. Net present value then arises to

$$\begin{aligned} NPV^{\tau} &= -150{,}000 + \left[9{,}600 - 0.4 \times \left(9{,}600 - \frac{150{,}000}{25}\right)\right] \\ &\quad \times \frac{1.024^{20} - 1}{0.024 \times 1.024^{20}} + (35{,}000 - 0.4 \times 5{,}000) \\ &\quad \times 1.024^{-20} = -1{,}046.57. \end{aligned}$$

In this case considering taxes on capital gains advises you not to carry out real investment.

7.3 Further Tax Base Adjustments

In the "Standard Model" all accruals are represented by depreciation allowances. However, there are numerous accruals that affect tax bases in real-world tax systems. Provisions, prepaid expenses and deferred income, valuation of inventory at historical costs and fair-value depreciation are just few examples. All examples mentioned cause timing effects. In the following numerical examples are provided.

7.3.1 Provisions

As one further adjustment provisions are considered. Provisions claimed for tax purposes might be provisions for pension payments to employees, liabilities on surety obligations, warranties, damage claims and litigation expenses.

Assume that in t_I a provision PRO for tax purposes is made. The reason why the provision was made does not occur and provision has to be released in t_{II} to the same amount it was made in t_I. We assume that $t_{II} > t_I$. Post-tax net present value is then defined as

$$\begin{aligned} NPV^{\tau} &= -I_0 + \sum_{t=1}^{n} \frac{CF_t - \tau \times (CF_t - D_t)}{(1 + i^{\tau})^t} + \tau \times PRO \\ &\quad \times \left(\frac{1}{(1 + i^{\tau})^{t_I}} - \frac{1}{(1 + i^{\tau})^{t_{II}}}\right). \end{aligned}$$

As a result, provisions that are not used cause a timing effect, leading to a greater post-tax net present value. Formally, there is no problem to design the effect of one provision. However, if there are provisions made in every period, determination of the effect in terms of post-tax net present value might not be profitable because the timing effects might be smaller than the tax planning costs. Moreover, remember we still handle with certainty. If we know what happens in the future certainly, we do not need to model provisions. In case of uncertainty, we need to assume parameters as probability of claiming and distribution of cash outflow due to the reason the provision was made for.

Example 7.2. Provisions

Daniel runs a small business in Texas where he sells burgers. Since he strives to provide the whole state with his burgers he wants to expand. Initial costs of expansion and future cash flows are

t	0	1	2	3	4
CF_t	-80,000	20,000	18,400	20,000	60,000

If his marginal tax rate is assumed to be 40%, interest rate is 8% and straight-line depreciation is applied, post-tax net present value is determined as:

t	0	1	2	3	4
CF_t	−80,000	20,000	18,400	20,000	60,000
D_t		20,000	20,000	20,000	20,000
IP_t		0	1,600	3,200	4,954
FI_t	0	20,000	40,000	61,920	108,892
TB_t		0	0	3,200	44,954
T_t		0	0	1,280	17,982
CF_t^τ	−80,000	20,000	20,000	21,920	46,972

The post-tax net present value is calculated as:

$$NPV^\tau = -I_0 + FI_n \times (q^\tau)^{-n} = -80{,}000 + 108{,}892 \times 1.048^{-4} = 10{,}272.$$

Suppose, an enactment of local authorities forces Daniel to install a special filter system in his kitchen. Because he does not care about the enactment he claims a provision for litigation expenses of 10,000 in $t = 2$ which is deductible for tax purposes. Due to elections the enactment is abolished in $t = 3$ and Daniel has to release the provision made in $t = 2$ to the amount of 10,000. Now, if full loss offset is assumed, post-tax net present value amounts to

t	0	1	2	3	4
CF_t	−80,000	20,000	18,400	20,000	60,000
D_t		20,000	20,000	20,000	20,000
IP_t		0	1,600	3,520	4,969
FI_t		20,000	44,000	62,112	109,093
PRO_t			−10,000	10,000	
TB_t		0	−10,000	13,520	44,969
T_t		0	−4,000	5,408	17,988
CF_t^τ	−80,000	20,000	24,000	18,112	46,981
NPV^τ	10,438				

Because tax payment is delayed from $t = 2$ to $t = 3$, post-tax net present value rises. It rises to the amount of $10{,}000 \times 0.4 \times (1.048^{-2} - 1.048^{-3}) \approx 166$ which just explains the difference of the post-tax net present values $10{,}438 - 10{,}272 = 166$.

7.3.2 Prepaid Expenses and Deferred Income

Prepaid expenses occur if cash outflow precedes expenses in financial or tax accounting terms. Two examples are prepaid rents and disagios.[1] Suppose, you are in year $t = 1$ and you pay a rent for $t = 2$. The cash outflow in $t = 1$ is neither deductible for tax purposes nor reduces profit. As expenses occur in $t = 2$, there is a time delay lasting in negative time effects. In case of disagios, the book value of your loan is L, however, received cash just amounts to $L \times (1-d)$, where d is the disagio rate. You do not have an actual cash outflow, however, cash inflow is not equal to the amount of your liability. As an immediate write-off is usually not granted for tax purposes, the disagio has to be depreciated over the useful life of the loan.

Deferred income is the corresponding case to prepaid expense. In this case cash inflow precedes earnings in the future. That might happen if the leaser pays the rent in advance.

Our "Standard Model" does not display that kind of accruals, because accruals are solely represented by depreciation. What assumption could be made to prevent consideration of prepaid expenses and deferred income? It is known that the impact of prepaid expenses on present value of tax liability corresponds with the impact of deferred income. If the amount of prepaid expenses is equal to the amount of deferred income there is no impact on post-tax net present value. That exception is implicitly assumed in our "Standard Model".

[1] Disagios are discussed later in Sect. 9.4 starting on p. 355.

Example 7.3. Leasing Rate as an Example for Deferred Income

Consider a lessee who pays his rent 1 year in advance leading to deferred income (from the perspective of the lessor). Assume your time horizon to be $n = 10$, the annual rent in arrears to be € 8,000, a marginal tax rate of 40% and an alternative financial investment that yields 8% before taxes. The advantage in terms of present value for the lessor of the tax liability if the rent is (fully) taxed at the end of the following year and the asset is completely written off is

$$\Delta PV = 8{,}000 \times 0.4 \times \left(\frac{1.048^{10} - 1}{0.048 \times 1.048^{10}} \times 1.048 - \frac{1.048^{10} - 1}{0.048 \times 1.048^{10}} \right)$$
$$= 1{,}197.66.$$

7.3.3 *Valuation of Inventory*

Usually, supplies or inventory is bought in one period and evolve to expenses due to the production process in another period. In this case cash outflow and expenses in terms of financial accounting diverge timely. In the "Standard Model" it is assumed that cash outflow for inventory and expenses occur in one financial period. Because of that there is no valuation problem because there is no capitalization of inventory at the end of the fiscal year. If there is timely divergence it is implicitly assumed that inventory is received on credit and credit is payed back at the time when inventory is sold.

If inventory has to be valued, there are several methods for valuation, e.g., valuation

(a) At cost of acquisition,
(b) At cost of manufacture, or
(c) At going-concern-value.

Concerning the sequence of consumption, inventory might typically be valued using its average cost or the last-in-first-out-method (lifo) method. In Germany, in special cases the first-in-first-out-method (fifo) is allowed.

Example 7.4. Valuation of Inventory at Historical Cost

Suppose a carpenter buys timber in $t = 0$ for € 15,000 which is used to construct houses in $t = 1$. For construction in $t = 1$ the carpenter gets € 20,000. If the time horizon is $t = 4$ periods, the stream of cash inflow and cash outflow looks like

t	0	1	2	3	4
CF_t^{out}	–15,000	–15,000	–15,000	–15,000	
CF_t^{in}		20,000	20,000	20,000	20,000

Notice that in $t = 4$ the carpenter is not going to order more timber supplies as he stops working at the end of $t = 4$. If a marginal tax rate of 30% and a pre-tax interest rate of 6% is assumed and no depreciable capital assets are available, post-tax net present value in the case of our "Standard Model" is calculated as:

t	0	1	2	3	4
CF_t^{in}		20,000	20,000	20,000	20,000
CF_t^{out}	15,000	15,000	15,000	15,000	
CF_t	–15,000	5,000	5,000	5,000	20,000
TB_t	–15,000	5,000	5,000	5,000	20,000
T_t	–4,500	1,500	1,500	1,500	6,000
CF_t^τ	–10,500	3,500	3,500	3,500	14,000
NPV^τ	11,052				

In detail we get

$$NPV^\tau = -10{,}500 + 3{,}500 \times \frac{1.042^3 - 1}{0.042 \times 1.042^3} + \frac{14{,}000}{1.042^4}$$
$$= 11{,}052.$$

Remember that in this case we implicitly assume immediate write-off of the supplies.

If we now valuate the supplies at historical cost and therefore produce current assets there is a deferral of 1 year for tax purposes. In that case tax base in $t = 0$ is zero whereas in $t = 4$ due to expenses of timber bought in $t = 3$ tax base is €5,000. The following financial plan draws computation of post-tax net present value in case of valuating the supplies at historical cost.

t	0	1	2	3	4
CF_t^{in}		20,000	20,000	20,000	20,000
CF_t^{out}	15,000	15,000	15,000	15,000	
CF_t	–15,000	5,000	5,000	5,000	20,000
TB_t	0	5,000	5,000	5,000	5,000
T_t	0	1,500	1,500	1,500	1,500
CF_t^τ	–15,000	3,500	3,500	3,500	18,500
NPV^τ	10,369				

In detail we get

$$NPV^{\tau} = -15{,}000 + 3{,}500 \times \frac{1.042^3 - 1}{0.042 \times 1.042^3} + \frac{18{,}500}{1.042^4}$$
$$= 10{,}369.$$

As the cash outflow leads to tax deductible expenses in the following year, post-tax net present value drops from 11,052 to 10,369.

7.3.4 Fair Value Depreciation

Fair value depreciation is applied if the market value falls below the value at which the asset is capitalized. This might occur, e.g., in case of

1. Extensive use of plant & equipment,
2. Asset is completely or partially destroyed, e.g., by a natural disaster,
3. Consumption preferences of consumers change (inventory is outmoded),
4. Market value falls (important for financial assets), and
5. Technical progress.

Revaluation results in shifting depreciation to an earlier period of time and hence causes post-tax net present value to rise due to timing effects. If fair value depreciation is applied and if it is assumed that remaining historical costs are spread over the useful life, the adjustment of the "Standard Model" by implementing fair value depreciation (*FairVD*) can be formally described as (d = year of fair value depreciation ($d < n$))

$$NPV^{\tau} = -I_0 + \sum_{t=1}^{d} \frac{CF_t - \tau \times \left(CF_t - \frac{I_0}{n}\right)}{(q^{\tau})^t} + \tau \times FairVD_d \times (q^{\tau})^{-d}$$
$$+ \sum_{t=d+1}^{n} \frac{CF_t - \tau \times \left(CF_t - \frac{I_0 - d \times \frac{I_0}{n} - FairVD_d}{n-d}\right)}{(q^{\tau})^t},$$

where $FairVD_d$ stands for fair value depreciation in $t = d$. Remaining depreciation after fair value depreciation in d is represented by $\left(I_0 - d \times \frac{I_0}{n} - FairVD_d\right)$ spread over a period of time of $n-d$.

Example 7.5. Fair Value Depreciation

Long John loves hiking and climbing. He thinks about buying real property in Austria's mountains for 180,000 in order to have a fix basis for his trekking tours. Since he lives in France he does not need the accommodation during the whole year and wants to rent the property to tourists for 11,000 a year. Now John is 50 years old and he knows for sure that at the age of 70 he will not be able to make hiking tours any more and therefore sells the property in 20 years for 120,000. Acquisition costs and future cash flows are provided in the following table

t	0	1	2	3	...	19	20
CF_t	–180,000	11,000	11,000	11,000	...	11,000	131,000

Straight-line depreciation has to be spread over 60 years, marginal tax rate is assumed to be 30% and $i = 6\%$. Hence, annual depreciation is $D_t = \frac{180{,}000}{60} = 3{,}000$. It is assumed that John withdraws post-tax cash flows for consumption after each period. Post-tax net present value without fair value depreciation gives

t	0	1	2	3	...	19	20
CF_t	–180,000	11,000	11,000	11,000	...	11,000	131,000
D_t		3,000	3,000	3,000	...	3,000	3,000
BV_t		177,000	174,000	171,000	...	123,000	120,000
TB_t		8,000	8,000	8,000	...	8,000	8,000
T_t		2,400	2,400	2,400	...	2,400	2,400
CF_t^τ	–180,000	8,600	8,600	8,600	...	8,600	128,600
NPV^τ	–12,464						

Where post-tax net present value is easily calculated as:

$$NPV^\tau = -180{,}000 + 8{,}600 \times \frac{1.042^{19} - 1}{0.042 \times 1.042^{19}} + 128{,}600 \times 1.042^{-20}$$
$$= -12{,}464.$$

Notice capital gain in n is book value in n less selling price ($CG_n = BV_n - SP_n = 120{,}000 - 120{,}000 = 0$).

In $t = 2$, the property is damaged by an avalanche and John claims a fair value depreciation of 116,000 for his property in addition to the straight-line depreciation in $t = 2$. Fortunately, as a skilled craftsman he is able to fix the damage without any cash outflow and reduction of rent, respectively. If immediate full loss offset is assumed, post-tax net present value is determined as:

t	0	1	2	3	...	19	20
CF_t	−180,000	11,000	11,000	11,000	...	11,000	131,000
D_t		3,000	3,000	1,000	...	1,000	1,000
$FairVD_2$			116,000				
BV_t		177,000	58,000	57,000	...	41,000	40,000
TB_t		8,000	−108,000	10,000	...	10,000	90,000
T_t		2,400	−32,400	3,000	...	3,000	27,000
CF_t^τ	−180,000	8,600	43,400	8,000	...	8,000	104,000
NPV^τ	2,163						

Depreciation in the first two periods is 3,000. So book value after fair value depreciation at the end of $t = 2$ is

$$BV = 180{,}000 - 2 \times 3{,}000 - 116{,}000 = 58{,}000.$$

Because remaining useful life at the end of $t = 2$ is 58 years, depreciation from $t = 3, \ldots, 20$ is $\frac{58{,}000}{58} = 1{,}000$.

Because tax shield occurs earlier, post-tax net present value rises. NPV^τ is determined as:

$$NPV^\tau = -180{,}000 + \frac{8{,}600}{1.042} + \frac{43{,}400}{1.042^2} + 8{,}000 \times \frac{1.042^{17} - 1}{0.042 \times 1.042^{17}}$$
$$\times 1.042^{-2} + 104{,}000 \times 1.042^{-20}$$
$$= 2{,}163.$$

Notice that post-tax net present value is positive. Further, be sure to discount the present value of the annuity (from $t = 3, \ldots, 19$) for 2 years, not for 3 years. That is because present value of the annuity is calculated to the end of period $t = 2$. Capital gain in n is now 120,000 − 40,000 = 80,000 plus cash flow in n less depreciation in n gives $TB_n = 90{,}000$ as taxable base.

7.4 Loss Offset Restrictions

A further adjustment to our "Standard Model" deals with losses. We have assumed that losses are treated symmetrically to profits. That means immediate full loss offset is applied. Remember immediate full loss offset implicates that in the period in that losses occur a tax refund to the amount of the product of marginal tax rate and losses

($\tau \times TB_t$) is collected by the taxpayer. This status is also called symmetric taxation because negative income is "taxed" correspondingly to positive income. If marginal tax rates are used, symmetric taxation can be implemented easily as we have seen in our "Standard Model". In real-world tax systems, however, typically no tax refunds are granted. Moreover, often progressive tax rates are used and tax exempt amounts are applied. In that case it's not easy or it does not make sense to apply those rules to losses. If losses are not treated equally compared to positive income, losses and profit are taxed asymmetrically.

To justify our assumption of immediate full loss offset so far we might argue that we have always considered marginal investments. What does that mean? We are focused on additional investments, having already realized many other investments. From the other investments we generate enough positive taxable income to offset losses that occur by the additional investment alternative. However, that argument depends on the fact that additional investment projects are considered. In fact there is often no possibility of immediate deduction.

To our knowledge there is no tax system worldwide applying immediate loss offset. Each country defines its own legal rules to handle losses for tax purposes. Alternative real-world loss offset restrictions are discussed later on. The negative effect of restricted loss offset rules is at first a negative timing effect since tax liability is reduced in future periods. Saving taxes later instead of receiving a tax refund immediately affects net present value to be lower. If you have losses that amount to billions of Euros (see Table 7.2 on p. 277), timing effects cause net present values to fall heavily. However, the problem of existing loss offset rules is, that there are time restrictions to carry forward losses in many countries. That means if you are not able to offset your losses within say 5 years, your losses for offsetting purposes are lost.

As losses might occur in real investments, loss offset restrictions might lead to real investments being worse compared to financial investments. As we assumed a certain discount rate, losses do not occur at alternative financial investments. As net present value states the relative advantage of real investments compared to a certain financial investment, it is obvious that loss offset restrictions lead to lower net present value compared with a world without loss offset restrictions.

To handle the terms in the basic tax formula, Table 7.1 outlines the way to compute the tax base. Please note that the basic tax formula is presented in a very rough manner.

Table 7.1 Basic tax formula

	Item of tax formula	Explanation
	Gross Income	Sum of all items subject to tax
–	Deductions	Deductions concerning personal circumstances
=	Adjusted Gross Income	
–	Loss Offset	
=	Tax Base	

Table 7.2 Loss carry forward of corporations in Germany

Year	Loss carry forward in billion €	Δ
1992	128.32	
1995	239.45	86.61%
1998	285.37	19.18%
2001	380.23	33.24%
2004	473.37	24.50%

7.4.1 Loss Offset Restrictions in Germany

This subsection deals with loss offset restrictions in Germany. Later on we will see that loss offset restrictions are basically timing effects. Of course, loss offset restrictions might prevent deduction in preceding or future periods at all and hence cause tax base effects. But, let's focus on possible timing effects because in Germany no time restriction for deduction of current loss carry forwards is applied. Table 7.2 shows that timing effects might have a significant impact on a macroeconomic perspective. The table shows the amounts of loss carry forwards for corporations at the end of the year considered.[2] The column on the very right displays the relative change of loss carry forwards to the previous survey.

In 2004 there is an overall €473.37 billion loss carry forward. Assuming an interest rate of 8% and a corporate marginal tax rate – including local business taxes but neglecting the owner's level – of 30%, a 1 year deferral results in an increase of present value in terms of tax liability of $0.3 \times 473.37 \times (1 - 1.056^{-1}) =$ €7.53 billion (!) which is not just peanuts.

Now, we want to give a brief introduction how complex loss offset rules might be. Remember that integrating detailed legal rules in our "Standard Model" is done for calculating taxes more precisely that reduce the overall objective (cash after taxes, ready for consumption) for an investor. Germany's loss offset restrictions consist of four parts:

1. Loss carry back time restriction
2. Loss carry back amount restriction
3. Loss carry forward without time restriction
4. Loss offset restriction depending on the adjusted gross income (AGI)

Let's first consider the loss carry back time restriction. § 10d (1) EStG (German Income Tax Code) states that losses can be carried back 1 year. However, there is an option to carry back losses. Taxpayers can elect to carry back or forward. The second restriction deals with the loss carry back amount restriction that also can be found in § 10d (1) EStG. The loss carry back amount restriction states that just losses up to €511,500 can be carried back. The loss carry forward is determined as the third restriction because losses that cannot be carried back are not

[2] Source: Statistisches Bundesamt, Körperschaftsteuerstatistik 2004, p. 12.

tax deductible immediately. However, there is no time restriction for loss carry forwards in Germany. Losses, therefore, can be carried forward to infinity. The fourth restriction is implemented because of the fear of the government of a high variance concerning tax revenue. The restriction is also called minimum tax (not comparable with the Alternative Minimum Tax (AMT) in the US, which is in fact a separate calculation of taxable income in addition to the conventional calculation) because future taxable income is (with exceptions) not reduced to zero. Losses are deductible in the future up to € 1 million, limited to the adjusted gross income (AGI). If adjusted gross income exceeds € 1 million and loss carry forward exceeds € 1 million too, just 60% of adjusted gross income that exceed € 1 million is deductible.

Formal speaking loss carry back *LCB* is described as:

$$LCB_t = \min\{511{,}500; \max\{TB_{t-1}; 0\}; \max\{-AGI_t; 0\}\} \tag{7.5}$$

where TB_{t-1} represents taxable income of the previous period. Notice that AGI_t has to be negative to represent losses. Loss carry back is restricted to negative AGI_t.

For determination of loss carry forward *LCF* in t we have to consider the loss carry back used and the amount of loss carry forward of the previous period (just in case loss carry back does not occur). *LCF* is then the sum of loss carry forward in $t-1$ less negative *AGI* less loss carry back in t less loss offset (LO) in t.

$$LCF_t = LCF_{t-1} - \min\{0; AGI_t\} - LCB_t - LO_t, \tag{7.6}$$

where $LCF_0 = 0$. Loss offset LO in t is at first restricted to the loss carry forward of the previous period LCF_{t-1}. Second, deduction is restricted to positive *AGI* and third offset is restricted to € 1 million plus 60% of *AGI* that exceeds € 1 million.

$$\begin{aligned} LO_t = \min\{&LCF_{t-1}; \max\{AGI_t; 0\}; 1{,}000{,}000 \\ &+ 0.6 \times [\max\{AGI_t; 0\} - 1{,}000{,}000]\}. \end{aligned} \tag{7.7}$$

The tax base TB_t depends on the existence of loss offsets or loss carry backs.

$$TB_t = \max\{CF_t - D_t + i \times FI_{t-1} - LO_t; 0\} - LCB_t. \tag{7.8}$$

Example 7.6. Loss Offset Restrictions in Germany

A German investor faces a real investment alternative in Germany that induces acquisition costs of $I_0 = 8{,}550{,}000$ and yields the following return in terms of cash

t	1	2	3	4	5	6
CF_t	2,500,000	1,900,000	–2,500,000	3,500,000	3,000,000	3,700,000

To determine net cash flow in t, Germany's loss offset restrictions formally derived in (7.5)–(7.8) are applied. To calculate the parameters in the following financial plans, the parameters are briefly discussed.

Adjusted gross income represents the sum of cash flow plus interest payments received less depreciation. Financial investment FI_t consists of the financial investment of the previous period plus interest paid in t plus cash flow in t less taxes paid in t.

First compute NPV^τ in absence of any loss offset restrictions. Tax liability in that case is represented by the product of the marginal tax rate and tax base TB_t, no matter if tax base is positive or negative. If we neglect loss offset restrictions in our model then taxable income equals adjusted gross income. After-tax cash flows then are the sum of pre-tax cash flow plus interest payments less tax liability.

$$\begin{aligned} AGI_t &= CF_t + i \times FI_{t-1} - D_t \\ FI_t &= CF_t + (1+i) \times FI_{t-1} - T_t \\ T_t &= \tau \times TB_t \\ TB_t &= AGI_t \\ CF_t^\tau &= CF_t + i \times FI_{t-1} - T_t. \end{aligned}$$

We assume financial investment in $t = 0$ to be zero ($FI_0 = 0$). Marginal tax rate is assumed to be 45% and interest rate is 10%. Moreover, straight-line depreciation is applied over 6 years. The corresponding financial plan then gives

t	1	2	3	4	5	6
CF_t	2,500,000	1,900,000	−2,500,000	3,500,000	3,000,000	3,700,000
D_t	1,425,000	1,425,000	1,425,000	1,425,000	1,425,000	1,425,000
FI_t	2,016,250	3,813,394	3,289,380	6,036,546	8,659,806	11,812,346
IP_t	0	201,625	381,339	328,938	603,655	865,981
AGI_t	1,075,000	676,625	−3,543,661	2,403,938	2,178,655	3,140,981
TB_t	1,075,000	676,625	−3,543,661	2,403,938	2,178,655	3,140,981
T_t	483,750	304,481	−1,594,647	1,081,772	980,395	1,413,441
CF_t^τ	2,016,250	1,797,144	−524,014	2,747,166	2,623,260	3,152,540

Notice that because $FI_0 = 0$, interest payments received in $t = 1$ are necessarily zero. In $t = 3$ a tax refund of 1,594,647 occurs. Using the after-tax discount rate of $i^\tau = 5.5\%$, NPV^τ is computed by discounting FI_n and, hence, gives

$$NPV^{\tau} = -I_0 + FI_6 \times (1 + i^{\tau})^{-n}$$
$$= -8{,}550{,}000 + 11{,}812{,}346 \times 1.055^{-6} = 16{,}855.$$

Pre-tax net present value is −243,447.

Now, Germany's loss offset restrictions are considered. Therefore, tax liability and taxable income have to be adjusted (remember, Germany's loss offset restrictions are presented in a formal manner earlier). Tax liability is now restricted to positive taxable income. Additionally, tax refund due to a loss carry back has to be considered. Since we defined T_t to be negative, tax refund is $-\tau \times LCB_t$. Taxable income is adjusted by loss carry back. We assume loss carry forward and taxable income in $t = 0$ to be zero ($LCF_0 = TB_0 = 0$). Taxable income has to be defined in $t = 0$ because of a possible loss carry back.

t	1	2	3	4	5	6
CF_t	2,500,000	1,900,000	−2,500,000	3,500,000	3,000,000	3,700,000
D_t	1,425,000	1,425,000	1,425,000	1,425,000	1,425,000	1,425,000
FI_t	2,016,250	3,813,394	1,924,908	5,389,251	8,549,159	11,695,613
IP_t		201,625	381,339	192,491	538,925	854,916
AGI_t	1,075,000	676,625	−3,543,661	2,267,491	2,113,925	3,129,916
LCB_t			511,500			
LCF_t			3,032,161	1,271,666		
LO_t				1,760,495	1,271,666	
TB_t	1,075,000	676,625	−511,500	506,996	842,259	3,129,916
T_t	483,750	304,481	−230,175	228,148	379,017	1,408,462
CF_t^{τ}	2,016,250	1,797,144	−1,888,486	3,464,343	3,159,908	3,146,454

As there is no loss in $t = 1{,}2$, after-tax cash flows are equal in case of loss offset restrictions and in case of absence of loss offset restrictions. Differences start beginning with $t = 3$. Losses in $t = 3$ occur to the amount of −3,543,661. As adjusted gross income in the previous period is positive, loss carry back is possible. However, loss carry back is restricted to 511,500. Since loss carry back causes tax authorities to change the tax declaration of the previous period, tax refund in $t = 3$ is $0.45 \times 511{,}500 = 230{,}175$. At the same time loss carry forward is reduced by 511,500 to $LCF_3 = 3{,}543{,}661 - 511{,}500 = 3{,}032{,}161$. Loss offset in $t = 4$ then accounts for

$$LO_4 = \min\{3{,}032{,}161; \max\{2{,}267{,}491; 0\}; 1{,}000{,}000$$
$$+ 0{,}6 \times [\max\{2{,}267{,}491; 0\} - 1{,}000{,}000]\}$$
$$= 1{,}760{,}495.$$

Loss carry forward in $t = 4$ is, hence, reduced to $LCF_4 = 3{,}032{,}161 - 1{,}760{,}495 = 1{,}271{,}666$. In $t = 5$ loss offset is calculated as:

$$\begin{aligned} LO_5 = \min\{&1{,}271{,}666; \max\{2{,}113{,}925; 0\}; 1{,}000{,}000 \\ &+ 0{,}6 \times [\max\{2{,}113{,}925; 0\} - 1{,}000{,}000]\} \\ = {}&1{,}271{,}666. \end{aligned}$$

If loss offset restrictions are considered, after-tax net present value is reduced to $NPV^{\tau} = -8{,}550{,}000 + 11{,}695{,}613 \times 1.055^{-6} = -67{,}805$. The example shows that neglecting loss offset restrictions might distort investment decisions. In the previous example, real investment is carried out if loss offset restrictions are neglected (because of positive post-tax net present value) and real investment is not carried out if loss offset restrictions are considered.

Example 7.7. Flat Tax vs. Loss Offset Possibility

The following example is based on the assumptions made in Ex. 7.6. However, we now go further and make our model a little bit more realistic and implement legal treatment of capital income in Germany. In Germany, capital income is taxed at a marginal tax rate of $\tau^{flat} = 25\%$. This tax rate is applicable just for capital income on the personal level. Capital income of a business entity organized as a sole proprietorship or partnership does not enjoy the reduced marginal tax rate. For that reason a German investor has to decide to withdraw his money from his business and invest in a financial investment on the private level in order to enjoy a 25% marginal tax rate. In the case of investing on the business level, interest payments received can be used for loss offset purposes. First, consider the case of no loss offset restrictions where the investor decides to withdraw after-tax cash flow at the end of each period and reinvest the money withdrawn in a financial investment with an after-tax return of $i^{\tau} = 10\% \times (1 - 25\%) = 7.5\%$.

t	1	2	3	4	5	6
CF_t	2,500,000	1,900,000	–2,500,000	3,500,000	3,000,000	3,700,000
D_t	1,425,000	1,425,000	1,425,000	1,425,000	1,425,000	1,425,000
FI_t	2,016,250	3,853,719	3,408,998	6,230,923	8,989,492	12,339,954
$IP_t^{\tau,flat}$		151,219	289,029	255,675	467,319	674,212
AGI_t	1,075,000	475,000	–3,925,000	2,075,000	1,575,000	2,275,000
TB_t	1,075,000	475,000	–3,925,000	2,075,000	1,575,000	2,275,000
T_t	483,750	213,750	–1,766,250	933,750	708,750	1,023,750
CF_t^{τ}	2,016,250	1,837,469	–444,721	2,821,925	2,758,569	3,350,462

Notice that interest payments received are not included in AGI_t. In the financial plan above, interest payments received are post-tax interest payments $IP_t^{\tau,flat}$ where the marginal tax rate of 25% is applied. E.g., $IP_2^{\tau,flat}$ is determined as $IP_2^{\tau,flat} = 2{,}016{,}250 \times 0.1 \times (1-0.25) = 151{,}219$. Because discount rate rises to $i^{\tau^{flat}} = 0.1 \times (1-0.25) = 0.075$, post-tax net present value falls to $NPV^{\tau} = -8{,}550{,}000 + 12{,}339{,}954 \times 1.075^{-6} = -554{,}185$ compared to 16,855 in the case where financial and real investment returns are considered to be treated equally.

Second, the table below draws the case of determination of post-tax net present value applying Germany's loss offset restrictions. We still assume that the financial investment is carried out on the personal level. Now, consider loss carry back in $t = 3$. As the interest payments received are not part of AGI in $t = 2$, the loss carry back falls to 475,000 – because the loss carry back is restricted to positive AGI in $t = 2$ – compared to 511,500 in the case of a financial investment on the business entity level. This causes time differences because losses are offset later. Post-tax net present value falls to $NPV^{\tau} = -8{,}550{,}000 + 12{,}124{,}383 \times 1.075^{-6} = -693{,}866$ which is of course mainly caused by applying a discount rate of $i^{\tau,flat} = 0.075$.

t	1	2	3	4	5	6
CF_t	2,500,000	1,900,000	−2,500,000	3,500,000	3,000,000	3,700,000
D_t	1,425,000	1,425,000	1,425,000	1,425,000	1,425,000	1,425,000
FI_t	2,016,250	3,853,719	1,856,498	5,302,235	8,596,403	12,124,383
$IP_t^{\tau,flat}$		151,219	289,029	139,237	397,668	644,730
AGI_t	1,075,000	475,000	−3,925,000	2,075,000	1,575,000	2,275,000
LCB_t			475,000			
LCF_t			3,450,000	1,805,000	460,000	
LO_t				1,645,000	1,345,000	460,000
TB_t	1,075,000	475,000	−475,000	430,000	230,000	1,815,000
T_t	483,750	213,750	−213,750	193,500	103,500	816,750
CF_t^{τ}	2,016,250	1,837,469	−1,997,221	3,445,737	3,294,168	3,527,980

7.4.2 *Loss Offset Restriction in Selected Countries*

Because immediate full loss offset is a simplification that is not granted in any country's tax system worldwide, we provide a brief overview over existing loss offset rules in selected countries in Table 7.3.

As we can see there are more loss carry back restrictions than loss carry forward restrictions. E.g., in Austria, Greece, Italy, Luxembourg, Spain, and Sweden there is no loss carry back allowed. Losses have to be carried forward obligatory. In France losses can be carried back for 3 years, in the US for 2 years. All other countries

Table 7.3 Loss offset rules in selected countries

Country	Loss carry back		Loss carry forward	
	Years	Max. amount	Years	Max. offset
Austria	–	–	∞	75% of *AGI*
France	3	∞	∞	∞
Germany	1	511,500	∞	€ 1 million + 60% of *AGI* exceeding € 1 million
Greece	–	–	5	∞
Ireland	1	∞	∞	∞
Italy	–	–	5	∞
Luxembourg	–	–	∞	∞
Spain	–	–	15	∞
Sweden	–	–	∞	∞
United Kingdom	1	∞	∞	∞
United States	2	∞	20	∞

AGI: Adjusted gross income

applying loss carry back allow loss carry back for just 1 year. Germany is the only exception where the loss carry back amount is limited.

On the other hand, loss carry forward is applied in all other countries. If there was no loss offset at all, taxpayers would be treated quite hard since the government profits from positive income, however, does not take part in losses. In most countries, loss carry forward is neither time restricted nor restricted in the amount. Just Austria and Germany apply amount restrictions, however, losses can be carried forward infinitely. Greece, Italy, Spain, and US apply time restrictions for loss carry forwards. If losses cannot be offset, up to that time no tax refund occurs at all.

Example 7.8. Loss Offset Restrictions in Selected Countries

In the following we want to illustrate the effects of the loss offset restriction of the countries considered in Table 7.3. We assume the cash flow structure of the real investment considered as equal in all countries considered. Cash flow stream is supposed to be $I_0 = 1{,}500{,}000$ and further

t	1	2	3	4	5	6
CF_t	300,000	300,000	400,000	–1,800,000	1,600,000	1,550,000

Suppose $\tau = 40\%$ and $i = 10\%$. In this case pre-tax NPV is –39,828.

To reduce the differences solely to loss offset restrictions marginal tax rate and interest rate are assumed to be equal in all countries. Table 7.4 shows the financial plan in case of immediate full loss offset. Consider $t = 4$. Because of the loss of $-1{,}954{,}859$ there is a tax refund of 781,944. Using

Table 7.4 Immediate full loss offset

t	1	2	3	4	5	6
CF_t	300,000	300,000	400,000	–1,800,000	1,600,000	1,550,000
D_t	250,000	250,000	250,000	250,000	250,000	250,000
IP_t		28,000	57,680	95,141	2,849	109,020
FI_t	280,000	576,800	951,408	28,493	1,090,202	2,185,614
AGI_t	50,000	78,000	207,680	–1,954,859	1,352,849	1,409,020
TB_t	50,000	78,000	207,680	–1,954,859	1,352,849	1,409,020
T_t	20,000	31,200	83,072	–781,944	541,140	563,608
CF_t^τ	280,000	296,800	374,608	–922,915	1,061,709	1,095,412

the after-tax discount rate of $i^\tau = 0.1 \times (1 - 0.4) = 0.06$, NPV^τ is computed by discounting FI_n and, hence, gives

$$\begin{aligned} NPV^\tau &= -I_0 + FI_n \times (1 + i^\tau)^{-n} \\ &= -1{,}500{,}000 + 2{,}185{,}614 \times 1.06^{-6} = 40{,}772. \end{aligned}$$

Because of immediate full loss offset AGI_t is equal to TB_t.

In the following, we consider groups of countries whose loss offset restrictions lead to the same post-tax net present value. The first group is represented by Greece, Italy, Luxembourg, Spain, and Sweden. The loss offset restrictions of those countries is characterized by the absence of loss carry back possibilities. However, Greece, Italy, and Spain apply a timing restriction for loss carry forwards. As our example does not need to carry losses forward for more than 2 years, loss offset restrictions in Greece, Italy, and Spain lead to the same result as in Luxembourg and Sweden. Loss offset can formally be described as:

$$LO_t = \min\{LCF_{t-1}; \max\{AGI_t; 0\}\}$$

and restricted to loss carry forward in $t-1$ and positive AGI in t. Loss carry forward in t is then calculated as:

$$LCF_t = -\sum_{k=t-\delta}^{t-1} \min\{AGI_k; 0\} - \sum_{k=t-\delta}^{t-1} \sum_{z=t-\delta}^{t-1} LO_z^{AGI_k} - \min\{AGI_t; 0\} - LO_t,$$

where $\delta \in [5; 15]$ and hence represents the loss carry forward timing restriction of Greece, Italy, and Spain. Loss carry forward in t is restricted to loss carry forward in $t-1$ less negative adjusted gross income, less loss offset in t. Loss carry forward in $t-1$ is the sum of the negative adjusted gross income of the last δ periods

$$-\sum_{k=t-\delta}^{t-1} \min\{AGI_k; 0\}$$

minus the loss offset of that periods assigned to negative AGI in $k = t - \delta, \ldots, t-1$. Because of the loss carry forward time restriction loss offset has to be assigned to a specific adjusted gross income

$$\sum_{k=t-\delta}^{t-1} \sum_{z=t-\delta}^{t-1} LO_z^{AGI_k}.$$

Further, the sum of loss offsets assigned to AGI_k has to be less or equal to the loss $\min\{AGI_k; 0\}$ which occurred in period k

$$\sum_{z=t-\delta}^{t-1} LO_z^{AGI_k} \leq -\min\{AGI_k; 0\}.$$

The financial plan summarized in Table 7.5 calculates post-tax cash flows under consideration of loss offset restrictions in Greece, Italy, Luxembourg, Spain, and Sweden.

Notice that loss carry forward in $t = 6$ is zero and

$$LCF_4 = 1{,}954{,}859$$
$$LO_5^{AGI_4} = 1{,}274{,}655$$
$$LO_6^{AGI_4} = 680{,}204.$$

The post-tax net present value is determined as:

$$\begin{aligned} NPV^\tau &= -I_0 + FI_n \times (q^\tau)^{-n} \\ &= -1{,}500{,}000 + 2{,}119{,}558 \times 1.06^{-6} = -5{,}795. \end{aligned}$$

Table 7.5 Loss offsetting in Greece, Italy, Luxembourg, Spain, and Sweden

t	1	2	3	4	5	6
CF_t	300,000	300,000	400,000	−1,800,000	1,600,000	1,550,000
D_t	250,000	250,000	250,000	250,000	250,000	250,000
IP_t		28,000	57,680	95,141	−75,345	77,120
FI_t	280,000	576,800	951,408	−753,451	771,204	2,119,558
AGI_t	50,000	78,000	207,680	−1,954,859	1,274,655	1,377,120
LCF_t				1,954,859	680,204	
LCB_t						
LO_t					1,274,655	680,204
TB_t	50,000	78,000	207,680	0	0	696,916
T_t	20,000	31,200	83,072	0	0	278,766
CF_t^τ	280,000	296,800	374,608	−1,704,859	1,524,655	1,348,354

The next financial plan deals with the situation in the United Kingdom and Ireland. In that countries loss carry back for one period and no time or amount restriction in terms of loss carry forward is applied. Loss offset, loss carry back, and loss carry forward in this case evolve to

$$\begin{aligned} LCF_t &= LCF_{t-1} - \min\{AGI_t; 0\} - LO_t \\ LO_t &= \min\{LCF_{t-1}; \max\{AGI_t; 0\}\} \\ LCB_t &= \min\{\max\{TB_{t-1}; 0\}; \max\{-AGI_t; 0\}\}. \end{aligned}$$

As there is now a tax refund in $t = 4$ of $TB_3 \times \tau = 207{,}680 \times 0.4 = 83{,}072$, post-tax net present value must rise in comparison to the situation of Greece, Italy, Luxembourg, Spain, and Sweden. Table 7.6 shows that result.

Post-tax net present value now is

$$NPV^\tau = -1{,}500{,}000 + 2{,}130{,}025 \times 1.06^{-6} = 1{,}584.$$

However, there is just an advantage of the loss carry back rule if there is no loss in previous periods. If there are solely losses in previous periods, net present value would be the same as in the case of Greece, Italy, Luxembourg, Spain, and Sweden.

Now, consider the case of the US displayed in Table 7.7. As we have a two period loss carry back, post-tax net present value must be higher than in the case of the United Kingdom and Ireland. That is because in our example the 20 year time restriction for loss carry forward does not bind and loss carry back is fully applicable.

Table 7.6 Loss offsetting in the United Kingdom and Ireland

t	1	2	3	4	5	6
CF_t	300,000	300,000	400,000	–1,800,000	1,600,000	1,550,000
D_t	250,000	250,000	250,000	250,000	250,000	250,000
IP_t		28,000	57,680	95,141	–67,038	86,258
FI_t	280,000	576,800	951,408	–670,379	862,583	2,130,025
AGI_t	50,000	78,000	207,680	–1,954,859	1,282,962	1,386,258
LCF_t				1,747,179	464,217	
LCB_t				207,680		
LO_t					1,282,962	464,217
TB_t	50,000	78,000	207,680	–207,680	0	922,041
T_t	20,000	31,200	83,072	–83,072	0	368,816
CF_t^τ	280,000	296,800	374,608	–1,621,787	1,532,962	1,267,442

Table 7.7 Loss offsetting in the US

t	1	2	3	4	5	6
CF_t	300,000	300,000	400,000	–1,800,000	1,600,000	1,550,000
D_t	250,000	250,000	250,000	250,000	250,000	250,000
IP_t		28,000	57,680	95,141	–63,918	89,690
FI_t	280,000	576,800	951,408	–639,179	896,903	2,133,956
AGI_t	50,000	78,000	207,680	–1,954,859	1,286,082	1,389,690
LCF_t				1,669,179	383,097	
LCB_t				285,680		
LO_t					1,286,082	383,097
TB_t	50,000	78,000	207,680	–285,680	0	1,006,593
T_t	20,000	31,200	83,072	–114,272	0	402,637
CF_t^τ	280,000	296,800	374,608	–1,590,587	1,536,082	1,237,053

NPV^τ is computed as 4,355. Tax refund of loss carry back in $t = 3$ gives

$$\begin{aligned} T_4 &= \tau \times LCB_4 = \tau \times (TB_2 + TB_3) \\ &= 0.4 \times (78{,}000 + 207{,}680) \\ &= 114{,}272. \end{aligned}$$

As expected, NPV^τ exceeds the one in the United Kingdom and Ireland.

Loss offset restrictions in France go one step further and allow loss carry back for three periods. Table 7.8 draws the situation in France due to our assumptions.

NPV^τ is computed as 6,131. Now, the loss carry back in $t = 4$ results in a tax refund in $t = 4$ of

$$\begin{aligned} T_4 &= \tau \times LCB_4 = \tau \times (TB_1 + TB_2 + TB_3) \\ &= 0.4 \times (50{,}000 + 78{,}000 + 207{,}680) \\ &= 134{,}272. \end{aligned}$$

In Austria there is no loss carry back, however, there is no time restriction for loss carry forward. Loss offset is restricted to 75% of the positive adjusted gross income in t and hence can be described as:

$$LO_t = \min\{LCF_{t-1}; 0.75 \times \max\{AGI_t; 0\}\}.$$

The financial plan in Table 7.9 represents the case of Austria based on our assumptions.

NPV^τ is computed as –11,187. Notice the situation in $t = 5$. Loss offset is restricted to $LO_5 = 0.75 \times 1{,}274{,}655 = 955{,}991$.

Table 7.8 Loss offsetting in France

t	1	2	3	4	5	6
CF_t	300,000	300,000	400,000	–1,800,000	1,600,000	1,550,000
D_t	250,000	250,000	250,000	250,000	250,000	250,000
IP_t	0	28,000	57,680	95,141	–61,918	91,890
FI_t	280,000	576,800	951,408	–619,179	918,903	2,136,476
AGI_t	50,000	78,000	207,680	–1,954,859	1,288,082	1,391,890
LCF_t				1,619,179	331,097	
LCB_t				335,680		
LO_t					1,288,082	331,097
TB_t	50,000	78,000	207,680	–335,680	0	1,060,793
T_t	20,000	31,200	83,072	–134,272	0	424,317
CF_t^τ	280,000	296,800	374,608	–1,570,587	1,538,082	1,217,573

Table 7.9 Loss offsetting in Austria

t	1	2	3	4	5	6
CF_t	300,000	300,000	400,000	–1,800,000	1,600,000	1,550,000
D_t	250,000	250,000	250,000	250,000	250,000	250,000
IP_t	0	28,000	57,680	95,141	–75,345	64,374
FI_t	280,000	576,800	951,408	–753,451	643,738	2,111,910
AGI_t	50,000	78,000	207,680	–1,954,859	1,274,655	1,364,374
LCF_t				1,954,859	998,868	
LCB_t						
LO_t					955,991	998,868
TB_t	50,000	78,000	207,680	0	318,664	365,506
T_t	20,000	31,200	83,072	0	127,466	146,202
CF_t^τ	280,000	296,800	374,608	–1,704,859	1,397,189	1,468,172

The last setting deals with the situation in Germany. Loss offset restrictions for that case are already described earlier. The result based on the known assumptions is stated in Table 7.10.

NPV^τ is computed as –332. Consider loss offset in $t = 5$. We get

$$LO_5 = 1{,}000{,}000 + 0.6 \times (1{,}282{,}962 - 1{,}000{,}000) = 1{,}169{,}777.$$

Summary

The table given later summarizes the results of the different loss offset restrictions applied in the selected countries on NPV^τ. Compared to after-tax NPV based on an immediate full loss offset, NPV^τ changes between –85% and –127%. This illustrates the timing effect of loss offset restrictions quite well. However, notice that relative changes do not reflect decision criteria at all.

Table 7.10 Loss offsetting in Germany

t	1	2	3	4	5	6
CF_t	300,000	300,000	400,000	−1,800,000	1,600,000	1,550,000
D_t	250,000	250,000	250,000	250,000	250,000	250,000
IP_t	0	28,000	57,680	95,141	–67,038	81,731
FI_t	280,000	576,800	951,408	–670,379	817,309	2,127,308
AGI_t	50,000	78,000	207,680	−1,954,859	1,282,962	1,381,731
LCF_t				1,747,179	577,402	
LCB_t				207,680		
LO_t					1,169,777	577,402
TB_t	50,000	78,000	207,680	–207,680	113,185	804,329
T_t	20,000	31,200	83,072	–83,072	45,274	321,732
CF_t^τ	280,000	296,800	374,608	−1,621,787	1,487,688	1,309,999

Method of loss offset restriction	NPV^τ	Δ in total to $NPV^{\tau,full}$	Δ relative to $NPV^{\tau,full}$
immediate full loss offset $NPV^{\tau,full}$	40,772		
Sweden/Luxembourg/Spain/Italy	–5,796	–46,567	–114%
United Kingdom/Ireland	1,583	–39,188	–96%
United States	4,355	–36,417	–89%
France	6,131	–34,641	–85%
Austria	–11,187	–51,959	–127%
Germany	–332	–41,103	–101%

Example 7.9. Case Study: Linde Group

In almost all countries worldwide, tax reports of companies and individuals are not publicly available. But it is very important for investors to gather information about the tax position of companies. An important example is to find out whether a company has tax loss carry forwards, because they influence future tax payments and future net cash flows heavily. One possibility to find that information is to have a look at Financial Reports. According to many Financial Accounting systems (e.g., IFRS), companies must report deferred tax positions. The most important reason for recognition of deferred tax assets or deferred tax liabilities are differences in income recognition between tax accounting and financial accounting. But there is an additional reason to recognize deferred tax assets: If there is a tax loss carry forward then the company has to build a deferred tax asset in the amount of the expected tax saving. A loss carry forward of € 1 million which can be offset in the next year causes a deferred tax asset of $1{,}000{,}000 \times \tau$. If the tax rate $\tau = 30\%$ then the deferred tax asset is $1{,}000{,}000 \times 0.3 = 300{,}000$. If a loss carry forward cannot be used any longer, for example, because no future profits are expected or because the period of the loss carry forward expires, a valuation allowance has to be made.

Let's have a look at the Linde Group, a German DAX company. Linde Group Financial Report 2005, p. 94, states deferred tax assets on tax loss carry forwards and tax credits in 2005 of € 112 million less valuation allowance of € 75 million. In 2004 there were € 152 million of deferred tax assets less valuation allowance of € 67 million.

The Financial Report 2005 states:

> ... (it is) no longer probable that the deferred tax asset will be utilized. A valuation allowance of € 75 million (2004: € 67 million) has therefore been recognized against the deferred tax assets to reduce the potential tax savings of € 234 million (2004: € 182 million), as it is not probable that the underlying tax loss carry forwards and tax credits of € 209 million (2004: € 171 million) and deductible temporary differences of € 25 million (2004: € 11 million) will be utilized. Of the total potential tax savings less the valuation allowances of € 234 million (2004: € 182 million), € 75 million (2004: € 64 million) may be carried forward for up to 10 years and € 132 million (2004: € 118 million) may be carried forward for longer than 10 years.

in € million	2005	2004
May be carried forward for up to 10 years	85	94
May be carried forward for longer than 10 years	49	108
May be carried forward indefinitely	222	142
	356	344

Based on that information only 356 − 234 =€ 122 million can be carried forward in 2005. About € 234 million (!) of the original loss carry forward are lost without being tax deductible.

Linde calculates with a tax rate of 32%. This means that potential tax savings of € 234 million×0.32 =€ 75 million are lost.

Let us discuss further economic effects of loosing this loss carry forward.

(a) What is the present value effect of this situation compared to a company which offsets the loss in 2005? What assumptions do you need to answer this question? What kind of tax effect occurs?
(b) What is the effect on the tax base in 2005?
(c) What is the effect on the 2005 cash flow?
(d) What is the effect on IFRS net profits in 2005 and on the earnings per share ratio?
(e) What would be the 2005 present value effect if a loss of € 234 million was not offset in 2005, but was carried forward and be offset in 2006?

Additional information to answer these questions can be found in the Linde Financial Report 2005 on p. 29:

in € million	2005
Earnings before taxes on income (EBT)	789
Taxes on income	279
Earnings after taxes on income	510
Minority interests	–9
Net income after minority interests	501

Assume the marginal tax rate to be 32%. The average number of shares in 2005 was 119,864,046 and earnings per share were € 4.19.

(a) The present value effect of loosing the loss carry forward of € 234 million is exactly the loss of the potential tax saving of € 234 million × 0.32 =€ 75 million. You always need to know the tax rate a company uses to calculated deferred taxes. Sometimes, companies use the tax rate of the home country of the head quarter, but in most cases the tax rate is an average tax rate of the countries were they have business activities. A tax base effect occurs because the total tax base is increasing in case of a denied loss offset.
(b) The effect on the tax base is € 234 million.
(c) The effect on net cash flows equals the present value effect: € 234 million × 32% = € 75 million.
(d) Again, the effect on IFRS net profits in 2005 equals the net cash flow effect. The income decreases by € 75 million. Without loosing the loss carry forward, income of € 501 million would be € 75 million higher. This causes an increase in earnings and earnings per share by 15%!

Earnings per share 2005 (in €)	4.19
Net income after minority interests (in million €)	501
+ value of loss offset (in million €)	75
Corrected net income (in million €)	576
Corrected earnings per share (in €)	$\frac{576{,}000{,}000}{119{,}864{,}046} = 4.81$
Increase in earnings per share	$\frac{4.81}{4.18} - 1 = 15\%$

(e) In contrast to the previous questions, we have a timing effect. The sum of tax bases remains equivalent. To calculate the present value effect, we need to know or assume the tax rate (32%) and the after-tax interest rate, for example 5%. The effect of delaying a loss offset instead of completely loosing it is very large: Profits and cash flow decrease by about €3.6 million instead of €75 million!

$$PV^\tau = -75{,}000{,}000 + \frac{75{,}000{,}000}{1.05} = -3{,}571{,}429.$$

7.4.3 *The Combined Effect of Loss Offset Restrictions and Tax Base Adjustments*

In the last sections, we have seen two different extensions of the Standard Model which influence the after-tax net present value. Now, we want to combine those two effects. We will see that tax base adjustments, for example provisions, are not necessarily advantageous when losses occur and loss offset restrictions exist. To better understand this, we refer to our examples from Sects. 7.3.1 and 7.3.4.

Example 7.10. Provisions and Losses

Let's get back to Ex. 7.2. Daniel wants to know tax effects very precisely. To determine the effect of the provision, he includes loss offset restrictions applicable in the US because there is no other positive income beside the investment alternative considered. In that case post-tax net present value gives:

t	0	1	2	3	4
CF_t	–80,000	20,000	18,400	20,000	60,000
D_t		20,000	20,000	20,000	20,000
IP_t		0	1,600	3,200	4,954
FI_t		20,000	40,000	61,920	108,892
PRO_t			–10,000	10,000	
AGI_t		0	–10,000	13,200	44,954
LCB_t					
LCF_t			10,000		
LO_t				10,000	
TB_t		0	–10,000	3,200	44,954
T_t		0	0	1,280	17,982
CF_t^τ	–80,000	20,000	20,000	21,920	46,972
NPV^τ	10,272				

If you first consider post-tax net present value, you recognize the same amount as in the case where no provision is considered. The reason is that there is no loss carry back from $t = 2$ to $t = 1$, because in $t = 1$ there is no positive taxable income. Claiming the provision leads to a loss carry forward in $t = 2$ and does not result in a tax refund. Then in $t = 3$ loss offset is possible. However, at the same time provision is released, tax refund and deduction of the provision occur in the same period and hence do not result in a lower tax present value.

Example 7.11. Fair Value Depreciation and Losses

We refer to Ex. 7.5 where fair value depreciation reduced income heavily. Now, we want to integrate loss offset restrictions. Because investment takes place in Austria, it seems appropriate to consider Austria's loss offset restrictions (double tax treaty assigns taxable income of real property to Austria not to France) that are characterized by no loss carry back and limited loss offset in future periods to 75% of adjusted gross income (see Table 7.3 on p. 283 and Table 7.9 on p. 288 for more details). The following table shows the calculation of NPV^τ if Austria's loss offset restrictions are considered.

t	0	1	2	3	...	16	17	18	19	20
CF_t	–180,000	11,000	11,000	11,000	...	11,000	11,000	11,000	11,000	131,000
D_t		3,000	3,000	1,000	...	1,000	1,000	1,000	1,000	1,000
$FairVD_5$			116,000							
BV_t		177,000	58,000	57,000	...	44,000	43,000	42,000	41,000	40,000
AGI_t		8,000	–108,000	10,000	...	10,000	10,000	10,000	10,000	90,000
LCF_t	0	0	108,000	100,500	...	3,000	0	0	0	0
LO_t		0	0	7,500	...	7,500	3,000	0	0	0
TB_t		8,000	–108,000	2,500	...	2,500	7,000	10,000	10,000	90,000
T_t		2,400	0	750	...	750	2,100	3,000	3,000	27,000
CF_t^τ		8,600	11,000	10,250	...	10,250	8,900	8,000	8,000	104,000
NPV^τ	–5,627									

Now net present value is again negative, however, greater than in the case of no fair value depreciation.

7.5 Varying Marginal Tax Rates and Progressive Tax Rates

The assumptions of our "Standard Model" reduce tax rate functions to constant marginal tax rates applicable for real investments and financial investments equally. However, real-world tax systems are quite dynamic and as tax rates are often adjusted by politicians to suggest voters that something is done to reduce tax burden, tax rates change almost annually. Usually, nontax experts are impressed by discussions about tax rates. "Tax cut cum base broadening" which means tax rates are reduced while tax bases are extended is a common means to attract investments.

Tax rates are also often used for discussions about simplifying taxation. However, tax experts do not focus on tax rate discussions to simplify taxation because they know that computing taxable base might last days, weeks, months, or even years, while applying progressive tax rate functions on the tax base in order to determine tax liability takes a few seconds. Therefore, discussions about simplifying tax systems have to start with computation of the tax base.

First consider varying marginal tax rates over time. We do not have to make substantial adjustments to the "Standard Model", but the post-tax discount rate in t is now a product on the basis of previous post-tax discount rates. Integrating periodic marginal tax rates lets the "Standard Model" evolve to

$$NPV^{\tau} = -I_0 + \sum_{t=1}^{n} \frac{CF_t - \tau_t \times (CF_t - D_t)}{\prod_{k=0}^{t}(1 + i \times (1 - \tau_k))}. \tag{7.9}$$

Example 7.12. Varying Tax Rates

Suppose the following cash flow structure of a real investment alternative, straight-line depreciation over 5 years, $i = 8\%$ and $\tau_1 = 20\%$, $\tau_2 = 30\%$, $\tau_3 = 40\%$, $\tau_4 = 35\%$, $\tau_5 = 30\%$:

t	1	1	2	3	4	5
CF_t	−500,000	110,000	115,000	120,000	125,000	151,000

If the option to tax capital income at the flat rate in Germany is neglected, post-tax net present value is determined as:

t	1	1	2	3	4	5
CF_t	−500,000	110,000	115,000	120,000	125,000	151,000
D_t		100,000	100,000	100,000	100,000	100,000
TB_t		10,000	15,000	20,000	25,000	51,000
T_t		2,000	4,500	8,000	8,750	15,300
CF_t^{τ}	−500,000	108,000	110,500	112,000	116,250	135,700
q_t^{τ}		1.0640	1.0560	1.0480	1.0520	1.0560
$DF_t = (\prod_{k=0}^{t} q_k^{\tau})^{-1}$		1.0640^{-1}	1.1236^{-1}	1.1775^{-1}	1.2387^{-1}	1.3081^{-1}
PV_t^{τ}		101,504	98,346	95,115	93,845	103,737
NPV^{τ}	−7,453					

The corresponding discount factors DF_t are calculated as:

$$DF_1 = (1 + 0.08 \times (1 - 0.2))^{-1} = 1.0640^{-1}$$
$$DF_2 = (1.0640 \times (1 + 0.08 \times (1 - 0.3)))^{-1} = 1.1236^{-1}$$
$$DF_3 = (1.0640 \times 1.0560 \times (1 + 0.08 \times (1 - 0.4)))^{-1} = 1.1775^{-1}$$
$$DF_4 = (1.0640 \times 1.0560 \times 1.0480 \times (1 + 0.08 \times (1 - 0.35)))^{-1} = 1.2387^{-1}$$
$$DF_5 = (1.0640 \times 1.0560 \times 1.0480 \times 1.0520 \times (1 + 0.08 \times (1 - 0.3)))^{-1} = 1.3081^{-1}.$$

Moreover, real-world tax systems usually provide a progressive tax rate function. But how is the correct discount rate determined? In that case we have to determine the annual marginal tax rate applied to the returns of the financial investments explicitly. To determine annual marginal tax rates, future value is calculated as a byproduct. If we determine the after-tax future value, we do not need to determine after-tax net present values based on complicated methods. Instead, we can base our decision on the after-tax future values.

7.6 Tax Options

Real-world tax codes usually include innumerable tax options. Tax options make tax planning more complicated because in order to determine the optimal choice, all alternatives have to be calculated. Options can be integrated into our "Standard Model" by implementing dummy variables. Often alternatives are reduced to two options. That fact results in using binary variables to display alternatives. The intention of the following example is to show how to handle tax options and sensitize you to be careful with using max or min operations in your models while optimizing gradually.

Example 7.13. Tax Options

Suppose the following cash flow stream

t	0	1	2	3	4
CF_t	–600,000	1,200,000	150,000	0	200,000

Interest rate is $i = 8\%$ and straight-line depreciation is applied over 4 years. Further, the German progressive tax rate function shown in Table 4.3 on p. 142 is applied.

If we take the progressive German tax rate function and the German loss offset restrictions as adjustments to our "Standard Model" into account then the following financial plan shows how future value is determined.

t	0	1	2	3	4
CF_t	–600,000	1,200,000	150,000	0	200,000
D_t		150,000	150,000	150,000	150,000
IP_t		0	59,456	74,868	82,201
FI_t		743,194	935,850	1,027,518	1,268,950
AGI_t		1,050,000	59,456	–75,132	132,201
LCB_t				59,456	
LO_t					15,676
LCF_t				15,676	
TB_t		1,050,000	59,456	– 59,456	116,525
T_t		456,806	16,800	–16,800	40,769
CF_t^τ	–600,000	743,194	192,656	91,668	241,432

In this case T_t is calculated as:

$$T_t = T(TB_t),$$

where $T(\cdot)$ represents the German tax rate function. In detail T_t is calculated as:

$$\begin{aligned} T_1 &= 1{,}050{,}000 \times 0.45 - 15{,}694 = 456{,}806 \\ T_2 &= 59{,}456 \times 0.42 - 8{,}172 = 16{,}800 \\ T_3 &= -16{,}800 \quad \text{(tax refund due to the loss carry back)} \\ T_4 &= 116{,}525 \times 0.42 - 8{,}172 = 40{,}769. \end{aligned}$$

Now consider $t = 3$. Negative adjusted gross income AGI can just be offset to the amount of 59,456 as a loss carry back which equals taxable income of the preceding year. Loss carry back results in a tax refund exactly to the same amount as the tax liability in $t = 2$. Loss carry forward of 15,676 in $t = 3$ is offset in $t = 4$. Financial investment in $t = 4$ equals the after-tax future value $FI_4 = FV^\tau = 1{,}268{,}950$.

Let's go a step further and consider Germany's flat tax on capital income. Application of the flat tax rate is actually a tax option. You have the choice to assess your whole income or to choose the flat rate of $\tau^{flat} = 25\%$ on capital income and assess remaining income. To choose, we have to model both situations and if optimizing gradually year by year, minimal tax liability in t gives

$$T_t = \min\{T_t^{\alpha=1}; T_t^{\alpha=0}\}, \tag{7.10}$$

where α is a binary variable and is 0 if all income is assessed and 1 if capital income is taxed at the flat rate of 25%

$$\alpha = \left\{ \begin{matrix} 0 & \text{assessment} \\ 1 & \text{flat tax} \end{matrix} \right\}.$$

Tax base TB_t refers to the tax base on which the progressive tax rate function is applied, while T_t refers to the sum of the progressive tax and the flat tax.

The following plan now shows again determination of future value.

t	0	1	2	3	4
CF_t	–600,000	1,200,000	150,000	0	200,000
D_t		150,000	150,000	150,000	150,000
IP_t		0	59,456	75,023	81,025
FI_t		743,194	937,786	1,012,809	1,278,467
AGI_t		1,050,000	59,456	–74,977	131,025
LCB_t					
LO_t					74,977
LCF_t				74,977	
$TB_t^{\alpha=0}$		1,050,000	59,456	0	56,048
$T_t^{\alpha=0}$		456,806	16,800	0	15,367
$TB_t^{\alpha=1}$		1,050,000	0	0	0
$T_t^{\alpha=1}$		456,806	14,864	18,756	20,256
α_t		0/1	1	0	0
CF_t^{τ}	–600,000	743,194	194,592	75,023	265,658

Tax base is calculated as:

$$TB_t = CF_t - D_t + (1 - \alpha_t) \times IP_t - LO_t$$

and tax liability then gives

$$T_t = T(TB_t) + \alpha \times 0.25 \times IP_t.$$

In $t = 1$ there are no interest payments because $FI_0 = 0$. Hence, tax base and tax liability in both cases ($\alpha = 0; \alpha = 1$) are equal. In $t = 2$ tax liability in case of $\alpha = 1$ is less than in the case of $\alpha = 0$. This is because other income equals zero

$$CF_2 - D_2 = 150{,}000 - 150{,}000 = 0$$

and hence income tax just consists of

$$T_2^{\alpha=1} = 0.25 \times IP_2 = 0.25 \times 59{,}456 = 14{,}864.$$

Notice, if assessment is chosen in $t = 2$, taxable income would be

$$TB_2 = 150{,}000 - 150{,}000 + 59{,}456 = 59{,}456,$$

which consists of the interest payments. The income tax then would be

$$T_2^{\alpha=0} = 59{,}456 \times 0.42 - 8{,}172 = 16{,}800.$$

In the case of assessment, average tax rate can be used to choose optimal α_2. Average tax rate here is

$$\frac{16{,}800}{59{,}456} = 28.27\%$$

and hence exceeds the flat tax of 25%.

Now consider $t = 3$. As there is no assessment of interest payments in $t = 2$ (which results in a tax base of zero), loss carry back in $t = 3$ cannot be claimed. Therefore, losses that occur in $t = 3$ have to be offset in $t = 4$. Since tax base in case of assessment is zero, there is no income tax liability in $t = 3$. $\alpha_3 = 0$ is optimal in $t = 3$.

In $t = 4$ income tax in case of assessment and flat tax is

$$\begin{aligned} T_4^{\alpha=0} &= \max\{(200{,}000 - 150{,}000 + 81{,}025 - 74{,}977) \times 0.42 - 8{,}172; 0\} \\ &= 15{,}368 \\ T_4^{\alpha=1} &= \max\{(200{,}000 - 150{,}000 - 74{,}977) \times 0.42 - 8{,}172; 0\} \\ &\quad + 0.25 \times 81{,}025 \\ &= 20{,}256. \end{aligned}$$

As assessment leads to a lower tax liability, $\alpha_3 = 0$ is optimal. In case of $\alpha_3 = 1$, there would be left a loss carry forward at the end of the time horizon of

$$LCF_4^{\alpha=1} = 74{,}977 - (200{,}000 - 150{,}000) = 24{,}977.$$

The optimal vector for α_t is (0/1, 1, 0, 0). Using this approach, the after-tax future value is $FV^\tau = 1{,}278{,}467$.

However, the previous approach does not necessarily lead to the maximum future value. Year by year optimization where optimization is started in $t = 0$ and then successively applied in each period up to n does not take interaction of periods into account. To solve that problem, maximization of future value is formally described as:

$$\max_{\alpha_t} \quad FV^{\tau} = \sum_{t=1}^{n} CF_t^{\tau} \times (1 + i^{\tau})^{n-t}.$$

Further conditions as calculation of loss carry back, loss carry forward, loss offset, tax base, post-tax cash flow, and financial investment are already discussed earlier. Now, α_t is explicitly considered as a decision parameter. In each period α_t maybe 0 or 1. This fact results in $2^n = 2^4 = 16$ possible ways to calculate future value. Since n is just 4 we can find the optimal vector for α easily. However, the greater n, the more time consuming the search for the optimal vector. If there is more than one choice – suppose two – we already would have $4^4 = 256$ possible ways to calculate maximum future value. Complete enumeration therefore just suits for finding the optimal solution if the time restriction for computing does not bind. Determination of a solution without complete enumeration is part of current research.

But now have a look at the optimal solution presented in the following financial plan at first. Notice, that the optimal vector for α_t is different to the previous case and at the same time, the future value is greater now. The reason for that is taxation in $t = 2$. Now, assessment is chosen despite lasting in a greater tax liability than in the case of flat rate taxation. However, that disadvantage is overcompensated by a possible loss carry back in $t = 3$. Now, a loss carry back takes place in $t = 3$. In our previous example, a loss offset was only possible 1 year later, in $t = 4$.

In $t = 4$ assessment is optimal. The optimal vector for α_t in this case is $(0/1, 0, 0, 1)$. The after-tax future value is $FV^{\tau} = 1{,}282{,}138$.

t	0	1	2	3	4
CF_t	–600,000	1,200,000	150,000	0	200,000
D_t		150,000	150,000	150,000	150,000
IP_t		0	59,456	74,868	82,202
FI_t		743,194	935,851	1,027,519	1,282,138
AGI_t		1,050,000	59,456	–75,132	132,202
LCB_t				59,456	
LO_t					15,676
LCF_t				15,676	
$TB_t^{\alpha=0}$		1,050,000	59,456	–59,456	116,526
$T_t^{\alpha=0}$		456,806	16,800	–16,800	40,769
$TB_t^{\alpha=1}$		1,050,000	0	0	34,324
$T_t^{\alpha=1}$		456,806	14,864	18,717	27,583
α_t		0/1	0	0	1
CF_t^{τ}		743,194	192,657	91,668	254,619

In $t = 4$ income tax in case of assessment is

$$T_4^{\alpha=0} = (200{,}000 - 150{,}000 + 82{,}202 - 15{,}676) \times 0.42 - 8{,}172$$
$$= 40{,}769.$$

In case of flat rate taxation TB_4 gives

$$TB_4^{\alpha=1} = 200{,}000 - 150{,}000 - 15{,}676 = 34{,}324.$$

Tax on € 34,324 is

$$T(\cdot) = \left(228.74 \times \frac{34{,}324 - 13{,}469}{10{,}000} + 2{,}397\right) \times \frac{34{,}324 - 13{,}469}{10{,}000} + 1{,}038$$
$$= 7{,}032.$$

Total tax in case of flat rate taxation then gives

$$T_4^{\alpha=1} = 7{,}032 + 0.25 \times 82{,}202 = 27{,}583.$$

In addition to the timing effect, rising FV^{τ} can be based on the character of the progressive tax rate function and on the amount chosen for the loss carry back. If you have a look at the tax rate function you will realize that there is a personal exemption of € 8,004. That means that the first € 8,004 of taxable income are not taxed at all. If income is slightly above € 8,004, the marginal tax rate is very low compared to the top marginal tax rate of 45%.

The second argument to include loss carry back as a decision variable in our future value function is the trade off between current tax refund that results from claiming loss carry back, and future reduction in tax liability due to a greater loss carry forward. If, e.g., taxable income is low in $t - 1$, average tax rate is low, too, compared to a possible greater average tax rate in $t + 1$ that, hence, leads to greater reduction of tax liability. Of course, timing effects do play a role, too.

Considering those facts explains why loss carry back up to the allowed maximum amount is not optimal. If you carry back less than the allowed maximum of TB_{t-1}, there remains still positive income in $t - 1$, but taxes are quite low. But this causes an advantage: The loss carry forward LCF_t is higher and can be used in the following years from $t + 1$ on. If the marginal tax rate is higher in $t + 1$ than in $t - 1$ taking the loss carry back into account then limiting the loss carry back is advantageous. As we compare different points of time, we have to discount the marginal tax rate of $t + 1$ in order to compare it to the marginal tax rate calculated in t when the loss carry back takes place.

Reducing taxable income of the previous period to less than € 8,004 does not lead to an additional tax refund in $t = 3$. Smaller loss carry backs resulting in a positive tax base calculated in $t = 3$ as a correction for period $t = 2$ may lead to reduced tax refunds compared to the full loss carry back.

Our future value function is described as:

$$\max_{LCB_t, \alpha_t} \quad FV^\tau = \sum_{t=1}^{n} CF_t^\tau \times (1 + i^\tau)^{n-t}.$$

The optimal solution for α_t and LCB_t is presented in the following financial plan. The optimal vector of α_t does not change compared to the previous assumptions. However, now optimal LCB_3 is smaller compared to the previous example. The marginal tax rate calculated in $t = 3$ as a correction for $t = 2$ is identical to the discounted marginal tax rate of $t = 4$ if the loss carry back is $LCB_3 = 43{,}927$. This amount can be calculated using Excel Solver, for example. The marginal tax rate relevant for the loss carry back is 24.91%, and the discounted marginal tax rate of $t = 4$ is also $26.41\% \times (1 + 0.08 \times (1 - 0.25))^{-1} = 24.91\%$.

The loss carry back $LCB_3 = 43{,}927$ causes a recalculation of year two's tax base: Now, the tax base $TB_2 = 59{,}456 - LCB_3 = 59{,}456 - 43{,}927 = 15{,}528$. Tax on this income according to the German progressive tax rate function is $T_2 = 1{,}541$. We paid $T_2 = 16{,}800$, but now the new calculation is 1,541 only. Therefore, our tax refund is 16,800 – 1,541 = 15,259. Be aware that our tax refund calculations were slightly simplified in the previous sections! Simplification leads to identical results as long as we have constant tax rates or if the loss carry back is identical to the previous year's tax base.

The remaining loss carry forward is $LCF_3 = 75{,}132 - 43{,}927 = 31{,}205$. This amount is offset in $t = 4$.

t	0	1	2	3	4
CF_t	600,000	1,200,000	150,000	0	200,000
D_t		150,000	150,000	150,000	150,000
IP_t		0	59,456	74,868	82,078
FI_t		743,194	935,850	1,025,976	1,285,155
AGI_t		1,050,000	59,456	–75,132	132,078
LCB_t				43,927	
LO_t					31,205
LCF_t				31,205	
$TB_t^{\alpha=0}$		1,050,000	59,456	–43,927	100,873
$T_t^{\alpha=0}$		456,806	16,800	–15,259	34,195
$TB_t^{\alpha=1}$		1,050,000	0	0	18,795
$T_t^{\alpha=1}$		456,806	14,864	18,717	22,899
α_t		0/1	0	0	1
CF_t^τ		743,194	192,656	90,127	259,179

In $t = 4$ income tax in case of assessment is

$$T_4^{\alpha=0} = (200{,}000 - 150{,}000 + 82{,}078 - 31{,}205) \times 0.42 - 8{,}172 = 34{,}195.$$

In case of flat rate taxation TB_4 gives

$$TB_4^{\alpha=1} = 200{,}000 - 150{,}000 - 31{,}205 = 18{,}795,$$

which results in a tax liability of

$$T(\cdot) = \left(228.74 \times \frac{18{,}795 - 13{,}469}{10{,}000} + 2{,}397\right) \times \frac{18{,}795 - 13{,}469}{10{,}000} + 1{,}038$$
$$= 2{,}380.$$

Total tax then gives

$$T_4^{\alpha=1} = 2{,}380 + 0.25 \times 82{,}078 = 22{,}899.$$

If α_t and LCB_t are optimized, FV^τ rises to 1,285,155.

7.7 Handling Uncertainty

One Achilles heel of our "Standard Model" is the problem of certainty. Certainty is assumed particularly concerning interest rates, tax rates, and cash flows.

The least problem are interest rates, because long-term government bonds are available. Therefore, interest rates can be assumed to be known for up to 30 years. Another problem we do not discuss is that the alternative financial investment should represent adequate risk to the evaluated real investment alternative.

Tax rates cause considerable problems. First, taxes are levied on business returns (real investment returns) in the enumerator and on capital income in the denominator. Now, tax law seems to behave very dynamic. Especially, tax rates are subject to changes because tax rate functions are an illustrative parameter for the general public to measure tax burden. Therefore, it is no wonder that tax rates are used for politics. Second, if tax rates vary over time, nominator and denominator might be addressed in different ways. Often, business income is taxed at a progressive rate, whereas the trend for taxation of financial income goes to a flat tax rate. Hence, you have two uncertain tax rate parameters to deal with. Of course, tax bases might also change over time.

The main problem, however, is caused by forecasting future cash flows. Since reality is stochastic, dynamic and complex, it is almost impossible to give a precise forecast. In Chap. 6 we discussed the predictive ability of profits. However, approximation might be reduced to a very short time horizon. One reasonable basis to predict future cash flows might be provided by long-term contracts which occur, e.g., at renting contracts of real property.

Example 7.14. Uncertain Cash Flows

Let's consider the following example to imagine the impact of uncertainty. In Table 7.11 you find two possible uncertain cash flow streams of investment A where probability of occurrence is $\alpha = 0.5$ and the certain cash flow stream of investment B – where cash flows of investment B are the mean of cash flows of investment A.

If capital market rate is $i = 10\%$, pre-tax net present values are

$$NPV^{A,\alpha} = -300{,}000 + \frac{30{,}000}{1.1} + \frac{30{,}000}{1.1^2} + \frac{30{,}000}{1.1^3} + \frac{330{,}000}{1.1^4} = 0$$

$$NPV^{A,(1-\alpha)} = -300{,}000 + \frac{100{,}000}{1.1} + \frac{100{,}000}{1.1^2} + \frac{92{,}000}{1.1^3} + \frac{75{,}000}{1.1^4} = -6{,}099$$

$$NPV^{B} = -300{,}000 + \frac{65{,}000}{1.1} + \frac{65{,}000}{1.1^2} + \frac{61{,}000}{1.1^3} + \frac{202{,}500}{1.1^4} = -3{,}050.$$

Mean of pre-tax net present value of investment A if $\alpha = 0.5$ is

$$\text{mean } NPV^{A} = 0.5 \times 0 + 0.5 \times (-6{,}099) = -3{,}050$$

which is equivalent to the pre-tax net present value of investment B.

In Table 7.12 the post-tax case with $\tau = 30\%$, straight-line depreciation over 4 years and immediate full loss offset is depicted. Again, mean of post-tax net present value of investment A is equivalent to post-tax net present value of investment B.

Table 7.11 Pre-tax case

t	0	1	2	3	4
$CF_t^{A,\alpha}$	–300,000	30,000	30,000	30,000	330,000
$NPV^{A,\alpha}$	0				
$CF_t^{A,(1-\alpha)}$	–300,000	100,000	100,000	92,000	75,000
$NPV^{A,(1-\alpha)}$	–6,099				
CF_t^{B}	–300,000	65,000	65,000	61,000	202,500
NPV^{B}	–3,050				
mean NPV^{A}	–3,050				

Table 7.12 Post-tax case, immediate full loss offset

t	0	1	2	3	4
$CF_t^{A,\alpha}$	–300,000	30,000	30,000	30,000	330,000
D_t		75,000	75,000	75,000	75,000
TB_t		–45,000	–45,000	–45,000	255,000
T_t		–13,500	–13,500	–13,500	76,500
CF_t^{τ}		43,500	43,500	43,500	253,500
$NPV^{\tau,A,\alpha}$	7,552				
$CF_t^{A,(1-\alpha)}$	–300,000	100,000	100,000	92,000	75,000
D_t		75,000	75,000	75,000	75,000
TB_t		25,000	25,000	17,000	0
T_t		7,500	7,500	5,100	0
CF_t^{τ}		92,500	92,500	86,900	75,000
$NPV^{\tau,A,(1-\alpha)}$	–4,605				
CF_t^{B}	–300,000	65,000	65,000	61,000	202,500
D_t		75,000	75,000	75,000	75,000
TB_t		–10,000	–10,000	–14,000	127,500
T_t		–3,000	–3,000	–4,200	38,250
CF_t^{τ}		68,000	68,000	65,200	164,250
$NPV^{\tau,B}$	1,473				
mean $NPV^{\tau,A}$	1,473				

The after-tax net present values of projects A and B are identical: $NPV^{\tau,B} = 1{,}473$ and the mean $NPV^{\tau,A} = 1{,}473$.

Now, Germany's loss offset restrictions are introduced in Table 7.13 (for Germany's loss offset restrictions see Sect. 7.4.1 on p. 277). We assume that in case of negative cash flows additional funds are provided. Therefore, we do not calculate negative or positive financial investments in the financial plans. Loss offset restrictions cause the mean of both post-tax net present values of investment A to be negative, whereas post-tax net present value of investment B is positive.

Now the after-tax net present values of projects A and B vary from each other: $NPV^{\tau,B} = 402$ and the mean $NPV^{\tau,A} = -792$. Which investment is carried out, depends on the investor's utility function. However, this is a nontax cost of tax planning.[3]

Even if the investor is risk-neutral – as we assumed in calculating mean NPVs – we cannot determine financial plans based on average cash flows. Instead, we have to calculate after-tax net present values for all different possible cash flow structures. Afterward, we can build the mean after-tax net present value based on those financial plans. This is caused by asymmetric taxation of losses and profits.

[3] See *Scholes* et. al [1], pp. 170–201.

Table 7.13 Post-tax case, German loss offset rules

t	0	1	2	3	4
$CF_t^{A,\alpha}$	–300,000	30,000	30,000	30,000	330,000
D_t		75,000	75,000	75,000	75,000
AGI_t		–45,000	–45,000	–45,000	255,000
LCF_t		45,000	90,000	135,000	0
LO_t		0	0	0	135,000
TB_t		0	0	0	120,000
T_t		0	0	0	36,000
CF_t^{τ}		30,000	30,000	30,000	294,000
$NPV^{\tau,A,\alpha}$	3,021				
$CF_t^{A,(1-\alpha)}$	–300,000	100,000	100,000	92,000	75,000
D_t		75,000	75,000	75,000	75,000
TB_t		25,000	25,000	17,000	0
T_t		7,500	7,500	5,100	0
CF_t^{τ}		92,500	92,500	86,900	75,000
$NPV^{\tau,A,(1-\alpha)}$	–4,605				
CF_t^B	–300,000	65,000	65,000	61,000	202,500
D_t		75,000	75,000	75,000	75,000
AGI_t		–10,000	–10,000	–14,000	127,500
LCF_t		10,000	20,000	34,000	0
LO_t		0	0	0	34,000
TB_t		0	0	0	93,500
T_t		0	0	0	28,050
CF_t^{τ}		65,000	65,000	61,000	174,450
$NPV^{\tau,B}$	402				
mean $NPV^{\tau,A}$	–792				

Example 7.15. Stochastic Cash Flows

Assume a real investment alternative with initial costs of $I_0 = 800{,}000$. Further assume $i = 10\%$, a marginal tax rate on business income of $\tau = 45\%$ and a flat rate tax on capital income of $\tau^{flat} = 25\%$, leading to $(1 + i^{\tau}) = 1 + i \times (1 - \tau^{flat}) = 1.075$. Time horizon is supposed to be $n = 4$ and application of straight-line depreciation leads to annual depreciation of $D = \frac{800{,}000}{4} = 200{,}000$.

Suppose cash flows to be identically independent normally distributed. If mean is represented by μ and variance by σ^2, distribution of cash flows can be described as:

$$CF_t \underset{iid}{\sim} N(\mu, \sigma^2).$$

If we want to generate 5,000 cash flow streams (simulations) with $n = 4$ each, we need to have 20,000 values of cash flow. Let's assume μ to be 1,000,000 and σ to be 6,000,000.[4] For each of the cash flow streams, we calculate after-tax net present values NPV^{τ}. Figure 7.1 shows the frequency of occurrence of after-tax net present values if immediate full loss offset is assumed. Figure 7.2 shows frequency of occurrence of after-tax net present values if Germany's loss offset restrictions are applied (for Germany's loss offset restrictions see Sect. 7.4.1 starting on p. 277). Due to loss offset restrictions, timing effects as well as tax base effects occur. If there is a loss carry forward at the end of $t = n$, they get lost and do not result in future tax refunds. If you compare Figs. 7.1 and 7.2, it's well demonstrated that distribution moves to the left, that is because the mean NPV^{τ} is lower if Germany's loss offset restrictions are applied.

The following table summarizes mean and standard deviation in case of before-tax *NPV* and after-tax *NPV* if immediate full loss offset or Germany's loss offset restrictions are supposed. Notice that in case of applying Germany's loss offset restrictions, mean NPV^{τ} is negative.

	μ	σ
Pre-tax *NPV*	2,402,450	9,608,360
Immediate full loss offset	1,394,840	11,103,500
Loss offset restrictions	–795,460	11,509,700

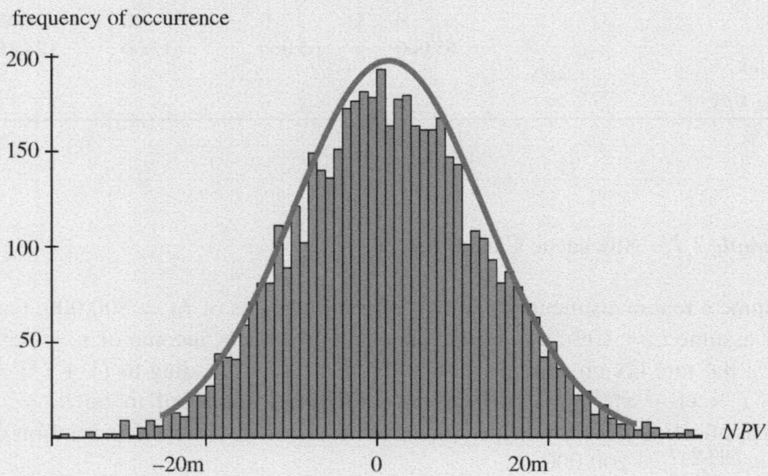

Fig. 7.1 Distribution of NPV^{τ} if immediate full loss offset is assumed

[4] To generate the cash flow values, we used the random generator of normally distributed values of Mathematica 6.0 with a seed value of 1.

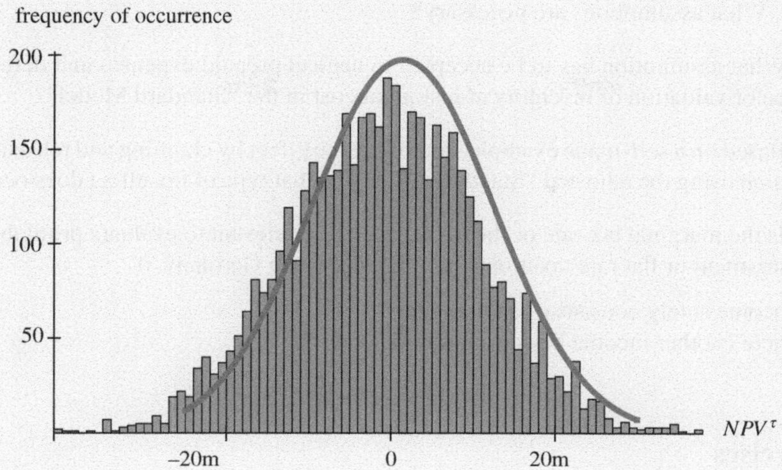

Fig. 7.2 Distribution of NPV^{τ} if Germany's loss offset restrictions are applied

Questions

7.1. Show how capital gains taxation can be implemented to adjust the "Standard Model" using a self-created example covering four periods. Assume that planning horizon is greater than useful life of the real investment.

7.2. Explain how the "Standard Model" could be adjusted with respect to

(a) Valuation of inventory at acquisition cost,
(b) Prepaid expenses and deferred income,
(c) Provisions,
(d) Fair value depreciation

in order to make the model more realistic?

7.3. How does the assumption of immediate full loss offset affect post-tax net present value compared to currently implemented loss offset restrictions?

7.4. Develop a self-made numerical example and show that post-tax net present value

(a) falls,
(b) stays constant,
(c) rises

if loss offset restrictions are applied compared to the case of immediate full loss offset. What assumptions are necessary?

7.5. What assumption has to be accepted to neglect prepaid expenses and deferred income or valuation of inventory at historical cost in the "Standard Model"?

7.6. Based on a self-made example, determine the effect by claiming and releasing a provision using the adjusted "Standard Model". What type of tax effect does occur?

7.7. Is the marginal tax rate or the average tax rate relevant to evaluate profitability of assessment or flat rate taxation of capital income in Germany, if

(a) income solely consists of capital gains,
(b) there is other income beside capital gains?

Exercises

Solutions are provided starting on p. 395.

7.8. Capital Gains

Suppose a real investment alternative with initial costs of $I_0 = 100{,}000$ that results in the following certain future stream of cash flows:

t	0	1	2	3	4
CF_t	–100,000	25,000	26,000	27,000	31,000

Assume $i = 6\%$, $\tau = 40\%$ and straight-line depreciation. In $t = 4$, the investor sells the asset for $SP_n = 5{,}000$. The investor withdraws all cash flow after taxes at the end of each period. Determine

(a) the post-tax net present value if capital gains are tax exempt.
(b) the post-tax net present value if capital gains are taxed at the rate of $\tau = 40\%$.
(c) The maximum tax rate on capital gains that causes the investor to be indifferent between the real investment and the alternative financial investment.

7.9. Loss Offset Restrictions in Germany

Given the following structure of adjusted gross income (in million €), determine tax liability in each period if Germany's loss offset restrictions are applied.

t	1	2	3	4	5	6	7	8
AGI_t	0.6	–4.0	2.6	–1.0	2.0	0.6	–0.4	0.5

(a) Use the legal German progressive tax rates (see Table 4.3 on p. 142) without optimizing loss carry back.
(b) What happens if loss carry back is optimized in such a way that the tax-free amount of € 8,004 is not carried back?

Neglect modelling FI_t and NPV^{τ}.

7.10. Loss Offset Restrictions in Selected Countries

Assume the following certain future stream of cash flows with initial costs of $I_0 = 1{,}200{,}000$.

t	0	1	2	3	4	5	6
CF_t	–1,200,000	300,000	800,000	400,000	–1,600,000	300,000	2,000,000

Suppose $\tau = 40\%$, $i = 10\%$ and straight-line depreciation. If the investor wants to maximize future value, determine

(a) Pre-tax net present value.
(b) Post-tax net present value if immediate full loss offset is applied.
(c) Post-tax net present value if loss offset restrictions in

1. Sweden, Luxembourg, Spain, and Italy,
2. United Kingdom and Ireland,
3. The US,
4. France,
5. Austria,
6. Germany

are applied.

7.11. Provisions

Kenneth Layth runs a small business where he produces snow shovels in the legal framework of a sole proprietorship. In 2009 he had a big delivery to Home Depot. During the year 2009 it became obvious that there are some quality problems with the shovels. In 2010, Layth expects costs of litigation of € 75,000. In fact, in 2010 he only faced costs of € 10,000. If Layth's personal marginal tax rate is $\tau^p = 40\%$ and pre-tax rate of return of an alternative secure financial investment is $i = 8\%$, compute the advantage of the tax liability in terms of present value.

7.12. Provisions and Loss Offset Restrictions

Assume a time horizon of $n = 3$ and the following cash flow stream:

t	0	1	2	3
CF_t	–90,000	30,000	28,200	80,000

Straight-line depreciation is assumed, the interest rate is $i = 6\%$ and the marginal tax rate is $\tau = 30\%$.

(a) Determine the post-tax future value for the real investment.
(b) Now determine the post-tax future value if a provision of € 10,000 is claimed in $t = 2$ and released to the same amount in $t = 3$ and Germany's loss offset restrictions are applied. Provide a brief interpretation of your result.

7.13. Changing Marginal Tax Rates

An investor is offered a real investment that would cost € 150,000 in $t = 0$ and yield € 40,000 annually for the next 5 years. Straight-line depreciation is applied. Total cash after taxes is withdrawn at the end of each period. In $t = n = 5$ the real investment is worthless and is scrapped. The investment opportunity is a marginal investment because the investor has lots of other real investments running. The interest rate is $i = 50\%$. For the following 5 years, the investor knows that his marginal income tax rates on business income will be $\tau_1 = 50\%$, $\tau_2 = 40\%$, $\tau_3 = 30\%$, $\tau_4 = 20\%$, and $\tau_5 = 20\%$ whereas tax rates on capital income will be $\tau_1^{CI} = 15\%$, $\tau_2^{CI} = 20\%$, and $\tau^{CI} = 25\%$ for $t = 3,4,5$. It is assumed that capital income does not qualify for business income (the financial investment is not a business asset). As a result, lower tax rates for business income in $t = 4,5$ cannot be claimed for capital income. Is the investor advised to carry out the investment?

7.14. Progressive Tax Rates

A real investment opportunity with acquisition costs of $I_0 = 200{,}000$ promises the following certain stream of future cash flows

t	0	1	2	3	4	5
CF_t	–200,000	45,000	45,000	60,000	65,000	75,000

The capital market rate is supposed to be $i = 10\%$. Further, straight-line depreciation is applied. The investor wants to maximize his wealth (future value).

(a) Is the real investment carried out if a marginal tax rate of $\tau = 45\%$ for both business income and capital income is applied?
(b) Is the real investment carried out in case a marginal tax rate of $\tau = 45\%$ is applied for business income whereas capital income is taxed at a flat rate of $\tau^{flat} = 25\%$?
(c) Is the real investment carried out in case Germany's progressive tax rate function (see Table 4.3 on p. 142) is applied to business income, whereas capital income is taxed at a flat rate of $\tau^{flat} = 25\%$? Neglect the option of assessment of capital income if the marginal tax rate is less than 25%.

Use the post-tax future value as your decision criterion.

7.15. Uncertainty

An investor is offered a real investment opportunity yielding the following certain future cash flows in $t = 1{,}2$ and uncertain cash flows in $t = 3$. The parameter ϕ represents the probability of the two outcomes

t	0	1	2	3
CF_t	−90,000	33,000	36,300	$\phi \times 43{,}923 + (1 - \phi) \times 35{,}937$

The investor is risk neutral and carries out the decision on the basis of the mean of the net present value. The interest rate is $i = 10\%$ and $\tau = 40\%$. Straight-line depreciation is applied. The investor withdraws all cash flow after taxes at the end of each year.

(a) Determine the value for ϕ that causes pre-tax net present value to be zero.
(b) Determine the value for ϕ that causes post-tax net present value to be zero.
(c) Does taxation boost or discriminate real investment in this case?

7.16. Including Value Added Taxes (VAT)

Alex wants to start a business offering seminars for business games. The software he needs to purchase costs €23,800 including VAT of €3,800 (19%). He expects an annual cash flow of €6,426, including 19% VAT. Hence, the stream of cash flows is

t	0	1	2	3	4	5
CF_t	−23,800	6,426	6,426	6,426	6,426	6,426

The capital market rate is $i = 10\%$ and $\tau = 45\%$. Straight-line depreciation is applied. Alex withdraws all money for consumption at the end of each year. VAT liability in each year amounts to $\frac{6{,}426}{1.19} \times 0.19 = 1{,}026$.

(a) Determine the post-tax net present value considering VAT. Notice in this case, the asset is capitalized at €20,000 because Alex gets a refund of €3,800 in $t = 0$.
(b) Now, tax law offers an option for VAT purposes where the investor does not have to pay VAT on sales. However, he cannot claim input VAT for initial costs (in this case €3,800). Is the option profitable for Alex if annual sales stay at €6,426?

Reference

1. Scholes, M.S., Wolfson, M.A., Erickson, M., Maydew, E.L., Shevlin, T.: Taxes and Business Strategy. A Planning Approach. 4th edn., Prentice Hall, Upper Saddle River (2009)

Chapter 8
Standard Model of Business Valuation

Abstract This chapter deals with the problem of selling or buying a sole proprietorship or partnership (asset deal). The investor and the seller have to calculate the marginal price they are willing to pay or to accept, respectively. We derive simple models of firm valuation and show how taxation affects investment decisions in terms of buying or selling firms. After reading this chapter, you will be able to conduct simple business evaluations for both sides of the transaction – purchasers and sellers.

8.1 Introduction

The tax consequences arising from selling and buying businesses depend on the legal form of the company. In case of corporations, shares of the purchased company are capitalized. For tax purposes, the book value of shares usually remains constant over time (share deal). Compared to an asset deal, a share deal causes less complicated tax consequences, because there is no goodwill depreciation for tax purposes.

In case of sole proprietorships or partnerships, assets are bought and capitalized. The assets and an eventual goodwill are depreciated over time. In case of an asset deal, the stake in the purchased business entity is mirrored in the balance sheet of the purchaser. In some countries, there is an option to treat share deals (buying corporations) like asset deals for tax purposes. In those cases, our models can be transferred to corporation transactions. Figure 8.1 shows significant differences between an asset and a share deal.

To determine marginal prices, no matter in what decision setting, we always have to consider possible alternatives. Therefore, we have to identify the real investment option and the alternative financial investment. In the case considered in this chapter, the real investment option of a potential buyer is to invest in a sole proprietorship or partnership. The alternative is assumed to be a financial investment with a certain fixed interest rate.

The value of the firm depends on the buyer's/seller's return on the alternative investment. The buyer's price limit (marginal price of the buyer) for the firm is the

DOI 10.1007/978-3-642-03284-4_8,

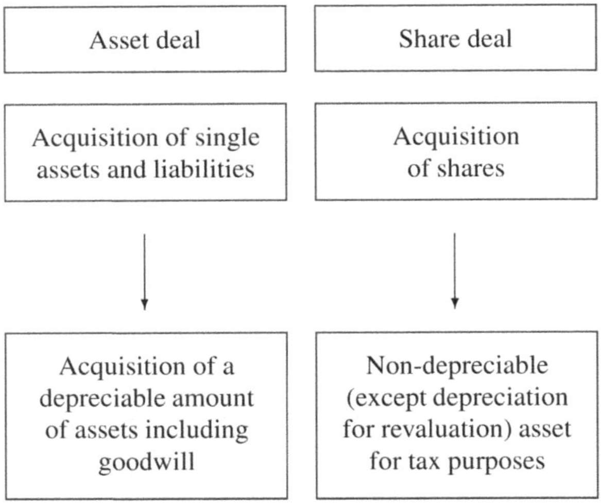

Fig. 8.1 Comparison of asset and share deal for tax purposes

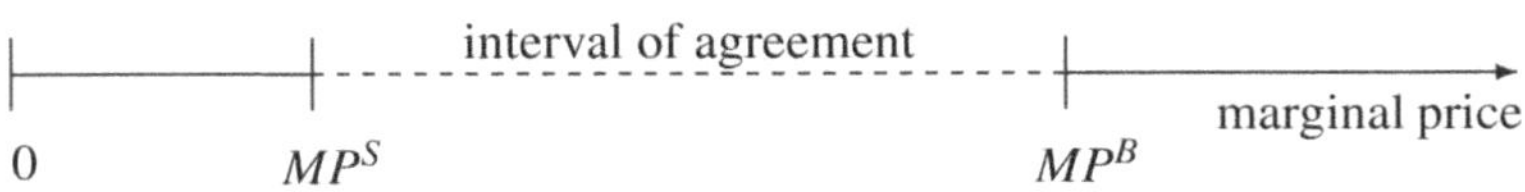

Fig. 8.2 Positive interval of agreement

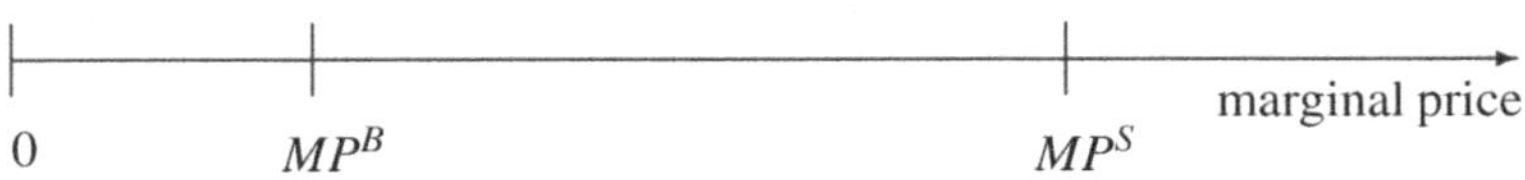

Fig. 8.3 Absence of an interval of agreement

price that leads to indifference between buying the firm and choosing the financial investment alternative. The owner's price limit for the firm is the price that leads to indifference between selling the firm and keeping the firm (marginal price of the seller).

In terms of net present value, this means that the net present value has to be zero. In a buyer or seller situation, the marginal price does not necessarily reflect the price that finally leads to a transaction. Obviously this is the case, if the marginal price of the seller MP^S is less or equal to the marginal price of the buyer MP^B. Figure 8.2 shows a positive interval of agreement, which occurs if $MP^B > MP^S$. In that case, the transaction is carried out. The price has to be negotiated and lies between the two marginal prices. The final price paid depends on the specific negotiations, but the minimum and maximum prices will be found using our models. The case without a positive interval of agreement is depicted in Fig. 8.3.

Table 8.1 Relationship between purchase price and goodwill

	Purchase price
–	Goodwill
=	Fair market value of net assets
–	Step-up of net assets
=	Book value of net assets (= Book value of equity)

Taking these considerations into account, we are facing two main questions:

1. How much is a potential buyer willing to pay at maximum without facing a disadvantage from the deal in comparison to the alternative financial investment? → marginal buyer's price.
2. What is the amount that a potential seller has to realize at least without facing a disadvantage compared to the case where no selling occurs? → marginal seller's price.

8.2 Marginal Price, Goodwill, and Going-Concern-Value

Calculating marginal prices is generally possible for all investment decision settings. Especially, they are used in cases of business valuation.

If stakes of a partnership or a sole proprietorship are sold, the buyer is usually willing to pay more than the book value of the underlying equity. Purchasing the business entity and paying more than the book value of the equity leads to a step-up of all assets' book values to the fair market value. If the purchase price cannot be reached by stepping up all assets, the difference between the fair market value of the equity or going-concern-value of the assets, respectively, and the purchase price is called goodwill. The going-concern-value of the assets is the value of the business assets in an ongoing entity. It typically deviates from the value of the single assets in case of liquidating the business. Goodwill represents an intangible asset. The relationship between goodwill, going-concern-value, and the book value of net assets is shown in Table 8.1.

Example 8.1. Calculating Goodwill

Suppose, Franz, Paul, and Norbert are stakeholders of "The Tax Consultants", a company which is organized as a partnership. The operating business consists of consulting tax authorities in considerably difficult tax issues. Franz holds 60%, Paul 30%, and Norbert 10% of the stakes. As Paul becomes onerous, Franz and Norbert pressure him to sell his stake to Ekkehard. The balance sheet looks like this:

Balance sheet

capital assets	6,000	equity	1,500
current assets	500	liabilities	5,000
total assets	6,500	total equity and liabilities	6,500

Capital assets are completely represented by immovable assets. Those assets could be sold for 8,000 in total. The current assets' book value equals their fair market value of 500. As Ekkehard is a sly old fox, he is willing to pay 1,500 for Paul's stake, knowing that the stake is worth much more. Paul's book value of equity is $1{,}500 \times 30\% = 450$ and represents the book value of the net of assets. Summing up all assets gives 6,500 less liabilities of 5,000, which leads to a net of assets of $1,500$ also represented by the book value of equity. Now, Paul's share of the fair market value of capital assets amounts to $8{,}000 \times 30\% = 2{,}400$. Subtracting the share of the book value $6{,}000 \times 30\% = 1{,}800$ leads to the reserves of $2{,}400 - 1{,}800 = 600$ slumbering in these immovable assets. Hence, we get

	30% share of Paul	100% total
Purchase price	1,500	5,000
− Book value of net assets	450	1,500
− Step-up of net assets	600	2,000
= Goodwill	450	1,500

In real world tax systems, goodwill that is realized in an asset deal is allowed to be depreciated for tax purposes. For example, in Germany and Austria as well as in the US, the economic life of goodwill for tax purposes is 15 years. Now, the depreciation of goodwill produces a tax shield that amounts to goodwill depreciation D^{GW} times tax rate τ.

Example 8.2. Tax Shield of Goodwill Depreciation

Assume the parameters of Ex. 8.1. If the economic life of goodwill is assumed to be 15 years, annual depreciation accounts for $D^{GW} = \frac{450}{15} = 30$ and results in tax savings of $30 \times 40\% = 12$, if the tax rate is assumed to be $\tau = 40\%$. If $i = 10\%$ and $i^{\tau} = 6\%$, the present value of tax savings at the time of purchasing is

$$PV_0 = 12 \times \frac{1.06^{15} - 1}{0.06 \times 1.06^{15}} = 116.55.$$

These tax savings lead to the fact that goodwill depreciation and step-up depreciation affect the marginal purchase price. However, the marginal purchase price determines goodwill depreciation as well. To be able to solve the implicit equation more easily, we assume that tax rates are constant over time.

Example 8.3. Effect of Depreciation Allowances on the Marginal Purchase Price

Suppose, an investment project generates the following future cash flow stream of

t	1	2	3	4
CF_t	220	320	280	260

After-tax cash flows are invested at the capital market rate of $i = 5\%$. The investment decision is made by using the assumptions of the "Standard Model" under consideration of taxation. The marginal purchase price excluding taxation is simple to derive, because it is just represented by the present value of the future cash flows generated by the investment.

$$PV_0 = \frac{220}{1.05} + \frac{320}{1.05^2} + \frac{280}{1.05^3} + \frac{260}{1.05^4} = 955.55.$$

A potential buyer is not willing to pay more than 955.55 for the considered real investment project.

Let's extend the example by two tax systems

(a) A tax system with a common comprehensive tax and a marginal tax rate of $\tau = 50\%$ for financial and real investment income, respectively.
(b) A tax system with a marginal tax rate of $\tau = 50\%$ for real investment income and a flat tax of $\tau^{flat} = 25\%$ for financial investment income.

Now, we are looking for the maximum marginal purchase price an investor is willing to pay to be indifferent between the real investment and the alternative financial investment. Hence, we want to derive the marginal purchase price of the buyer $MP^B = I_0$ so that

$$MP^B = I_0 = PV_0^{\tau}. \tag{8.1}$$

For reasons of simplification, let's assume that the book value of the assets bought is zero and that the fair market value as well as the goodwill of the investment project is depreciated over 4 years. The market value of assets plus goodwill will be equal to the marginal price the buyer will pay. Therefore, they will be equal to I_0. Based on these assumptions, depreciation D_t accounts for $\frac{I_0}{4}$ and the financial plan looks like this:

t	1	2	3	4
CF_t	220	320	280	260
D_t	$\frac{I_0}{4}$	$\frac{I_0}{4}$	$\frac{I_0}{4}$	$\frac{I_0}{4}$
$TB_t = CF_t - D_t$	$220 - \frac{I_0}{4}$	$320 - \frac{I_0}{4}$	$280 - \frac{I_0}{4}$	$260 - \frac{I_0}{4}$
$T_t = \tau \times TB_t$	$110 - \frac{I_0}{8}$	$160 - \frac{I_0}{8}$	$140 - \frac{I_0}{8}$	$130 - \frac{I_0}{8}$
$CF_t - T_t$	$110 + \frac{I_0}{8}$	$160 + \frac{I_0}{8}$	$140 + \frac{I_0}{8}$	$130 + \frac{I_0}{8}$

Case (a): Discounting $CF_t^\tau = CF_t - T_t$ at a rate of $i^\tau = i \times (1-\tau) = 2.5\%$ leads to

$$\begin{aligned} PV_0^\tau = {} & 107.32 + 0.121951 \times I_0 + 152.29 + 0.118977 \times I_0 + 130.00 \\ & + 0.116075 \times I_0 + 117.77 + 0.113244 \times I_0. \end{aligned} \tag{8.2}$$

(8.2) is reduced to

$$PV_0^\tau = 507.38 + 0.470247 \times I_0. \tag{8.3}$$

From (8.1) we know that $PV_0^\tau = I_0 = MP^B$. In (8.3), we can replace PV_0^τ and I_0 by MP^B and solve for MP^B

$$\begin{aligned} MP^B &= 507.38 + 0.470247 \times MP^B \\ MP^B &= \frac{507.38}{1 - 0.470247} = 957.77. \end{aligned}$$

We can double check our result by referring to the NPV-formula. Since the after-tax net present value in case of marginal prices is defined as $NPV^\tau = -I_0 + PV_0^\tau \stackrel{!}{=} 0$, we can derive NPV^τ from (8.3) and, hence, get

$$\begin{aligned} NPV^\tau &= -I_0 + 507.38 + 0.470247 \times I_0 = 0 \\ &= 507.38 - 0.529753 \times I_0 = 0. \end{aligned} \tag{8.4}$$

Applying tax system (a), (8.4) leads to a marginal price of

$$I_0^{(a)} = \frac{507.38}{0.529753} = 957.77.$$

Case (b): Taking tax system (b) into account, CF_t^τ is discounted at a rate of $i^\tau = 5\% \times (1 - 0.25) = 3.75\%$. Therefore, the discounted cash flows are

$$PV_0^\tau = 106.02 + 0.120482 \times I_0 + 148.64 + 0.116127 \times I_0 + 125.36 + 0.111930 \times I_0 + 112.20 + 0.107884 \times I_0. \quad (8.5)$$

(8.5) is reduced to

$$PV_0^\tau = 492.22 + 0.456423 \times I_0.$$

The resulting NPV^τ is

$$\begin{aligned} NPV^\tau &= -I_0 + 492.22 + 0.456423 \times I_0 = 0 \\ &= 492.22 - 0.543577 \times I_0 = 0. \end{aligned} \quad (8.6)$$

(8.6) leads to a marginal price applying tax system (b)

$$I_0^{(b)} = \frac{492.22}{0.543577} = 905.52.$$

The results of Ex. 8.3 show what we already know from the tax paradox discussed in Sect. 3.4 starting on p. 97. The post-tax marginal price can be higher or lower than the price before taxes. The assumptions of tax system (b) in Ex. 8.3 comprise a lower marginal tax rate for financial investments as for real investments. As the alternative financial investment experiences lower taxation, it suggests preference of financial investments over real investments. Hence, the marginal price drops from pre-tax $PV_0 = 955.55$ to 905.52 under tax system (b), whereas it increases to 957.77 under tax system (a).

Now, let's derive a model for a more complex decision setting (*Wagner/Rümmele* [1]). In the setting, we have a seller who is willing to sell his stake in his business entity and a purchaser who wants to take over the stake. If we derive the possible investment alternatives for the purchaser, we get

(a) Purchasing the stake in the business entity.
(b) Carrying out an alternative financial investment.

Notice, the alternative financial investment is represented by a taxable financial investment at the capital market rate of i, resulting in a net present value of zero. This consideration leads to a marginal purchase price that just sets the net present value of the future cash flows of the business entity exactly to zero.

The decision setting of the seller consists of the following alternatives

(a) Selling the stake in the business entity
(b) Keeping the stake in the business entity and realizing its post-tax future cash flows.

A possible transaction also induces tax consequences. The purchaser has to step-up the assets taken over and eventually capitalize a goodwill. The seller has to tax the capital gain out of the disposal of the business entity, which is the difference between the payments received and the book value of his stake.

We use the so-called two-phase-model. In the first phase, cash flows are explicitly given. The second phase is usually represented by an infinite stream of constant cash flows, because it is quite unrealistic to estimate more detailed cash flows for periods far in the future. Therefore, the structure of our model is

t	1	...	n	$n+1$	...	n_{GW}	$n_{GW}+1$	...	∞
CF_t	CF_1	...	CF_n	CF_{n+1}	...	...	...	...	CF_∞

where n represents the useful life of the step-up. This implicitly assumes that either there is one asset that is stepped-up or all assets stepped-up have the same useful life. n_{GW} stands for the economic life of goodwill which is assumed to be longer than the depreciation of the step-ups ($n_{GW} > n$).

One might argue, that the scheduled depreciation of the assets purchased is not considered so far. However, that lack is justified by the simple assumption that the total amount of replaced investment is equivalent to the depreciation allowances (not step-up depreciation) of the assets in every single period. It is important to mention that from now on, the cash outflow for replacement investments is already deducted in the presented cash flow structure for the rest of this chapter.

Example 8.4. Replacement Investments

Suppose, the book value of capital assets of a business entity amounts to 100,000 and capital assets are represented by ten identical machines. The useful life of all ten machines is estimated to be $n = 10$ periods and every machine costs 10,000. All machines presented in the balance sheet are purchased at the same time. Therefore, annual depreciation amounts to $\frac{10,000}{10} =$ 1,000 per machine or 10,000 in total. Now, if one machine is purchased every period, the purchase price of 10,000 (if inflation is neglected) just equals depreciation. If a tax base consists of cash flows before replacement investments CF_t^{before} less depreciation of capital assets, the tax base equals cash flows after replacement investments ($TB_t = CF_t^{\text{after}}$), and both numbers equal exactly the cash flow-equivalent tax base that arises, if replacement investments are not considered explicitly.

t	1	2	3	4
CF_t^{before}	40,000	45,000	65,000	23,000
I_t	10,000	10,000	10,000	10,000
D_t	10,000	10,000	10,000	10,000
TB_t/CF_t^{after}	30,000	35,000	55,000	13,000

8.3 Decision Setting of the Purchaser

To determine the final marginal price of the purchaser, we have to distinguish two cases.

1. The marginal price of the buyer (MP^B) is lower than the going-concern-value GCV of the assets purchased ($MP^B < GCV$). In that case, there are step-ups, but no goodwill appears.
2. The marginal price of the buyer exceeds the going-concern-value ($MP^B > GCV$). In that case there are step-ups and an additional goodwill occurs.

As an overall assumption, we suppose that the marginal price of the buyer always exceeds the book value of equity (BV)

$$MP^B > BV.$$

8.3.1 *Marginal Price of Purchaser is Lower than Going-Concern-Value*

As already mentioned, we have to step-up the assets purchased proportionally. Further, the amount of step-up is depreciated over the economic life. No goodwill occurs. Under these assumptions, tax base arises to

$$TB_t = \left\{ \begin{array}{ll} CF_t - \frac{MP^B - BV}{n} & \text{for } 1 \leq t \leq n \\ CF_t & \text{for } t > n \end{array} \right\} . \tag{8.7}$$

Please be aware, that the useful life of assets n can deviate from the period n in which cash flows are planned in detail, as described in the two-phase-model.

Calculating the marginal price of the buyer implies determination of the present value of future cash flows taking depreciation of step-ups into account, but (in the case considered) neglecting goodwill depreciation. If $\sum_{t=1}^{\infty}(CF_t - T_t) \times (q^\tau)^{-t}$ reflects the present value, the marginal price of the buyer is

$$\begin{aligned} MP^B &= \sum_{t=1}^{\infty}(CF_t - T_t) \times (q^\tau)^{-t} \\ &= \underbrace{\sum_{t=1}^{n}\left[CF_t - \tau \times \left(CF_t - \frac{MP^B - BV}{n}\right)\right] \times (q^\tau)^{-t}}_{\text{first phase}} \\ &\quad + \underbrace{\sum_{t=n+1}^{\infty} CF_t \times (1-\tau) \times (q^\tau)^{-t}}_{\text{second phase}} . \end{aligned}$$

Splitting the term represented by the first phase, we get

$$MP^B = \sum_{t=1}^{n} \tau \times \frac{MP^B - BV}{n} \times (q^\tau)^{-t} + \sum_{t=1}^{n} CF_t \times (1-\tau) \times (q^\tau)^{-t} \quad (8.8)$$
$$+ \sum_{t=n+1}^{\infty} CF_t \times (1-\tau) \times (q^\tau)^{-t}.$$

As cash flows are constant ($CF_t = CF_\infty$) to infinity in the second phase, the present value of net cash flows of the second phase can be expressed as the present value of an infinite annuity. Using the results from (2.19) on p. 20, the present value of the infinite cash flow structure starting from n would be

$$PV_n^\tau = \sum_{t=1}^{\infty} CF_\infty \times (1-\tau) \times (q^\tau)^{-t} = \frac{CF_\infty \times (1-\tau)}{i^\tau}. \quad (8.9)$$

To get the present value in $t = 0$, the present value of the infinite annuity in n has to be discounted by n-periods. Hence, the present value in $t = 0$ of the annuity starting in n is

$$PV_0^\tau = \sum_{t=n+1}^{\infty} CF_\infty \times (1-\tau) \times (q^\tau)^{-t} \times (q^\tau)^{-n} = \frac{CF_\infty \times (1-\tau)}{i^\tau} \times (q^\tau)^{-n}. \quad (8.10)$$

Example 8.5. Taxing an Infinite Stream of Cash Flows

Please have a look at the formula for the infinite annuity for a second. If financial and real investments are taxed equally, taxes do not affect the present value of an infinite annuity. Considering (8.9), we get

$$PV^\tau = \frac{CF_\infty \times (1-\tau)}{i^\tau} = \frac{CF_\infty \times (1-\tau)}{i \times (1-\tau)} = \frac{CF_\infty}{i} = PV.$$

The pre-tax net present value equals the post-tax net present value.

Moreover, because $\frac{MP^B - BV}{n}$ is constant, the first part of (8.8), $\sum_{t=1}^{n} \tau \times \frac{MP^B - BV}{n} \times (q^\tau)^{-t}$ can also be expressed as the present value of an annuity using the present value factor of an annuity in arrears

$$\sum_{t=1}^{n} \tau \times \frac{MP^B - BV}{n} \times (q^\tau)^{-t} = \tau \times \frac{MP^B - BW}{n} \times \frac{(q^\tau)^n - 1}{i^\tau \times (q^\tau)^n}. \quad (8.11)$$

Using the results of (8.10) and (8.11), (8.8) simplifies to

$$MP^B = \tau \times \frac{MP^B - BV}{n} \times \frac{(q^\tau)^n - 1}{i^\tau \times (q^\tau)^n} + \sum_{t=1}^{n} CF_t \times (1-\tau) \times (q^\tau)^{-t} + \frac{CF_\infty \times (1-\tau)}{i^\tau \times (q^\tau)^n}.$$

Now, solving for MP^B leads to

$$MP^B - \frac{\tau \times MP^B}{n} \times \frac{(q^\tau)^n - 1}{i^\tau \times (q^\tau)^n} = -\tau \times \frac{BV}{n} \times \frac{(q^\tau)^n - 1}{i^\tau \times (q^\tau)^n} + \sum_{t=1}^{n} \frac{CF_t \times (1-\tau)}{(q^\tau)^t} + \frac{CF_\infty \times (1-\tau)}{i^\tau \times (q^\tau)^n}.$$

Finally, we get

$$MP^B = \frac{1}{1 - \frac{\tau}{n} \times \frac{(q^\tau)^n - 1}{i^\tau \times (q^\tau)^n}} \times \left(-\tau \times \frac{BV}{n} \times \frac{(q^\tau)^n - 1}{i^\tau \times (q^\tau)^n} + \sum_{t=1}^{n} \frac{CF_t \times (1-\tau)}{(q^\tau)^t} + \frac{CF_\infty \times (1-\tau)}{i^\tau \times (q^\tau)^n} \right). \quad (8.12)$$

If CF_t stays constant for all $t = 1, \ldots, \infty$ $(CF_t = CF_\infty)$, (8.12) simplifies to

$$MP^B = \frac{-\tau \times \frac{BV}{n} \times \frac{(q^\tau)^n - 1}{i^\tau \times (q^\tau)^n} + \frac{CF_\infty \times (1-\tau)}{i^\tau}}{1 - \frac{\tau}{n} \times \frac{(q^\tau)^n - 1}{i^\tau \times (q^\tau)^n}}.$$

Example 8.6. Calculating MP^B if $BV \leq MP^B < GCV$

Suppose, Wilhelm is a successful tax consultant. Approaching his 40th birthday, he has earned enough money to spend the rest of his life playing golf and tennis. As a result, he wants to sell his office which is known for exclusively rich clients. A potential buyer is found in Franz. Franz expects the future cash flows to be (in k€)

t	1	2	3	4	5	6	...	∞
CF_t	100	150	200	250	300	400	...	400

The book value of capital assets is assumed to be 3,000,000 and the going-concern-value 6,000,000, respectively. The capital market interest rate is $i = 10\%$, the tax rate is assumed to be 40% on real investment and financial investment alike, and the economic life of step-ups is $n = 6$ periods.

First, we have a look at the pre-tax marginal price, which is same for both, the buyer and the seller.

$$\begin{aligned} PV &= \sum_{t=1}^{\infty} CF_t \times q^{-t} \\ &= \frac{100{,}000}{1.1} + \frac{150{,}000}{1.1^2} + \frac{200{,}000}{1.1^3} + \frac{250{,}000}{1.1^4} + \frac{300{,}000}{1.1^5} + \frac{400{,}000}{0.1 \times 1.1^5} \\ &= 3{,}205{,}854. \end{aligned}$$

Now, Franz's after-tax marginal buyer's price can be derived in two ways. First, we can use a financial plan and second, we can use the formula derived in (8.12). Let's start with the financial plan method. The depreciation of step-ups is

$$D_t^{SU} = \frac{MP^B - BV}{n}$$

as we assume that $BV \leq MP^B < GCW$. All numbers in the table are given in k€.

t	1	2	3	4	5
CF_t	100	150	200	250	300
D_t^{SU}	$\frac{MP^B-3{,}000}{6}$	$\frac{MP^B-3{,}000}{6}$	$\frac{MP^B-3{,}000}{6}$	$\frac{MP^B-3{,}000}{6}$	$\frac{MP^B-3{,}000}{6}$
TB_t	$100-\frac{MP^B-3{,}000}{6}$	$150-\frac{MP^B-3{,}000}{6}$	$200-\frac{MP^B-3{,}000}{6}$	$250-\frac{MP^B-3{,}000}{6}$	$300-\frac{MP^B-3{,}000}{6}$
T_t	$240-\frac{MP^B}{15}$	$260-\frac{MP^B}{15}$	$280-\frac{MP^B}{15}$	$300-\frac{MP^B}{15}$	$320-\frac{MP^B}{15}$
CF_t^τ	$-140+\frac{MP^B}{15}$	$-110+\frac{MP^B}{15}$	$-80+\frac{MP^B}{15}$	$-50+\frac{MP^B}{15}$	$-20+\frac{MP^B}{15}$
PV_0^τ	–132.075 + 0.062893 $\times MP^B$	–97.900 + 0.059333 $\times MP^B$	–67.170 + 0.055975 $\times MP^B$	–39.605 0.052806 $\times MP^B$	–14.945 0.049871 $\times MP^B$

t	6	7	8	...	∞
CF_t	400	400	400		400
D_t^{SU}	$\frac{MP^B-3{,}000}{6}$	0	0	...	0
TB_t	$400-\frac{MP^B-3{,}000}{6}$	400	400	...	400
T_t	$360-\frac{MP^B}{15}$	160	160	...	160
CF_t^τ	$40+\frac{MP^B}{15}$	240	240	...	240
PV_0^τ	$28.198 + 0.046997 \times MP^B + \frac{240}{0.06 \times 1.06^6}$				

If we sum up PV_0^τ (in k€), we get (in €)

$$MP^B = 2{,}496{,}346 + 0.327822 \times MP^B$$
$$MP^B = 3{,}713{,}815.$$

The step-up amount is

$$MP^B - BV = 3{,}713{,}815 - 3{,}000{,}000 = 713{,}815.$$

The depreciation of the step-up in $t = 1, \ldots, 6$ amounts to

$$\frac{MP^B - BV}{n} = \frac{3{,}713{,}815 - 3{,}000{,}000}{6} = 118{,}969.$$

Now, using (8.12), the marginal buyer price and step-up depreciation $\frac{MP^B - BV}{n}$ amount to

$$MP^B = \frac{1}{1 - \frac{0.4}{6} \times \frac{1.06^6 - 1}{0.06 \times 1.06^6}} \times \left(-0.4 \times \frac{3{,}000{,}000}{6} \times \frac{1.06^6 - 1}{0.06 \times 1.06^6} + \sum_{t=1}^{n} \frac{CF_t \times (1 - 0.4)}{1.06^t} + \frac{400{,}000 \times (1 - 0.4)}{0.06 \times 1.06^6} \right)$$
$$= 1.4877 \times (-983{,}464.87 + 659{,}968.82 + 2{,}819{,}842.16)$$
$$MP^B = 3{,}713{,}815.$$

Notice that the step-up depreciation overstates cash flows in $t = 0$, because

$$\frac{MP^B - BV}{n} = 118{,}969 > CF_1 = 100{,}000.$$

At this point it is important to mention that the implicit assumption of immediate full loss offsets is made. Otherwise, a simple analytical solution as presented here would not be possible if losses occur.

8.3.2 Marginal Price of Purchaser Exceeds Going-Concern-Value

In this case, ($MP^B \geq GCV$) the amount of step-ups is $GCV - BV$. Step-ups that exceed the GCV are not allowed, because the book value of the assets in the new company would have values higher than their going-concern-values. As in the first case, depreciation of step-ups has to be considered. The useful life of step-ups is assumed to be n periods. In addition to the first case, goodwill has to be capitalized and depreciated according to the straight-line method over a period of n_{GW} years. We assume that $n_{GW} > n$.[1] Tax base then will be calculated as:

$$TB_t = \begin{Bmatrix} CF_t - \frac{GCV-BV}{n} - \frac{MP^B - GCV}{n_{GW}} & \text{for} \quad 1 \leq t \leq n \\ CF_t - \frac{MP^B - GCV}{n_{GW}} & \text{for } n < t \leq n_{GW} \\ CF_t & \text{for} \quad t > n_{GW} \end{Bmatrix}.$$

Therefore, the marginal buyer price is calculated as:

$$\begin{aligned} MP^B &= \sum_{t=1}^{\infty}(CF_t - T_t) \times (q^\tau)^{-t} \\ &= \underbrace{\sum_{t=1}^{n}\left[CF_t - \tau \times \left(CF_t - \frac{GCV - BV}{n} - \frac{MP^B - GCV}{n_{GW}}\right)\right] \times (q^\tau)^{-t}}_{\text{first part}} \\ &\quad \underbrace{+ \sum_{t=n+1}^{n_{GW}}\left[CF_t - \tau \times \left(CF_t - \frac{MP^B - GCV}{n_{GW}}\right)\right] \times (q^\tau)^{-t}}_{\text{second part}} \qquad (8.13) \\ &\quad \underbrace{+\frac{CF_\infty \times (1 - \tau)}{i^\tau \times (q^\tau)^{n_{GW}}}}_{\text{third part}}. \end{aligned}$$

The first part reflects the present value of post-tax cash flows from $t = 1, \ldots, n$ that is the useful life of the step-ups. During that phase, two different types of depreciation affect the tax base: First, depreciation of step-ups and second, depreciation of goodwill. The second part of the formula reflects the present value of post-tax cash flows that arise after full depreciation of step-ups until the period of full depreciation of goodwill (years $t = n + 1, \ldots, n_{GW}$). The third part is already known from (8.10). Transformation of (8.13) leads to

$$MP^B = \sum_{t=1}^{n} \tau \times \frac{GCV - BV}{n} \times (q^\tau)^{-t}$$

[1] This assumption is true for many types of assets. If assets comprise buildings with a long remaining useful life, the assumption is not true and the formulas have to be adjusted. The mechanisms remain the same, though.

$$+\sum_{t=1}^{n}\tau\times\frac{MP^B-GCV}{n_{GW}}\times(q^\tau)^{-t}+\sum_{t=n+1}^{n_{GW}}\tau\times\frac{MP^B-GCV}{n_{GW}}\times(q^\tau)^{-t}$$
$$+\sum_{t=1}^{n}CF_t\times(1-\tau)\times(q^\tau)^{-t}+\sum_{t=n+1}^{n_{GW}}CF_t\times(1-\tau)\times(q^\tau)^{-t}$$
$$+\frac{CF_\infty\times(1-\tau)}{i^\tau\times(q^\tau)^{n_{GW}}}$$

$$=\sum_{t=1}^{n}\tau\times\frac{GCV-BV}{n}\times(q^\tau)^{-t}+\sum_{t=1}^{n_{GW}}\tau\times\frac{MP^B-GCV}{n_{GW}}\times(q^\tau)^{-t}$$
$$+\sum_{t=1}^{n_{GW}}CF_t\times(1-\tau)\times(q^\tau)^{-t}+\frac{CF_\infty\times(1-\tau)}{i^\tau}\times(q^\tau)^{-n_{GW}}$$

$$=\tau\times\frac{GCV-BV}{n}\times\frac{(q^\tau)^n-1}{i^\tau\times(q^\tau)^n}+\tau\times\frac{MP^B-GCV}{n_{GW}}\times\frac{(q^\tau)^{n_{GW}}-1}{i^\tau\times(q^\tau)^{n_{GW}}}$$
$$+\sum_{t=1}^{n_{GW}}CF_t\times(1-\tau)\times(q^\tau)^{-t}+\frac{CF_\infty\times(1-\tau)}{i^\tau}\times(q^\tau)^{-n_{GW}}. \tag{8.14}$$

Solving (8.14) for MP^B gives

$$MP^B-\tau\times\frac{MP^B}{n_{GW}}\times\frac{(q^\tau)^{n_{GW}}-1}{i^\tau\times(q^\tau)^{n_{GW}}} \tag{8.15}$$
$$=\tau\times\frac{GCV-BV}{n}\times\frac{(q^\tau)^n-1}{i^\tau\times(q^\tau)^n}-\tau\times\frac{GCV}{n_{GW}}\times\frac{(q^\tau)^{n_{GW}}-1}{i^\tau\times(q^\tau)^{n_{GW}}}$$
$$+\sum_{t=1}^{n_{GW}}CF_t\times(1-\tau)\times(q^\tau)^{-t}+\frac{CF_\infty\times(1-\tau)}{i^\tau}\times(q^\tau)^{-n_{GW}}.$$

The left-hand side of (8.15) is simplified to

$$MP^B\times\left(1-\tau\times\frac{1}{n_{GW}}\times\frac{(q^\tau)^{n_{GW}}-1}{i^\tau\times(q^\tau)^{n_{GW}}}\right)=\ldots.$$

Solving for MP^B, we finally get

$$MP^B=\frac{1}{1-\frac{\tau}{n_{GW}}\times\frac{(q^\tau)^{n_{GW}}-1}{i^\tau\times(q^\tau)^{n_{GW}}}}\times\left(\sum_{t=1}^{n_{GW}}(1-\tau)\times CF_t\times(q^\tau)^{-t}\right. \tag{8.16}$$

$$+\frac{CF_\infty \times (1-\tau)}{i^\tau \times (q^\tau)^{n_{GW}}} + \tau \times \frac{GCV-BV}{n} \times \frac{(q^\tau)^n - 1}{i^\tau \times (q^\tau)^n}$$

$$-\tau \times \frac{GCV}{n_{GW}} \times \frac{(q^\tau)^{n_{GW}} - 1}{i^\tau \times (q^\tau)^{n_{GW}}}\Bigg).$$

If CF_t stays constant for all $t = 1, \ldots, \infty$, (8.16) is simplified to

$$MP^B = \frac{\tau \times \frac{GCV-BV}{n} \times \frac{(q^\tau)^n-1}{i^\tau \times (q^\tau)^n} - \tau \times \frac{GCV}{n_{GW}} \times \frac{(q^\tau)^{n_{GW}}-1}{i^\tau \times (q^\tau)^{n_{GW}}} + \frac{CF_t \times (1-\tau)}{i^\tau}}{1 - \tau \times \frac{1}{n_{GW}} \times \frac{(q^\tau)^{n_{GW}}-1}{i^\tau \times (q^\tau)^{n_{GW}}}}.$$

Example 8.7. Calculating MP^B if $MP^B \geq GCV$

Suppose the following assumptions, where τ represents the marginal tax rate for returns on real investments and τ^{flat} is applied to financial yields.

$i = 5\%$ $BV = 800{,}000$
$\tau = 50\%$ $GCV = 960{,}000$
$\tau^{flat} = 25\%$ $i^{\tau,flat} = 3.75\%$
$n = 5$

Pre-tax cash flow stream in k€

t	1	2	3	4	5	6	...	∞
CF_t	550	500	450	400	350	300	...	300

The pre-tax marginal prices of the purchaser and the seller are equivalent, hence

$$PV_0 = MP^B = MP^S$$
$$= \frac{550{,}000}{1.05} + \frac{500{,}000}{1.05^2} + \frac{450{,}000}{1.05^3} + \frac{400{,}000}{1.05^4} + \frac{350{,}000}{1.05^5} + \frac{300{,}000}{0.05 \times 1.05^5}$$
$$= 6{,}670{,}523.$$

To determine the post-tax MP^B, we assume $MP^B > GCV$. In this case, the annual depreciation of step-ups D_t^{SU} will be

$$D_t^{SU} = \frac{GCV - BV}{n} = \frac{960{,}000 - 800{,}000}{5} = 32{,}000$$

for $t = 1, \ldots, n$. The way of calculating post-tax cash flows is displayed in the following table. D_t^{GW} represents the depreciation of goodwill. Again, all numbers in the table are given in k€.

t	1	2	3	4	5
CF_t	550	500	450	400	350
D_t^{SU}	32	32	32	32	32
D_t^{GW}	$\frac{MP^B-960}{15}$	$\frac{MP^B-960}{15}$	$\frac{MP^B-960}{15}$	$\frac{MP^B-960}{15}$	$\frac{MP^B-960}{15}$
TB_t	550–32–$\frac{MP^B-960}{15}$	500–32–$\frac{MP^B-960}{15}$	450–32–$\frac{MP^B-960}{15}$	400–32–$\frac{MP^B-960}{15}$	350–32–$\frac{MP^B-960}{15}$
T_t	$0.5\times\left(582-\frac{MP^B}{15}\right)$ $=291-\frac{MP^B}{30}$	$0.5\times\left(532-\frac{MP^B}{15}\right)$ $=266-\frac{MP^B}{30}$	$0.5\times\left(482-\frac{MP^B}{15}\right)$ $=241-\frac{MP^B}{30}$	$0.5\times\left(432-\frac{MP^B}{15}\right)$ $=216-\frac{MP^B}{30}$	$0.5\times\left(382-\frac{MP^B}{15}\right)$ $=191-\frac{MP^B}{30}$
CF_t^τ	$259+\frac{MP^B}{30}$	$234+\frac{MP^B}{30}$	$209+\frac{MP^B}{30}$	$184+\frac{MP^B}{30}$	$159+\frac{MP^B}{30}$
PV_0^τ	249.637 + 0.032129 $\times MP^B$	217.390 + 0.030967 $\times MP^B$	187.147 + 0.029848 $\times MP^B$	158.805 + 0.028769 $\times MP^B$	132.269+ 0.027729 $\times MP^B$

t	6	...	15	16	...	∞
CF_t	300	...	300	300	...	300
D_t^{SU}	0	...	0	0	...	0
D_t^{GW}	$\frac{MP^B-960}{15}$	...	$\frac{MP^B-960}{15}$	0	...	0
TB_t	$364-\frac{MP^B}{15}$	...	$364-\frac{MP^B}{15}$	300	...	300
T_t	182 – $\frac{1}{30}\times MP^B$	...	182 – $\frac{1}{30}\times MP^B$	150	...	150
CF_t^τ	118 + $\frac{1}{30}\times MP^B$	...	118 + $\frac{1}{30}\times MP^B$	150	...	150
PV_0^τ	94.614 + 0.026727 $\times MP^B$	...	67.930 + 0.019189 $\times MP^B$	2,302.71		

The marginal purchase price then gives

$$MP^B = 4{,}054{,}134.84 + 0.3771765 \times MP^B$$
$$= 6{,}509{,}284.$$

Knowing MP^B, we can complete the financial plan (amounts in k€) with the correct numbers ($D_t^{GW} = \frac{6{,}509{,}284-960}{15} = 369.95$).

t			n			$n+1$	...	n_{GW}	n_{GW}	...	∞
t	1	2	3	4	5	6	...	15	16	...	∞
CF_t	550.00	500.00	450.00	400.00	350.00	300.00	...	300.00	300.00	...	300.00
D_t^{SU}	32.00	32.00	32.00	32.00	32.00	0.00	...	0.00	0.00	...	0.00
D_t^{GW}	369.95	369.95	369.95	369.95	369.95	369.95	...	369.95	0.00	...	0.00
TB_t	148.05	98.05	48.05	−1.95	−51.95	−69.95	...	−69.95	300.00	...	300.00
T_t	74.03	49.03	24.03	−0.98	−25.98	−34.98	...	−34.98	150.00	...	150.00
CF_t^τ	475.97	450.97	425.97	400.98	375.98	334.98	...	334.98	150.00	...	150.00

Remember, the pre-tax marginal purchase price is 6,670,523. As we assumed preferred taxation of financial returns, financial investment turns out to be slightly better than the real investment alternative. Why is the post-tax marginal purchase price not lower than it actually is? The answer is quite simple. Remember the discussion of the income tax paradox in Sect. 3.4 starting on p. 97.[2] The post-tax net present value is lower than the pre-tax net present value if the present value of depreciation is lower than the present value of economic depreciation. The present value of step-up depreciation is

$$PV_0^{D^{SU}} = 32{,}000 \times \frac{1.0375^5 - 1}{0.0375 \times 1.0375^5} = 143{,}464$$

and the present value of goodwill depreciation ($\frac{MP^B - GCV}{n_{GW}} \times PVAR$) is

$$PV_0^{D^{GW}} = \frac{6{,}509{,}284 - 960{,}000}{15} \times \frac{1.0375^{15} - 1}{0.0375 \times 1.0375^{15}} = 4{,}186{,}120.$$

Hence, the present value of depreciation in total is

$$PV_0^D = 143{,}464 + 4{,}186{,}120 = 4{,}329{,}584.$$

[2] See also the end of Sect. 5.4 starting on p. 201.

Calculating the present value of economic depreciation, we know that economic depreciation of an infinite annuity is zero. Therefore, we just have to consider economic depreciation of $t = 1, \ldots, 6$ and get (numbers in k€)

t	0	1	2	3	4	5	6
CF_t		550.00	500.00	450.00	400.00	350.00	300.00
PV_t	6,670.52	6,454.05	6,276.75	6,140.59	6,047.62	6,000.00	6,000.00
ED_t		216.47	177.30	136.16	92.97	47.62	0.00
PV^{ED}	615.14						

Remember, to calculate ED_t, the pre-tax interest rate is used, whereas PV^{ED} is determined using the post-tax interest rate. As the present value of economic depreciation is 615,141 and depreciation of step-ups and goodwill amounts to 4,329,584, the post-tax marginal purchase price should exceed the pre-tax marginal purchase price. However, preferred taxation of financial investments overcompensates the advantage of depreciation and therefore, the after-tax marginal buyer's price is lower than the pre-tax marginal price.

8.4 Marginal Price of the Seller

The determination of the marginal price of the seller MP^S is not as time-consuming as in the case of the purchaser. Because there is no depreciation of goodwill or step-up depreciation, the result of the equation is part of the calculation of the final result. However, the problem still persists how to handle capital gains for tax purposes. In real world tax systems, profits that stem from business entity transactions are usually taxable. If capital gains are taxed at the same marginal tax rate as returns on real investments, tax arises to

$$\tau \times (MP^S - BV),$$

where BV stands for the initial acquisition costs or the book value of equity, respectively. The capital gain of the seller is the difference between the price he receives (MP^S) and the book value. To determine the marginal price of the seller, we have to set the post-tax marginal price of seller ($MP^S - T$) equal to the present value of the future cash flows of the business.

$$MP^S - \tau \times (MP^S - BV) = \sum_{t=1}^{n} \frac{CF_t \times (1-\tau)}{(q^\tau)^t} + \frac{CF_\infty \times (1-\tau)}{i^\tau \times (q^\tau)^n} \tag{8.17}$$

The right-hand side represents the value the seller will have if he decides to keep the business. Solving (8.17) for MP^S gives

$$MP^S = \frac{\sum_{t=1}^{n} \frac{CF_t \times (1-\tau)}{(q^\tau)^t} + \frac{CF_\infty \times (1-\tau)}{i^\tau \times (q^\tau)^n} - \tau \times BV}{1-\tau}. \tag{8.18}$$

Equation (8.18) implicitly assumes that the marginal seller's price exceeds the book value of equity. If the marginal seller's price is less than the book value of equity and immediate full loss offset is assumed, we get

$$MP^S + \tau \times (BV - MP^S) = \sum_{t=1}^{n} \frac{CF_t \times (1-\tau)}{(q^\tau)^t} + \frac{CF_\infty \times (1-\tau)}{i^\tau \times (q^\tau)^n}. \tag{8.19}$$

Notice, that the left-hand side changes compared to (8.17). Again, solving (8.19) for MP^S results in

$$MP^S = \frac{\sum_{t=1}^{n} \frac{CF_t \times (1-\tau)}{(q^\tau)^t} + \frac{CF_\infty \times (1-\tau)}{i^\tau \times (q^\tau)^n} - \tau \times BV}{1-\tau},$$

which is equal to (8.18). Immediate full loss offset implies a marginal investment decision, meaning that the seller has carried out other investments and is always able to offset the losses occurred with other positive income. Offsetting a loss leads to a tax refund of $\tau \times (BV - MP^S)$.

Example 8.8. Calculating the Marginal Price of the Seller

Based on Ex. 8.7, we assume a pre-tax cash flow stream in k€ of

t	1	2	3	4	5	6	...	∞
CF_t	550	500	450	400	350	300	...	300

First, we compute the seller's marginal price using our formula derived in (8.18). We get

$$\begin{aligned} MP^S &= \frac{\sum_{t=1}^{5} \frac{CF_t \times (1-0.5)}{1.0375^t} + \frac{300 \times (1-0.5)}{0.0375 \times 1.0375^5} - 0.5 \times 800{,}000}{1-0.5} \\ &= \frac{1{,}016{,}981 + 3{,}327{,}511 - 400{,}000}{1-0.5} \\ &= 7{,}888984. \end{aligned}$$

Deriving the present value of future cash flows with a financial plan (numbers in k€) leads to

t	1	2	3	4	5	6	...	∞
CF_t	550.00	500.00	450.00	400.00	350.00	300.00	300.00	300.00
T_t	275.00	250.00	225.00	200.00	175.00	150.00	150.00	150.00
CF_t^τ	275.00	250.00	225.00	200.00	175.00	150.00	150.00	150.00
PV^τ	265.06	232.25	201.47	172.61	145.58			3,327.51
PV_0^τ	4,344.49							

Now, determination of the marginal seller's price leads to

$$MP^S = \frac{4{,}344{,}492 - 0.5 \times 800{,}000}{1 - 0.5} = 7{,}888{,}984.$$

Because $MP^B = 6{,}509{,}284 < MP^S = 7{,}888{,}984$, no transaction occurs. The purchaser is not willing to pay more than €6,509,284, and the seller is not willing to sell for less than €7,888,984. So the purchaser does not accept to pay the minimum amount the seller demands in order to be indifferent between selling and keeping the business entity.

The results of Exs. 8.7 and 8.8 show us that – under the assumptions made – no transaction of the considered business entity occurs.

Under which assumptions would the transaction take place? Suppose, the going-concern-value of assets equals their book value ($BV = GCV$) and there is no step-up in the book value of assets. If the price for the business entity exceeds GCV, the difference represents the seller's taxable profit as well as depreciable goodwill for the purchaser. However, profit is taxed immediately, whereas the depreciation of goodwill is spread over its useful life, leading to a disadvantage in terms of present value. A transaction will only occur if the present value of profit taxation is equal or less than the present value of future tax savings from goodwill depreciation. If the marginal tax rate on capital gains from the transfer is τ^{CG} and the marginal price for the business entity is MP, the following condition must hold so that a transaction occurs

$$\tau^{CG} \times (MP - BV) \leq \tau \times \frac{MP - BV}{n_{GW}} \times \frac{(q^\tau)^{n_{GW}} - 1}{i^\tau \times (q^\tau)^{n_{GW}}}. \tag{8.20}$$

Reducing (8.20) and integrating the fact, that

$$n_{GW} > \frac{(q^\tau)^{n_{GW}} - 1}{i^\tau \times (q^\tau)^{n_{GW}}} \qquad i^\tau > 0,$$

gives

$$\tau^{CG} < \tau.$$

The marginal tax rate on capital gains has to be strictly lower than the marginal tax rate of other income in order to guarantee that a transaction occurs. This result holds true only under the assumptions mentioned earlier.

Example 8.9. Critical Capital Gains Tax

In order to determine the critical capital gains tax that ensures a transaction, we refer to Exs. 8.7 and 8.8. First, we have to set (8.18) equal to MP^B and then we solve for τ^{CG}

$$MP^B = \frac{\sum_{t=1}^{n} \frac{CF_t \times (1-\tau)}{(q^\tau)^t} + \frac{CF_\infty \times (1-\tau)}{i^\tau \times (q^\tau)^n} - \tau^{CG} \times BV}{1 - \tau^{CG}}$$

$$MP^B \times (1 - \tau^{CG}) + \tau^{CG} \times BV = \sum_{t=1}^{n} \frac{CF_t \times (1-\tau)}{(q^\tau)^t} + \frac{CF_\infty \times (1-\tau)}{i^\tau \times (q^\tau)^n}$$

$$MP^B - MP^B \times \tau^{CG} + \tau^{CG} \times BV = \sum_{t=1}^{n} \frac{CF_t \times (1-\tau)}{(q^\tau)^t} + \frac{CF_\infty \times (1-\tau)}{i^\tau \times (q^\tau)^n}$$

$$\tau^{CG} \times (BV - MP^B) = \sum_{t=1}^{n} \frac{CF_t \times (1-\tau)}{(q^\tau)^t} + \frac{CF_\infty \times (1-\tau)}{i^\tau \times (q^\tau)^n} - MP^B$$

$$\tau^{CG} = \frac{\sum_{t=1}^{n} \frac{CF_t \times (1-\tau)}{(q^\tau)^t} + \frac{CF_\infty \times (1-\tau)}{i^\tau \times (q^\tau)^n} - MP^B}{(BV - MP^B)}.$$

The maximum marginal tax rate on capital gains that ensures a transaction is

$$\tau^{CG} = \frac{1{,}016{,}981 + 3{,}327{,}511 - 6{,}509{,}284}{800{,}000 - 6{,}509{,}284} = 0.3792.$$

Hence, maximum τ^{CG} is 37.92%.

In many countries, capital gains from selling large stakes in businesses are taxed at a reduced tax rate. Sometimes, those reductions are only granted if the seller has reached a minimum age.

8.5 Extension

Let's go back to the purchaser. In his case, we assumed replacement investments to be equal to the depreciation of assets.[3] Therefore, there was no scheduled depreci-

[3] Notice, depreciation of replacement investments does not have anything to do with depreciation of step-ups or goodwill.

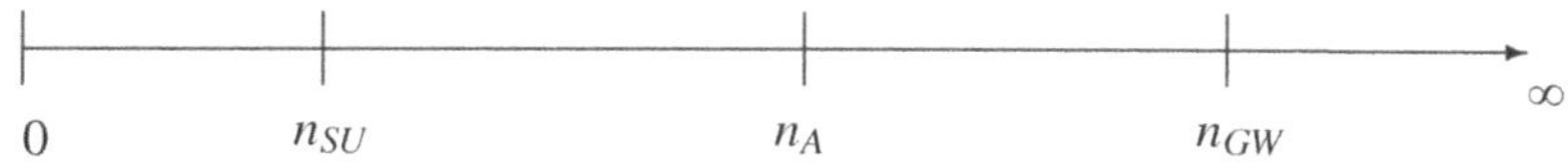

Fig. 8.4 Time line of depreciation

ation of assets $D_t = \frac{BV}{n}$. If that assumption is removed, we have to deal with three types of depreciation

1. Scheduled depreciation of assets,
2. Depreciation of step-ups,
3. Depreciation of goodwill.

The time line of depreciation is depicted in Fig. 8.4, where n_A stands for the useful life of the assets at the moment of transaction. However, useful life of some assets that are not stepped-up might be shorter than useful life of the assets that are stepped-up.

For convenience, in the following we assume that all assets are depreciated over the same period of time as step-ups are depreciated ($n_{SU} = n_A = n$). The marginal purchase price then accounts for

$$\begin{aligned} MP^B &= \sum_{t=1}^{\infty}(CF_t - T_t) \times (q^\tau)^{-t} \\ &= \underbrace{\sum_{t=1}^{n}\left[CF_t - \tau \times \left(CF_t - \frac{BV}{n} - \frac{GCV\text{–}BV}{n} - \frac{MP^B - GCV}{n_{GW}}\right)\right] \times (q^\tau)^{-t}}_{\text{first part}} \\ &\quad + \underbrace{\sum_{t=n+1}^{n_{GW}}\left[CF_t - \tau \times \left(CF_t - \frac{MP^B - GCV}{n_{GW}}\right)\right] \times (q^\tau)^{-t}}_{\text{second part}} \\ &\quad + \underbrace{\sum_{t=n_{GW}+1}^{\infty} CF_t \times (1-\tau) \times (q^\tau)^{-t}}_{\text{third part}}. \end{aligned} \tag{8.21}$$

The first part reflects the present value of post-tax cash flows from $t = 1, \ldots, n$, this is the period of depreciation of step-ups and assets. During that period, three different types of depreciation affect the tax base: (1) scheduled depreciation of assets, (2) depreciation of step-ups, and (3) depreciation of goodwill. The second part reflects the present value of post-tax cash flows that arise after full depreciation of assets and step-ups until the period of full depreciation of goodwill ($t = n + 1, \ldots, n_{GW}$).

The third part represents the post-tax present value of the infinite annuity of after-tax cash flows.

Because of the assumption of equal useful life of assets and step-ups, depreciation in the first part of (8.21) is simplified to

$$-\frac{BV}{n} - \frac{GCV - BV}{n} = \frac{-BV - GCV + BV}{n} = \frac{GCV}{n}.$$

Transformation of (8.21) leads to

$$\begin{aligned}
MP^B &= \sum_{t=1}^{n} \tau \times \frac{GCV}{n} \times (q^\tau)^{-t} + \sum_{t=1}^{n} \tau \times \frac{MP^B - GCV}{n_{GW}} \times (q^\tau)^{-t} \\
&\quad + \sum_{t=n+1}^{n_{GW}} \tau \times \frac{MP^B - GCV}{n_{GW}} \times (q^\tau)^{-t} + \sum_{t=1}^{n} CF_t \times (1-\tau) \times (q^\tau)^{-t} \\
&\quad + \sum_{t=n+1}^{n_{GW}} CF_t \times (1-\tau) \times (q^\tau)^{-t} + \sum_{t=n_{GW}+1}^{\infty} CF_t \times (1-\tau) \times (q^\tau)^{-t} \\
&= \sum_{t=1}^{n} \tau \times \frac{GCV}{n} \times (q^\tau)^{-t} + \sum_{t=1}^{n_{GW}} \tau \times \frac{MP^B - GCV}{n_{GW}} \times (q^\tau)^{-t} \\
&\quad + \sum_{t=1}^{n_{GW}} CF_t \times (1-\tau) \times (q^\tau)^{-t} + \frac{CF_\infty \times (1-\tau)}{i^\tau} \times (q^\tau)^{-n_{GW}} \\
&= \tau \times \frac{GCV}{n} \times \frac{(q^\tau)^n - 1}{i^\tau \times (q^\tau)^n} + \tau \times \frac{MP^B - GCV}{n_{GW}} \times \frac{(q^\tau)^{n_{GW}} - 1}{i^\tau \times (q^\tau)^{n_{GW}}} \qquad (8.22) \\
&\quad + \sum_{t=1}^{n_{GW}} CF_t \times (1-\tau) \times (q^\tau)^{-t} + \frac{CF_\infty \times (1-\tau)}{i^\tau} \times (q^\tau)^{-n_{GW}}.
\end{aligned}$$

Solving (8.22) for MP^B gives

$$\begin{aligned}
MP^B &- \tau \times \frac{MP^B}{n_{GW}} \times \frac{(q^\tau)^{n_{GW}} - 1}{i^\tau \times (q^\tau)^{n_{GW}}} \qquad (8.23) \\
&= \tau \times \frac{GCV}{n} \times \frac{(q^\tau)^n - 1}{i^\tau \times (q^\tau)^n} - \tau \times \frac{GCV}{n_{GW}} \times \frac{(q^\tau)^{n_{GW}} - 1}{i^\tau \times (q^\tau)^{n_{GW}}} \\
&\quad + \sum_{t=1}^{n_{GW}} CF_t \times (1-\tau) \times (q^\tau)^{-t} + \frac{CF_\infty \times (1-\tau)}{i^\tau} \times (q^\tau)^{-n_{GW}}.
\end{aligned}$$

The left-hand side of (8.23) is simplified to

$$MP^B \times \left(1 - \tau \times \frac{1}{n_{GW}} \times \frac{(q^\tau)^{n_{GW}} - 1}{i^\tau \times (q^\tau)^{n_{GW}}}\right) = \ldots . \tag{8.24}$$

Solving for MP^B, we finally get

$$\begin{aligned} MP^B = & \frac{1}{1 - \frac{\tau}{n_{GW}} \times \frac{(q^\tau)^{n_{GW}-1}}{i^\tau \times (q^\tau)^{n_{GW}}}} \times \left(\sum_{t=1}^{n_{GW}} (1-\tau) \times CF_t \times (q^\tau)^{-t}\right. \\ & + \frac{CF_\infty \times (1-\tau)}{i^\tau} \times (q^\tau)^{-n_{GW}} + \tau \times \frac{GCV}{n} \times \frac{(q^\tau)^n - 1}{i^\tau \times (q^\tau)^n} \\ & \left. - \tau \times \frac{GCV}{n_{GW}} \times \frac{(q^\tau)^{n_{GW}} - 1}{i^\tau \times (q^\tau)^{n_{GW}}}\right). \end{aligned} \tag{8.25}$$

If CF_t stays constant for all $t = 1, \ldots, \infty$, (8.25) is simplified to

$$MP^B = \frac{\tau \times \frac{GCV}{n} \times \frac{(q^\tau)^n - 1}{i^\tau \times (q^\tau)^n} - \tau \times \frac{GCV}{n_{GW}} \times \frac{(q^\tau)^{n_{GW}} - 1}{i^\tau \times (q^\tau)^{n_{GW}}} + \frac{CF_t \times (1-\tau)}{i^\tau}}{1 - \tau \times \frac{1}{n_{GW}} \times \frac{(q^\tau)^{n_{GW}-1}}{i^\tau \times (q^\tau)^{n_{GW}}}}.$$

In the case of the seller, the formula is adjusted to the depreciation of assets. Therefore, the marginal seller's price is

$$\begin{aligned} MP^S - \tau \times (MP^S - BV) = & \sum_{t=1}^{n} \left(CF_t \times (1-\tau) + \tau \times \frac{BV}{n}\right) \times (q^\tau)^{-t} \\ & + \frac{CF_\infty \times (1-\tau)}{i^\tau \times (q^\tau)^n}. \end{aligned}$$

Solving for MP^S yields

$$MP^S = \frac{\sum_{t=1}^{n} (CF_t \times (1-\tau) + \tau \times \frac{BV}{n}) \times (q^\tau)^{-t} + \frac{CF_\infty \times (1-\tau)}{i^\tau \times (q^\tau)^n} - \tau \times BV}{1-\tau}. \tag{8.26}$$

Example 8.10. Marginal Prices if Assets are Depreciated

Taking the assumptions of Ex. 8.7 and supposing a useful life of assets of $n = 5$, the marginal price of the purchaser according to (8.25) is

$$
\begin{aligned}
MP^B &= \frac{1}{1-\frac{0.5}{15}\times\frac{1.0375^{15}-1}{0.0375\times 1.0375^{15}}}\times\left(\sum_{t=1}^{15}(1-0.5)\times CF_t\times 1.0375^{-t}\right.\\
&\quad+\frac{300{,}000\times(1-0.5)}{0.0375\times 1.0375^{15}}+0.5\times\frac{960{,}000}{5}\times\frac{1.0375^{5}-1}{0.0375\times 1.0375^{5}}\\
&\quad\left.-0.5\times\frac{960{,}000}{15}\times\frac{1.0375^{15}-1}{0.0375\times 1.0375^{15}}\right)\\
&= 1.6055914\\
&\quad\times(1{,}016{,}981+1{,}024{,}805+2{,}302{,}706+430{,}393-362{,}089)\\
&= 7{,}085{,}147.
\end{aligned}
$$

Using (8.26), the marginal price of seller is

$$
\begin{aligned}
MP^S &= \frac{\sum_{t=1}^{5}(CF_t\times(1-0.5)+\tau\times\frac{800{,}000}{5})\times 1.0375^{-t}}{1-0.5}\\
&\quad+\frac{\frac{300{,}000\times(1-0.5)}{0.0375\times 1.0375^{5}}-0.5\times 800{,}000}{1-0.5}\\
&= \frac{1{,}375{,}642+3{,}327{,}511-400{,}000}{1-0.5}\\
&= 8{,}606{,}306.
\end{aligned}
$$

Again, no transaction occurs, because $MP^S > MP^B$.

Questions

8.1. Explain the substantial differences between asset and share deals.

8.2. Give at least five examples, why going-concern-values might exceed book values.

8.3. As you can see in actual balance sheets, goodwill plays an important role in financial and tax accounting. What might drive an investor to pay more than the going-concern-value for a business entity?

8.4. Why is there no transaction interval if the basic Standard Model for firm valuation is used? What has to be introduced to remove that lack? Give at least two examples.

8.5. Explain formally, why goodwill is a dependent variable and a variable that influences marginal prices at the same time in the case of computing the marginal prices of sole proprietorships or partnerships.

8.6. Derive the marginal price of a purchaser and a seller in the case of a sole proprietorship or partnership. Assume going-concern-value to be greater than the book value.

Exercises

Solutions are provided starting on p. 397.

8.7. Income Tax Paradox

Using a self-made numerical example, show that marginal prices rise if the tax rate rises. Explain the specific reasons for the appearance of the income tax paradox when computing marginal prices. Use the infinite annuity for justification.

8.8. Marginal Price of Seller and Purchaser

John is a lawyer and approaches his 70th birthday. At this time of his life, he still looks ahead. The rest of his life, he wants to do world trips and just enjoy life. Because of that, he wants to sell his office if somebody is willing to pay enough. As John has been a lawyer, he has been not familiar working with data. He asks you as his grandchild to calculate the marginal price for him for free. John's marginal tax rate of $\tau = 35\%$ stays constant over time. An alternative financial investment yields 8%. Real investments and financial investments are taxed equally. Replacement investments (computers and office furniture) equal the depreciation of assets; therefore, no scheduled depreciation is taken into account. The book value of net assets is €800,000. Going-concern-value (because of his classic car to impress his clients) is €3,000,000. Straight line depreciation of step-up is spread over 5 years. As you are a smart mathematician, you immediately realize that no goodwill occurs. As John signed contracts in the long run, future cash flows of his business can be determined with certainty (in k€) as:

t	1	2	3	4	5	6	7	8	9	10	11	...	∞
CF_t	50	60	70	80	90	100	110	120	130	140	150	...	150

(a) Determine John's marginal selling price.
(b) Your friend Eddie is interested in purchasing the office from John and because of your reputation, Eddie asks you as a friend to calculate his maximum bid for free. Calculate Eddie's marginal price, if Eddie's marginal tax rate is 35%, too. What does the step-up amount to? Is the transaction carried out?
(c) What happens c.p., if John's marginal tax rate is 25%?
(d) Does the transaction occur if c.p. John's marginal tax rate is 35% and a marginal tax rate of $\tau^{CG} = 20\%$ for capital gains is levied?

(e) Take the assumptions of (b). Calculate the maximum value of τ^{CG} for which the transaction still occurs.
(f) Again, consider the assumptions made in (b). Calculate the minimal amount of capital gain that has to be tax exempt that a transaction sill occurs.
(g) Step back to the assumptions made in (c). What's the maximum amount that you might charge your grandfather for calculating his marginal price without being guilty of distorting the transaction considered?

8.9. Marginal Price of Seller and Purchaser
George owns a small sole proprietorship. His operating business deals with processing metal. He owns only one numerically controlled machine (CNC-Machine). Because he is tired of working with metal, he wants to sell his business and asks you to determine the value of his company. He tells you that he makes €50,000 of revenues in cash every year and that he is sure that his business will generate that amount to infinity. His marginal tax rate is 25% and the interest is supposed to be 4%. The book value of his machine accounts for €300,000. An expertise shows that he could sell the machine at the book value. There are no further capital or current assets and no liabilities. For simplification, assume the replacement investments to be equal to the depreciation of assets. What is the marginal price of George and a potential purchaser facing the same marginal tax rate as George? Suppose, the marginal purchase price exceeds *GCV* and legal straight-line depreciation of goodwill is spread over 15 years.

8.10. Marginal Price of Seller and Purchaser
Sophie is a successful businesswoman in the energy sector. Her stake in the partnership "Electricity 4-ever" amounts to 30%. She wants to spend more time with her children and therefore is looking for somebody who is willing to purchase her stake in "Electricity 4-ever". The balance sheet shows a book value of net assets of €600,000. The going-concern-value is determined as €1,000,000. Sophie's marginal tax rate is 40% and stays constant over time and she can invest money at a pre-tax yield of 6%. Since the partnership signed only long-run contracts, future cash flows of the company are €100,000 for $t = 1, \ldots, \infty$. Real investments and financial investments are taxed equally. Replacement investments equal depreciation of assets. Depreciation of step-up is equally spread over 4 years (straight-line depreciation). Legal straight-line depreciation of goodwill for tax purposes is supposed to last 15 years.

(a) Calculate the minimum price for which Sophie is willing to sell her stake.
(b) Todd is interested in purchasing Sophie's stake. Determine Todd's marginal price if his marginal tax rate is 40% and

  (ba) MP^B is assumed to be less than *GCV*,
  (bb) MP^B is assumed to exceed *GCV*.

  What's the correct price? Is the transaction carried out?
(c) Determine Todd's marginal price if the legal depreciation of goodwill for tax purposes is supposed to be 6 years.

8.11. Marginal Price of Seller and Purchaser

Helmut studied engineering in the late fifties. After his studies, he started to produce copiers. He improved his product and now owns an appreciable product line being able to produce high-tech copier. He steadily expanded his business and today, he owns a remarkable factory complex with a production line capable of producing high-tech copiers. Now, at the end of his life, he needs to sell his sole proprietorship to an investor, because he does not have any children that could continue his business. The initial costs of his production line, being the only asset, were €500,000. The current book value of the production line amounts to €275,000. The production line was acquired 9 years ago and its useful life is estimated to be 20 years in total. There are no liabilities. If he sold his production line he would get €400,000. Helmut's marginal tax rate is 30% and an alternative financial investment yields 6%. Due to his contracts being set up for a long time horizon, he can predict future cash flows to be €75,000 for $t = 1, \ldots, \infty$ with certainty.

(a) Calculate the amount that an investor has to pay Helmut for his business entity in order to make him indifferent between selling and keeping the business.
(b) Suppose, Helmut finds an appropriate investor in Chris, who is a young and talented engineer. If Chris' marginal tax rate is 30%, the step-up depreciation is spread over 5 years to equal amounts and legal depreciation of goodwill is supposed to take place over 15 years, what amount is Chris willing to pay Helmut at maximum?

8.12. Marginal Price of Seller and Purchaser

After her studies of business management in Austria and Italy, back in the US, Hillary was tired of drinking bad tasting filtered American coffee. She therefore opened a couple of coffee shops, organized as a sole proprietorship, where fine Italian coffee is sold. As Hillary thinks that she has already worked enough for the rest of her life, she is looking for an investor for her small empire. One day, coffee specialist Harald shows up and thinks about buying the company. The book value of the business is supposed to be €150,000. If Hillary sold her capital and current assets to different parties, she would receive €200,000. Replacement investments equal depreciation of assets. Assets are straight-line depreciated over 5 years. Both, Harald and Hillary estimate the certain future cash flow stream to be €50,000 for $t = 1, \ldots, \infty$. Suppose, that $MP^B > BV$. What amount is Harald willing to pay at maximum, if his marginal tax rate is 50%, capital income is taxed at 25% and $i = 8\%$? Assume immediate full loss offset.

References

1. Wagner, F. W., Rümmele, P.: Ertragsteuern in der Unternehmensbewertung: Zum Einfluss von Steuerrechtsänderungen. Die Wirtschaftsprüfung 433–441 (1995)

Chapter 9
Taxation and Financing Decisions

Abstract The preceding chapters neglect the fact that investors might have to acquire external funds to carry out their desired investment alternatives. This chapter deals with the problem of financing investments with equity or debt. We show that taxation can distort financing decisions. Moreover, we analyze alternative sources of debt financing after taxes. After studying this chapter, you will be able to evaluate financing options according to their profitability.

9.1 Introduction

Once in your life, you are thinking about buying real property. Suppose, you have finished your studies in business administration and you get paid well by your employer. As your paycheck exceeds your living expenses each month, you are able to save enough money for an investment in real property. You decide to buy an apartment in Munich. The real investment returns constant rents of € 15,000 annually. However, as living in Munich is very expensive, real property is quite expensive, too. A real estate agent offers you an apartment for I_0 = € 315,000. In $t = 0$ you know, that in $t = n = 20$, you will sell the property for SP_{20} = € 315,000 to be able to build your own house to live in. Assuming an interest rate of $i = 4.5\%$, the pre-tax net present value amounts to

$$NPV = -I_0 + CF \times \frac{(1+i)^n - 1}{i \times (1+i)^n} + SP_n \times (1+i)^{-n}$$

$$= -315{,}000 + 15{,}000 \times \frac{1.045^{20} - 1}{0.045 \times 1.045^{20}} + 315{,}000 \times 1.045^{-20}$$

$$= 10{,}731.55.$$

Suppose, you face a marginal tax rate of $\tau = 40\%$ and the legal useful life of the property is $n_A = 50$ years. Moreover, capital gains from the disposal of the property

D. Schanz and S. Schanz, *Business Taxation and Financial Decisions*,
DOI 10.1007/978-3-642-03284-4_9, © Springer-Verlag Berlin Heidelberg 2011

in $n = 20$ are subject to tax. If $i^\tau = 0.045 \times (1 - 0.4) = 0.027$ and $q^\tau = 1 + i^\tau$, the post-tax net present value yields

$$NPV^\tau = -I_0 + \left[CF - \tau \times \left(CF - \frac{I_0}{n_A}\right)\right] \times \frac{(q^\tau)^n - 1}{i^\tau \times (q^\tau)^n}$$

$$+ \left[SP_n - \tau \times \left(SP_n - \left[I_0 - n \times \frac{I_0}{n_A}\right]\right)\right] \times (q^\tau)^{-n}$$

$$= -315{,}000 + \left[15{,}000 - 0.4 \times \left(15{,}000 - \frac{315{,}000}{50}\right)\right] \times \frac{(q^\tau)^{20} - 1}{i^\tau \times (q^\tau)^{20}}$$

$$+ \left[315{,}000 - 0.4 \times \left(315{,}000 - \left[315{,}000 - 20 \times \frac{315{,}000}{50}\right]\right)\right] \times (q^\tau)^{-20}$$

$$= 16{,}654.82.$$

Depreciation is defined as $D_t = \frac{I_0}{n_A}$, the tax base is determined as $TB_t = CF_t - \tau \times (CF_t - D_t)$, and the taxable capital gain CG_n is $CG_n = I_0 - (I_0 - \sum_{t=1}^{n} D_t)$, where $(I_0 - \sum_{t=1}^{n} D_t = I_0 - n \times D_t)$ represents the book value in n. So far, carrying out the offered real investment options after consideration of taxation is profitable.

Now, assume that you cannot raise funds by your own to acquire the real property offered. Suppose, you only have equity to the amount of € 125,000 and need to ask for a bank loan of € 315,000 – € 125,000 = € 190,000. Suppose, you get a bullet loan. In that case, you have to pay a constant amount of interest up to $n = 20$. The loan is amortized at $n = 20$. Assume the borrowing rate to be $\rho = 7\%$. The pre-tax net present value of your loan is calculated as:

$$NPV^L = 190{,}000 - 0.07 \times 190{,}000 \times \frac{1.045^{20} - 1}{0.045 \times 1.045^{20}}$$

$$-190{,}000 \times 1.045^{-20}$$

$$= -61{,}787.70.$$

At first, there is a cash inflow when you receive the loan. In the following periods, you have cash outflows because of your interest payments. In $n = 20$, you have to pay back the amount of the loan in total.

If you determine the post-tax net present value of the loan, you have to take into account that interest payments on debt are deductible for tax purposes. Borrowing money and repayment of the loan are not tax deductible. The post-tax net present value is ($i^\tau = 0.027$, $q^\tau = 1.027$)

$$
\begin{aligned}
NPV^{\tau,L} &= 190{,}000 - 0.07 \times (1 - 0.4) \times 190{,}000 \times \frac{1.027^{20} - 1}{0.027 \times 1.027^{20}} \\
&\quad -190{,}000 \times 1.027^{-20} \\
&= -43{,}601.15.
\end{aligned}
$$

If the post-tax net present value of the equity financed real property and the post-tax net present value of debt are combined, we get the net present value of our partly debt financed investment alternative

$$NPV^{\tau} = 16{,}543.82 - 43{,}601.15 = -27{,}057.33.$$

As the net present value is negative, you are advised not to realize your dream of owning real property.

This simple example shows how financing can affect investment decisions, if taxation is taken into account. Once more, we experienced that taxes distort investment decisions. Therefore, financing questions cannot be neglected when determining the profitability of investment options. The following sections derive how and why financing alternatives affect investment decisions if investors face cash restrictions.

9.2 Integrating Debt Financing in Decision Criteria

Financing costs have to be explicitly considered in investment decision modeling. However, consideration of financing costs in the discount factor seems to be impossible. Hence, investment and financing has to be considered separately. We implicitly assumed that approach in our initial example in Sect. 9.1. Therefore, the net present value of the total investment consists of the sum of the net present value of the investment alternative financed by equity plus the net present value of the financing vehicle.

	Net present value of investment alternative financed by equity (unlevered investment)
+	Net present value of financing vehicle
=	Net present value of total investment

If ρ represents the interest rate for debt, A_t the annual amortization of debt, and L_t the book value of debt or liabilities, respectively, the pre-tax net present value of debt (loan) is defined as:

$$NPV^{L} = L_0 - \sum_{t=1}^{n} (\rho \times L_{t-1} + A_t) \times q^{-t}.$$

Let's have a look at ρ. We know that lending and borrowing do not necessarily result in the same interest rates. Usually, the following condition is satisfied

$$i < \rho.$$

This means that the lending rate is always lower than the borrowing rate. Under that condition, it is true that

$$NPV^L < 0.$$

The pre-tax net present value of debt is zero if $i = \rho$.

To calculate the post-tax net present value, we have to determine the parts of the loan that are tax deductible. In all known current tax systems, L_0 is not taxed. Correspondingly, an amortization is not deductible. Hence, only interest payments on debt are considered as deductible. Those tax rules lead to a post-tax net present value of debt of

$$NPV^{\tau,L} = L_0 - \sum_{t=1}^{n} (\rho \times (1-\tau) \times L_{t-1} + A_t) \times (q^\tau)^{-t}. \tag{9.1}$$

You see that the interest payments are calculated based on the borrowing rate ρ, while the net present value is determined by discounting all numbers at a rate of $i^\tau = q^\tau - 1$, because this rate represents the opportunity costs of the investor.

Combining the post-tax net present value of the full equity financed investment alternative and the net present value of debt gives

$$\begin{aligned} NPV^\tau = & \underbrace{-I_0 + \sum_{t=1}^{n} [CF_t - \tau \times (CF_t - D_t)] \times (q^\tau)^{-t}}_{NPV \text{ of equity financed investment}} \\ & \underbrace{+ L_0 - \sum_{t=1}^{n} [\rho \times L_{t-1} \times (1-\tau) + A_t] \times (q^\tau)^{-t}}_{NPV \text{ of financing vehicle}}. \end{aligned}$$

Example 9.1. Debt Financing in Case of a Bullet Loan

An investor needs to purchase a new machine to meet the expectations of his contractual partner. Initial costs for the machine are $I_0 = 60{,}000$. Future cash flow returns during the useful life of four periods (straight-line depreciation) are considered as certain because of the signed contract. They are

t	0	1	2	3	4
CF_t	-60,000	15,300	16,500	18,500	21,500

If the capital market interest rate is assumed to be $i = 7\%$, the pre-tax net present value will be $NPV = 214.56$ and the post-tax net present value will be $NPV^{\tau} = 347.48$, if a marginal tax rate of $\tau = 30\%$ is applied.

1. First, let's have a look at the NPV^{τ} calculation by treating the equity financed investment and the debt financing separately. Cash flows of the equity financed investment are derived in the following table

t	0	1	2	3	4
CF_t	–60,000	15,300	16,500	18,500	21,500
D_t		15,000	15,000	15,000	15,000
TB_t		300	1,500	3,500	6,500
T_t		90	450	1,050	1,950
CF_t^{τ}		15,210	16,050	17,450	19,550

The after-tax net present value is

$$NPV^{\tau} = -60{,}000 + \frac{15{,}210}{1.049} + \frac{16{,}050}{1.049^2} + \frac{17{,}450}{1.049^3} + \frac{19{,}550}{1.049^4} = 347.48.$$

Now, suppose the investor faces a cash restriction that forces him to take a bullet loan of 45,000 at $\rho = 9\%$ until $n = 4$. As a bullet loan leads to constant interest payments on debt over time and the amortization occurs in period n, the pre-tax net present value yields

$$\begin{aligned} NPV^L &= 45{,}000 - 0.09 \times 45{,}000 \times \frac{1.07^4 - 1}{0.07 \times 1.07^4} \\ &\quad -45{,}000 \times 1.07^{-4} \\ &= -3{,}048.49. \end{aligned}$$

The post-tax net present value is

$$\begin{aligned} NPV^{\tau,L} &= 45{,}000 - 0.09 \times (1 - 0.3) \times 45{,}000 \times \frac{1.049^4 - 1}{0.049 \times 1.049^4} \\ &\quad -45{,}000 \times 1.049^{-4} \\ &= -2{,}239.15. \end{aligned}$$

The post-tax net present value of the investment is

$$NPV^{\tau} = 347.48 - 2{,}239.15 = -1{,}891.67.$$

2. Second, the determination of the total post-tax net present value in one financial plan is illustrated in the following table. It is important to mention, that an immediate full loss offset is assumed.

t	0	1	2	3	4
CF_t	–60,000	15,300	16,500	18,500	21,500
D_t		15,000	15,000	15,000	15,000
CF^L	45,000				
BV_t^L	45,000	45,000	45,000	45,000	0
IP_t^L		–4,050	–4,050	–4,050	–4,050
A_t					–45,000
TB_t		–3,750	–2,550	–550	2,450
T_t		–1,125	–765	–165	735
CF_t^τ	–15,000	12,375	13,215	14,615	–28,285
NPV^τ	–1,892				

IP_t^L denotes interest payments triggered by the loan.

3. If we calculate the total post-tax net present value using a financial plan where the financial investment is considered separately, we get

t	0	1	2	3	4
CF_t	–60,000	15,300	16,500	18,500	21,500
D_t		15,000	15,000	15,000	15,000
CF^L	45,000				
BV_t^L	45,000	45,000	45,000	45,000	0
IP_t^L		–4,050	–4,050	–4,050	–4,050
A_t					–45,000
FI_t		12,375	26,196	42,095	15,873
IP_t		0	866	1,834	2,947
TB_t		–3,750	–1,684	1,284	5,397
T_t		–1,125	–505	385	1,619
CF_t^τ	–15,000	12,375	13,821	15,899	–26,222
NPV^τ	–1,892				

In some countries, for example in Austria and in Germany, capital income is taxed at a lower rate than other income. The marginal tax rate on capital income in these countries is 25%. However, there is no corresponding cut of the deductibility of interest payments on debt. In fact, arbitrage possibilities might occur because of that. Let $i = 4\%$ and $\rho = 5\%$ (notice that we have a real world condition that satisfies $i < \rho$). Moreover, the marginal tax rate applied on capital income is supposed to be 25%, whereas interest payments on debt are deductible at a marginal tax rate of 45%. Hence, we face post-tax interest rates of

$$i^{\tau} = 0.04 \times (1 - 0.25) = 3\%$$
$$\rho^{\tau} = 0.05 \times (1 - 0.45) = 2.75\%.$$

Suddenly, we face a post-tax condition that satisfies $i^{\tau} > \rho^{\tau}$. It is easy to see, that we are in the lucky situation of a "free lunch". Suppose, you are endowed with funds of equity of € 1. The initial costs for your real investment alternative are € 1 and the time horizon is supposed to be 1 year. Now, the best thing you can do is to go to your bank and borrow € 1 in order to finance your real investment alternative. Your funds of equity are invested at a pre-tax rate of 4% at the capital market. One year later, you have to pay back € 1 to your bank and pay interest of € 0.05 on that debt. However, debt is deductible for tax purposes and, hence, results in a reduction of your tax liability of $0.45 \times 0.05 =$ € 0.0225. In total, your net cash outflow in $t = 1$ is $1 + 0.05 - 0.0225 =$ € 1.0275.

On the other hand, your financial investment yields 4% and you have to pay taxes of $0.04 \times 0.25 =$ € 0.01. Your net cash inflow in $t = 1$ from your financial investment is $0.04 - 0.01 =$ € 0.03. Now, if you take the 0.03 net return and pay your net interest on debt, you are left with $0.03 - 0.0275 =$ € 0.0025, which is called a "free lunch".

t	0	1
Financial investment:		
CF_t	–1.0000	1.0000
IP_t		0.0400
T_t		0.0100
CF_t^{τ}	–1.0000	1.0300
Loan:		
CF_t^L	1.0000	
IP_t^L		–0.0500
A_t		–1.0000
T_t		0.0225
$CF_t^{\tau,L}$	1.0000	–1.0275
Total CF_t^{τ}	0.0000	0.0025
NPV^{τ}	0.0024	

To be in a situation of a "free lunch", the following condition must hold

$$\rho \times (1 - \tau) < i \times (1 - \tau^{flat}) \Leftrightarrow \rho < i \times \frac{(1 - \tau^{flat})}{(1 - \tau)},$$

where τ^{flat} represents the marginal tax rate on capital income. If that condition is satisfied, it is profitable to replace equity by debt.

9.3 Types of Loans

This section deals with different types of loans or loan equivalents. In detail, we focus on

1. Bullet loans
2. Loans with amortization by installments
3. Annuity loans
4. Loans with disagios
5. Leasing contracts

The basic types of loans (1–3) will be discussed in this section; disagios and leasing contracts will be covered in Sects. 9.4 and 9.5.

9.3.1 Bullet Loan

Bullet loans are characterized by constant (annual) interest payments. The loan is amortized at the end of the contract period. Since interest payments IP_t are constant over time, interest payments and amortization can be described as

$$IP_t = IP = \rho \times L_0 \quad \forall \quad t = 1, ..., n$$

$$A_t = \begin{Bmatrix} 0 & \text{for } t = 1, ..., n-1 \\ L_0 & \text{for } t = n \end{Bmatrix}.$$

The post-tax net present value of a bullet loan consists of

$$\begin{array}{ll|l} NPV^{\tau,L} = & L_0 & \text{raising the loan} \\ & -\sum_{t=1}^{n} [\rho \times (1-\tau) \times L_0] \times (q^\tau)^{-t} & NPV^\tau \text{ of interest payments} \\ & -L_0 \times (q^\tau)^{-n} & NPV^\tau \text{ of amortization.} \end{array} \tag{9.2}$$

Because of constant interest payments, (9.2) simplifies to

$$\begin{aligned} NPV^{\tau,L} &= L_0 - \rho \times (1-\tau) \times L_0 \times \frac{(q^\tau)^n - 1}{i^\tau \times (q^\tau)^n} - L_0 \times (q^\tau)^{-n} \\ &= L_0 \times \left[1 - (q^\tau)^{-n} - \rho \times (1-\tau) \times \frac{(q^\tau)^n - 1}{i^\tau \times (q^\tau)^n}\right]. \end{aligned}$$

9.3.2 Amortization by Installments

Loans amortized by installments are characterized by periodic constant amortization. Periodic amortization reduces the outstanding debt constantly. The annual amortization (A_t) is

$$A_t = A = \frac{L_0}{n}.$$

Interest payments are calculated on the remaining debt of the previous period ($t-1$). The interest on debt in t for $t > 0$ is determined as:

$$IP_t = \rho \times L_{t-1},$$

where $L_{t-1} = (L_0 - (t-1) \times A)$. The post-tax net present value of a loan amortized by installments is

$$NPV^{\tau,L} = L_0 - \sum_{t=1}^{n} \left(\rho \times (1-\tau) \times L_{t-1} + \frac{L_0}{n} \right) \times (q^{\tau})^{-t}.$$

9.3.3 Annuity Loans

Annuity loans are characterized by constant annual annuity payments, where the annuity contains both interest and amortization. Within the first periods, the percentage of interest contained in the annuity is higher than at the end of the time horizon. Over time, the composition of the annuity changes in favor of the amortization. If *ANN* denotes constant periodic payments, the annuity is calculated as:

$$ANN = \frac{L_0}{PVAR(n,\rho)} = L_0 \times \frac{\rho \times (1+\rho)^n}{(1+\rho)^n - 1},$$

where $PVAR(n, \rho)$ represents the present value factor of an annuity in arrears dependent on the maturity of the loan and the interest payments on debt. Notice, that the present value factor is not calculated by using the interest rate i. The decreasing interest payments are described by

$$IP_t = \rho \times L_{t-1}.$$

The increasing amortization is described by

$$A_t = ANN - IP_t = ANN - \rho \times L_{t-1} = A_1 \times (1+\rho)^{t-1}.$$

As a result, the remaining debt in t is determined by

$$L_t = L_{t-1} - A_t = L_0 - A_1 \times \frac{(1+\rho)^t - 1}{\rho}.$$

Now, the net present value of an annuity loan is

$$NPV^{\tau,L} = L_0 - \sum_{t=1}^{n} [\rho \times L_{t-1} \times (1-\tau) + A_t] \times (q^{\tau})^{-t},$$

which is equivalent to (9.1).

Example 9.2. Post-Tax Net Present Values of Different Types of Loans

Suppose, you raise a bullet loan to finance a real property that will be rented to a third party. We assume full deductibility of interest payments on debt. Further assumptions are

$$\begin{aligned} i &= 5\% & \rho &= 6\% \\ \tau^{flat} &= 25\% & \tau &= 50\% \\ i^{\tau} &= 3.75\% & \rho^{\tau} &= 3\% \\ L_0 &= 150{,}000 & n &= 5. \end{aligned}$$

1. Bullet loan

   The pre-tax financial plan for a bullet loan then is

t	0	1	2	3	4	5
CF_t	150,000	–9,000	–9,000	–9,000	–9,000	–159,000
NPV	–6,495					

The pre-tax net present value is $NPV = -6{,}495 < 0$. A negative result was expected, since $\rho > i$. The post-tax financial plan of the bullet loan is derived as:

t	0	1	2	3	4	5
IP_t		–9,000	–9,000	–9,000	–9,000	–9,000
L_0, A_n	150,000					–150,000
TB_t		–9,000	–9,000	–9,000	–9,000	–9,000
T_t		–4,500	–4,500	–4,500	–4,500	–4,500
CF_t^{τ}	150,000	–4,500	–4,500	–4,500	–4,500	–154,500

The post-tax net present value is

$$\begin{aligned} NPV^{\tau,L} &= 150{,}000 - (150{,}000 \times 0.06 \times (1-0.5)) \times \frac{1.0375^5 - 1}{0.0375 \times 1.0375^5} \\ &\quad -150{,}000 \times 1.0375^{-5} \\ &= 5{,}043.67. \end{aligned}$$

2. Loan amortized by installments

Now, consider a loan amortized by installments. The pre-tax financial plan is

t	0	1	2	3	4	5
L_t	150,000	120,000	90,000	60,000	30,000	0
A_t		−30,000	−30,000	−30,000	−30,000	−30,000
IP_t		−9,000	−7,200	−5,400	−3,600	−1,800
CF_t	150,000	−39,000	−37,200	−35,400	−33,600	−31,800
NPV	−4,023					

The pre-tax net present value based on the current assumptions evolves to $NPV = -4.023 < 0$. Again, the result could be expected, because of $\rho > i$. However, the pre-tax net present value of a loan amortized by installments exceeds the pre-tax net present value of the bullet loan. Taking taxes into account, the post-tax financial plan of the loan amortized by installments is

t	0	1	2	3	4	5
L_t	150,000	120,000	90,000	60,000	30,000	0
A_t		−30,000	−30,000	−30,000	−30,000	−30,000
IP_t		−9,000	−7,200	−5,400	−3,600	−1,800
TB_t		−9,000	−7,200	−5,400	−3,600	−1,800
T_t		−4,500	−3,600	−2,700	−1,800	−900
CF_t^{τ}	150,000	−34,500	−33,600	−32,700	−31,800	−30,900

Calculating the post-tax net present value, we get

$$NPV^{\tau,L} = 150{,}000 - \frac{34{,}500}{1.0375} - \frac{33{,}600}{1.0375^2} - \frac{32{,}700}{1.0375^3} - \frac{31{,}800}{1.0375^4} - \frac{30{,}900}{1.0375^5}$$
$$= 3{,}100,$$

which is less than in the case of the bullet loan.

3. Annuity loan

In the case of an annuity loan, we first have to calculate the annuity. Taking the assumptions into account, we get

$$ANN = 150{,}000 \times \frac{0.06 \times 1.06^5}{1.06^5 - 1} = 35{,}609.46.$$

Hence, the pre-tax financial plan can be derived as:

t	0	1	2	3	4	5
L_t	150,000	123,391	95,185	65,286	33,594	0
ANN_t		–35,609	–35,609	–35,609	–35,609	–35,609
A_t		–26,609	–28,206	–29,898	–31,692	–33,594
IP_t		–9,000	–7,403	–5,711	–3,917	–2,016
CF_t	150,000	–35,609	–35,609	–35,609	–35,609	–35,609
NPV	–4,170					

The pre-tax net present value of $-4,170$ is still negative. Taking taxes into account, we get a post-tax financial plan for deriving the post-tax net cash flows as follows

t	0	1	2	3	4	5
L_t	150,000	123,391	95,185	65,286	33,594	0
ANN_t		–35,609	–35,609	–35,609	–35,609	–35,609
A_t		–26,609	–28,206	–29,898	–31,692	–33,594
IP_t		–9,000	–7,403	–5,711	–3,917	–2,016
TB_t		–9,000	–7,403	–5,711	–3,917	–2,016
T_t		–4,500	–3,702	–2,856	–1,959	–1,008
CF_t^τ	150,000	–31,109	–31,908	–32,754	–33,651	–34,602

Calculating the post-tax present value in case of the annuity loan leads to

$$NPV^{\tau,L} = 150{,}000 - \frac{31{,}109}{1.0375} - \frac{31{,}908}{1.0375^2} - \frac{32{,}754}{1.0375^3} - \frac{33{,}651}{1.0375^4} - \frac{34{,}602}{1.0375^5}$$
$$= 3{,}216.$$

The pre-tax and post-tax present values of the three different types of loans considered are provided in the following table

	NPV^L	$NPV^{\tau,L}$
bullet loan	–6,495	5,044
amortization by installments	–4,023	3,100
annuity loan	–4,170	3,216

The summary leads to the following pre-tax rank order

bullet loan < annuity loan < amortization by installment

However, the post-tax rank order advises to choose

bullet loan > annuity loan > amortization by installment

which is right away the reverse order compared to the pre-tax rank order. What causes the reversal? If $\rho > i$, the fastest possible amortization is optimal. This leads to the result that in a pre-tax view, annuity loans are preferred over bullet loans, because the amortization of bullet loans does not occur until $t = n$. The present value of interest payments on debt is less negative in the case of annuity loans than in the case of bullet loans. Exactly the same result causes bullet loans to be less profitable than annuity loans in the post-tax setting.

Let's have a look at the internal rates of return. Clearly, in the pre-tax setting, the internal rate of return has to be ρ. The post-tax internal rates of return are $\rho^\tau = 3\%$ in each case as depicted in the following table

	i^*	$i^{*,\tau}$
bullet loan	6%	3%
amortization by installments	6%	3%
annuity loan	6%	3%

Obviously, the internal rate of return stays constant over all alternatives within the pre- and post-tax setting, respectively. The criterion of the internal rate of return states indifference between all three alternatives, which is – considering the results of the net present value criterion – not true.

Summary: If $\rho > i$, early amortization is favorable before taxes. In that case, the amortization by installments is the best alternative, and an annuity loan is favorable compared to a bullet loan. The result of the after-tax case is the opposite. Tax rate effects based on tax shields cause bullet loans to be more profitable compared to annuity loans and especially compared to loans with amortization by installments. For tax purposes, late amortization of debt is favorable. Interest rate effects or tax rate effects may prevail.

9.4 Disagios

Usually, loans are not paid out at their nominal value, because financial institutions charge a percentage of the nominal value of the loan as a fee (disagio). That disagio has to be taken into account when calculating the total amount needed for financing investments. If disagios are charged as a percentage of the nominal value, the cash received is

$$CF = (1 - d) \times L,$$

where d represents the disagio factor. Suppose, you need to finance your initial investment I_0 with debt in total. Taking the disagio into account, you need to raise funds of debt of

$$L = \frac{I_0}{(1-d)}.$$

For accounting purposes, disagios have to be capitalized as an accrued item (prepaid expenses) and have to be depreciated during maturity or treated as expenses immediately. The treatment depends on local GAAP or tax accounting. If the disagio is capitalized, the question of the appropriate method of depreciation will arise. Of course, it depends on the characteristics of the underlying loan which method of depreciation should be used. If we face a bullet loan, one might argue that full depreciation should occur at the time of maturity. However, straight-line depreciation could be justified, too, because interest payments are charged on an annual basis. In case of amortization by installments, it is getting more difficult to determine a "correct" annual depreciation. In the following, we discuss three types of depreciation:

1. The straight-line depreciation
2. The declining balance depreciation according to the exact method based on the effective interest rate (= internal rate of return)
3. The declining balance depreciation according to the sum of digits-method as an approximation to the exact method

If the declining balance depreciation is used, there will be basically two possibilities to allocate the disagio to different years of the loan. First, the exact method, that is determination of the effective interest rate and second, a simpler approximation of the exact method which is called the sum of digits-method. Calculating the declining balance methods is more complicated than the straight-line method, because we do not know the effective interest rate of the loan. We know the rate ρ, which is defined explicitly in the loan contract, but the effective interest rate ρ^* exceeds ρ, because the disagio builds an additional interest component.

9.4.1 Straight-Line Depreciation of the Disagio

If the straight-line method is used, annual constant depreciation D would be a proportional fraction of the disagio

$$D_t = D = \frac{d \times L}{n}.$$

Example 9.3. Straight-Line Method

Suppose, we need funds of € 84,600 for financing the acquisition costs of our favorable real investment with a useful life of 3 years. The financial institution we negotiated with, offered us a borrowing rate of $\rho = 5\%$ and a disagio rate of $d = 6\%$. Further, the amortization of the loan has to occur by constant installments. We accepted. The capital market rate is $i = 4\%$. Hence, the nominal value of our liability is

$$L = \frac{I_0}{1-d} = \frac{84{,}600}{0.94} = 90{,}000.$$

The absolute disagio amount $L \times d$ is $90{,}000 \times 0.06 = 5{,}400$. The marginal tax rate for real investments is assumed to be $\tau = 50\%$ and capital income is taxed at a flat rate of $\tau^{flat} = 25\%$. If the straight-line method is used for depreciation, the annual depreciation will be

$$D_t^{disagio} = \frac{5{,}400}{3} = 1{,}800.$$

The net present value of the loan including the disagio can be derived from the following table.

t	0	1	2	3
CF_0^L	84,600			
BV_t^L	90,000	60,000	30,000	0
A_t		–30,000	–30,000	–30,000
IP_t^L		–4,500	–3,000	–1,500
$BV_t^{disagio}$	5,400	3,600	1,800	0
$D_t^{disagio}$		1,800	1,800	1,800
TB_t		–6,300	–4,800	–3,300
T_t		–3,150	–2,400	–1,650
$CF_t^{\tau,L}$	84,600	–31,350	–30,600	–29,850
$NPV^{\tau,L}$	–1,997.31			

$$NPV^{\tau} = 84{,}600 - \frac{31{,}350}{1.03} - \frac{30{,}600}{1.03^2} - \frac{29{,}850}{1.03^3} = -1{,}997.31. \quad (9.3)$$

Disagios will become more transparent if we look at double-entry bookkeeping again. Accounting records concerning the disagio are

(a) At the beginning of $t = 1$:

Dr	interest expense	5,400			
			Cr	liabilities	5,400

(b) At the end of the first year, 3,600 of the interest expenses have to be carried to the following years:

Dr prepaid expense	3,600		
		Cr interest expense	3,600

(c) In $t = 2{,}3$:

Dr interest expense	1,800		
		Cr prepaid expense	1,800

The net present value of the loan without disagio is

t	0	1	2	3
CF_0	84,600			
BV_t	84,600	56,400	28,200	0
A_t		–28,200	–28,200	–28,200
IP_t		–4,230	–2,820	–1,410
TB_t		–4,230	–2,820	–1,410
T_t		–2,115	–1,410	–705
CF_t^τ	84,600	–30,315	–29,610	–28,905
$NPV^{\tau,loan}$	805.53			

$$NPV^{\tau,loan} = 84{,}600 - \frac{30{,}315}{1.03} - \frac{29{,}610}{1.03^2} - \frac{28{,}905}{1.03^3} = 805.53. \quad (9.4)$$

The net present value is positive, which was expected, because $i^{\tau,flat} > \rho^\tau$. Correspondingly, the net present value after taxes of the disagio is

t	0	1	2	3
CF_0	0			
BV_t	5,400	3,600	1,800	0
A_t		–1,800	–1,800	–1,800
IP_t		–270	–180	–90
$BV_t^{disagio}$	5,400	3,600	1,800	0
$D_t^{disagio}$		1,800	1,800	1,800
TB_t		–2,070	–1,980	–1,890
T_t		–1,035	–990	–945
CF_t^τ	0	–1,035	–990	–945
$NPV^{\tau,disagio}$	–2,802.83			

The after-tax cash flow CF_t^τ consists of the tax refund, the amortization and the interest payments for the part of the loan related to the disagio $CF_t^\tau = A_t + IP_t - T_t$.

$$NPV^{\tau,disagio} = -\frac{1{,}035}{1.03} - \frac{990}{1.03^2} - \frac{945}{1.03^3} = -2{,}802.83.$$

Of course, the sum of the post-tax net present value of the loan and the disagio is equal to the post-tax net present value determined in (9.3)

$$NPV^{\tau,loan} + NPV^{\tau,disagio} = 805.53 - 2{,}802.83 = -1{,}997.31. \quad (9.5)$$

9.4.2 *Declining Balance Depreciation of the Disagio: Exact Method*

If it seems to be more appropriate to allocate interest expenses (= disagio depreciation) to different years based on the declining balance method, one possibility is to choose the exact method. Applying the exact method, the effective interest rate (= internal rate of return) of the loan is used to allocate the depreciation.[1]

Allocation of the depreciation to the different years takes place on the basis of the internal rates of return. Depreciation is always the difference between the effective interest payment based on the cash amount paid out (= liability less disagio) and actual interest paid to the bank. Example 9.4 demonstrates how this method works.

Example 9.4. Exact Method for Depreciating Disagios

To follow this example, you need to remember the method of computing the internal rate of return discussed in Sect. 2.4.3, starting on p. 28 (Newton's Solution). As an alternative, you can use the internal rate of return function of your calculator or Excel. If you choose the second method, you can skip Newton's Solution and continue to read the second part of this example, starting on p. 361.

---

[1] For a better understanding of the internal rate of return, see the discussion in Sect. 2.4.2, starting on p. 23. Under the assumptions of a simple cash flow structure of a loan, where the sign of cash flows only changes once after year $t = 0$, we typically can find one single internal rate of return. If there are different solutions, e.g., positive and negative ones, choose the positive one.

To determine the internal rate of return i^* (or – in this case – the effective borrowing rate ρ^*), we have to focus on the cash flow stream from and to the financial institution until maturity. Notice, that in this case, calculating the internal rate of return has nothing to do with taxes, because we want to find out the effective interest rate we pay to the bank *before* taxes. We then use this result for deriving our tax payments, but taxes do not change the allocation of interest costs to periods any more.

We use our assumptions from Ex. 9.3 on p. 356. In $t = 0$, we receive funds of € 84,600 from the financial institution. In the following periods, we have to pay the installments and interest of 5% on remaining debt of the preceding year. Annual installments are $\frac{90{,}000}{3} = 30{,}000$. The present value of our loan using the effective interest rate i^* for discounting cash flows is

$$f(i^*) = 84{,}600 - \frac{(30{,}000 + 0.05 \times 90{,}000)}{(1+i^*)} - \frac{(30{,}000 + 0.05 \times 60{,}000)}{(1+i^*)^2} - \frac{(30{,}000 + 0.05 \times 30{,}000)}{(1+i^*)^3}. \tag{9.6}$$

We are looking for i^* so that the condition

$$f(i^*) \stackrel{!}{=} 0$$

is satisfied. In order to use Newton's Solution, we need to calculate the first derivative of (9.6) with respect to i^*

$$\frac{\partial f(i^*)}{\partial i^*} = \frac{34{,}500}{(1+i^*)^2} + \frac{66{,}000}{(1+i^*)^3} + \frac{94{,}500}{(1+i^*)^4}.$$

Then we follow these steps:

1. Estimation of a starting point i_0 : $i_0 = 0.07$ (i^* has to exceed ρ) and definition of an interruption value (e.g., $|\Delta i| < 0.0001$).
2. Determination of the function value at i_0, $f(i_0)$

$$f(0.07) = 84{,}600 - \frac{34{,}500}{1.07} - \frac{33{,}000}{1.07^2} - \frac{31{,}500}{1.07^3} = -2{,}179.85.$$

3. Determination of the function value of the first derivative of the net present value $f'(i_0)$

$$f'(0.07) = \frac{34{,}500}{1.07^2} + \frac{66{,}000}{1.07^3} + \frac{94{,}500}{1.07^4} = 156{,}102.89$$

4. Determination of i_1

$$i_1 = 0.07 - \frac{-2{,}179.85}{156{,}102.89} = 0.08396.$$

The interruption criterion does not bind, because $|\Delta i| = 0.07 - 0.08396 = 0.01396 > 0.0001$. Therefore, we repeat steps two to four

$$f(0.08396) = 84{,}600 - \frac{34{,}500}{1.08396} - \frac{33{,}000}{1.08396^2} - \frac{31{,}500}{1.08396^3} = -46.24$$

$$f'(0.08396) = \frac{34{,}500}{1.08396^2} + \frac{66{,}000}{1.08396^3} + \frac{94{,}500}{1.08396^4} = 149{,}634.12$$

$$i_2 = 0.08396 - \frac{-46.24}{149{,}634.12} = 0.08427.$$

The interruption criterion still does not bind, therefore we repeat steps two to four

$$f(0.08427) = 84{,}600 - \frac{34{,}500}{1.08427} - \frac{33{,}000}{1.08427^2} - \frac{31{,}500}{1.08427^3} = 0.12$$

$$f'(0.08427) = \frac{34{,}500}{1.08427^2} + \frac{66{,}000}{1.08427^3} + \frac{94{,}500}{1.08427^4} = 149{,}494.65$$

$$i_3 = 0.08427 - \frac{0.12}{149{,}494.65} = 0.08427.$$

Now, the interruption criterion binds ($\Delta = |i_3 - i_2| = 0.0000008 < 0.0001$). The internal rate of return accounts for $i^* = 8.427\%$. Let's check the result

$$f(0.08427) \approx 0.$$

An alternative way to calculate i^* is using a calculator or Excel. The exact internal rate of return is $i^* = 0.08426917$.

Let's get back to our disagio. Our nominal borrowing rate ρ is 5% based on the nominal loan of €90,000, but our effective borrowing rate is $\rho^* = 8.426917\%$ based on the cash outflow of €84,600. In effect, the disagio plus paying 5% interest is identical to paying 8.426917% interest on a loan of €84,600 without a disagio.

The post-tax net present value of the loan without disagio does not change compared to Ex. 9.3.

For calculating the after-tax net present value, we need to know the allocation of the disagio depreciation to the years $t = 1,2,3$. Depreciation in $t = 1$ is the difference between the effective interest payment based on the cash payout of € 84,600 and interest paid to the bank of € 4,500.

$$D_1^{disagio} = 84{,}600 \times 0.08426917 - 4{,}500 = 7{,}129.17 - 4{,}500 = 2{,}629.17.$$

In $t = 2$, the depreciation is again the difference between the effective interest payment based on the notional value of the loan according to the effective interest rate-method and interest paid to the bank of € 3,000. The notional value of the loan is $84{,}600 \times 1.08426917 - 30{,}000 - 4{,}500 = 57{,}229.17$. Amortization of 30,000 and interest payments of 4,500 are subtracted, because they are really paid toward the bank. Depreciation is

$$D_2^{disagio} = 57{,}229.17 \times 0.08426917 - 3{,}000 = 4{,}822.65 - 3{,}000 = 1{,}822.65.$$

The notional value of the loan at the end of $t = 2$ is $57{,}229.17 \times 1.08426917 - 30{,}000 - 3{,}000 = 29{,}051.83$. In $t = 3$, interest paid to the bank is 1,500. Depreciation is

$$D_3^{disagio} = 29{,}051.83 \times 0.08426917 - 1{,}500 = 2{,}448.17 - 1{,}500 = 948.17.$$

The notional value of the loan at the end of $t = 3$ is $29{,}051.83 \times 1.08426917 - 30{,}000 - 1{,}500 = 0$. The sum of disagio depreciations is

$$\sum_{t=1}^{3} D_t^{disagio} = 2{,}629.17 + 1{,}822.65 + 948.17 = 5{,}400,$$

which equals the disagio amount. The post-tax net present value of the disagio is

t	0	1	2	3
CF_0	0.00			
BV_t	5,400.00	3,600.00	1,800.00	0.00
A_t		–1,800.00	–1,800.00	–1,800.00
IP_t		–270.00	–180.00	–90.00
$BV_t^{disagio}$	5,400.00	2,770.83	948.17	0.00
$D_t^{disagio}$		2,629.17	1,822.65	948.17
TB_t		–2,899.17	–2,002.65	–1,038.17
T_t		–1,449.59	–1,001.33	–519.09
CF_t^{τ}	0.00	–620.42	–978.68	–1,370.92
$NPV^{\tau,disagio}$	–2,779.42			

$$NPV^{\tau,disagio} = -\frac{620.42}{1.03} - \frac{978.68}{1.03^2} - \frac{1{,}370.92}{1.03^3} = -2{,}779.42.$$

The post-tax net present value in total, taking (9.4) into account, is

$$NPV^{\tau,loan} + NPV^{\tau,disagio} = 805.53 - 2{,}779.42 = -1{,}973.89. \tag{9.7}$$

The accounting records concerning the disagio are comparable to the straight-line depreciation method. The only difference lies in the depreciation amounts in $t = 1,2,3$.

9.4.3 *Declining Balance Depreciation of the Disagio: Sum of Digits-Method*

The sum of digits-method is a declining balance depreciation method that can be used as an approximation to the exact method provided in the previous example. The sum of digits-method is much more common, because it represents an easy way to calculate the declining balance depreciation. The main assumption of the sum of digits-method is that the amount of depreciation falls by a constant amount each period. Therefore, the method is also called arithmetic declining balance depreciation.

To calculate the sum of digits S, you sum up the years n of the duration of the loan from $t = 1$ to $t = n$.

$$S = \sum_{t=1}^{n} t. \tag{9.8}$$

A faster way to calculate the sum according to (9.8) is the following Gauß' solution

$$S = \sum_{t=1}^{n} t = \frac{n \times (n+1)}{2}. \tag{9.9}$$

In each year, a fraction of $\frac{n-t+1}{S}$ of the disagio is depreciated. If the disagio is $d \times L_0$, annual depreciation yields

$$D_t^{disagio} = \frac{n-t+1}{S} \times (d \times L_0) = \frac{(n-t+1) \times 2}{n \times (n+1)} \times (d \times L_0). \tag{9.10}$$

Example 9.5. Sum of Digits-Method

Recall the assumptions made in Ex. 9.4. If the duration of the loan is $n = 3$ years, the sum of years is based on (9.9)

$$S = \sum_{t=1}^{3} t = \frac{n \times (n+1)}{2} = \frac{3 \times 4}{2} = 6.$$

The absolute amount of the disagio is $d \times L_0 = 0.06 \times 90{,}000 = 5{,}400$. Therefore, the depreciation in $t = 1$ according to (9.10) yields

$$D_1^{disagio} = \frac{n - t + 1}{S} \times (d \times L_0) = \frac{3 - 1 + 1}{6} \times 5{,}400 = 2{,}700.$$

In $t = 2$ and $t = 3$, depreciation of the disagio is

$$D_2^{disagio} = \frac{3 - 2 + 1}{6} \times 5{,}400 = 1{,}800$$
$$D_3^{disagio} = \frac{3 - 3 + 1}{6} \times 5{,}400 = 900.$$

Each year, the depreciation decreases by the constant amount of 900. An analytical derivation for this constant difference will be given at the end of this section.

The depreciation and the weights of depreciation allowances are displayed in the following table.

year	weight	depreciation	Δ to previous year
1	$\frac{3}{6}$	$\frac{3}{6} \times 5{,}400 = 2{,}700$	–
2	$\frac{2}{6}$	$\frac{2}{6} \times 5{,}400 = 1{,}800$	900
3	$\frac{1}{6}$	$\frac{1}{6} \times 5{,}400 = 900$	900
		5,400	

The post-tax net present value of the disagio is

t	0	1	2	3
CF_0	0			
BV_t	5,400	3,600	1,800	0
A_t		−1,800	−1,800	−1,800
IP_t		−270	−180	−90
fraction		$\frac{3}{6}$	$\frac{2}{6}$	$\frac{1}{6}$
$BV_t^{disagio}$	5,400	2,700	900	0
$D_t^{disagio}$		2,700	1,800	900
TB_t		−2,970	−1,980	−990
T_t		−1,485	−990	−495
CF_t^τ	0	−585	−990	−1,395
$NPV^{\tau,disagio}$	−2,777.75			

The tax base consists of the interest payments, and the depreciation of the disagio $TB_t = IP_t - D_t$. After-tax cash flows include amortization of the loan, interest payments and tax refunds $CF_t^\tau = A_t + IP_t - T_t$. The post-tax net present value is

$$NPV^{\tau,disagio} = -\frac{585}{1.03} - \frac{990}{1.03^2} - \frac{1,395}{1.03^3} = -2,777.75.$$

Taking (9.3) into account, the total post-tax net present value is

$$NPV^{\tau,loan} + NPV^{\tau,disagio} = 805.53 - 2,777.75 = -1,972.23. \quad (9.11)$$

The result shows, that the sum of digits-method is a reasonable approximation to the exact method.

The next table summarizes the post-tax net present values of the three methods ((9.5), (9.7) and (9.11))

	NPV^τ	Δ to exact method
straight-line depreciation	−1,997.31	−23.49
declining balance depreciation		
- exact method	−1,973.89	
- sum of digits-method	−1,972.23	1.59

The after-tax net present values based on declining balance depreciation of the disagio are less negative than the after-tax net present value based on straight-line depreciation of the disagio. This is an expected result, because the declining balance depreciation accelerates depreciation allowances and therefore causes a higher present value of tax refunds.

How is the constant decrease of the depreciation – in our example, 900 – derived? The constant difference of depreciation allowances is defined as:

$$\Delta_D = const. = D_t - D_{t+1} = \frac{BV_0 - BV_n}{\frac{n\times(n+1)}{2}}, \tag{9.12}$$

where $BV_0 - BV_n$ represents the accumulated depreciation allowances. In case of a disagio, $BV_0 - BV_n$ equals the absolute disagio amount. The book value of the disagio in $t = n$ is always zero.

Proof. To prove (9.12), let's start with the depreciation allowances that have to sum up to $BV_0 - BV_n$

$$\begin{aligned} BV_0 - BV_n = {} & D_1 + (D_1 - \Delta_D) + (D_1 - 2\times\Delta_D) + (D_1 - 3\times\Delta_D) \\ & + \ldots + (D_1 - (n-1)\times\Delta_D). \end{aligned} \tag{9.13}$$

Notice, that $D_2 = (D_1 - \Delta_D)$, $D_3 = (D_1 - 2\times\Delta_D)$, and so on.

Simplifying (9.13) gives

$$\begin{aligned} BV_0 - BV_n = {} & D_1 + D_1 + D_1 + D_1 + \ldots + D_1 \\ & -\Delta_D - 2\times\Delta_D - 3\times\Delta_D - \ldots - (n-1)\times\Delta_D, \end{aligned}$$

which can be further simplified to

$$BV_0 - BV_n = n\times D_1 - \Delta_D \times \underbrace{(1+2+3+\ldots+(n-1))}_{\Psi}. \tag{9.14}$$

Now, concentrate on the term represented by Ψ. For simplifying the term, we can use the Gauß rule we applied before. By the way, do you recall the Gauß story you have probably heard from your teacher in high school? One time, the later mathematician Gauß behaved bad in school. The teacher told him to sum up all the numbers from one to one hundred, hoping for a few minutes of calm. The teacher thought that little Gauß would need a while to give the correct answer. After a few moments, Gauß told the teacher the correct answer. What happened? Suppose, that $n = 10$. In that case, Ψ would be

$$\Psi = 1+2+3+4+5+6+7+8+9+10.$$

Gauß recognized that the numbers can be sorted as follows

$$\Psi = \underbrace{10}_{10} + \underbrace{(1+9)}_{10} + \underbrace{(2+8)}_{10} + \underbrace{(3+7)}_{10} + \underbrace{(4+6)}_{10} + \underbrace{5}_{\frac{10}{2}}. \tag{9.15}$$

Equation (9.15) leads to

$$\Psi = n \times \left(\frac{n}{2}\right) + n \times \frac{1}{2} = \frac{n \times (n+1)}{2}. \tag{9.16}$$

Using (9.16), (9.14) is simplified to

$$BV_0 - BV_n = n \times D_1 - \Delta_D \times \frac{n \times (n-1)}{2}. \tag{9.17}$$

Solving (9.17) for Δ_D leads to

$$\Delta_D = \frac{(BV_0 - BV_n) - n \times D_1}{-\frac{n \times (n-1)}{2}}. \tag{9.18}$$

According to the sum of digits-method, D_1 is defined as:

$$D_1 = n \times \Delta_D. \tag{9.19}$$

This rule is required, because this equation guarantees that in $t = n$, $D_n = \Delta_D$ which is necessary for achieving constant differences in depreciation allowances. Combining (9.18) and (9.19) gives

$$\Delta_D = \frac{(BV_0 - BV_n) - n \times n \times \Delta_D}{-\frac{n \times (n-1)}{2}}. \tag{9.20}$$

Solving (9.20) for Δ_D yields

$$\begin{aligned}
\Delta_D &= \frac{(BV_0 - BV_n)}{-\frac{n \times (n-1)}{2}} + \frac{n \times \Delta_D}{\frac{(n-1)}{2}} \\
\Delta_D - \frac{n \times \Delta_D}{\frac{(n-1)}{2}} &= \frac{(BV_0 - BV_n)}{-\frac{n \times (n-1)}{2}} \\
\frac{\Delta_D \times \frac{(n-1)}{2} - n \times \Delta_D}{\frac{(n-1)}{2}} &= \frac{(BV_0 - BV_n)}{-\frac{n \times (n-1)}{2}} \\
\frac{\frac{\Delta_D \times (n-1)}{2} - \frac{2 \times n \times \Delta_D}{2}}{\frac{(n-1)}{2}} &= \frac{(BV_0 - BV_n)}{-\frac{n \times (n-1)}{2}}
\end{aligned}$$

$$
\begin{aligned}
\frac{\Delta_D \times (n-1) - 2 \times n \times \Delta_D}{(n-1)} &= \frac{(BV_0 - BV_n)}{-\frac{n \times (n-1)}{2}} \\
\frac{\Delta_D \times (n-1-2 \times n)}{(n-1)} &= \frac{(BV_0 - BV_n)}{-\frac{n \times (n-1)}{2}} \\
\frac{\Delta_D \times (-n-1)}{(n-1)} &= \frac{(BV_0 - BV_n)}{-\frac{n \times (n-1)}{2}} \\
\Delta_D &= \frac{(BV_0 - BV_n)}{-\frac{n \times (n-1)}{2}} \times \frac{(n-1)}{(-n-1)} \\
\Delta_D &= \frac{(BV_0 - BV_n)}{-\frac{n \times (-n-1)}{2}} \\
\Delta_D &= \frac{(BV_0 - BV_n)}{\frac{n \times (n+1)}{2}}.
\end{aligned}
$$

□

9.5 Leasing

In a leasing contract, a lessee rents an investment object from the lessor instead of buying it.

> A lease is an agreement whereby the lessor conveys the right to use an asset for an agreed period of time to the lessee in return for a (series of) payment(s).

There are several nontax advantages of leasing over buying, such as:

1. Liquidity is preserved, because there are no acquisition costs.
2. Leverage is avoided, if acquisition costs have to be debt financed.
3. The balance sheet structure does not change.
4. Less capital is locked up.
5. Lending limits are not affected.
6. Leasing provides a secure basis for calculation, because leasing rates are known because of the contract.
7. No reserves for replacement investments have to be made.

From the viewpoint of the lessee, the leasing contract combines acquisition and financing of an investment object in one contract. Because of that characteristic, separation of the investment and the financing (loan) is not possible. For evaluation of leasing contracts, an integrated consideration of all cash inflows and outflows related to the leasing contract is necessary.

Tax effects of leasing depend on the specific conditions of the contract. The main question for both financial accounting and tax accounting is: Which party should be regarded as the owner of the leasing object? The answer is decisive for the attribution of the object and depreciation to the lessor or lessee. Typically, there is an attribution to the beneficial owner rather than to the legal proprietor ("substance over form") using a catalog of criteria. The classification of the leasing objects is basically comparable under IAS 17 and the German tax code. IAS 17 distinguishes between

1. Finance lease: Transfers substantially all the risk and reward of ownership of the asset to the lessee.
2. Operating lease: Other than finance lease.

The following characteristics usually indicate a finance lease contract, if one of them is fulfilled (see IAS 17.10.)

1. The lease transfers ownership of the asset to the lessee by the end of the lease term.
2. The lessee has the option to purchase the asset at a price that is expected to be sufficiently lower than the fair value at the date the option becomes exercisable.
3. The lease term is for the major part of the economic life of the asset even if title is not transferred.
4. At the inception of the lease the present value of the minimum lease payments amounts to at least substantially all of the fair value of the leased asset.
5. The leased assets are of such a specialized nature that only the lessee can use them without major modifications.

Under German tax rules, we distinguish between operating leasing and finance leasing as follows. First, finance leasing occurs if

(a) The contract is signed for a specific period of time and is not callable during the minimum term of lease and
(b) Leasing payments during the minimum term of lease cover at least the acquisition costs of the asset and all related costs of the lessor.

Leasing contracts not qualified as finance leasing are operating leasing contracts.

Second, we must have a closer look at the contract conditions in case of finance leasing to find out who capitalizes and depreciates the asset. We have to distinguish contracts with a purchase option at the end of the minimum term of lease and contracts without a purchase option.

1. Finance leasing contracts without a purchase option:
   (a) The lessor has to capitalize the asset if the minimum term of lease is at least 40% and does not exceed 90% of the useful life of the leasing asset.
   (b) The lessee has to capitalize the asset if the minimum term of lease is less than 40% or exceeds 90% of the useful life of the leasing asset.
2. Finance leasing contracts including a purchase option:
   (a) The lessor has to capitalize the asset if the minimum term of lease is at least 40% or does not exceed 90% of the useful life and the purchase price at the end of the minimum lease term is not less than the book value if straight-line depreciation is applied.

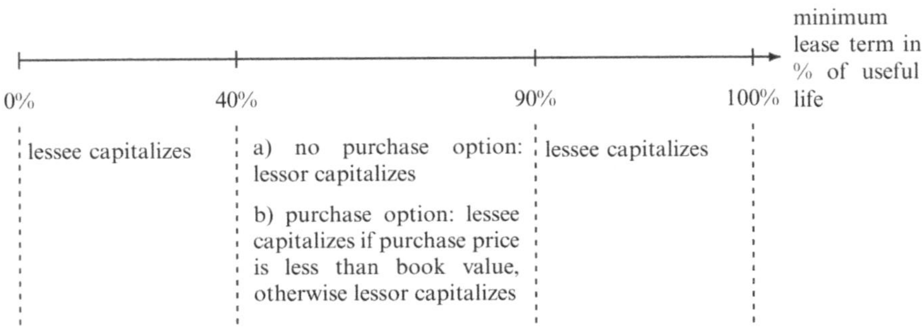

Fig. 9.1 Capitalization in case of finance leasing

(b) The lessee has to capitalize the asset if the minimum term of lease is less than 40% or exceeds 90% of the useful life.

(c) The lessee has to capitalize the asset if the minimum term of lease is at least 40% and does not exceed 90% of the useful life and the purchase price at the end of the minimum lease term is less than the book value if straight-line depreciation is applied.

Figure 9.1 summarizes capitalization in case of finance leasing.

Moreover, leased assets of such a specialized nature that only the lessee can use them without major modifications, are always capitalized by the lessee.

Those rules are comparable in many countries, but details may differ. As a result, capitalization of leased assets might differ from country to country.

9.5.1 *Operating Lease*

In case of an operating lease, the lessor capitalizes and depreciates the asset. The leasing payments *LP* are operating revenues of the lessor. The cash outflows for the lessor are the acquisition costs of the investment. The cash inflow is represented by the leasing payments and a potential selling price in $t = n$. For tax purposes, received leasing payments are reduced by depreciation of the initial investment. In $t = n$, capital gains are taxed, if a selling price SP_n exceeds the book value of the asset $BV_n = I_0 - \sum_{t=1}^{n} D_t$. To evaluate the profitability of a leasing contract from the lessor's perspective, the application of the "Standard Model" is possible. The post-tax net present value for the lessor ($NPV^{\tau,lessor}$) is

$$\begin{aligned} NPV^{\tau,lessor} &= -I_0 + \sum_{t=1}^{n} [LP_t - \tau \times (LP_t - D_t)] \times (q^\tau)^{-t} \\ &\quad + \left[SP_n - \tau \times \left(SP_n - I_0 + \sum_{t=1}^{n} D_t\right)\right] \times (q^\tau)^{-n}. \end{aligned} \tag{9.21}$$

In case of the lessee, leasing payments are tax deductible operating expenses. Moreover, the tax base is affected by the cash inflow generated by the real investment. In fact, from the lessee's perspective, the tax base is equal to his cash flows, as there are no accruals or deferrals. Service payments for leasing contracts are immediately tax deductible and will be neglected in the following. The lessee's post-tax net present value ($NPV^{\tau,lessee}$) is

$$NPV^{\tau,lessee} = \sum_{t=1}^{n}(CF_t - LP_t) \times (1-\tau) \times (q^{\tau})^{-t}. \tag{9.22}$$

Notice, that there are no payments in $t = n$ for the leasing asset, because the lessor and not the lessee is the legal owner and can sell the leasing asset.

To make implications of leasing contracts more transparent, let's have a look at the accounting records in case the lessor has to capitalize the leasing asset.

(a) Accounting records in case of the lessor

1. In $t = 0$, the lessor purchases the asset (assuming equity financing):

Dr plant & equipment	
	Cr cash account

2. In $t = 1, \ldots, n$, accounting records of depreciation and receipt of rents:

Dr depreciation	
	Cr plant & equipment

Dr cash account	
	Cr rental income

3. If the lessor sells the asset at the end of the contract period and $BV > 0$, the accounting records are:

Dr cash account	
	Cr plant & equipment
	Cr other income

Depending on tax accounting or financial accounting, tax payments have to be considered.

(b) Accounting records of the lessee are the same for all periods. Only the leasing expenses and cash inflow (sales revenue) have to be considered.

Dr	leasing expenses		
		Cr	cash account

Dr	cash account		
		Cr	sales revenue

Example 9.6. Operating Lease

In the following, we refer to the German tax rules for capitalizing leasing assets. Bill owns a big leasing company, where he buys assets and rents the assets to other companies. One day, he signed a leasing contract with George. George rents a machine over a period of 5 years. During that period, he expects to earn $CF_t = 21{,}000$ each year with the leased machine. The useful life of the machine is 10 years. Bill has to pay $I_0 = 134{,}000$ of acquisition costs and receives an annual rent of $LP_t = 20{,}000$. In $t = 6$, Bill sells the machine for $SP_6 = 80{,}000$ to a third person. The marginal income tax rate is assumed to be $\tau = 40\%$ for both Bill and George. The capital market interest rate is $i = 6\%$. It is assumed that Bill and George withdraw total cash flows after taxes at the end of each period.

Before we start to determine the post-tax net present values for the lessor (Bill) and the lessee (George), we have to evaluate, whether the leasing contract qualifies for an operating leasing contract or a finance leasing contract and who has the right to depreciate the asset. Because the sum of rents in $t = 1, \ldots, 5$ ($5 \times 20{,}000 = 100{,}000$) does not exceed the acquisition costs, the contract is considered as an operating leasing contract. Bill has to capitalize the machine and claims the depreciation.

Let's evaluate the leasing contract for Bill and George separately. Bill's financial plan is

t	0	1	2	3	4	5	6
I_0, SP_6	–134,000						80,000
LP_t		20,000	20,000	20,000	20,000	20,000	
D_t		13,400	13,400	13,400	13,400	13,400	13,400
BV_t		120,600	107,200	93,800	80,400	67,000	53,600
TB_t		6,600	6,600	6,600	6,600	6,600	13,000
T_t		2,640	2,640	2,640	2,640	2,640	5,200
CF_t^τ		17,360	17,360	17,360	17,360	17,360	74,800
NPV^τ	4,658						

Bill has to depreciate the asset ($D_t = \frac{134{,}000}{10} = 13{,}400$). In $t = 6$, capital gains are subject to tax. The capital gain amounts to $SP_6 - BV_6 = 80{,}000 - 53{,}600 = 26{,}400$. The post-tax interest rate is $i^\tau = 3.6\%$. The post-tax net present value for the lessor equals

$$NPV^{\tau,lessor} = -134{,}000 + 17{,}360 \times \frac{1.036^5 - 1}{0.036 \times 1.036^5} + [80{,}000 - 0.4 \times (80{,}000 - 53{,}600 - 13{,}400)] \times 1.036^{-6} = 4{,}658.$$

In Bill's case, the leasing contract is profitable. The accounting records for the lessor are

(a) Purchasing the asset in $t = 0$:

Dr	plant & equipment	134,000			
			Cr	cash account	134,000

(b) Receiving rents and claiming depreciation in $t = 1, \ldots, 5$:

Dr	cash account	20,000			
			Cr	rental income	20,000

Dr	depreciation	13,400			
			Cr	plant & equipment	13,400

(c) Selling the asset in $t = 6$:

Dr	cash account	80,000			
			Cr	plant & equipment	53,600
			Cr	other income	26,400

Notice, that for financial accounting purposes, tax liabilities are expenses. For tax accounting, taxes usually do not qualify as tax deductible expenses.

How about George? His financial plan is

t	0	1	2	3	4	5	6
CF_t		21,000	21,000	21,000	21,000	21,000	
LP_t		–20,000	–20,000	–20,000	–20,000	–20,000	
TB_t		1,000	1,000	1,000	1,000	1,000	
T_t		400	400	400	400	400	
CF_t^τ		600	600	600	600	600	
NPV^τ	2,701						

The post-tax net present value for the lessee is

$$NPV^{\tau,lessee} = 600 \times \frac{1.036^5 - 1}{0.036 \times 1.036^5} = 2{,}701.$$

The leasing contract is profitable for George, too. George has to pay the rents of $LP_t = 20{,}000$, but receives returns of $CF_t = 21{,}000$. There is no depreciation or capital gain. The accounting records for the lessee are the same in each period

Dr	cash account	21,000			
			Cr	sales revenue	21,000

Dr	leasing expenses	20,000			
			Cr	cash account	20,000

9.5.2 *Finance Lease*

If leasing is characterized as a finance lease, the leasing contract is reinterpreted as acquisition of an asset plus a loan contract (annuity loan). Attribution of the leasing asset to the lessor or lessee depends on the specific details of the contract. As an example, we have presented the German rules for attribution at the beginning of Sect. 9.5.

If the leasing asset is attributed to the lessee, the lessee capitalizes and depreciates the underlying asset. The lessor is still the legal owner of the asset, but the lessee is qualified as beneficial owner. The separation of legal ownership and capitalization of the asset results in splitting up the leasing payments *LP* into interest payments *IP* and amortization payments A.

$$LP_t = IP_t + A_t.$$

The fraction of LP_t that represents the interest payments is tax deductible. The fraction of LP_t referring to the amortization payments is not deductible, which is identical to treatment of payments in case of a loan. However, instead of deducting the amortization payments, the lessee can claim depreciation allowances although he is not the legal owner.

Separating leasing payments into interest and amortization for accounting purposes (e.g., IAS 17.25) is based on the exact method[2] or the sum of digits-method[3].

Now, in case the asset is attributed to the lessee, the post-tax net present value for the lessee is computed as:

$$NPV^{\tau,lessee} = \sum_{t=1}^{n} [CF_t - LP_t - \tau \times (CF_t - D_t - IP_t)] \times (q^{\tau})^{-t}.$$

The lessor cannot claim any depreciation allowances. Corresponding to the restriction of deduction of interest payments for the lessee, the lessor only has to pay taxes on the fraction that represents interest payments. The after-tax net present value $NPV^{\tau,lessor}$ for the lessor is

$$NPV^{\tau,lessor} = -I_0 + \sum_{t=1}^{n} [LP_t - \tau \times IP_t] \times (q^{\tau})^{-t} + SP_n \times (1-\tau) \times (q^{\tau})^{-n}.$$

If the lessor sells the asset, he has to pay taxes on the total selling price, because he had not capitalized the asset and has no book value.

If we have a finance lease contract, where the asset is attributed to the lessor, then the after-tax net present values for the lessor and the lessee are calculated according to (9.21) and (9.22) on p. 370. Tax consequences are exactly the same as in case of operating leasing.

Let's look at the accounting records in case the lessee has to capitalize the underlying asset. In this setting, the lessor purchases the asset, however, the lessee has to capitalize it, although he had no cash outflow for the initial cost of the asset.

The lessor has to capitalize receivables to the amount of the initial costs of the asset. Plant and equipment is removed from the lessor's accounts.

(a) Accounting records in case of the lessor

1. In $t = 0$, the lessor purchases the asset (assuming equity financing) and capitalizes receivables:

Dr	plant & equipment		
		Cr	cash account

Dr	receivables		
		Cr	plant & equipment

[2] See p. 359.

[3] See p. 363.

2. In the following periods, the part of the leasing payment, which is qualified as amortization, reduces the receivables. The remaining part is allocated to interest income:

Dr	cash account		
		Cr	receivables
		Cr	interest income

(b) Accounting records in case of the lessee

1. In $t = 0$, the lessee has to capitalize the leasing asset and corresponding liabilities:

Dr	plant & equipment		
		Cr	liabilities

Corresponding to the receivables of the lessor, the lessee has to capitalize liabilities to the amount of the initial costs of the asset.

2. In the following periods, a fraction of the leasing payments is classified as amortization. They reduce the liabilities. The remaining part is a tax deductible interest expense. Additionally, the lessee can claim depreciation, because he capitalizes the leasing asset:

Dr	liabilities		
Dr	interest expenses		
		Cr	cash account

Dr	depreciation		
		Cr	plant & equipment

Moreover, the lessee has cash inflow from his sales:

Dr	cash account		
		Cr	sales revenue

Example 9.7. Finance Lease

Assume, two parties sign a leasing contract for a movable asset. The contract is not callable during the minimum lease term. The useful life of the asset is supposed to be 5 years, whereas the contract is signed for (case A) 4 years or (case B) 5 years. The acquisition costs of the asset are $I_0 = 120{,}000$. For depreciation allowances the straight-line method is applied. At the end of the contract, the asset will be sold to a third party. The selling price for the asset in $t = 4$ is $SP_4 = 40{,}000$ (case A) or in $t = 5$ $SP_5 = 20{,}000$ (case B), respectively. The capital market interest rate is assumed to be $i = 5\%$ and the marginal tax rate is $\tau = 50\%$. Further, we assume that the interest is subject to the marginal tax rate of $\tau = 50\%$. All cash flows after taxes are withdrawn at the end of each period.

Case A: $n = 4$ Years

Leasing payments are agreed to be $LP_t = 40{,}000$. The lessee calculates with cash flows of $CF_t = 50{,}000$ annually. In case of $n = 4$, we have $\sum_{t=1}^{n} LP_t = 4 \times 40{,}000 = 160{,}000 > 120{,}000 = I_0$. The sum of leasing payments exceeds the acquisition costs. Consequently, the leasing contract is classified as a finance lease. The lease term is substantially shorter than the asset's life ($\frac{4}{5} = 80\%$). Therefore, the asset has to be capitalized by the lessor and tax consequences are comparable to operating leasing contracts. The after-tax cash flow from the lessor's perspective can be taken from the following financial plan. On the one hand, the leasing rents received are fully taxable, on the other hand, the lessor can claim the depreciation.

t	0	1	2	3	4
I_0, SP_4	–120,000				40,000
LP_t		40,000	40,000	40,000	40,000
D_t		24,000	24,000	24,000	24,000
BV_t		96,000	72,000	48,000	24,000
TB_t		16,000	16,000	16,000	32,000
T_t		8,000	8,000	8,000	16,000
CF_t^{τ}	–120,000	32,000	32,000	32,000	64,000

The post-tax net present value for the lessor equals

$$\begin{aligned} NPV^{\tau,lessor} &= -120{,}000 + 32{,}000 \times \frac{1.025^4 - 1}{0.025 \times 1.025^4} \\ &\quad + [40{,}000 - 0.5 \times (40{,}000 - 24{,}000)] \times 1.025^{-4} \\ &= 29{,}374. \end{aligned}$$

The leasing contract is profitable for the lessor.

The cash flows after taxes from the lessee's perspective are shown in the following table. Corresponding to the treatment for tax purposes in case of the lessor, leasing payments are fully tax deductible. The lessee cannot claim the depreciation, because the lessor has to capitalize the asset.

t	0	1	2	3	4
CF_t		50,000	50,000	50,000	50,000
LP_t		40,000	40,000	40,000	40,000
TB_t		10,000	10,000	10,000	10,000
T_t		5,000	5,000	5,000	5,000
CF_t^{τ}		5,000	5,000	5,000	5,000

Discounting the after-tax cash flows results in a post-tax net present value of

$$NPV^{\tau,lessee} = 5{,}000 \times \frac{1.025^4 - 1}{0.025 \times 1.025^4} = 18{,}810.$$

The lessee is advised to sign the contract, because he can earn a positive post-tax net present value. The accounting records are analogous to Ex. 9.6.

Case B: $n = 5$ Years

Leasing payments are agreed to be $LP_t = 36{,}000$. The lessee calculates with certain cash flows of $CF_t = 45{,}000$ each year. In case of $n = 5$, the sum of leasing payments is $\sum_{t=1}^{n} LP_t = 5 \times 36{,}000 = 180{,}000 > 120{,}000 = I_0$. This is again a finance leasing contract. In contrast to our example with $n = 4$ years, the lease term equals the asset's life of 5 years. Therefore, the asset has to be capitalized and depreciated by the lessee. Now, we have to split up the leasing payments into interest expenses and acquisition costs of the asset. The sum of interest payments during the contract period is defined as the sum of the leasing payments less the acquisition costs

$$\sum_{t=1}^{n} IP_t = \sum_{t=1}^{n} LP_t - I_0 = 5 \times 36{,}000 - 120{,}000 = 60{,}000.$$

The fraction of leasing payments that is characterized as interest payments is tax deductible from the lessee's perspective and is subject to tax for the lessor. The problem is to allocate the sum of interest payments of 60,000 to the periods of the leasing contract. Basically, we use the exact method or the sum of digits-method. For reasons of simplification, in this case we refer to the sum of digits-method discussed in Sect. 9.4.3. The sum of digits is

$$S = \sum_{t=1}^{n} t = \frac{n \times (n+1)}{2} = \frac{5 \times 6}{2} = 15.$$

The annual deductible interest payments are then calculated as:

$$IP_t = \frac{n-t+1}{S} \times \left(\sum_{t=1}^{n} LP_t - I_0\right) = \frac{5-t+1}{15} \times 60{,}000.$$

t	1	2	3	4	5
LP_t	36,000	36,000	36,000	36,000	36,000
Fraction	$\frac{5}{15}$	$\frac{4}{15}$	$\frac{3}{15}$	$\frac{2}{15}$	$\frac{1}{15}$
IP_t	20,000	16,000	12,000	8,000	4,000
A_t	16,000	20,000	24,000	28,000	32,000

The part of the leasing payment which exceeds interest payments is qualified as amortization of a loan given by the lessor ($A_t = LP_t - IP_t$).

In $t = 5$, the book value of the asset $BV_5 = 0$ which results in a fully taxable selling price SP_5 for the lessor. The financial plan from the lessor's perspective is

t	0	1	2	3	4	5
I_0, SP_5	–120,000					20,000
LP_t		36,000	36,000	36,000	36,000	36,000
IP_t		20,000	16,000	12,000	8,000	4,000
A_t		16,000	20,000	24,000	28,000	32,000
TB_t		20,000	16,000	12,000	8,000	24,000
T_t		10,000	8,000	6,000	4,000	12,000
CF_t^{τ}	–120,000	26,000	28,000	30,000	32,000	44,000

$$NPV^{\tau,lessor} = -120{,}000 + \frac{26{,}000}{1.025} + \frac{28{,}000}{1.025^2} + \frac{30{,}000}{1.025^3} + \frac{32{,}000}{1.025^4} + \frac{44{,}000}{1.025^5}$$
$$= 27{,}755.$$

The accounting records for the lessor

(a) Purchase in $t = 0$:

Dr	plant & equipment	120,000			
			Cr	cash account	120,000

Dr	receivables	120,000			
			Cr	plant & equipment	120,000

Notice, that the acquisition costs of the asset are capitalized as receivables. Plant & equipment is removed from the lessor's accounts.

(b) Accounting records in $t = 1, \ldots, 4$ (the amount allocated to interest income and to amortization changes each year):

Dr	cash account	36,000			
			Cr	interest income	20,000
			Cr	receivables	16,000

(c) Accounting records in $t = 5$:

Dr	cash account	36,000			
			Cr	interest income	4,000
			Cr	receivables	32,000

Dr	cash account	20,000			
			Cr	other income	20,000

The lessee has to capitalize the asset and he claims the depreciation. The fraction of leasing payments that causes taxable income for the lessor is correspondingly tax deductible from the lessee's perspective. The post-tax cash flows for the lessee are

t	0	1	2	3	4	5
CF_t		45,000	45,000	45,000	45,000	45,000
D_t		24,000	24,000	24,000	24,000	24,000
LP_t		36,000	36,000	36,000	36,000	36,000
IP_t		20,000	16,000	12,000	8,000	4,000
A_t		16,000	20,000	24,000	28,000	32,000
TB_t		1,000	5,000	9,000	13,000	17,000
T_t		500	2,500	4,500	6,500	8,500
CF_t^τ		8,500	6,500	4,500	2,500	500

$$NPV^{\tau,lessee} = \frac{8{,}500}{1.025} + \frac{6{,}500}{1.025^2} + \frac{4{,}500}{1.025^3} + \frac{2{,}500}{1.025^4} + \frac{500}{1.025^5} = 21{,}365.$$

The accounting records for the lessee are

(a) Capitalizing the asset in $t = 0$:

Dr	plant & equipment	120,000			
			Cr	liabilities	120,000

(b) The accounting records for cash flows earned with the asset, reducing liabilities, interest expenses, and depreciation in $t = 1$:

Dr	cash account	45,000			
			Cr	sales revenue	45,000

Dr	liabilities	16,000			
Dr	interest expenses	20,000			
			Cr	cash account	36,000

Dr	depreciation	24,000			
			Cr	plant & equipment	24,000

(c) The accounting records in $t = 2, \ldots, 5$ are analogous to $t = 1$.
(d) When the lessee returns the asset to the lessor in $t = 5$, the book value of the asset is zero.

Questions

9.1. Please have a look at Table 3.1 on p. 89. Consider the part that reflects the debit interest rate. How many different post-tax credit interest rates can be distinguished in your home country?

9.2. Provide examples, why firms have to access debt financing to carry out desired investments.

9.3. Show formally that the pre-tax net present value of a bullet loan will normally be negative. However, under specific assumptions, it can be positive in the post-tax case. What assumptions have to be made?

9.4. How can disagios be treated for tax purposes?

9.5. Are there differences concerning the treatment of disagios for financial accounting purposes and tax purposes in Germany? How are disagios treated in your home country?

9.6. What kind of leasing contracts can be distinguished? Which characteristics are assigned to each case? Which characteristics can be identified for tax purposes in Germany? What are the characteristics in your home country?

9.7. Look at the characteristics for capitalization of the leasing asset in case of finance leasing. They are provided at the beginning of Sect. 9.5, starting on p. 368. What do you think why is the asset capitalized by the lessee, if the minimum lease term is less than 40% or exceeds 90% of the useful life of the asset?

9.8. Which implications do occur, if the leasing asset is capitalized by (a) the lessor (b) the lessee?

Exercises

9.9. Post-Tax Interest Rate

An investor wants to purchase a real property. The useful life of the property is 10 years, the acquisition costs amount to €500,000, from which 40% are assigned to the land. The building is amortized by straight-line depreciation. The investor rents the building. Rents are expected to stay constant over time and amount to €72,000 every year. In $t = 10$, the property will be sold for 40% of its acquisition costs. The capital market interest rate is $i = 10\%$ and the constant marginal tax rate is $\tau = 25\%$. The investor needs to finance 50% of the acquisition costs by debt. His bank offers him a bullet loan with a borrowing rate of $\rho = 11\%$. The loan does not include a disagio.

(a) Suppose, the acquired property qualifies as a business asset which results in fully deductible interest payments. Is the investment carried out?
(b) Now, assume the property does not qualify as a business asset, because a head of family purchases the property and moves in with his whole family. If he did not purchase the property, he would have to pay an annual rent of €72,000. Because the family uses the property itself, the interest payments on the loan are not tax deductible. Is the head of the family advised to purchase the property?
(c) Suppose, the asset qualifies as a business asset. What happens, if the interest payments on the loan are only deductible up to 80%?

9.10. Evaluating Different Types of Loans

Assume a real investment alternative yielding the following certain future cash flow stream

t	0	1	2	3	4
CF_t	–300,000	80,000	90,000	95,000	110,000

The capital market interest rate is $i = 8\%$ and the marginal tax rate is $\tau = 40\%$. We assume straight-line depreciation. The cash flows after taxes are withdrawn at the end of each period. Please assume immediate full loss offset.

(a) Determine the relative additional pre-tax consumption potential if the real investment is carried out.
(b) Determine the post-tax net present value.
(c) The investor can only raise funds of 50% of the acquisition costs. The bank offers the following financing alternatives:

(c1) A bullet loan with $\rho = 11\%$ and $d = 0\%$.
(c2) A loan amortized by constant equal installments with $\rho = 12\%$ and $d = 0\%$.

(c3) A loan amortized by constant equal installments with $\rho = 9\%$ and $d = 6.25\%$.
(c4) An annuity loan with $\rho = 9.76\%$ and $d = 0\%$.

What is the post-tax rank order of the four loans offered? Which offer is the best one? Is the real investment carried out?

(d) Based on the assumptions of (c), what happens, if interest income at the personal level is taxed at a flat tax rate of $\tau^{flat} = 25\%$, whereas real investment income is still taxed at a rate of $\tau = 40\%$?

9.11. Arbitrage With Debt Financing?
A real investment yields the following cash flows

t	0	1	2	3	4
CF_t	–600,000	160,000	185,000	200,000	210,000

The capital market interest rate is supposed to be $i = 10\%$ and the marginal tax rate is $\tau = 50\%$. The straight-line method is applied for depreciation. Cash flows after taxes are withdrawn at the end of each period.

(a) Determine the post-tax net present value.
(b) Now, assume that the investor needs to finance 40% of the acquisition costs with external funds. He gets the following offer from his bank: A bullet loan with a borrowing rate $\rho = 11\%$ and a disagio rate of $d = 0\%$. What is the post-tax net present value of the loan? Is the real investment carried out?
(c) The government introduces a flat tax rate on interest income of $\tau^{flat} = 25\%$. How is the post-tax net present value of the loan in (b) affected? Is the real investment carried out?

9.12. Disagios
Assume a loan that is amortized by annual constant installments. The nominal loan amounts to €600,000 – disbursed with a disagio rate of $d = 5\%$ – and the maturity of the loan is $n = 4$. The borrowing rate is $\rho = 8\%$ and the capital market interest rate is $i = 6\%$. The marginal tax rate is $\tau = 30\%$.

(a) Determine the pre-tax net present value.
(b) Determine the post-tax net present value if the disagio is depreciated by applying the straight-line method.
(c) Determine the post-tax net present value if the disagio is depreciated by applying the sum of digits-method.
(d) Determine the post-tax net present value if the disagio is depreciated by applying the exact method.

9.13. Financing Restrictions
A real investment alternative yields the following future cash flows

t	0	1	2	3	4
CF_t	–320,000	80,000	90,000	95,000	120,000

The capital market interest rate is $i = 4\%$ and the marginal tax rate is $\tau = 20\%$. Depreciation is $D_t = 80{,}000$ for $t = 1, \ldots, 4$.

(a) Determine the post-tax net present value if the investment is fully financed with equity.
(b) Suppose, you are facing financing restrictions that force you to raise external funds to the amount of 90% of the acquisitions costs. A bank offers you two possibilities

(ba) A bullet loan with the following conditions: $\rho = 6.5\%$, $d = 0\%$.
(bb) A loan amortized by annual constant installments: $\rho = 7.9\%$, $d = 0\%$.

In case of (ba)

(1) Determine the post-tax net present value of the bullet loan.
(2) Determine the post-tax net present value of the real investment and the financing alternative in one financial plan.

In case of (bb)

(1) Determine the post-tax net present value of the loan. Which loan leads to a higher post-tax net present value?
(2) What happens if the borrowing rate for a short term liability (one period) is $\rho^{short} = 18\%$?

9.14. Prepayment Penalty
Sometimes, investors want to get rid of their existing liabilities as soon as possible. They may find more profitable ways to acquire funds or are in a lucky position to have enough cash to pay back debt. Assume the following future cash flows of a real investment opportunity

t	0	1	2	3	4
CF_t	–200,000	90,000	68,000	55,000	50,000

Assume straight-line depreciation over 4 years. Suppose, $i = 6\%$ and $\tau = 40\%$. The cash flows after taxes are withdrawn at the end of each period.

(a) Determine the post-tax future value of the equity financed real investment. Is the investor advised to carry out the real investment?
(b) Suppose, 60% of the acquisition costs have to be debt financed. You receive an offer for a loan. The loan is amortized by constant annual installments ($A_t = A$) with the following conditions: $\rho = 12\%$ and $d = 0\%$. Is the investor still advised to carry out the investment?
(c) The investor is considering premature amortization of the loan. The prepayment is assumed to be restricted in $t = 2$ to $2 \times A$ or in $t = 3$ to $2 \times A$. The bank is willing to accept the prepayment under the following conditions: If prepayment in $t = 2$ amounts to twice the annual installment, the bank will charge a prepayment penalty of €3,500; if prepayment in $t = 3$ amounts to

twice the annual installment, a prepayment penalty of € 1,500 will be charged. What is the investor going to do?

9.15. Leasing

An investor (Marcus) calculates with future cash flows in $t = 1, \ldots, 6$ of annually € 170,000 if he can realize his business idea. For his idea, he needs to acquire an expensive machine ($I_0 = 750{,}000$) with a useful life of $n = 6$. Marcus asks whether Holger is willing to buy the machine and lease it to him, if he pays him $LP_t = 140{,}000$ for $t = 1, \ldots, 6$. Holger assumes straight-line depreciation. Both Marcus and Holger calculate with $i = 8\%$ and $\tau = 50\%$. The cash flows after taxes are withdrawn at the end of each period.

(a) Who has to capitalize the machine, if Marcus and Holger sign a leasing contract which is rescindable during the minimum lease term of 6 years? Use the characteristics provided at the beginning of Sect. 9.5, starting on p. 368 for evaluation.
(b) Determine Marcus' post-tax net present value, if Holger signs the contract. Is Holger willing to sign the contract under these conditions?
(c) Provide the accounting records in $t = 0$ and $t = 1$ for the lessor and the lessee.
(d) Now, assume Marcus has the option to purchase the machine from Holger at the end of $t = 4$ for € 270,000. The useful life of the machine is not affected by the purchase. Marcus has to finance the purchase with external funds. His bank offers him a bullet loan with a borrowing rate of $\rho = 10\%$ and $d = 0\%$. Are both willing to sign the leasing contract?
(e) Based on (d), provide accounting records for Marcus and Holger in $t = 4{,}5{,}6$.

9.16. Purchase-Equivalent Leasing Payment

An investor has to decide whether he wants to purchase or lease a machine. Acquisition costs would be $I_0 = 400{,}000$ and the useful life is $n = 5$. In case of purchasing the machine, the investor has access to a loan that equals the acquisitions cost and is amortized over 4 years by constant installments. The borrowing rate is $\rho = 10\%$. The capital market interest rate is $i = 8\%$ and the marginal income tax rate is $\tau = 25\%$. Determine the leasing payment, if the minimum lease term is 5 years and if the lessor has to capitalize the asset (straight-line depreciation). The cash flows after taxes are withdrawn at the end of each period.

9.17. Leasing

An investor wants to lease a machine with a useful life of 6 years and acquisition costs of $I_0 = 96{,}000$. The minimum lease term is supposed to be 6 years and the annual leasing payments are € 19,500. At the end of $t = 6$, the lessor sells the machine for € 30,000 to a third person. The capital market interest rate is $i = 5\%$ and the marginal tax rate is $\tau = 40\%$.

(a) Based on the characteristics provided at the beginning of Sect. 9.5, starting on p. 368, who has to capitalize the asset?
(b) Determine the post-tax net present value of the lessor and the lessee applying

(1) The sum of digits-method.
(2) The exact method.

(c) Provide the accounting records in $t = 0, 1, 6$ for both the lessor and the lessee if the sum of digits-method is applied.
(d) Now, suppose the minimum lease term is only 4 years, however, the lessee's time horizon is still 6 years. The leasing payments are now € 29,250. At the end of $t = 4$, the lessee can purchase the asset for € 30,000. In $t = 6$, the lessee sells the asset for € 30,000. The sum of digits-method is applied.

(1) Who has to capitalize the asset?
(2) Determine the post-tax net present value for both the lessor and the lessee, if the lessee buys the asset from the lessor at the end of $t = 4$.
(3) Based on (2), provide accounting records for the lessor and the lessee in $t = 4, 5, 6$.

9.18. Leasing

Donald wants to acquire a machine with a useful life of 5 years and acquisition costs of € 1,500,000. The real investment opportunity promises the following stream of certain future cash flows

t	0	1	2	3	4	5
CF_t	–1,500,000	350,000	450,000	450,000	500,000	550,000

The capital market interest rate is $i = 8\%$. The constant marginal income tax rate is $\tau = 50\%$. The investment is depreciated applying the straight-line method. Capital income is taxed at a flat rate of $\tau^{flat} = 25\%$. Donald withdraws all cash flows after taxes to reinvest them at the capital market. An immediate full loss offset is assumed.

(a) Is Donald advised to carry out the investment, if acquisition costs are completely equity financed?

Now, suppose Donald does not have any equity. There are two mutual exclusive financing alternatives to finance the machine:

(b) The first choice is a mix of debt and a dormant equity holding. 50% of the acquisition costs are financed by a bullet loan with $\rho = 6\%$ and $d = 6.25\%$ (sum of digits-method) and 50% are financed by Dagobert as dormant equity. Dagobert receives $\rho = 10\%$ on the equity provided by him. Determine the post-tax net present value of the financing alternative.
(c) The second choice is an annuity loan with $\rho = 11\%$ and $d = 0\%$. Determine the post-tax net present value of the financing alternative.
(d) Which financing alternative is profitable? Determine the total post-tax net present value of the real investment and the best financing alternative.

Right before Donald signs the contract, he receives an offer from a lessor. The offer contains a minimum lease term of 5 years and constant annual leasing payments of €390,000. There is no purchase or prolongation option. After the minimum lease term, the asset will be handed out to the lessor.

(e) Who has to capitalize the asset?
(f) Determine the post-tax net present value of the leasing contract for Donald by applying the sum of digits-method. Does the leasing option lead to a higher post-tax net present value than the financing options above?
(g) Determine the maximum constant annual leasing payment that Donald can pay if he carries out the real investment.

Solutions

Solutions of Exercises of Chap. 2

2.25 Interest Computation
1,184.34

2.26 Interest Computation
13,097.46

2.27 Interest Computation
$i_{t=1,\ldots,5} = 4.56\%$, $i_{t=6,\ldots,8} = 6.27\%$.

2.28 Annuities
(a) $FV = 4{,}491.49$, (b) $FV = 4{,}760.98$.

2.29 Annuities
(a) $FV = 26{,}982.33$, (b) $FV = 25{,}944.55$.

2.30 Annuities
(a) Carl has to save € 3,701.09 annually, (b) Carl has to save € 5,527.48 annually.

2.31 Annuities
$ANN = 40{,}121.29$

2.32 Annuities
(a) For $n = 29.91$, the present value is € 135,000. As the person is already retired the person is not advised to pay the € 135,000, (b) the present value of the rent to infinity is $\frac{12{,}000}{0.1} = 120{,}000$, a present value of € 135,000 will never be reached. Again, the person is not advised to pay the amount.

2.33 Annuities
$ANN = 3{,}600.00$

2.34 Net Present Value
(a) $i = 5\%$, $CF = (-520; 100; 200; 300)$, $NPV = 15.79$; (b) same cash flow structure as in (a) but $i = 10\%$, $NPV = -38.41$; (c) $i = 10\%$, $CF = (-520; 0; 0; 520 \times (1+i)^3)$, $NPV = 0$.

2.35 Economic Depreciation
$ED_t = PV_{t-1} - PV_t$; loss of consumption possibility; $CF = (-100; 30; 50; 40)$, $i = 5\%$, $ED = (24.58; 45.80; 38.10)$.

2.36 Alternative Decision Criteria
(a) $NPV = -23.53$; (b) $FV = 117.26$; (c) $NFV = -28.61$; (d) $PV_0 = 96.47$, $PV_1 = 61.29$, $PV_2 = 84.35$, $PV_3 = 28.57$, $PV_4 = 0$; (e) $ANN = 4.82$; (f) $ANN = 27.20$; (g) $i^* = -3.11\%$; (h1) $r^B = 0.21\%$; (h2) $r^B = -0.58\%$.

2.37 Formal Derivation of an Annuity
See Sect. 2.4 on p. 19.

2.38 Present Value: Own Example
(a) $i = 5\%$, $CF = (-100; -40; 60; 80)$, $PV = (85.43; 129.71; 76.19; 0.00)$; (b) $i = 5\%$, $CF = (-100; 30; -20; 100)$, $PV = (96.81; 71.66; 95.24; 0.00)$; (c) $i = 5\%$, $CF = (-100; 5; 5; 105)$, $PV = (100; 100; 100; 0.00)$.

2.39 Present Value: Own Example
$i = 5\%$, $CF = (-100; 3.38; 20; -30; 40; 50)$, $PV = (67.53; 67.53; 50.90; 83.45; 47.62; 0.00)$.

2.40 Economic Profit
$EP_t = i \times PV_{t-1} = \Delta PV_t + CF_t$; (a) The level of cash flow rises: $CF_t \uparrow \rightarrow EP_t \uparrow$; (b) The interest rate rises: $i \uparrow \rightarrow EP_t \uparrow$; (c) The present value rises: $PV_{t-1} \uparrow \rightarrow EP_t \uparrow$.

2.41 Formal Derivation of the Marginal Rate of Substitution
See (2.36) on p. 44.

2.42 Evaluating Profitability

	A	B	FI	?
1. $NPV^A < NPV^B < 0$			x	
2. $r^{B,B} > i > r^{B,A}$		x		
3. $SUM^A < SUM^B < 0$				x
4. $NPV^A > SUM^B > 0$				x
5. $NPV^{A-B} > 0$				x
6. $i > r^{B,B} > r^{B,A}$			x	
7. $r^{B,B} > r^{B,A} > i$		x		
8. $NPV^{A-B} > 0$ and $NPV^A > 0$	x			
9. $NPV^{A-B} < 0$				x
10. $NPV^{B-A} < 0$ and $NPV^A > 0$	x			

2.43 Evaluating Profitability
(a) $PV_0 = 600.00$; (b) $PV_0 = 855.36$; (c) $PV_0 = 594.62$; (d) $PV_0 = 587.73$.

2.44 Modified Rate of Return

(a) $NPV^A = 13.61$, $r_A^B = 7.36\%$, $NPV^B = 10.55$, $r_B^B = 7.70\%$; (b) $NPV^A = 13.61$, $r_A^B = 7.36\%$, $NPV^B = 10.55$, $r_B^B = 7.56\%$; (c) $NPV^A = 13.61$, $r_A^B = 7.36\%$, $NPV^B = 10.55$, $r_B^B = 7.28\%$.

2.45 Modified Rate of Return

(a) $NPV^A = 49.72$, $NPV^B = 129.09$; (b) $r_A^B = 11.34\%$, $r_B^B = 13.39\%$; (c) $r_A^B = 11.06\%$, $r_B^B = 12.69\%$; (d) Rank order is not affected, because capital market rate is used for discounting and compounding; (e) CF_2 can be interpreted as a negative return from the real investment, which would justify compounding. It also could be interpreted as initial costs (acquisition costs), which would qualify for discounting. Another distinction would be the question, if negative cash flows can be covered by earlier returns on the real investment (this would be true for investment B) – which results in compounding – or not (this is true for investment A), which results in discounting, because it might have to be debt financed.

2.46 Fisher–Hirshleifer Model

(a) $f(I_0) = 20 \times \sqrt{W_0 - I_0}$; (b) $C_0 = 171.43$, $C_1 = 106.91$, $I_0 = 28.57$, $i^* = 274.18\%$, $U(C_0, C_1) = 538{,}615{,}447$; (c) Investor A: $C_0 = 211.98$, $C_1 = 77.73$, $F_0 = -94.62$, $I_0 = 82.64$, $NPV = 82.64$, $U(C_0, C_1) = 740{,}411{,}799$, $\Delta U(C_0, C_1) = 201{,}796{,}352$; Investor B: $C_0 = 70.66$, $C_1 = 233.18$, $F_0 = 46.70$, $I_0 = 82.64$, $NPV = 82.64$; (d) $C_0 = 202.08$, $C_1 = 80.83$, $F_0 = -71.52$, $I_0 = 69.44$, $U(C_0, C_1) = 660{,}836{,}563$.

2.47 Withdrawals and Wealth Maximization

(a) $NPV^A = 7{,}346.22$, $NPV^B = 5{,}860.82$; (b) $PV^A = 127{,}346.22$, $\max W_t^A = 10{,}187.70$, $PV^B = 125{,}860.82$, $\max W_t^B = 10{,}068.87$; (c) $\max W_t^A = 38{,}448.47$, $\max W_t^B = 38{,}000$; (d) $FV^A = 173{,}253.12$, $FV^B = 171{,}232.26$; (e) $NPV^A = 4{,}668.82$, $NPV^B = 5{,}467.08$.

Solutions of Exercises of Chap. 3

3.19 Evaluating Profitability after Taxes

	A	B	FI	?
1. $NPV^A > NPV^B > 0$				x
2. $NPV^A > NPV^B > 0$ and $NPV^{\tau,A} > NPV^{\tau,B}$				x
3. $NPV^A < NPV^B < 0$ and $NPV^{\tau,A} > NPV^{\tau,B} > 0$	x			
4. $NPV^{\tau,A} > NPV^B > 0$				x
5. $NPV^{\tau,A} < NPV^{\tau,B} < 0$			x	
6. $NPV^{\tau,A} > SUM^{\tau,B} > 0$				x
7. $NPV^{\tau,A-B} > 0$				x
8. $NPV^A < NPV^B < 0$ and $PV^{D,A} > PV^{ED,A}$ and $NPV^{\tau,B} < 0$	x			
9. $NPV^A > NPV^B > 0$ and $PV^{D,A} < PV^{ED,A}$ and $PV^{D,B} < PV^{ED,B}$				x

3.20 Standard Model

(a) $NPV = 9{,}069.05$, $NPV^{\tau} = 7.982.20$; (b) $FV^{\tau} = 164{,}644.80$; (c) marginal investment.

3.21 Standard Model and Depreciation

(a) $NPV^{\tau,A} = 7.14$, $NPV^{\tau,B} = 5.00$, $NPV^{\tau,c} = 2.93$, $NPV^{\tau,D} = 0.85$, $NPV^{\tau,E} = -1.23$, $NPV^{\tau,F} = 3.30$, $NPV^{\tau,G} = -5.32$; (b) $NPV^{\tau} = 0.00$; (c) $NPV^{\tau} = 0.00$.

3.22 Standard Model and Income Tax Paradox

(a) $NPV^{A} = 110.65, NPV^{B} = 109.45$.
(b) Post-tax net present values:

	$NPV^{\tau,A}$	$NPV^{\tau,B}$
$\tau = 0\%$	110.65	109.45
$\tau = 10\%$	98.92	101.50
$\tau = 20\%$	87.29	93.00
$\tau = 30\%$	75.77	83.91
$\tau = 40\%$	64.39	74.18
$\tau = 50\%$	53.15	63.79
$\tau = 60\%$	42.09	52.67
$\tau = 100\%$	0.00	0.00

3.23 Standard Model and Income Tax Paradox

(a) Post-tax net present values with different marginal tax rates are:

	NPV^{τ}
$\tau = 0\%$	−1,122.60
$\tau = 10\%$	−726.36
$\tau = 20\%$	−378.66
$\tau = 30\%$	−84.21
$\tau = 40\%$	151.91
$\tau = 50\%$	324.19
$\tau = 60\%$	426.64
$\tau = 100\%$	0.00

(b) $\tau = 33.28\%$.

3.24 Maximizing Withdrawals

(a) $NPV^{\tau} = 341{,}628.23$; (b) $NPV^{\tau} = 273{,}414.33$; (c) $W_2 = 1{,}217{,}510.33$, $NPV^{\tau} = 253{,}551.39$.

3.25 Maximizing Withdrawals or Future Value

(a) $NPV^{A} = 51{,}299.77$, $NPV^{B} = 51{,}592.79$; (b) $NPV^{\tau,A} = 29{,}749.83$, $NPV^{\tau,B} = 29{,}270.18$; (c) $NPV^{\tau,A} = 29{,}235.16$, there is no change for investment B compared to (b), because no loans are needed.

3.26 Marginal and Average Tax Rates

(a) Part I: $T'(TB) = 0$, Part II: $T'(TB) = 0.0000182434 \times TB - 0.006021736$, Part III: $T'(TB) = 0.0000045748 \times TB + 0.1779585$, Part IV: $T'(TB) = 0.42$, Part V: $T'(TB) = 0.45$, $T'(8{,}004) = 0.14$; (b) $T(45{,}000) = 10{,}807.10$, marginal income tax rate = 38.39%, average income tax rate = 24.16%, income after taxes = 34,129.90, net income after accepting the job should at least be 34,129.9 + 3,500 = 37,629.9, $T(50{,}000) = 12{,}847.00$, income after taxes = 37,153.00. Holger will not accept the job.

3.27 Fisher–Hirshleifer Model

(a) $f(I_0) = 20 \times \sqrt{I_0} - \tau \times (20 \times \sqrt{I_0} - I_0)$; (b) $f(I_0) = 20 \times \sqrt{I_0} \times (1 - \tau) + \tau \times (W_0 - I_0)$; (c) Investor A: $C_0 = 191.72$, $F_0 = -68.28$, $C_1 = 70.30$, $I_0 = 76.56$, $NPV^\tau = 55.68$; Investor B: $C_0 = 63.92$, $F_0 = 59.52$, $C_1 = 210.94$, $I_0 = 76.56$, $NPV^\tau = 55.68$; (d) $C_0 = 194.61$, $F_0 = -77.25$, $C_1 = 69.41$, $I_0 = 82.64$, $NPV^\tau = 59.47$.

Solutions of Exercises of Chap. 4

4.9 German Individual Income Tax

(a) €0, (b) €705.10, (c) €2,701.05, (d) €12,847.05, (e) €119,306.

4.10 Marginal and Average Tax Rates

Marginal tax rates: (a) 0%, (b) 21.29%, (c) 26.96%, (d) 40.68%, (e) 45%.
Average tax rates: (a) 0%, (b) 5.88%, (c) 13.51%, (d) 25.69%, (e) 39.77%.

4.11 German Splitting Method

€1,197.57

4.12 German Splitting Method

€15,693.80

4.13 US Individual Income Tax

(a) \$230.00, (b) \$630.00, (c) \$1,726.25, (d) \$7,256.25, (e) \$82,235.75.

4.14 Marginal and Average Tax Rates

Marginal tax rates: (a) 10%, (b) 10%, (c) 15%, (d) 25%, (e) 33%.
Average tax rates: (a) 2.88%, (b) 5.25%, (c) 8.63 %, (d) 14.51%, (e) 27.41%.

4.15 Taxation of Capital Income

Total tax if the flat tax is applied: €565.78. Total tax if the progressive tax rate is applied: €501.32.

4.16 Taxation of Capital Income

Total tax if the flat tax is applied: €5,875.57. Total tax if the progressive tax rate is applied: €5,943.18. An increase in salary does not change the result.

Solutions of Exercises of Chap. 5

5.32 Cash Flow Tax and Fisher–Hirshleifer Model

Investor A: $C_0 = 193.38$, $C_1 = 70.91$, $F_0 = -51.24$, $I_0 = 82.64$, $NPV^{\tau} = 57.85$;

Investor B: $C_0 = 64.46$, $C_1 = 212.73$, $F_0 = 77.67$, $I_0 = 82.64$, $NPV^{\tau} = 57.85$.

5.33 Cash Flow Tax and ACE Tax

(a) $NPV = 291{,}413.83$, $r^B = 27.22\%$; (b) $NPV^{\tau} = 161{,}797.14$; (c) $NPV^{\tau} = 160{,}277.61$; (d) $r^{\tau,B} = 27.22\%$; (e) $NPV^{\tau} = 160{,}277.61$.

5.34 ACE Tax and Losses

(a) $NPV = 616{,}466.90$; (b) $NPV^{\tau} = 431{,}526.83$; (c) $NPV^{\tau} = 431{,}526.83$; (d) $NPV^{\tau} = 431{,}526.83$.

5.35 Adjusted Cash Flow Tax

(a) $NPV = 104.77$; (b) $NPV^{\tau} = 62.86$; (c) $NPV^{\tau} = 62.86$.

5.36 ACE Tax and Cash Flow Tax

(a) $NPV^{\tau} = 47{,}746.06$; (b) $NPV^{\tau} = 47{,}746.06$; (c) $NPV^{\tau} = 47{,}746.06$; (d) $NPV^{\tau} = 47{,}746.06$; (e) $NPV^{\tau} = 53{,}244.79$.

5.37 Johansson/Samuelson Tax

(a) $NPV = 29.90$; (b) $NPV^{\tau} = 29.90$; (c) $NPV^{\tau} = 29.90$.

Solutions of Exercises of Chap. 6

6.17 Corporate Tax Systems

1. Slovakia: $\tau^c = 19\%$, taxable dividend = 202.5, and total tax burden = 47.5
2. Ireland: $\tau^c = 12.5\%$, taxable dividend = 218.75, and total tax burden = 96.88
3. Austria: $\tau^c = 25\%$, taxable dividend = 187.5, and total tax burden = 109.38
4. Malta: $\tau^c = 35\%$, taxable dividend = 250, and total tax burden = 75
5. United Kingdom: $\tau^c = 28\%$, taxable dividend = 200, and total tax burden = 110

6.18 Avoidance of Triple Taxation

Corporate income tax rate in Germany is $\tau^c = 15\%$, whereas flat rat on personal level is $\tau^p = 25\%$. In Germany, triple taxation is avoided by an exemption of 95% of dividends received. Hence, the amount ready for consumption for Mr. Thatcher is € 137,131.35.

6.19 Standard Model for Corporations

1. *NPV* before taxes on corporate level: $NPV = 1.32$
2. *NPV* before taxes from the owner's perspective

(a) Retention: $NPV = 1.32$
(b) Immediate distribution: $NPV = 1.32$

3. $NPV^{\tau,c}$ after taxes neglecting the owner's level

(a) Retention: $NPV^{\tau,c} = 1.11$
(b) Immediate distribution: $NPV^{\tau,c} = 1.11$

4. $NPV^{\tau,p}$ after taxes from the owner's perspective

1. Financing by retained earnings
(a) Retention: $NPV^{\tau,p} = -0.20$
(b) Immediate distribution: $NPV^{\tau,p} = 0.15$

2. Financing by new equity
(a) Retention: $NPV^{\tau,p} = -5.01$
(b) Immediate distribution: $NPV^{\tau,p} = -4.97$

Solutions of Exercises of Chap. 7

7.8 Capital Gains
(a) $NPV^{\tau} = 713.14$; (b) $NPV^{\tau} = -1{,}023.02$; (c) $\tau^{CG} = 16.43\%$.

7.9 Loss Offset Restrictions in Germany

(a) Loss offset without optimizing loss carry back:

t	1	2	3	4
AGI_t	600,000	−4,000,000	2,600,000	−1,000,000
LCB_t		511,500	0	511,500
LCF_t		−3,488,500	−1,528,500	−2,017,000
LO_t		0	1,960,000	0
TB_t	600,000	−3,488,500	640,000	−488,500
T_t	−254,306	0	−272,306	0
TB_t after LCB_t	88,500	−3,488,500	128,500	−488,500
T_t after LCB_t	−28,998	0	−45,798	0
Refund		225,308	0	226,508

t	5	6	7	8
AGI_t	2,000,000	600,000	−400,000	500,000
LCB_t	0	0	174,996	0
LCF_t	−417,000	0	−225,004	0
LO_t	1,600,000	417,000	0	225,004
TB_t	400,000	183,000	−225,004	274,996
T_t	−164,306	−68,688	0	−108,054
TB_t after LCB_t	400,000	8,004	−225,004	274,996
T_t after LCB_t	−164,306	0	0	−108,054
Refund	0	0	68,688	0

(b) Loss offset if loss carry back is subject to optimization. Compared to case (a) just $t = 6, \ldots, 8$ are subject to changes:

t	...	6	7	8
AGI_t		600,000	−400,000	500,000
LCB_t		0	183,000	0
LCF_t		0	−217,000	0
LO_t		417,000	0	217,000
TB_t		183,000	−217,000	283,000
T_t		−68,688	0	−111,656
TB_t after LCB_t		0	−217,000	283,000
T_t after LCB_t		0	0	−111,656
Refund		0	68,688	0

7.10 Loss Offset Restrictions in Selected Countries

(a) NPV=256,812.95; (b) NPV^τ=211,953.39; (c) 1. NPV^τ=154,648.77, 2. NPV^τ = 164,723.66, 3. NPV^τ = 186,965.45, 4. NPV^τ = 190,518.45, 5. NPV^τ = 76,633.09, 6. NPV^τ = 164,723.66.

7.11 Provisions

$PV = 75{,}000 \times \tau^p - \frac{(75{,}000-10{,}000)\times\tau^p}{1+0.08\times(1-\tau^p)} = 5{,}190.84$

7.12 Provisions and Loss Offset Restrictions

(a) FV^τ = 127,520.00; (b) FV^τ = 127,520.00.

7.13 Changing Marginal Tax Rates

NPV^τ = 13,615.54

7.14 Progressive Tax Rates

(a) $FV^{\tau,real}$ = 275,879.10, $FV^{\tau,FI}$ = 261,392.00; (b) $FV^{\tau,real}$ = 286,167.62, $FV^{\tau,FI}$ = 287,125.87; (c) $FV^{\tau,real}$ = 315,417.11, $FV^{\tau,FI}$ = 287,125.87.

7.15 Uncertainty

(a) ϕ = 0.5000; (b) ϕ = 0.4366; (c) Taxation boosts real investments because $NPV^\tau > NPV$ at $\phi = 0.4366$.

7.16 Including Value Added Taxes (VAT)

(a) NPV^τ = −1,602.33; (b) NPV^τ = 439.42.

Solutions of Exercises of Chap. 8

8.7 Income Tax Paradox Refer to Ex. 8.7 on p. 328, but use identical tax rates $\tau = \tau^{\text{flat}}$.

8.8 Marginal Price of Seller and Purchaser
(a) $MP^S = 2{,}001{,}400.72$; (b) $MP^B = 1{,}917{,}814.26$; no transaction takes place because $MP^S > MP^B$; (c) $MP^S = 1{,}793{,}347.84$; now transaction takes place; (d) $MP^S = 1{,}776{,}138.09$; transaction takes place; (e) $\tau^{CG} = 30.14\%$; (f) minimum amount = 155,232.00; (g) maximum amount = 124,466.42.

8.9 Marginal Price of Seller and Purchaser
$MP^S = 1{,}566{,}666.67$, $MP^B = 1{,}485{,}966.52$

8.10 Marginal Price of Seller and Purchaser
(a) $MP^S = 713{,}333.33$; (ba) $MP^B = 685{,}080.50$, correct price because $MP^B < GCV$; (bb) $MP^B = 651{,}018.44$, transaction is not carried out; (c) $MP^B = 677{,}709.09$, transaction does not take place.

8.11 Marginal Price of Seller and Purchaser
(a) $MP^S = 1{,}760,715.04$ (b) $MP^B = 1{,}614{,}538.59$.

8.12 Marginal Price of Seller and Purchaser
$MP^B = 788{,}000.83$

Solutions of Exercises of Chap. 9

9.9 Post-Tax Interest Rate
(a) Post-tax net present value of equity financed investment: $NPV^\tau = 19{,}179.76$; post-tax net present value of loan: $NPV^\tau = -12{,}870.15$; (b) Post-tax net present value (initial cost and present value of saved rents which are not tax deductible): $NPV^\tau = 91{,}252.61$; post-tax net present value of the loan: $NPV^\tau = -60{,}060.71$; (c) Post-tax net present value of loan: $NPV^\tau = -22{,}308.26$.

9.10 Evaluating Different Types of Loans
(a) $NPV^\tau = 7{,}501.91$; (b) equity financing $NPV^\tau = 6{,}078.06$; (c1) $NPV^\tau = -9{,}618.71$; (c2) $NPV^\tau = -8{,}203.38$; (c3) $NPV^\tau = -8{,}625.08$; (c4) $NPV^\tau = -3{,}769.26$; (d) Post-tax cash flow streams do not change; equity financing, τ^{flat}=25%: $NPV^\tau = -2{,}567.52$; (d1) $NPV^\tau = -3{,}118.60$; (d2) $NPV^\tau = -4{,}011.71$; (d3) $NPV^\tau = -4{,}395.32$; (d4) $NPV^\tau = 502.46$.

9.11 Arbitrage With Debt Financing?
(a) $NPV^\tau = -1{,}195.49$; (b) $NPV^\tau = -4{,}255.14$; (c) Post-tax net present value of the loan is positive: $NPV^\tau = 16{,}076.77$. Post-tax net present value of the equity

financed real investment drops to $NPV^\tau = -35{,}218.55$ so that in total NPV^τ is negative and investment is not carried out.

9.12 Disagios

(a) $NPV = -56{,}744.72$; (b) $NPV^\tau = -41{,}228.54$; (c) $NPV^\tau = -41{,}061.41$; (d) $i^* = 10.427\%, NPV^\tau = -41{,}077.59$.

9.13 Financing Restrictions

(a) $NPV^\tau = 22{,}592.50$; (ba) (1) $NPV^\tau = -21{,}308.48$; (2) $NPV^\tau = 1{,}284.02$; (bb) (1) $NPV^\tau = -21{,}102.88$; (2) Total $NPV^\tau = -533.11$.

9.14 Prepayment Penalty

(a) $NPV^\tau = 19{,}145.30$; (b) $NPV^\tau = -10{,}068.71$; (c) prepayment in $t = 2$: $NPV^\tau = 9{,}028.81$, prepayment in $t = 3$: $NPV^\tau = 9{,}204.72$.

9.15 Leasing

(a) Holger has to capitalize the asset; (b) Holger: $NPV^\tau = -55{,}416.87$, Marcus: $NPV^\tau = 78{,}632.05$; (d) Holger: $NPV^\tau = -46{,}789.79$, Marcus: $NPV^\tau = 65{,}165.09$.

9.16 Purchase-Equivalent Leasing Payment

The cash flow stream earned with the machine is unknown. However, we have to take the present value of the tax advantage due to depreciation into account; $NPV^\tau = -329{,}125.08$. Present value of the post-tax leasing payments: $PV = -78{,}133.11$. Leasing payment: $PV^\tau = -104{,}177.48$.

9.17 Leasing

(a) Finance leasing ($\sum_{t=1}^{n} LP_t > I_0$); minimum lease term is longer than 90% of useful life → lessee has to capitalize; (b) (1) sum of digits method, lessor, $NPV^\tau = 16{,}939.17$, lessee, $NPV^\tau = -63{,}194.43$; (2) exact method: $i^* = 5.963\%$, lessor: $NPV^\tau = 16{,}953.37$, lessee: $NPV^\tau : -63{,}208.63$; (d) (1) lessee has to capitalize, (2) lessor: $NPV^\tau = 20{,}796.65$, lessee: $NPV^\tau = -67{,}051.91$.

9.18 Leasing

(a) $NPV^\tau = 89{,}631.86$; (b) $NPV^\tau = 104{,}568.24$; (c) $NPV^\tau = 20{,}961.09$; (d) $NPV^\tau = 194{,}200.10$; (e) Finance leasing ($\sum_{t=1}^{n} LP_t > I_0$), minimum lease term is longer than 90% of useful life → lessee has to capitalize; (f) $NPV^\tau = 54{,}087.18$; (g) $LR_t^{max} = -460{,}990.40$.

Index

The manufacturer's authorised representative in the EU is Springer Nature Customer Service Centre GmbH, Europaplatz 3, 69115 Heidelberg, Germany. If you have any concerns regarding our products, please contact ProductSafety@springernature.com

Printed and bound by CPI Group (UK) Ltd, Croydon, CR0 4YY
25/09/2026
02222831-0005